Exploring the Political Economy and Social Philosophy of Vincent and Elinor Ostrom

Economy, Polity, and Society

The foundations of political economy—from Adam Smith to the Austrian school of economics, to contemporary research in public choice and institutional analysis—are sturdy and well established, but far from calcified. On the contrary, the boundaries of the research built on this foundation are ever expanding. One approach to political economy that has gained considerable traction in recent years combines the insights and methods of three distinct but related subfields within economics and political science: the Austrian, Virginia, and Bloomington schools of political economy. The vision of this book series is to capitalize on the intellectual gains from the interactions between these approaches in order to both feed the growing interest in this approach and advance social scientists' understanding of economy, polity, and society.

This series seeks to publish works that combine the Austrian school's insights on knowledge, the Virginia school's insights into incentives in non-market contexts, and the Bloomington school's multiple methods, real-world approach to institutional design as a powerful tool for understanding social behavior in a diversity of contexts.

Series Editors:

Virgil Henry Storr, associate professor of economics, George Mason University; senior fellow, F. A. Hayek Program for Advanced Study in Philosophy, Politics & Economics, Mercatus Center at George Mason University

Jayme S. Lemke, senior research fellow, Mercatus Center at George Mason University, George Mason University

Titles in the Series:

Interdisciplinary Studies of the Market Order: New Applications of Market Process Theory, edited by Peter J. Boettke, Christopher J. Coyne and Virgil Henry Storr

Knowledge and Incentives in Policy: Using Public Choice and Market Process Theory to Analyze Public Policy Issues, edited by Stefanie Haeffele

Exploring the Political Economy and Social Philosophy of James M. Buchanan, edited by Paul Dragos Aligica, Christopher J. Coyne, and Stefanie Haeffele

Exploring the Political Economy and Social Philosophy of F.A. Hayek, edited by Peter J. Boettke, Jayme S. Lemke and Virgil Henry Storr

Informing Public Policy: Analyzing Contemporary US and International Policy Issues through the Lens of Market Process Economics, edited by Stefanie Haeffele, Abigail R. Hall and Adam Millsap

Interdisciplinary Studies of the Political Order: New Applications of Public Choice Theory, edited by Donald J. Boudreaux, Christopher J. Coyne and Bobbi Herzberg

The Need for Humility in Policymaking: Lessons from Regulatory Policy, edited by Stefanie Haeffele and Anne Hobson

Commercial Society: A Primer on Ethics and Economics, by Cathleen A. Johnson, Robert F. Lusch and David Schmidtz

Exploring the Political Economy and Social Philosophy of Vincent and Elinor Ostrom, edited by Peter J. Boettke, Bobbi Herzberg and Brian Kogelmann

Exploring the Political Economy and Social Philosophy of Vincent and Elinor Ostrom

Edited by
Peter J. Boettke
Bobbi Herzberg
Brian Kogelmann

ROWMAN & LITTLEFIELD
Lanham • Boulder • New York • London

Published by Rowman & Littlefield
An imprint of The Rowman & Littlefield Publishing Group, Inc.
4501 Forbes Boulevard, Suite 200, Lanham, Maryland 20706
www.rowman.com

6 Tinworth Street, London, SE11 5AL, United Kingdom

British Library Cataloguing in Publication Information Available

Library of Congress Cataloging-in-Publication Data

Names: Boettke, Peter J., editor. | Herzberg, Bobbi, 1955- editor. | Kogelmann, Brian, 1989- editor.
Title: Exploring the political economy and social philosophy of Vincent and Elinor Ostrom / edited by Peter J. Boettke, Bobbi Herzberg, Brian Kogelmann.
Description: Lanham : Rowman & Littlefield, [2020] | Series: Economy, polity, and society | Includes bibliographical references and index. | Summary: "The interdisciplinary chapters in this volume explore and engage the work of Vincent and Elinor Ostrom, along with the Bloomington School of political economy more generally"—Provided by publisher.
Identifiers: LCCN 2020004793 (print) | LCCN 2020004794 (ebook) | ISBN 9781786614346 (cloth) | ISBN 9781786614353 (paperback) | ISBN 9781786614360 (epub)
Subjects: LCSH: Ostrom, Elinor—Political and social views. | Ostrom, Vincent, 1919–2012—Political and social views. | Institutional economics. | Public goods. | Decentralization in government.
Classification: LCC HB119.O88 E86 2020 (print) | LCC HB119.O88 (ebook) | DDC 320.092/2—dc23
LC record available at https://lccn.loc.gov/2020004793
LC ebook record available at https://lccn.loc.gov/2020004794

Contents

Introduction

Peter J. Boettke, Bobbi Herzberg, and Brian Kogelmann

The interdisciplinary chapters in this volume explore and engage the political economy and social philosophy of Elinor and Vincent Ostrom from a wide variety of contexts and several different disciplinary perspectives. The contributors come from philosophy, political economy, and sociology, among other disciplines. Consequently, the range of topics covered is extraordinarily wide, running the gamut from the European Union (EU), political parties, the Flint water crisis, regulating free speech, and much more. The hope is that these contributions demonstrate the continued relevance of the Ostroms' research program to a large variety of scholarly disciplines.

AN OVERVIEW OF THE OSTROMS' CAREER AND RESEARCH PROGRAM

Elinor Ostrom (1933–2012) and Vincent Ostrom (1919–2012) spent their lifetimes exploring the many ways in which average individuals come together to form institutions and solve complex social problems. Early life experiences shaped their approaches to work, community, and policy, more generally. Vincent spent his childhood on the family farm in Washington State, while Elinor grew up in the Los Angeles area during the Great Depression. In each case, they learned the lessons of human cooperation in economically difficult times in their communities. These lessons would shape the focus of their distinguished academic careers, as they sought to understand what allowed self-interested individuals to form cooperative social arrangements.

Elinor and Vincent met at UCLA, where Vincent served as a faculty member and Elinor was enrolled in the PhD program in political science.

Each faced significant challenges as they sought to eventually fit in the discipline: Vincent, from questions of academic freedom regarding his work in policy at Wyoming and UCLA, and Elinor, because of limits placed by continuing gender attitudes in the academe. Despite the challenges, they persevered to achieve at the highest levels of their fields.

In 1965, Vincent joined the faculty in political science at Indiana University and, with hard work, Elinor was hired shortly thereafter. It was probably the best decision Indiana University ever made. They would build an intellectual home (now the Ostrom Workshop) to bring scholars together across disciplines and methodologies. The model for this design was inspired by their work with a master woodworking craftsman in Indiana. They appreciated how, in the shop, a master and a novice could learn from one another as they worked side by side on a shared project. This would shape their approaches to teaching, their mentorship, and their own ongoing efforts to learn new methods from a wide array of colleagues and disciplines. An example of this institutional design in their own work is found in the mini-conference they held at the end of each semester. The conference was organized as a Saturday event structured around panels of two to three papers each. Instead of presenting your own paper, however, the Ostroms assigned a student/discussant charged with sympathetically laying out the argument posed by the author, before turning to the usual role of critique. Each term, it was common for the Ostroms to assign their own papers to one of the newer graduate students in a sincere desire to see what new insights he or she could bring. From day one, they treated all who passed through the workshop as members of their extended family—loved and respected, but always expected to carry their own weight. This ongoing exercise in cooperation emerged from, but also reinforced, the Ostrom attitude regarding the capacity of humans to socially coordinate action under the "right" institutions.

Over four decades, Elinor and Vincent Ostrom combined careful analytic theory, laboratory tests, and extensive field studies to push the understanding of constitutional and institutional theory to new levels. These efforts led to numerous honors and awards which ranged from Elinor's selection as corecipient of the 2009 Sveriges Riksbank Prize in Economic Science in honor of Alfred Nobel to Vincent's selection to deliver the 2005 John Gauss Lecture at APSA. For those who knew them, their success was not a surprise, but it was certainly well deserved and grounded in a rich intellectual tradition. It is our hope that works such as the chapters included in this volume will continue the conversations about institutions and human interactions that the Ostroms so enjoyed.

The intellectual contributions of the Ostroms can and have been the subject of entire books (e.g., Aligica and Boettke 2009). As such, the summary of their work offered in this introduction will necessarily be incomplete. One constant theme running throughout much of the Ostroms' work is a rejection of the simple paradigms and dichotomies characterizing the intellectual landscape. Consider, for instance, the common distinction between public and private goods. Private goods are those goods that are rivalrous and excludable. A good is rivalrous if person A's consumption of the good prevents person B from consuming it—for instance, if A consumes an apple, then B cannot consume it. A good is excludable if it is not too difficult to prevent someone from consuming it. To give an example, it is not hard for an apple seller to prevent A from consuming her apples. Public goods, by contrast, are those goods that are nonrivalrous and nonexcludable. Since they are nonrivalrous, one person consuming a public good does not prevent another person from consuming it. Since they are nonexcludable, it is hard to prevent persons from consuming public goods. The classic example of a public good is a lighthouse. Person A using a lighthouse does not prevent person B from using it; and it is hard to prevent persons from using a lighthouse to steer their ships to shore.

In the mid-twentieth century, the public-private good distinction characterized much of the debate in economics concerning the nature of market failure and the need for government intervention. Yet the Ostroms rejected this dichotomy as too simplistic (Ostrom and Ostrom [1977] 1999). For instance, consider goods that are nonrivalrous but excludable. These are goods where one person's consumption does not prevent the consumption of another (like public goods), *but* it is relatively easy to exclude others (like private goods). The Ostroms called these *toll goods*, and they include things like theaters, nightclubs, utilities, and so on. Or, consider goods that are rivalrous but nonexcludable. These are goods where one person's consumption prevents the consumption of another (like private goods), *but* it is relatively hard to exclude others from using them (like public goods). These are called *common pool resources* (CPRs) and include things like fisheries, water basins, timber forests, and so on. Developing this new typology of goods, the Ostroms demonstrate that things are more complicated than the simple public-private good distinction.

CPRs would play a central role in Elinor's research program specifically, and would offer another chance to reject a common dichotomy. CPRs are ripe for abuse. If I catch a fish, then you cannot catch that fish. And, since CPRs are nonexcludable, it is very difficult for you to prevent me from catching fish. Everyone recognizes this, and we all have an incentive to catch as many fish as we can before the fishery runs out; this, quite clearly, will lead to overfishing. Such a phenomenon is known as a *tragedy of the commons*. Before Elinor's important contributions, there were two proposed ways of addressing such tragedies. First, one could (if possible) implement a scheme of property rights, thereby transforming a CPR into individuated private goods. Since they have the capacity to exclude, property owners now have an incentive to use their resources sustainably. Or, one could allow the state to regulate consumption of CPRs, allowing only sustainable levels of consumption. If a CPR did not adopt either strategy—that is, regulation by the state or market privatization—then common wisdom held that a tragedy would result.

But common wisdom was incorrect. In her examination of CPRs that were successfully used in a sustainable manner over long periods of time, Elinor found that the institutional milieu characterizing these CPRs was neither pure private property rights nor regulation by Leviathan. Rather, successfully managed CPRs were governed by a complex mix of institutions that didn't fall neatly into either camp. As she phrases it: "Many successful CPR situations are rich mixtures of 'private-like' and 'public-like' institutions defying classification in a sterile dichotomy" (Ostrom 1990, 14). This institutional heterogeneity does not mean, though, that successful CPRs are not subject to careful scholarly analysis. One of Elinor's key contributions was the development of the design principles, or principles that characterize successfully managed CPRs.

This rejection of the state–market distinction goes beyond the analysis of CPRs. In her Nobel Prize address, Elinor begins by noting that "the market was seen as the optimal institution for the production and exchange of private goods. For nonprivate [public] goods, on the other hand, one needed 'the' government to impose rules and taxes to force self-interested individuals to contribute necessary resources and refrain from self-seeking activities" (Ostrom 2010, 642). But even so, "Undertaking empirical studies of how citizens, local public entrepreneurs, and public officials engage in diverse ways of providing, producing, and managing public service industries and common property regimes at multiple scales has generated substantial knowledge that is not explained by the two models of optimal organizational forms" (Ostrom 2010, 643). Considering the explanatory failures of the dichotomous state–market paradigm, the Ostroms introduced the idea of *polycentric* governance systems.

The idea of polycentricity was initially explored in a paper on metropolitan governance by Vincent Ostrom, Charles Tiebout, and Robert Warren. The authors begin by noting that metropolitan governance usually consists of "overlapping jurisdictions" of authority, "duplication of functions" concerning the provision of public goods and services, and "many centers of decision making that are formally independent of each other" (Ostrom, Tiebout, and Warren 1961, 831). This is opposed to monocentric or "gargantuan" approaches to governance, where authority, decision-making, and the provision of public goods and services are limited to one centralized governance unit, such that this one single unit's jurisdiction does not overlap with any other unit's jurisdiction. Monocentric governance structures are akin to one of the "optimal" organizational forms that Elinor decries—*the* state. Polycentric forms of governance are clearly distinct from this paradigm, in that authority is dispersed, fractured, and overlapping. And yet, polycentric governance systems are also clearly not markets, making them distinct from the other paradigm constituting the market–state dichotomy. We thus have a distinct form of governance that cannot be classified as either the state or the market. Exploring the idea of polycentric governance would be a key contribution of Vincent (e.g., Ostrom [1972] 1999).

The final theme running throughout the Ostroms' research program worth mentioning in this brief introduction is the idea of *self-governance*. A fundamental assumption often made by scholars of collective action is that "individuals are viewed as if they are in a trap and cannot get out without some external authority imposing a solution" (Ostrom 1990, 216). In other words, persons cannot solve their own problems in the absence of some kind of help from experts who, acting as a deus ex machina, come in and save the day. This paradigm too is rejected by the Ostroms. As Elinor notes in her work on CPR's: "Instead of presuming that individuals sharing a commons are inevitably caught in a trap from which they cannot escape, I argue that the capacity of individuals to extricate themselves from various types of dilemma situations *varies* from situation to situation" (Ostrom 1990, 14). Self-governance was also at the heart of Vincent's work. In asking whether a genuinely democratic society is possible, Vincent responds that it is, but *only if* self-governance is possible: "Democratic ways of life turn on self-organizing and self-governing capabilities rather than presuming that something called 'the Government' governs" (Ostrom 1997, 4). One way of viewing the Ostroms' broad and diverse research program is as offering a positive, yet qualified, answer to this question: self-governance *is* possible, but the conditions under which this is so are fragile and thus worthy of further inquiry.

AN OVERVIEW OF THE VOLUME

This volume is broken into three parts. In the first part, "Theory in the Ostroms," the chapters are focused on theoretical aspects of the Ostroms' research program. The first chapter, "On the Dynamic Nature of Goods," explores the typology of goods offered by the Ostroms. In particular, the author Veeshan Rayamajhee argues that we should not think of goods as fixed as either private goods, public goods, toll goods, or CPRs. Rather, how to classify a particular good depends on the context in which it is offered; importantly, when the context changes, so also might the proper classification of the good. What is a private good in some contexts might be a toll good in others. To highlight this, Rayamajhee presents three cases from Chicago, New Orleans, and Indonesia to discuss the dynamic nature of post-disaster goods and services and the shuffling of goods classification based on their shifting natures. The goal of this exercise is to highlight the diversity, heterogeneity, and fluidity of goods and services that are needed in any post-disaster scenario.

In chapter 2, "The Culture in the Ostroms," Mili Kalia examines the concept of culture as it appears in the Ostroms' work. Culture seems to play an important part in the Ostromian framework, but there have been few attempts by scholars to rigorously understand the role of culture within their work. This chapter seeks to fill this gap. It does so by showing that the study of culture through the discipline of sociology has much to offer the Ostroms, and that sociologists have much to learn from the Ostroms as well.

In chapter 3, "Social Services as Impure Public Goods," Roland Fritz examines to what extent social services typically provided by the welfare state can be classified within the Ostroms' typology of goods. He argues that while excludability from social service provision is not accepted in most societies for political reasons, rivalry of consumption still holds and manifests itself through nonprice rationing mechanisms. Hence, social services are best understood as CPRs. Fritz draws on Elinor's design principles for the successful and sustainable use of CPRs. By applying these principles to questions of social services, the author attempts to identify problems with their provision in contemporary welfare states and ends up arguing for more decentralized and participatory mechanisms in order to improve policy outcomes.

Part II of the volume, "Applications of Polycentricity," consists of chapters applying the concept of polycentricity to various topics in political economy. In chapter 4, "Polycentric Party Governance," Nicholas F. Jacobs applies the theory of polycentricity to the study of political leadership and party organization in the United States. Political parties are essential institutional arenas for the production of political leaders. Jacobs argues that polycentric party systems are capable of providing citizens necessary levels of choice over potential political leaders when the rules governing party competition nourish a system of multiple, independent centers of decision-making competing for power over the nomination process. Jacobs further shows that the US party system is becoming more centralized and losing vital elements of polycentric order, even as more people become involved in the democratic process.

In chapter 5, "Governing the (Banking) Commons," Pablo Paniagua Prieto contributes to the literature on banking stability by suggesting that a polycentric banking system can better deal with the provision of banking services—such as safeguarding from bank runs and providing emergency liquidity—than a monocentric system. The need to govern bank runs must incorporate the institutionalization of a lender of last resort to allow the expansion of liquidity. By using the Ostroms' insights on institutional diversity and polycentricity, Prieto challenges conventional wisdom and suggests that central banks are neither essential nor superior to polycentric arrangements in the governance of bank runs.

Chapter 6, "The Political Economy of the European Union," examines to what extent the EU is a polycentric order. The author, Jan P. Vogler, argues that the division of power within the EU largely mirrors the ideals of polycentricity. In addition to an analysis of the EU's institutional framework, Vogler investigates polycentric governance "in action" by analyzing (1) the sovereign debt crisis and (2) the international refugee crisis. When facing these major political-economic challenges, the EU's response consisted of a mix of centralized and decentralized initiatives. As one might expect from a polycentric system of governance, only the *combination* of policies initiated at both levels successfully addressed the consequences of the crises.

Part III examines collective action problems, analyzing them through the Ostromian framework of self-governance. In chapter 7, "The Inmate's Dilemma," Joanna Carroll examines how prison inmates organize strikes in the face of constant monitoring, difficult communication, and high levels of distrust. Using insights from Elinor's work, Carroll argues that leadership, innovations in communication tactics, and repetition of strikes are the most essential components to successful collective action among inmates. These elements allow trust to be built as well as spread ideology in order to increase inmates' preferences for participating in a strike.

Chapter 8, "The Cantinas Network of Terra do Meio," is written by V. Miranda Chase, Raquel Rodrigues dos Santos, and Augusto Postigo. The chapter explores the Cantinas Network of Terra do Meio in Brazil, a social institution that provides market access for nontimber forest products. Relying on participant observation during years of experience in the field, the authors use the Ostroms' institutional development framework to better understand the Cantinas. The analysis shows that the Cantinas emerged out of a social context marked by strong rules-in-use which influence participants' decisions. They argue that the Cantinas Network is successful in promoting economic growth and forest conservation because it is a resilient institution that respects local norms. As circumstances change, actors adopt new strategies without losing focus of their larger goal.

In chapter 9, "Community, State, and Market," Wanlin Lin draws on Elinor's work on social capital to facilitate our understanding of community governance in the context of transitional authoritarian regimes. Existing research on the institutional effects of social capital has primarily focused on democratic regimes or systems with weak governments rather than transitional authoritarian regimes, which have been underexplored. This chapter fills this lacuna by examining the forms and interaction of the three structural dimensions of social capital and applying them to explore the redevelopment of urban villages as a coordination problem in China's village communities. Doing so expands our understanding of the relationship between community, market, and state in transitional authoritarian regimes.

Chapter 10, "Under Emergency Management," examines the influence and limitations of community residents during the period of emergency management when the City of Flint switched its water source to the Flint River, and the consequences of lead contamination that followed. Author Sawyer Phinney finds that citizens' engagement regarding water provision services was limited due to emergency management law. Failure to incorporate localized knowledge throughout the process created the conditions that led to unsafe drinking water in Flint. This then created strong incentives for Flint residents to self-organize and utilize social capital by creating their own monitoring mechanisms to measure water quality, while also partnering with researchers and external scientists across the United States to complement local claims of lead contamination—which, in the end, motivated the return to a cleaner water source.

In chapter 11, "The Expressive Commons," Alexander Schaefer examines free speech as a collective action problem. To increase expressive freedom, the toleration of disagreeable expressions is required. Increasing the agreeableness of one's expressive environment may require a reduction in the overall expressive freedom of one's society. Analyzing the choice calculus of this trade-off reveals that the individual bears only a fraction, or none, of the cost of improving the agreeableness of his or her expressive environment, while the benefit of doing so is far more concentrated. The pool of acceptable expressions, therefore, generates a collective action problem, leading us to predict overrestriction of free speech. In exploring potential solutions to this problem, the conceptual schema developed draws on the work of Elinor Ostrom. In short: where states and markets fail, informal self-organization may prevail.

The final chapter is titled: "Are American Immigrant Processing Institutions Surviving or Thriving?" The author, Emily VanMeter, uses an Ostromian framework to examine how US immigration institutions have responded to recent increases in US-Mexico border apprehensions. The author argues that the strain of increasing numbers of immigrants from Guatemala, Honduras, and El Salvador in recent years has only served to highlight preexisting institutional weaknesses. In response, we see the formation and persistence of volunteer-based collective action organizations which have attempted to fill institutional gaps and encourage change. The author ends by proposing a more federally decentralized approach to immigration in order to better meet the needs of border communities as well as the immigrants being processed.

REFERENCES

Aligica, Paul Dragos, and Peter J. Boettke. 2009. *Challenging Institutional Analysis and Development: The Bloomington School*. New York: Routledge.

Ostrom, Elinor. 1990. *Governing the Commons: The Evolution of Institutions for Collective Action*. Cambridge: Cambridge University Press.

———. 2010. "Beyond Markets and States: Polycentric Governance of Complex Economic Systems." *American Economic Review* 100: 641–672.

Ostrom, Vincent. [1972] 1999. "Polycentricity (Part 1)." In *Polycentricity and Local Public Economies*, edited by Michael D. McGinnis, 52–74. Ann Arbor: University of Michigan Press.

———. 1997. *The Meaning of Democracies and the Vulnerability of Democracies: A Response to Tocqueville's Challenge*. Ann Arbor: University of Michigan Press.

Ostrom, Vincent, Charles M. Tiebout, and Robert Warren. 1961. "The Organization of Government in Metropolitan Areas: A Theoretical Inquiry." *American Political Science Review* 55: 831–842.

Ostrom, Vincent, and Elinor Ostrom. [1977] 1999. "Public Goods and Public Choices." In *Polycentricity and Local Public Economies*, edited by Michael D. McGinnis, 75–103. Ann Arbor: University of Michigan Press.

Part I

THEORY IN THE OSTROMS

Chapter 1

On the Dynamic Nature of Goods

Applications in Post-Disaster Contexts

Veeshan Rayamajhee

A few days after a devastating 7.8 magnitude earthquake struck Nepal in 2015, the government (of Nepal) released an official statement demanding that "all donations be channeled into the Prime Minister's Disaster Relief Fund" (Francis 2015).[1] The move, motivated by concerns about "the number of groups in Nepal and around the world collecting donations without the government's permission," had implicit goals of reducing redundancy, precluding misallocation of funds, and curbing corruption (Nelson 2015). Exactly two months following the earthquake, the National Planning Commission of Nepal organized the International Conference on Nepal's Reconstruction (ICNR) to raise funds for relief, reconstruction, and recovery efforts (Baldry et al. 2017). Development partners and donors pledged over $4 billion in disaster assistance. However, it took the government another six months to form the National Reconstruction Authority (NRA) and formulate a "comprehensive five-year plan"—Post-Disaster Recovery Framework (PDRF)—to utilize funds to address post-disaster challenges. PDRF adopted a recovery vision of establishing "well-planned, resilient settlements, and a prosperous society" and tasked itself with ensuring "safe structures, social cohesion, access to services, livelihood support, and capacity building" (NRA 2016). In short, NRA became the monocentric governing body charged with all responsibilities of planning, implementing, and overseeing every aspect of post-disaster reconstruction and recovery. To put it differently, it [NRA] was to be *the* assessor of needs, and provider of all goods and services—private, public, or otherwise—that are associated with reconstruction and recovery from the earthquake. The lessons that Elinor Ostrom learned from rural agricultural villages in Nepal—that heterogeneous communities across the country have unique challenges and that they use a wide range of traditional norms and complex institutional rules to govern their social and economic affairs—were conveniently ignored. Instead, a one-nation-one-solution approach to post-disaster policymaking was adopted as the national mantra to control all aspects of production and provision of all post-disaster goods and services.[2]

An extensive body of literature has invalidated the omniscience presumption of expert-guided central planners or governments to elicit and respond to widely disseminated information regarding post-disaster needs of people (Boettke et al. 2007; Chamlee-Wright and Storr 2010a, 2010b; Leeson and Sobel 2008; Sobel and Leeson 2006, 2007; Sutter and Smith 2017). However, market-versus-state debates on post-disaster recovery are of limited use without an adequate consideration of the typology and nature of goods and services. The assessment of earthquake damages and/or reconstruction of an interstate highway require a very different policy approach than that of assessing and providing household needs. In fact, as we shift our focus away from broad macroeconomic considerations to the needs of individuals, households, and local communities, post-disaster challenges become increasingly idiosyncratic. As I have stated elsewhere, disaster damages pose unique challenges to each household, especially in communities characterized by ethnic, religious, and cultural heterogeneity (Rayamajhee and Bohara 2019c). Therefore, debates surrounding the *appropriate role* of the central government or markets can be misguided in that they stem from a simplistic private-public dichotomy of goods and services. I contend that most goods that are naively assumed to be public by many post-disaster aid programs in developing countries are quasi-public; they are characterized by varying degrees of excludability and subtractability, and often fall within the "neither state nor market" domain (Fritz, 2020). On the other hand, some goods that are typically considered private may require nonmarket provision mechanisms in cases where physical infrastructures or institutional structures that make markets feasible are absent.

This chapter remains agnostic as to whether or not state-led post-disaster assistance programs succeed or fail. Without other institutions to compare performances against, empirical studies that evaluate the welfare impacts of state-led post-disaster aid reveal very little. Moreover, the fact that one agency's involvement in Nepal may have helped prevent worse outcomes says nothing about alternative ways the funds could have been better allocated. A fitting analogy is one of throwing a pebble in a still pond: Such action always brings about ripples, but any plausible claim about its effectiveness requires comparison against ripples from other pebbles. When disaster assistance is treated as a packageable product with prohibitively substantial economies of scale, lumping the production and provision of the package under the jurisdiction of one agency follows naturally, regardless of the number of donor agencies involved and the diversity of goals.[3] For this exercise, we begin with an acknowledgment that national and international aid agencies will continue to design, implement, and supervise many aspects of post-disaster relief, reconstruction, and recovery in developing countries, regardless of the potentially perverse outcomes of such efforts. Given this reality, the questions this chapter asks and seeks to answer are as follows: What are the characteristics of goods and services that constitute a post-disaster relief package? Are such characteristics endogenous? Are they dynamic? The answers to these questions can then pave ways to systematically analyze the appropriate modality(-ies) of post-disaster aid dissemination. An accurate understanding of the nature of each good or service is a necessary first step before we begin to formulate a framework that maps institutional types and levels to the scale of its production and provision.

First, I begin with an analysis of the nature of goods and services from Samuelson onward. Then, I examine how the Ostroms' framework that was built on the public choice foundation expands the narrow private-public dichotomy and provides a realistic and inclusive taxonomy of goods and services. Second, I discuss the dynamic nature of goods and services based on their shifting degrees of excludability and subtractability. Because the nature of goods is institutionally contingent, I argue that post-disaster institutional changes can lead to changes in their nature and their typology. Third, I present three case studies from different man-made and natural disasters in Chicago, New Orleans, and Indonesia to provide empirical evidence for the dynamic nature of post-disaster goods and services. Then, I discuss the challenges that stem from the shuffling of goods and services across different quadrants within the good-classification table. Fourth, I discuss the implications that the dynamic nature of post-disaster goods and services have for future policy research and practice. The final section concludes.

BEYOND THE PRIVATE-PUBLIC DICHOTOMY OF GOODS

Samuelson's (1954) formal exposition of what he termed *collective consumption goods* laid the foundation for the modern theory of public goods. He categorizes consumption goods into two types—private and collective—based on their binary characterization as either rivalrous or nonrivalrous.[4] Although he viewed his theory as having "little to contribute to discussion of the appropriate role of government," *publicness* of a good has been *the* theoretical justification for its public provision by the state (Hammond 2015).[5] A major deficiency with this conceptualization of goods is that it deals only with polar cases with "little reference to the real world" (Enke 1955). In fact, a vast majority of goods provided by the government are not exclusively "enjoyed in common" in that one's consumption of such good leads to some subtraction, either in quality or quantity, for others[6] (Margolis 1955). In an effort to close the gap between Samuelson's "purely private" and "purely public" goods, Buchanan develops the theory of clubs (Buchanan 1965). While some goods and services can be reasonably called "private" even by the strictest criteria of rivalry and excludability, goods that satisfy the characteristics of collective consumption are hard to find. Instead, they exhibit varying but finite degrees of "publicness." By emphasizing on an individual's utility rather than the good or service itself, he makes a subtle case for the "rivalrousness" of all goods.[7] Club theory relies on the possibility of exclusion to attain optimal-sharing arrangements, which requires "flexible property arrangements" and "excluding devices" (p. 14). That is, for any given property rights regime and the state of technology with considerable excludability restrictions, club good theory closes some gaps in the private-public spectrum but not all gaps (Sandler 2013). An alternate theory that does not assume away excludability is needed to fill other gaps.

Taking the nature of goods and services as "the analytical entry point," scholars of the Bloomington institutionalism picked up where the Virginia School left off (Aligica and Boettke 2009). For the Ostroms, the typology of a good determined by the "jointness of use or consumption" on the abscissa and "exclusion" on the ordinate defines its nature (Ostrom and Ostrom 2002). This framework is a step forward toward understanding both of these attributes (subtractability and excludability) in degrees rather than "all-or-none" categories (p. 77). Understood this way, a good belongs to a specific typology only insofar as its degrees of subtractability and excludability place it to that specific quadrant. In other words, when these degrees change substantially, the nature of a good defined in terms of its publicness (or privateness) also changes. This mode of analyzing goods reflects the Ostroms' pragmatic bend since no prior theory of goods—Samuelsonian private-public theory or Buchanan's club theory—had room for rivalrous goods that are nonexcludable, namely the common pool resources (CPRs).

In the case of CPR, exclusion may not be possible for a number of reasons. Aligica and Boettke (2009) point out that technology and institutions can create forms of exclusion and at times destroy them (p. 40). In the Turkish villages of Bodrum and the Bay of Izmir, the lack of an overarching institutional mechanism to design appropriation rules and address internal conflicts meant that new entrants seeking opportunities for quick economic gains could not be excluded (Ostrom 1990, 145). This led to overfishing and rent expropriation. In fisheries in Nova Scotia and Newfoundland, exclusion was attained because many local villages devised their own rules to determine who can use local fisheries and how to harvest resources (p. 144). When exclusion is viewed as being endogenous, as E. Ostrom does, one can then begin to think about an alternative institutional framework—one based on institutional diversity and polycentricity—that does not erroneously assume a static, homogeneous nature of goods. Such framework serves as a better foundation for the analysis of the nature and provision of goods and services based on the unique position that each good occupies within the subtractability-excludability matrix. If we are to simply follow the logic that private goods are best suited for private provision by a number of firms competing in the marketplace, then any good that has some degree of privateness—that is, those goods that are not fully public—should be provided through some competitive mechanism. Even if we overlook studies that show that public goods can be more efficiently provided by private firms,[8] taking this logic seriously leads us to conclude that only purely public goods that are perfectly nonexcludable and nonrivalrous are suitable for monopolistic provision by the state.

The challenge then can be defined as that of institutional matching (Furton and Martin 2019). Framing the problem this way has an advantage over the market-versus-government-failure paradigm in that it facilitates more productive discussions, incites more relevant research questions, and allows one to synthesize insights from public choice and new institutional economics (p. 198). Viewed this way, the relevant question is no longer "what is (are) the appropriate criterion (criteria) for the provision of goods by the government?" For the Ostroms, the public economy does not mean government monopoly but instead a mixed economy with maximum participation of the private sector in the production and delivery of public goods and services (Ostrom and Ostrom 2002, 75). Even Oates's (1972) "decentralization theorem," which shows that "efficient public goods provision occurs at the lowest level of government that internalizes relevant externalities" (Boettke, Coyne, and Leeson 2011), assumes too much in that it still places all goods into two separate buckets—*private versus public*. By freeing us from this private-versus-public two-bucket trap, the Ostroms open up the possibility of several potential arrangements for the supply and delivery of public goods and services. An analysis of the nature of goods is a prerequisite before proceeding to the central question: What are the appropriate institutional arrangements best catered to provide a variety of goods and services in a dynamic economy where technology and institutions are constantly evolving?

DYNAMIC NATURE OF GOODS

Despite their insistence that exclusion and subtractability[9] are matters of degrees and not of dichotomies, the Ostroms frequently use a *4x4* matrix (figure 1.1) to present the taxonomy of goods.[10] After all, they are clear that these are not "all-or-none" categories (p. 77). To understand why, one needs to delve into their epistemic choices. First, their emphasis is not to get the model right for the purpose of overall generalizability, but to "cut through complexity and retain enough elements" to make sure that the model is " realistic and relevant for the situations under consideration[11]" (Aligica 2014, 74). Second, the specific taxonomy is best suited for analyzing a particular class of goods they were studying that are (a) difficult to exclude and (b) subtractable, namely CPRs. Third, this presentation serves a distinct purpose in that it pays homage to its public choice roots by providing a common framework to place both club goods and CPRs alongside private and public goods. Therefore, this taxonomy is not to be interpreted as a rigid framework that merely expands the traditional two-box classification of goods into a four-box one.

Viewed this way, the taxonomy of goods is not one with four distinct boxes that determine a good's "type" but instead is one defined by varying degrees of excludability and subtractability. This opens up possibilities for new ways of analyzing goods that are consistent with the dynamic economy of the real world marked by frequent technological and institutional innovations. In other words, if the nature of goods is defined by specific features that have no theoretical or empirical basis for remaining static, then, extending this logic to its end, we are left to conclude that a dynamic taxonomy of goods is the next "trivial" step. The only intermediary task we have left is to present cases where goods and services shift their nature.[12] Before proceeding, let us briefly discuss each of these two features.

Excludability

A good or service is excludable to the extent that nonpurchasers can be precluded from enjoying its benefits. It is possible to create incentives for the private provision of a public good by bundling its consumption with another good that is excludable (Demsetz 1970). Candela and Geloso (2018) show that such bundling arrangements can occur even without any involvement of the state. We leave aside such possibilities and assume that nonexcludability is a qualifying criterion for the public provision of goods and services. For our purpose, it is sufficient to show that excludability of a good, even by the least stringent standards, is not exogenous. Ostrom (2003), in trying to distinguish between public goods and CPRs, presents arguments to this effect. Collective action problems for these two categories of goods differ vastly "in regard to how costly or difficult it is to devise physical and institutional means to exclude others" (p. 241). In other words, it is possible, albeit with varying levels of difficulty, to devise "physical and institutional means" that allow one to tinker with degrees of excludability. It can be argued that profit opportunities in devising such means of exclusion drive entrepreneurs to provide private solutions to many public good problems. Cowen (1985) uses the provision of protection services as an example of a good that has dual modes of supplying (p. 59). The same service can be supplied either by a patrolman walking the beat or by burglar alarms (McCubbins and Schwartz 1984). The first is *a non-marketing mode* with higher difficulties of exclusion, whereas the second is *a marketing mode* where exclusion is feasible. Cowen (1985) contends that the publicness of every good is institutionally contingent.[13,14] That is, any good can be made more (or less) public by examining it in different institutional contexts. Movie theater is one such example of a good where exclusion is attained by requiring admission fees.[15] Changes in existing institutions can not only alter costs of exclusion but can also influence exclusion criteria (legal rules, cultural norms).

Rivalrousness/Subtractability

A rivalrous good is one that may be provided to an additional person at a very low marginal cost. The quantity (or quality) of a purely nonrivalrous good is not reduced (or subtracted) because of another person's use. Weather forecast, roads, fire station, and national security are presented as typical examples. Critiques point out that no good satisfies such criteria. Roads during heavy traffic are rivalrous, as additional users lead to more congestion (Cowen 1985). The very existence of intersections and stoplights proves that one person's use of the good necessarily interferes with that of another person (p. 55). Coyne (2015) makes a similar case for the rivalrousness of national defense. Because the same missile cannot protect two geographic areas within the nation, the use of that missile to protect New York City necessarily subtracts from (the possibility of) its use to protect Los Angeles (p. 374). That is not to argue that national defense is a private good, but rather that rivalrousness itself should be viewed as a continuum and not as dichotomies. Despite some degree of rivalrousness, it is safe to say that national defense exhibits a higher degree of nonrivalrousness than bread or pen. More importantly, rivalrousness of the same good is institutionally contingent. Cowen (1985), invoking Minasian (1964), presents television as an example of a good that can be changed from a public good into a private good by technological innovations (p. 55). Other elements of institutional contingency include level of use, appropriate choice of marginal unit, and the quantity or service capacity of a good (pp. 55, 56). Formal and informal governing institutions also influence the rivalrousness of goods. As a more perverse case, we may consider *Dalits* in part of the Indian subcontinent who are considered "untouchables." Under the highly segregated, discriminatory system of untouchability, goods that are typically deemed nonrivalrous, such as schools, temples, shrines, rivers, or bazaars, can become rivalrous. A Dalit's entry to such public places make these places "impure," thereby precluding a Brahmin priest from entering them. In other words, a good's degree of rivalrousness is not necessarily its intrinsic feature. Various factors such as the state of technology, or legal, political, religious, and cultural institutions can influence its level of rivalrousness.

Nature of Goods in a Post-Disaster Context

Chamlee-Wright (2010) characterizes a post-disaster context as one where "much of the order we take for granted is shattered" (p. 4). When a covariate shock of a considerable magnitude strikes, infrastructures and institutions that hold communities and nations together can collapse (Rayamajhee, Bohara, and Storr 2019). Because the attributes that determine the typology of goods are institutionally contingent as previously discussed, it must then be the case that post-disaster institutional shock leads to changes in the typology of goods. The precise direction of that change is an empirical question. However, it is not unreasonable to assume that the direction will generally be away from the status quo. To better understand the dynamics, let us use the Ostroms' *4*x*4* typology of goods presented in figure 1.1 as the starting point. For analytical simplicity, I slightly deviate from the convention and present a revised good-classification in figure 1.2. The origin *(0,0)* represents the point of maximum nonexcludability and nonrivalry/nonsubtractability, where the pure public good is situated. The top-right corner is the point of maximum excludability and rivalry, which is reserved for pure private goods. In the revised typology matrix, club goods, CPRs (impure), public goods, and (impure) private goods occupy, respectively, the top-left, bottom-right, bottom-left, and top-right quadrants.

Consider a good A_i that is to be produced and/or provided in a post-disaster context, where $i=0,1,2,3. . . .N-1$ represents a (x,y) coordinate in figure 1.2 such that high x and y values represent high degrees of subtractability and excludability, respectively; N indicates the number of feasible configurations that A_i can attain. Horizontal lines L_{Ht} and vertical lines L_{Vt} indicate thresholds at period t that determine excludability and subtractability, respectively. For instance, for A_i such that $i(x> L_{Vt}, y> L_{Ht})$, the good is considered private, and

Figure 1.1 Conventional Classification of Goods. *Source:* Ostrom et al 1994.

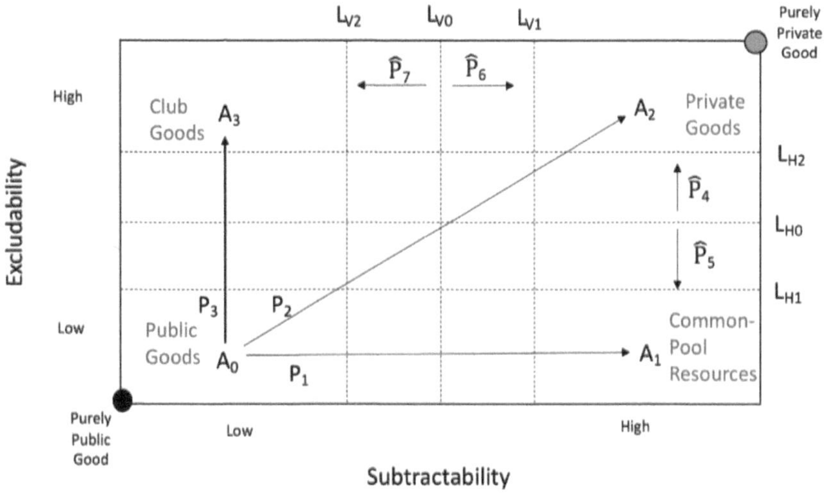

Figure 1.2 Dynamic Nature of Post-Disaster Goods and Services.

so on. In figure 1.2, A_0 is the original position of good A_i at a specific period. Alternate positions A_1, A_2, and A_3 are other feasible configurations of good A_i. For illustrative purposes, I assume $N=4$. After a shock (technological or institutional change), A_i can move from A_0 to A_1, A_2, A_3 with probabilities P_1, P_2, P_3, respectively. In other cases (not shown in figure 1.2), A_i can move from A_1 to A_0, A_2, A_3, from A_2 to A_0, A_1, A_3, or from A_3 to A_0, A_1, A_2 with different probabilities. Also assume $\sum_{i=1}^{N-1} P_i = 1$ for each A_i. On the other hand, L_{Ht} and L_{Vt} can shift from their original positions (L_{H0} and L_{V0}) to new positions (L_{Ht} and L_{Vt} , $t>0$) with corresponding probabilities of $\hat{P}_4$, $\hat{P}_5$, $\hat{P}_6$, and $\hat{P}_7$, respectively.[16] Also, for each L_{Ht} and L_{Vt}, $\sum_t \hat{P}_t = 1$. While I have limited the number of possible positions of A_i, L_{Ht}, and L_{Vt} to a bare minimum necessary for analysis, it should be noted that a large number of configurations are feasible with varying probabilities. Another crucial consideration to bear in mind is that figure 1.2 presents a one-shot ($n=1$) representation of $n \in [0,1,2,3,\ldots N-1]$ possible sequential moves. So, the analytical framework gets increasingly complex as I add additional goods and services and/or increase the number of sequential moves to $n>1$.

Now let us consider a shock that leads to changes in degrees of excludability and/or subtractability of goods and services. This can happen in a number of ways. Power outages following a natural disaster can disrupt or destroy security technology and other excluding devices that make the provision of many private or club goods feasible. A community gymnasium that relies exclusively on technology to exclude nonmembers may face the challenge of distinguishing former members from current members. That is, the services it provides become less excludable (shift: A_3 toward A_0). Disruption of internet service in private homes and its limited access in restaurants and local libraries decrease its excludability (shift: A_2 toward A_1). In other cases, technology can facilitate exclusion and create more club goods (Sandler 2013). Following the California wildfires, one website used community cams to provide many residents who fled their homes to safety a means to keep track of their properties, thereby making them more excludable than they would otherwise be (Hughes et al. 2008). In this specific scenario, the disaster made household properties nonexcludable (shift: A_2 toward A_1) but community efforts and entrepreneurial ingenuity increased excludability (shift: A_1 toward A_2). On the other hand, goods and services with considerably low marginal costs at higher levels of output can undergo an increase in their subtractability due to a disruption in supply chain or an overall reduction in supply. For instance, in a scenario characterized by waterborne disease pandemic, such as the one that occurred in post-2010-earthquake Port-au-Prince, Haiti, safe water can become a highly subtractable good owing to its limited supply (shift: A_0 toward A_1). The good (safe water) which was previously available as a nonsubtractable resource freely available from the Artibonite River became highly subtractable once the source was contaminated by cholera (Knox 2012).

On the other hand, economy-wide institutional changes that preclude legal enforcement of private property rights can shrink the domain of the private sector. A coercive takeover of any industry through nationalization schemes such as that of Carlos Andres Perez's economic plan *La Gran Venezuela* may be represented as an elimination of the entire upper-right quadrant in figure 1.2. Instead of moving all goods of any industry to a different quadrant individually, this industry-wide change is better represented by shifting both L_{Ht} upward and L_{vt} toward right until the top-right quadrant virtually disappears.[17] Interestingly, this depiction of an extreme scenario also provides a framework to explain why civil society and community-based organizations can become dormant as the public sphere expands (Boettke et al. 2007; Boettke, Coyne, and Leeson 2011; Rajan 2019).

CASES OF POST-DISASTER SHUFFLING OF GOOD-TYPOLOGY

Chicago Fire 1871

The Good

The Chicago fire of 1871 turned private assets valued at over $200 million at the time to ashes overnight, leaving more than a third of the city's inhabitants homeless (Andreas 1884; Skarbek 2014). In the wake of the destruction, volunteers gathered in one of the few remaining buildings in the city and identified three pressing needs that had to be addressed immediately: distribution of food to the victims, organizing citizen patrol for community safety, and the immediate restoration of businesses (CRAS 1874; Skarbek 2014). The list of other post-disaster needs included temporary housing, clothing, household necessities, swift transportation, and medical services (Skarbek 2014, 161–168). These are diverse goods and services of varying levels of excludability and subtractability in normal times, and are provided through different private and public institutional arrangements. Food, clothing, shelter, and household necessities (FCSH) are highly subtractable and excludable, and are therefore best suited for pure private provision. Compared to FCSH, medical services, transportation, and community safety (MTC) exhibit lower (higher) degrees of excludability (nonexcludability) and are less subtractable. Depending on the modes of production and/or provision, MTC are provided through different private, public, or club-like arrangements. To distinguish them from FCSH, we classify them as public, however it need not be necessarily so. On the other hand, the benefits of business restoration or the normal functioning of markets are highly nonexcludable and nonsubtractable, which is a distinctly *public* feature. In a modern economy, it is generally expected that the government ought to be responsible for establishing or maintaining certain institutional requisites essential for market operation.

Institutional Response

Skarbek (2014) provides a detailed account of the role of the Chicago Relief and Aid Society (henceforth CRAS), which she characterizes as "a voluntary association of agents with a stake in relief outcomes," in post-disaster relief efforts. CRAS board of directors comprised of members who had "deep collective interest in the community's welfare" (p. 173). Many had made fortunes in Chicago, all suffered losses from the fire, and were personally invested in ensuring that the city returned to prosperity. Members of the executive committee represented local businesses and cultural and religious communities, and they had "extensive experience and considerable specialized knowledge about operating large firms and social organizations within the community" (p. 172). Instead of attempting to take complete control of post-disaster response, Mayor Mason prudently handed over relief efforts to CRAS, and even ordered police commissioners not to interfere with the city's restoration and recovery attempts (Colbert and Chamberlin 2012). Despite Mayor Mason's request for noninterference, General Sheridan imposed martial law and enforced price controls (Sawislak 1995). This meant that price signals that are crucial to determine demands for specific goods and services were ineffective. This further exacerbated the already-interrupted flow of goods and services. In such a situation, the conventional classification of goods and services holds little meaning, as a forced publicness is imposed upon all goods and services (shift from A_1, A_2, A_3 toward A_0), subjecting them to problems of free riding and misappropriation.

Shifting of Goods and Services

In the absence of formal political or bureaucratic organization equipped to handle disaster relief, CRAS was able to "leverage organizational assets" and "constitutional rules" to effectively overcome challenges of moral hazard and free riding that could have further complicated disaster response (Skarbek 2014, 155). In such a situation, CRAS was able to mobilize local knowledge, expertise, and willpower to conduct an *appropriate bundling* of these goods and services as *disaster relief* and shift them to a quadrant where free-riding problem could be resolved. Once aid contributions have been made, they "exhibit features of a common pool resource" (Skarbek 2014, 156). That is, they are subtractable in consumption, but nonexcludable to disaster victims. Like many successful CPRs that Ostrom (1990) describes, CRAS was able to devise operational rules based on "strong pre-established principles" (p. 174). Exclusion was attained using appropriation rules that specified "who had rights to withdraw resources" from the collected aid funds and what the eligibility criteria were for receiving aid (p. 173). Locally instituted mechanisms for detecting fraudulent claims, "credible enforcement strategy" involving self-monitoring by fellow community members, and mobilization of local knowledge to assess needs and disseminate aid ensured that aid reached those populations that were "most in need" (p. 169).

Thus, owing to the institutional ingenuity of CRAS, heterogeneous goods that are traditionally deemed public (MTC) and private (FCSH) were bundled into one *disaster relief* package (now CPR). This rebundling is an institutional solution that CRAS deemed most appropriate under the circumstances where both government and markets were nonexistent or dysfunctional. Lack of private mechanisms such as storage facilities necessary for private provision of vegetables and other perishable items meant that a nonmarket, nongovernmental solution was needed. CRAS was able to use local expertise of Murray Nelson to transform a local skating rink into a frost-proof building for storage purposes (p. 173). On the other hand, the absence of local (and national) political and bureaucratic apparatus meant that security services were no longer appropriate for public provision. In that sense, both private and public goods had lost their privateness or publicness because of the changes in their degrees of excludability and subtractability. A new institutional solution was necessary to address a new situation where the conventional static classification of goods was unable to provide a practical framework to overcome this challenge. CRAS provided that solution by shifting goods and services to the CPR quadrant (A_2 to A_1 for FCHS, A_0 to A_1 for MTC).

Hurricane Katrina 2005

The Good

Chamlee-Wright and Storr (2009) report the case of Mary Queen of Vietnam (MQVN) community in New Orleans East after Hurricane Katrina in 2005, where the local Catholic church utilized "a bundle of club goods" to solve social coordination problems in the wake of the disaster. This "highly specific culturally and linguistically appropriate" bundle of goods included the following: (i) Vietnamese language training, (ii) religious services, (iii) occasional weekend markets for selling Vietnamese produce, arts, and crafts, (iv) informal social space, (v) meeting space for religious and nonreligious groups, (vi) organization structure for social coordination, (vii) community leadership for collective action, and (viii) ethnically appropriate charitable aid (p. 440). Additionally, because the group of church members also included local business owners and professionals, other secondary goods such as (ix) medical, (x) legal, and (xi) financial services came attached alongside the church bundle. Many of these services could be classified as private in peaceful times (e.g., medical, legal, and financial services) that are suitable for private provision by competing firms. On the other hand, some are typical club goods (e.g., meeting space for religious and nonreligious groups), whereas others are highly nonsubtractable and nonexcludable (e.g., weekend markets). While many "ethnically sensitive goods and services" can be typically transacted as private goods (in ethnic grocery stores and supermarts) within any specific ethnic in-group, the in-group itself may operate as a club in some instances. The MQVN Church also provided cultural services that were directly aimed at increasing their cultural capital—their "Vietnameseness[18]" (p. 441). In normal times, cultural capital can be characterized as being highly nonexcludable and nonsubtractable but many cultural services (e.g., language training) can be considered private goods.

Institutional Response

The MQVN community was founded by roughly 1,000 Roman Catholic refugees from North Vietnam who fled to the United States and settled in New Orleans East (Bankston and Zhou 2000; Grube and Storr 2014). The MQVN Catholic Church, referred by members of the community as *the center*, was "the center stage for social [and religious] activities," both before and after Katrina (Grube and Storr 2014). MQVN experienced the full brunt of the hurricane, which forced most residents to emigrate out of New Orleans East. When governments at the local, state, and national levels were mired in fraud and abuse of funds[19], the MQVN Church played a critical role in ensuring community return and facilitating redevelopment of New Orleans East (Boettke et al. 2007). The church was able to leverage its bonding and bridging social capital to effectively coordinate across local organizations and mobilize volunteers toward the goal of community's recovery. Chamlee-Wright and Storr (2010) document Father Vien's social entrepreneurial role in utilizing MQVN's shared histories and perspectives to forge a collective narrative. Fr. Vien possessed an endowment of "local knowledge" of their shared history of hardship that traced back to their North Vietnam times. He was able to expend that endowment toward unifying community and overcoming post-disaster challenges (p. 313). Moreover, Fr. Vien and other leaders of the MQVN Catholic Church had deep insights into the immediate needs of the community members. They understood their community's shared concerns that a steady flow of goods and services had to be restored to ensure community return and long-term recovery.

Shifting of Goods and Services

The bundle of club goods that the MQVN Church provided to its community members consists of heterogeneous elements that typically require diverse modes of production and/or provision. A few goods and services such as Vietnamese language training, ethnically appropriate charitable aid, and social space for informal gathering directly pertain to cultural capital (*Vietnameseness*), so it makes sense to bundle them together. But many other goods (e.g., medical, financial, and legal services) are not natural constituents of that bundle. However, in a post-disaster setting where infrastructures that support private or public provision of such goods and services are no longer intact, the MQVN Church served as a club and provided many of these services in the form of club goods (shift from A_0, A_1, A_2 to A_3). When profit-driven markets that operate based on price signals were missing, Fr. Vien and the church leaders were able to mobilize "their knowledge of place and time" to estimate demand for various market goods and services and appropriately bundle them (shift from A_2 to A_3). Bundling them as club goods then became an institutional innovation of sorts to achieve economies of scale that could facilitate the regular flow of goods and services.

The heterogeneity and interconnectedness of some of these goods require further attention. Let us reconsider *Vietnameseness*. In the aftermath of the hurricane, the MQVN Church facilitated the provision of various cultural services associated with increasing cultural capital among its members. In pre-Katrina MQVN, it would be impossible to exclude a nonmember from acquiring *Vietnameseness* if she/he was eager to do so. Nor can one person's *Vietnameseness* preclude someone else from acquiring it. However, the disaster altered the nature of *Vietnameseness* as a good. Because the community that made the good *public* was shattered, it lost its publicness. An existential threat meant that *Vietnameseness* was no longer as abundant. Since it has a positive value, the church then provided many *Vietnameseness*-related cultural services as club goods alongside other club goods. The "new" *Vietnameseness* (as a good), although nonsubtractable, is now excludable to some extent (shift from A_0 to A_3). Moreover, community members themselves are both producers and consumers of many of these goods and services. This means that a disruption within the community can interrupt both the production and consumption of such goods. For instance, it is very likely that both Vietnamese language tutors (providers) and the younger members of the community (potential consumers) were severely affected by the hurricane. Unlike in the case of market goods that are not location specific, language training service could not be supplanted from external markets. The MQVN Church remedied this by bundling it alongside other club goods that it provided (shift from A_2 to A_3). Note that the church continued to provide other club goods such as meeting space for religious and nonreligious groups (no shift).

Indonesian Tsunami 2004

The Good

Of all the places hit by the Indian Ocean earthquake and tsunami on December 26, 2004, the Indonesian province of Aceh was the worst affected. In a span of a few hours, 169,000 lives were lost; 141,000 private houses, 2,240 schools, and 2,676 bridges were destroyed; and 600,000 people became homeless (Kenny, Fan, and Palmer 2006). Also, 25,000 families needed relocating because the tsunami engulfed their lands and properties (Fan 2006). Once the waves settled, the most urgent task that lied ahead was the provision of shelter. Constructing houses for resettlement became the foremost priority of most aid agencies as well as provincial and national governments.

In a nondisaster context, a house is an archetypal private good. Doors or gates ensure that entry is restricted to members of the household. Property rights provide protection against forceful confiscation. If one household purchases a house, that specific house will no longer be available to another household. Similarly, most materials required to build a house are also private goods. Cement, sand, bricks, and timber are freely traded in Indonesian markets.

Institutional Response

When the tsunami struck coastal villages in Aceh, the province had already been undergoing a violent separatist conflict for over three decades. Martial law was in place, and only a select few aid organizations were allowed access in the first few days (Rand, Hirano, and Kelman 2011). As soon as government restrictions were lifted, aid organizations flooded Aceh, with over sixty agencies working on the ground. Political uncertainty and steep competition among aid agencies intensified pressures to spend funds quickly (Bhattacharjee et al. 2005; Kennedy et al. 2008). Most aid agencies lacked the "psychological and sociological texture of the Achenese" and were unable to use "local components and knowledge" (Lanti 2006). This meant increased consulting costs. Moreover, most international aid agencies, including Oxfam, had "at least one case of financial irregularities during the reconstruction" (Rand, Hirano, and Kelman 2011). On the other hand, citing "diminished capacity of the local government" in Aceh, the central government commissioned a special body *Badan Rehabilitasi dan Rekonstruksi Aceh dan Nias* (BRR) to plan, oversee, and manage reconstruction efforts (ibid). While donor agencies and BRR swamped Aceh, foreign investors, including those that were already operating in the region, shied away from making investments in the region.

Shifting of Excludability-Thresholds

In pre-tsunami Aceh, property rights were governed by "a hybrid of customs and laws" introduced over the feudal, colonial, and postindependence periods. Only 25 percent of land in Aceh was formally registered under government laws. The rest was governed by traditional *Adat* practices (Kenny, Fan, and Palmer 2006). The tsunami swept away government offices and destroyed all property documents.[20] Trees and paths that marked landholdings and artificial boundaries were gone, and the social institutions that complemented legal infrastructures were ruptured (ibid). Overnight, legal and social institutions that preserved the privateness of houses and landholdings were no longer intact. Moreover, rampant corruption in public administration and the fact that property documents no longer existed meant that any hopes of claiming legal ownership in the future were also lost. That is, houses and landholdings had lost their privateness entirely. It is no surprise that "no one chose to build their own house" even when presented with that option (Adams and Harvey 2006).

Given the tardiness of the local legal system, prohibitive costs of contract enforcement, and rampant corruption, not only was the legitimacy of ownership (of houses and landholdings) challenged but the markets for materials and labor required for reconstruction were also dysfunctional. Henderson and

Lee (2015) describe several adverse consequences associated with high risks of contract hazards in post-tsunami Aceh (p. 620). In many cases, builders can demand more money than was agreed upon contractually in an attempt to expropriate quasi-rents when the construction is midway. Because the costs of finding new builders and enforcing the original contract are prohibitive, the implementer usually has no choice but to cave in. For domestic builders, low-probability–high-intensity shocks present one-shot prisoner's dilemma games where incentives are aligned in ways that shirking becomes the dominant strategy.[21] Consequently, trust and reciprocity that are vital for market transactions to occur are greatly undermined.

Cowen's (1985) analysis that the nature of a good depends on (a) how much of the good is produced, and (b) how intense the demand is for the good is particularly relevant here (p. 53). The intense, highly inelastic demand for housing leads to increased demand for plumbers, carpenters, day labor, and materials. Moreover, when private citizens, domestic and international aid agencies, implementers, builders, and local and national governments are all competing for a finite pool of labor and capital, the equilibrium does not reflect the "true" demand for those goods in that international aid agencies and governments do not face realistic budget constraints.[22,23] In that sense, distorted incentives and price indifference faced by some players mean that the market is not allowed to function normally. All these factors distort the privateness of materials for reconstruction.

When legal infrastructures (e.g., courts and rule of law) and social (e.g., *Adat* practices) and cultural (e.g., norms of trust and reciprocity) institutions necessary for private transactions and contract enforcement are stripped away as in the case of Aceh, what constitutes the private sector is largely diminished. In the new post-tsunami scenario, the entire housing sector and its tertiary industries had lost their excludability. This can be presented as a case where the excludability threshold for the entire sector shifts upward (line L_{Ht} shifts upward from L_{H0} to L_{H2}), thereby shrinking the private sector. Note that this "new publicness" does not, however, mean that BRR was better equipped to fulfill housing needs. In fact, BRR's nonintrusive engagement or noninvolvement could have created incentives for the private provision of many goods and services (Vogler 2019). Instead, its subpar involvement led to a vacuum that was swiftly filled by a number of aid agencies all competing for a finite pool of aid monies toward building houses. The "new" good that had emerged—*aid* toward housing, construction materials—morphed into a perverse CPR; it was subtractable (finite amount of aid money) but nonexcludable to new appropriators (domestic and international aid agencies). Twenty-one percent of the houses that aid agencies built for tsunami-affected population remained unoccupied, whereas many beneficiaries received multiple houses from different aid agencies (AIPRD/LOGICA 2007; Rand,

Hirano, and Kelman 2011). These realities testify to the level of overextraction and free-riding problems associated with underperforming CPRs.

TOWARD INSTITUTIONAL MATCHING AND POLYCENTRIC GOVERNANCE

The forgoing cases emphasize the dynamic feature of post-disaster goods' classification—that is, the typology of goods is defined by existing technology and institutions, both of which are constantly evolving. Disasters are exogenous shocks that shake existing institutions, including, in many cases, those that facilitate market operations and the protection of property rights. Simultaneously, they also shock public institutions and hinder public good production and provision. The cases show that not only do goods move across boxes/quadrants in the good classification table, but the lines (separating the types) themselves become blurry or flexible. In such situations, a one-size-fits-all approach that does not account for the diversity and fluidity of post-disaster goods and services is ineffective, if not outright detrimental, to recovery and well-being. Therefore, instead of adhering to a static model of good classification, I emphasize the need to constantly reexamine the shifting nature of post-disaster goods and services. However, this need for reexamination should not be mistaken as a pursuit for *the right model* from a purely scientific rigor point of view. The Ostroms emphasize ideas, but not for the sake of mere theoretical, normative, and philosophical inquiry (Aligica 2014). What adds weight to their ideas is their "insistence on the fact that social scientists should try to think not only in terms of creating theory but also of applying it" (Aligica and Boettke 2009). So, the precision and scientific rigor of these models have to be evaluated alongside their associated trade-offs in terms of policy relevance (McGinnis 2018).

The Institutional Analysis and Development (IAD) framework that Ostrom proposed provides a "deceptively simple" yet powerful toolkit that allows us to navigate the complexities of the real world with multitiered, intertwined institutions that many technically sophisticated models in social sciences even fail to recognize (Aligica and Boettke 2009, 72). Once we rightly identify the nature of the good under consideration, along with relevant biophysical conditions, social and cultural attributes of the community, and formal and informal configurations of rules-in-use, we have the necessary tools to analyze different interlinked action situations within the IAD framework. We can then evaluate post-disaster challenges as social dilemmas involving a diverse array of private and public actors locked in a network of adjacent action situations (NAAS), where outcomes from one action situation influences rules in other interactions occurring in adjacent action situations (McGinnis 2011).

Such method of analysis can provide useful insights into the motivations and actions of actors in different positions and their associated outcomes. This line of inquiry can guide us to a better understanding of flexible institutional arrangements that are responsive to the changing nature of goods and services in post-disaster settings. In Elinor Ostrom's own words: "Unless institutional arrangements are able to respond to ever changing environments, the sustainability of situations is likely to suffer. Rural areas of developing countries are often faced with natural disasters and highly localized special circumstances. If an institutional arrangement is too inflexible to cope with these unique conditions, it is unlikely to prosper" (Ostrom 2011).

This chapter provides no panacea that can be applied based on bullet point instructions. In fact, Bloomington scholars warn against the lure of "panacea traps"—a naive presumption that a blueprint for the ideal governance structure (government ownership, privatization, community property) to solve all our problems exists (Ostrom 2007; Ostrom, Janssen, and Anderies 2007). Instead, what they offer is a "metatheoretical conceptual map" that provides us with diagnostic tools to determine how the nature of the good (or resource system), attributes of the community, and rules-in-use shape any given action situation where actors interact (ibid). However, the tools are only useful if the elements in the IAD framework are not misspecified. The cases presented in this chapter tell us that the standard view misspecifies the nature of most post-disaster goods and services. Two faulty conclusions derive from this premise. First, it provides a justification for the *Gargantua* approach to post-disaster policy analysis and practice. The assumed publicness of goods in a post-disaster scenario means that central planning authorities with presumed "unlimited cognitive capacity for information gathering and analysis" and "disinterestedness" ought to be in charge (McGinnis 2018; V. Ostrom 2008). Second, the crisis brought forth by disasters means that private actors find themselves in Hardin's "tragedy of the commons" situation, unable to establish or maintain self-governing institutions (Hardin 1968). This chapter refutes both conclusions.

Instead, the diversity of goods and their dynamic nature means that post-disaster policy responses should be directed toward identifying and working with a diverse set of possible institutional arrangements suited for their production and provision. A "polycentric system" of governance with "many [independent] centers of decision making," competing in some actions situations and cooperating in others, provides better analytical and policy tools to account for a wide diversity of institutions that operate in post-disaster contexts (V. Ostrom, Tiebout, and Warren 1961). This way of understanding post-disaster challenges using the "institutional matching" paradigm as opposed to the standard optimal resource allocation view steers us toward building a conceptual framework that matches institutional types and levels to the nature of the good or the type of collective action problem in hand. Within a polycentric framework, we can have a variety of formal and informal institutions (overlapping or disjoint) operating at different scales to produce and provide a wide variety of post-disaster goods and services and to overcome a diverse set of context-specific problems. Such an approach better reflects post-disaster scenarios of the real world where a wide variety of actors, including government agencies (local, regional, and national), businesses, domestic and international aid agencies, voluntary associations, and citizens, interact in diverse action situations. It also accounts for the crucial economic roles that social entrepreneurs and community's social capital play in many crises (Rayamajhee and Bohara 2019a, 2019b; Rayamajhee, Storr, and Bohara 2019).

CONCLUSION

What I seek to establish in this chapter is that goods and services—because their typology is institutionally contingent—can shift in their degrees of excludability and subtractability following a covariate shock. Because the rationale for private or public provision of goods and services stem from these two attributes, changes in their degrees must necessarily lead to changes in the institutional arrangements suitable for their continued provision. The forgoing cases from man-made and natural disasters demonstrate that bottom-up institutions that possess the knowledge of time and place are better equipped to understand the changing nature of goods and services during uncertain times and adjust their modes of provision accordingly. We find that there is a strong tendency for goods and services to move away from the classic private-public diagonal toward the club-CPR diagonal (refer to figure 1.2). This can happen because of two reasons. On the one hand, disasters can severely impact institutions that make markets feasible. On the other hand, bureaucratic slowness, political pressure to hide inefficiencies, and the lack of incentives and knowledge of government actors can cripple government institutions. In such situations, while external assistance is often necessary, local institutions that have context-specific knowledge and proper incentives to act quickly and appropriately are better equipped to handle crises. CRAS and the Catholic church of MQVN were able to utilize their rich social capital and local expertise to overcome coordination failure problems. CRAS leveraged their organizational assets and constitutional rules in a typical successful CPR fashion for the provision of disaster relief. The MQVN Church acted as a club to provide diverse and highly specialized goods and services, many of which are not typically considered club goods. Not only was the church able to provide these goods, but it was also able to use them for the higher purpose of ensuring community return. In the Aceh case, although the good (housing) did not change in terms of its degree of subtractability,[24] the failure of public institutions and the lack of market infrastructures made excludability near impossible, rendering good classification meaningless. In this case, donor implementers (often foreign) outperform both domestic implementers and the government. The lack of appropriate incentives and personal stake in the recovery process led the domestic implementers to engage in rent expropriation. This case tells us that what may seem like local governance from outside the sheath does not always correspond to self-governance.

Moreover, reconstruction and recovery efforts following a disaster are best characterized by coproduction processes—that is, active participation of disaster victims and other citizens is an important input into the production function (Rayamajhee, Storr, and Bohara 2019). The coordination of such coproduction processes becomes increasingly difficult as bureaucratic hierarchies get steeper. Sobel and Leeson (2007) attribute this difficulty to the knowledge problem that a central planner faces in a highly idiosyncratic post-disaster context. Another factor that exacerbates the coordination problem is one of the incentive misalignment that is created when large sums of disaster aid is flooded into one or few locations through the public sector (Boettke et al. 2007). Regardless of how benevolent the management of a central planning agency may be, one cannot assume that each government agent is motivated solely by the goals of efficiency and equity in post-disaster aid dissemination. This is especially true when we consider the fact that the performance of the agency is evaluated as a whole, and not as individuals or independently mobilized teams. Ostrom and her coauthors have shown that similar "perverse incentives" can plague development aid agencies working in post-disaster assistance (Gibson et al. 2005). In light of these considerations, efforts should be devoted to investigating polycentric approaches to post-disaster management where a variety of adaptive institutions compete and/or cooperate in a multitude of ways for the production and/or provision of a wide range of post-disaster goods and services.

My analysis that bottom-up institutions are more effective than central authorities for the provision of local public needs is consistent with theoretical and empirical studies in economics and public policy in a wide variety of nondisaster situations as well (e.g., Ostrom 1990). However, those in charge of post-disaster relief, reconstruction, and recovery often present "bottom-up" strategies that are designed, implemented, and monitored by a slew of experts and planners. Phrases like "local knowledge," "participatory approach," and "citizen science" appear in every white paper and recovery plan. The cases presented in this chapter tell us that bottom-up does not simply mean domestic or local. The litmus test for what constitutes "bottom-up" is self-governance. If de facto rules at the operational level are inadequate to address imminent challenges, "level-shifting" mechanisms to make changes in operational rules at collective choice and even constitutional levels through active participation of self-governing citizens must be in place (Ostrom 2009). Self-governance cannot be designed as an expert-guided "optimal" policy to be implemented through careful control from "benevolent" rulers. Amid terror and devastation brought forth by disasters lies an opportunity to observe, analyze, and understand diverse institutions at all levels and of all types. Disasters have a way of presenting and amplifying the inner workings of all such institutions. A careful examination of post-disaster recovery processes tells us that the entrepreneurial spirit of private, public, and social entrepreneurs and the sheer will of citizens are necessary conditions for successful rebounding. Any carefully crafted policies that threaten these conditions guide us not toward but away from recovery and prosperity. Any successful disaster recovery is always a story of many heroes—of private, public, and social entrepreneurs, of self-governing citizens—and never one of a single hero, the planner-rescuer.

NOTES

1. Peter Boettke, Bobbi Herzberg, Brian Kogelmann, Pablo Paniagua Prieto, and Virgil Storr provided helpful comments on earlier versions of this chapter. I am grateful to the participants of the Adam Smith Fellowship seminar research sequence for their friendship and enthusiasm. Without Peter Lipsey's timely instructions and assistance, the chapter would not exist.

2. Reports and recovery plans from government authorities incorporate best practices that include community participation and civic engagement, but such policies "cease on paper" and are rarely implemented in practice (Daly et al. 2017; Rayamajhee, Bohara, and Storr 2019).

3. Although governments often do not produce many goods and services included in the package, bundling diverse elements of the package allows them to not only handpick producers from among its allies in the private sector but also engage in rent-seeking behavior.

4. Samuelson, alongside Musgrave, is credited for the textbook definition of a public good as a good that is both nonrivalrous and nonexcludable. Although Samuelson's mathematical definition of public goods from his 1954 paper *The Pure Theory of Public Expenditure* is the most accepted formal model of public goods, the qualitative understanding of public goods owes more to Musgrave's work excludability criterion (Desmarais-Tremblay 2014). Musgrave (1969) was the first to use both criteria (nonrivalry and nonexcludability) for defining pure public goods (Pickhardt 2006).

5. Because individuals have incentives to hide their true valuation of collective consumption goods when opportunities to free ride on others exist, he contends that such goods are undersupplied by competitive markets. The implication of this

Samuelsonian dichotomy is that the "servant" of the "ethical observer," the state, ought to set the optimal taxes and subsidies to ensure optimal supply of such goods.

6. Examples include education, hospitals, highways, and even police and judicial services (p. 347).

7. He argues that the utility that an individual derives from the consumption of any good or service depends, regardless of its ultimate place on the private-public spectrum, upon the "number of other persons with whom he must share its benefits" (3). The task he undertook was then to determine the "membership margin" to attain the "most desirable cost and consumption sharing arrangement" (2). For each good, a unique optimal sharing threshold, N_j can be computed which indicates the degree of its "publicness."

8. For examples of this, see Candela and Geloso (2018); Koyama (2012); Tabarrok (1998), among others.

9. Rivalrousness and subtractability are used synonymously in the literature. E. Ostrom prefers to use subtractability when referring to CPRs.

10. Source: Ostrom, Gardner, Walker, and Walker (1994). Different variations of the same taxonomy can be found in Ostrom and Ostorm (2002) and elsewhere.

11. This in no way suggests that her approach was subjective and opportunistic. Aligica (2014) provides a detailed discussion of Ostrom's epistemic and methodological approaches in chapter 3. She makes a distinction between frameworks, theories, and models. Frameworks use the most general set of variables to evaluate all settings. A theory specifies relevant components of a framework to best describe a phenomenon. Several theoretical perspectives can be consistent with a single framework. Models only capture a narrow set of parameters and variables to illustrate or examine a theory or make predictions based on the theory (pp. 93, 94).

12. Note that the burden of proof required for the empirical validity for this claim is extremely low. We need to only convince readers that the observed cases of the shifting nature of goods are not exception but normal occurrences. However, to make a plausible countercase, one needs to show that no good ($n \rightarrow \infty$) has dynamic characteristics.

13. Cowen presents seven such "institutional elements of importance": (1) production technology, (2) quantity of production, (3) distribution mechanism of the product, (4) intensity of demand for the product, (5) definition of marginal unit, (6) definition of "consumption," and (7) different meanings of exclusion (p. 53).

14. Similar arguments have been presented by Aligica and Boettke (2009). As discussed earlier, they argue that technology and institutions can create or destroy forms of exclusion (p. 40).

15. With larger turnout, however, difficulties for exclusion increase (p. 61). It is possible during crowded times for a person to watch multiple shows by paying admission fees for one movie.

16. Because institutional changes can be incorporated into the analysis through changes in levels of excludability and subtractability, shifting L_{Ht} and L_{Vt} may seem redundant. However, we allow shifts in L_{Ht} and L_{Vt} to account for exogenous changes in these thresholds. If we adopt a narrow definition of institutions, these shifts can account for factors that are not accounted as institutional change. For example, shift in political rhetoric alone can lead to differences in the precise thresholds for L_{Ht} and L_{Vt}.

17. It may be helpful to distinguish the movement of goods across quadrants from the shrinking-expanding of quadrants. This can be defined as a function of the scale and scope of institutional changes. A formal exploration of this relationship is reserved for future work.

18. Vietnameseness, in this context, is analogous to "behavior conducive to upward mobility" (Bankston and Zhou 2000). There is a very unique type of bundling of goods occurring here. One good (cultural services) leads to another good (Vietnameseness), which can then lead to the final good (opportunities for upward mobility).

19. Boettke et al. (2007) note that the Government Accountability Office (GAO) reported fraud and abuse costs of up to $2 billion.

20. Fifteen tons of documents were shipped to the capital to be restored (Kenny, Fan, and Palmer 2006).

21. Henderson and Lee (2015) note that domestic implementers are likely to face this incentive because they "do not operate internationally" and because "in Aceh many (domestic implementers) were short-lived" (p. 621). In the case of domestic builders, there is reason to think that similar incentive structure exists, especially when donors and implementers are international. On the other hand, international implementers have incentives to perform regardless of domestic hurdles because they face "reputational costs" in the context of the repeated game of contracting in aid disasters (p. 620). This leads to increased costs in consulting and other fees, thereby substantially raising reconstruction costs.

22. In relative terms, international aid agencies and governments have endogenous budget constraints. Higher assessments of destruction and need is potentially positively associated with higher donations.

23. Henderson and Lee (2015) find that *donor-implementers* outperform *international implementers*, *domestic implementers*, and *BRR (government)* because they face proper incentives.

24. I do not find explicit indication of excludability and rivalrousness of the good (house) changing in the Aceh case.

REFERENCES

Adams, Leslie, and Paul Harvey. 2006. "Learning from Cash Responses to the Tsunami: Cash and Shelter." London: Humanitarian Policy Group, Overseas Development Institute.

AIPRD/LOGICA. 2007. "Technical Housing Quality Assessment Program." Canberra and Jakarta: Australia Indonesia Partnership for Reconstruction and Development and Local Governance and Infrastructure for Communities in Aceh.

Aligica, Paul Dragos. 2014. *Institutional Diversity and Political Economy: The Ostroms and Beyond*. New York: Oxford University Press.

Aligica, Paul Dragos, and Peter J. Boettke. 2009. *Challenging Institutional Analysis and Development: The Bloomington School*. New York: Routledge.

Andreas, A.T. 1884. *History of Chicago from the Earliest Period to the Present Time, Vol. 2 of 3: From 1857 Until the Fire of 1871*. University of Michigan Libraries. A. T. Alexander.

Baldry, Eileen, Hemant Ojha, and Krishna K. Shrestha. 2017. "Two Years after the Earthquake, Why Has Nepal Failed to Recover?" *The Conversation.* http://theconversation.com/two-years-after-the-earthquake-why-has-nepal-failed-to-recover-77552.

Bankston III, Carl L., and Min Zhou. 2000. "De Facto Congregationalism and Socioeconomic Mobility in Laotian and Vietnamese Immigrant Communities: A Study of Religious Institutions and Economic Change." *Review of Religious Research* 40 (4), 41 (4): 453–470.

Bhattacharjee, Abhijit, Vivek Rawal, Charlie Fautin, Judy-Leigh Moore, Sylvester Kalonge, and Vivien Margaret Walden. 2005. "Multi-Agency Evaluation of Tsunami Response: India and Sri Lanka." *CARE International, World Vision (WV), Oxfam GB, Catholic Relief Services (CRS).*

Boettke, Peter, Emily Chamlee-Wright, Peter Gordon, Sanford Ikeda, Peter T. Leeson, and Russell Sobel. 2007. "The Political, Economic, and Social Aspects of Katrina." *Southern Economic Journal* 74 (2): 363–376.

Boettke, Peter J., Christopher J. Coyne, and Peter T. Leeson. 2011. "Quasimarket Failure." *Public Choice* 149 (1–2): 209.

Buchanan, James M. 1965. "An Economic Theory of Clubs." *Economica* 32 (125): 1–14.

Candela, Rosolino A., and Vincent J. Geloso. 2018. "The Lightship in Economics." *Public Choice* 176 (3–4): 479–506.

Chamlee-Wright, Emily. 2010. *The Cultural and Political Economy of Recovery: Social Learning in a Post-Disaster Environment.* Routledge Advances in Heterodox Economics 12. New York: Routledge.

Chamlee-Wright, Emily, and Virgil Henry Storr. 2009. "Club Goods and Post-Disaster Community Return." *Rationality and Society* 21 (4): 429–458.

———. 2010a. "Expectations of Government's Response to Disaster." *Public Choice* 144 (1–2): 253–74. https://doi.org/10.1007/s11127-009-9516-x.

———. 2010b. "The Role of Social Entrepreneurship in Post-Katrina Community Recovery." *International Journal of Innovation and Regional Development* 2 (1/2): 149–164.

Colbert, Elias, and Everett Chamberlin. 2012. *Chicago and The Great Conflagration...* Cincinnati and New York: C.F. Vent 1831.

Cowen, Tyler. 1985. "Public Goods Definitions and Their Institutional Context: A Critique of Public Goods Theory." *Review of Social Economy* 43 (1): 53–63.

Coyne, Christopher J. 2015. "Lobotomizing the Defense Brain." *The Review of Austrian Economics* 28 (4): 371–396.

CRAS. 1874. "Report of the Chicago Relief and Aid Society of Disbursement of Contributions for the Sufferers of the Chicago Fire." Chicago: Chicago Relief Aid Society.

Daly, Patrick, Sabin Ninglekhu, Pia Hollenbach, Jennifer Duyne Barenstein, and Dori Nguyen. 2017. "Situating Local Stakeholders within National Disaster Governance Structures: Rebuilding Urban Neighbourhoods Following the 2015 Nepal Earthquake." *Environment and Urbanization* 29 (2): 403–424.

Demsetz, Harold. 1970. "The Private Production of Public Goods." *The Journal of Law and Economics* 13 (2): 293–306.

Desmarais-Tremblay, Maxime. 2014. "On the Definition of Public Goods. Assessing Richard A. Musgrave's Contribution." In Documents de Travail Du Centre d'Economie de La Sorbonne. Paris Cedex 13.

Enke, Stephen. 1955. "More on the Misuse of Mathematics in Economics: A Rejoinder." *The Review of Economics and Statistics* 37 (2): 131–133.

Fan, Lilianne. 2006. "The Struggle for Land Rights in Post-Tsunami and Post-Conflict Aceh, Indonesia." Presented at World Bank Land Policies and Legal Empowerment of the Poor Conference, Washington DC, November 2–3, 2006. Washington DC: World Bank.

Francis, Alys. 2015. "Anger as Corruption, Red Tape Holds up Nepal Earthquake Aid Delivery." *ABC News*, May 19, 2015. http://www.abc.net.au/news/2015-05-19/corruption,-red-tape-holds-up-nepal-earthquake-aid-delivery/6479052.

Fritz, Roland. 2020. "Social Services and Impure Public Goods: Ostromian Lessons for Service Provision in Welfare States." In *Exploring the Political Economy and Social Philosophy of Vincent and Elinor Ostrom*, edited by Peter J. Boettke, Bobbi Herzberg, and Brian Kogelmann. New York: Rowman and Littlefield International.

Furton, Glenn, and Adam Martin. 2019. "Beyond Market Failure and Government Failure." *Public Choice* 178: 197–216.

Gibson, Clark C., Krister Andersson, Elinor Ostrom, and Sujai Shivakumar. 2005. *The Samaritan's Dilemma: The Political Economy of Development Aid.* Oxford: Oxford University Press on Demand.

Grube, Laura, and Virgil Henry Storr. 2014. "The Capacity for Self-governance and Post-disaster Resiliency." *The Review of Austrian Economics* 27 (3): 301–324.

Hammond, J. Daniel. 2015. "Paul Samuelson on Public Goods: The Road to Nihilism." *History of Political Economy* 47 (suppl_1): 147–173.

Hardin, Garrett. 1968. "The Tragedy of the Commons." *Science* 162: 1243–1248.

Henderson, J. Vernon, and Yong Suk Lee. 2015. "Organization of Disaster Aid Delivery: Spending Your Donations." *Economic Development and Cultural Change* 63 (4): 617–664.

Hughes, Amanda L., Leysia Palen, Jeannette Sutton, Sophia B. Liu, and Sarah Vieweg. 2008. "Site-Seeing in Disaster: An Examination of on-Line Social Convergence." In *Proceedings of the 5th International ISCRAM Conference*, 44–54. Citeseer.

Kennedy, Jim, Joseph Ashmore, Elizabeth Babister, and Ilan Kelman. 2008. "The Meaning of 'Build Back Better': Evidence from Post-Tsunami Aceh and Sri Lanka." *Journal of Contingencies and Crisis Management* 16 (1): 24–36.

Kenny, Sean, Lilianne Fan, and Robin Palmer. 2006. "The Tsunami Two Years on: Land Rights in Aceh." *Oxfam Policy and Practice: Agriculture, Food and Land* 6 (3): 135–145.

Knox, Richard. 2012. "Water in the Time of Cholera: Haiti's Most Urgent Health Problem." NPR.Org, April 12, 2012. https://www.npr.org/sections/health-shots/2012/04/13/150302830/water-in-the-time-of-cholera-haitis-most-urgent-health-problem.

Koyama, Mark. 2012. "Prosecution Associations in Industrial Revolution England: Private Providers of Public Goods?" *The Journal of Legal Studies* 41 (1): 95–130.

Lanti, Irman G. 2006. "Indonesia: Accomplishments Amidst Challenges." *Southeast Asian Affairs* 2006 (1): 91–110.

Leeson, Peter T., and Russell S. Sobel. 2008. "Weathering Corruption." *The Journal of Law and Economics* 51 (4): 667–681.
Margolis, Julius. 1955. "A Comment on the Pure Theory of Public Expenditure." *The Review of Economics and Statistics* 37 (4): 347–349.
McCubbins, Mathew D., and Thomas Schwartz. 1984. "Congressional Oversight Overlooked: Police Patrols versus Fire Alarms." *American Journal of Political Science* 28 (1): 165–179.
McGinnis, Michael D. 2011. "Networks of Adjacent Action Situations in Polycentric Governance." *Policy Studies Journal* 39 (1): 51–78.
———. 2018. "Beyond a Precarious Balance: Improving the Scientific Rigor and Policy Relevance of Institutional Analyses from the Bloomington School." In *Ostrom's Tensions: Reexamining the Political Economy and Public Policy of Elinor C. Ostrom*, edited by Roberta Q. Herzberg, Peter J. Boettke, and Paul Dragos Aligica. Arlington, VA: Mercatus Center at George Mason University.
Minasian, Jora R. 1964. "Television Pricing and the Theory of Public Goods." *The Journal of Law and Economics* 7: 71–80.
Musgrave, Richard. 1969. "Provision for Social Goods." In *Public Economics*, edited by J. Margolis and H. Guitton. London: McMillan.
Nelson, Dean. 2015. "Nepal Aid Donors 'May Halt Fundraising' Amid Fears Government Will Seize Donations." May 1, 2015 sec. World. https://www.telegraph.co.uk/news/worldnews/asia/nepal/11577706/Nepal-aid-donors-may-halt-fundraising-amid-fears-government-will-seize-donations.html.
NRA. 2016. "Nepal Earthquake 2015 Post-Disaster Recovery Framework 2016-2020." Kathmandu: Government of Nepal.
Oates, Wallace E. 1972. *Fiscal Federalism*. New York: Harcourt Brace Jovanovich.
Ostrom, Elinor. 1990. *Governing the Commons*. Cambridge: Cambridge University Press.
———. 2003. "How Types of Goods and Property Rights Jointly Affect Collective Action." *Journal of Theoretical Politics* 15 (3): 239–270.
———. 2007. "A Diagnostic Approach for Going beyond Panaceas." *Proceedings of the National Academy of Sciences* 104 (39): 15181–15187.
———. 2009. *Understanding Institutional Diversity*. Princeton: Princeton University Press.
———. 2011. "Background on the Institutional Analysis and Development Framework." *Policy Studies Journal* 39 (1): 7–27.
Ostrom, Elinor, Marco A. Janssen, and John M. Anderies. 2007. "Going beyond Panaceas." *Proceedings of the National Academy of Sciences* 104 (39): 15176–15178.
Ostrom, Elinor, Roy Gardner, James Walker, and Jimmy Walker. 1994. *Rules, Games, and Common-Pool Resources*. Ann Arbor: University of Michigan Press.
Ostrom, Vincent. 2008. *The Intellectual Crisis in American Public Administration*. Tuscaloosa: University of Alabama Press.
Ostrom, Vincent, Charles M. Tiebout, and Robert Warren. 1961. "The Organization of Government in Metropolitan Areas: A Theoretical Inquiry." *American Political Science Review* 55 (4): 831–842.

Ostrom, Vincent, and Elinor Ostrom. 2002. "Public Goods and Public Choices." In *Polycentricity and Local Public Economies: Readings from the Workshop in Political Theory and Policy Analysis*, 75–103. Institutional Analysis. Ann Arbor: University of Michigan Press.

Pickhardt, Michael. 2006. "Fifty Years after Samuelson's 'The Pure Theory of Public Expenditure': What Are We Left With?" *Journal of the History of Economic Thought* 28 (4): 439–460.

Rajan, Raghuram. 2019. *The Third Pillar: How Markets and the State Leave the Community Behind.* London: Penguin Press.

Rand, Emily Christensen, Seki Hirano, and Ilan Kelman. 2011. "Post-Tsunami Housing Resident Satisfaction in Aceh." *International Development Planning Review* 33 (2): 187–211.

Rayamajhee, Veeshan, and Alok Bohara. 2019a. "Social Capital, Trust, and Collective Action in Post-Earthquake Nepal." *Working Paper.*

———. 2019b. "Do Voluntary Associations Reduce Hunger? An Empirical Exploration of the Social Capital-Food Security Nexus among Food Impoverished Households in Western Nepal." *Food Security* 1–11. https://doi.org/10.1007/s12571-019-00907-0.

———. 2019c. "Natural Disaster Damages and Their Link to Coping Strategy Choices: Field Survey Findings from Post-Earthquake Nepal." *Journal of International Development* 31 (4): 336–343.

Rayamajhee, Veeshan, Alok K. Bohara, and Virgil H. Storr. 2019. "Ex-Post Coping Responses and Post-Disaster Resilience: A Case from the 2015 Earthquake in Nepal." *Working Paper.*

Rayamajhee, Veeshan, Virgil H. Storr, and Alok Bohara. 2019. "Social Entrepreneurship, Coproduction, and Post-Disaster Recovery." *Working Paper.*

Samuelson, Paul A. 1954. "The Pure Theory of Public Expenditure." *The Review of Economics and Statistics*, 387–389.

Sandler, Todd. 2013. "Buchanan Clubs." *Constitutional Political Economy* 24 (4): 265–284.

Sawislak, Karen. 1995. *Smoldering City: Chicagoans and the Great Fire, 1871-1874.* Chicago: University of Chicago Press.

Skarbek, Emily C. 2014. "The Chicago Fire of 1871: A Bottom-up Approach to Disaster Relief." *Public Choice* 160 (1–2): 155–180.

Sobel, Russell S., and Peter T. Leeson. 2006. "Government's Response to Hurricane Katrina: A Public Choice Analysis." *Public Choice* 127 (1–2): 55–73.

———. 2007. "The Use of Knowledge in Natural-Disaster Relief Management." *The Independent Review* 11 (4): 519–532.

Sutter, Daniel, and Daniel J. Smith. 2017. "Coordination in Disaster: Nonprice Learning and the Allocation of Resources after Natural Disasters." *The Review of Austrian Economics* 30 (4): 469–492.

Tabarrok, Alexander. 1998. "The Private Provision of Public Goods via Dominant Assurance Contracts." *Public Choice* 96 (3–4): 345–362.

Vogler, Jan P. 2019. "The Entanglement of Public Bureaucratic Institutions." In *Interdisciplinary Studies of the Political Order: New Applications of Public Choice Theory*, edited by Donald J. Boudreaux, Christopher J. Coyne, and Bobbi Herzberg, 99–129. New York: Rowman and Littlefield International.

Chapter 2

The Culture in the Ostroms

Institutions, Rules, and Relational Rationality

Mili Kalia

Whatever fate or destiny the future may hold for human civilization, that future will be a product of human choice.

—Vincent Ostrom [1973] 2008, 1

CULTURE AND THE OSTROMS: WHY NOT CULTURE?

Culture plays an important part in the Ostromian framework, but there have been few attempts by scholars to understand the role of culture within their work (Hess and Ostrom 2003; Singleton 2017; V. Ostrom 1997; Megyesi and Mike 2016). In trying to understand the place of culture and in order to explain complexity of the modern human condition, Vincent Ostrom, in the preface of The Meaning of Democracy and the Vulnerability of Democracies (1997), presents himself with a troubling paradox—there is a growing desire among individuals in society to live private lives free from external control and interference. Concomitantly, there is continuing centralization of power in the hands of a few (the nation-state and/or markets). One of the ways to think through this paradox and reach necessary "constructive solutions," he notes, "requires us to rethink the place of the cultural and social sciences and humanities in human affairs" (Ostrom 1997, xiii). In many respects, since its inception, the culture question has been important for the Ostroms. However, a clear and systematic articulation of how and why culture matters, in their work, has not been presented in writing.[1]

There are a few reasons why we do not see a more comprehensive and systematic engagement with culture in their work. First is an acknowledgment between Vincent and Elinor Ostrom that culture is a difficult area within which we can develop generalizable theories. In a rare occasion, where they have come together to write on culture, they note their reservations regarding culture and theory building. However, they also indicate that there is a possibility of thinking and talking about culture but it can only happen through incorporating common elements in research framework that can only be developed via interdisciplinary work and gaining practical experience of social processes and order as they change. It is worth writing their statement in its entirety here:

> Over the course of these many years, the two of us have reached the conclusion that a single, general theory of culture, economics, government, law, or politics is not possible. Identifying common elements in theories of such subjects, however, is possible. Theory, like language, is subject to innovative developments. We cannot anticipate what the character of future innovation is likely to be. Thus we need to work with frameworks that identify the elements to be taken into consideration when constructing theory and building models. If used in the context of comparative analysis, we can build complementary modes of inquiry to extend our knowledge of what can be learned from human experience in diverse cultural traditions. We need not surrender to complete cultural relativism; but we do face difficult problems in coming to terms with the ways that human experience is conceptualized and in working with multiple criteria of performance. (V. Ostrom and Ostrom 1997, 80)

Secondly, Vincent and Elinor Ostrom developed their intellectual expertise and areas of specialization along different paths. Paul Dragos Aligica and Peter J. Boettke (2009, 55–56) have noted that their academic engagement was an interesting symbiotic relationship between two scholars, which in turn was an immediate response to prevailing academic and policy frameworks that were being used to make flawed predictions. While acknowledging their similar motivations, Aligica and Boettke also recognized another issue that may have precluded a comprehensive presentation and analysis of culture in their works. They note, "there was a keen awareness that to build viable and realistic theory of collective action meant more than extracting a set of generalizations from concrete cases; hence a very interesting evolution. On the one hand analytic and operational framework was advanced. . . . On the other hand, emulating the tradition of grand scale approach of Adam Smith's and Thomas Hobbes's efforts of building theory of a broad perspective of human condition, an entire vision of human action in its social milieu was conjured. The work of Elinor Ostrom illustrated mainly the first direction. The work of Vincent Ostrom illustrated mainly the second one." Both Vincent and Elinor Ostrom dedicated their intellectual efforts on different levels but in interdependent aspect. Marrying their thought in one systematic whole is a challenge[2] as the impetus to understand patterns of social order and change was similar, but, in terms of frameworks and spheres of empirical observations, was different.

Thirdly, there is considerable confusion, ambiguity, and disagreement as to what culture is. It must be emphasized that this ambiguity is not isolated or unique to the Ostromian framework, but not having a clear idea of what culture is, how it should be conceptualized, and/or not fully appreciating the underlying epistemological reasons for its continued existence and support in academic and nonacademic spheres significantly hinders productive conversations around the effects of culture.

A fourth related and an important issue is that there is little acknowledgment of the fact that culture is connected to rationality, which is also central in understanding how people make decisions and choices. This observation is not alien to the Ostroms or to the cultural theorists in anthropology, sociology, and psychology. Unfortunately, how culture and rationality come together has not been explored systematically using the Ostromian lens.

Fifthly, and related to aforementioned points, while there has been extensive application of Ostrom's Institutional Analysis and Development (IAD) framework, little attention has been paid to their call to incorporate multiple theoretical framework within the IAD framework in order to make their project truly interdisciplinary (V. Ostrom 1997; E. Ostrom 2010). It is particularly concerning how certain fields (primarily sociology) have been relatively silent despite some very notable mention of their contributions in some texts that are now considered key readings in the field of new institutionalism (Powell and DiMaggio 1991). This silence is particularly troubling as sociology has made some significant strides in explaining how culture determines social institutions, collective action and social interaction and order since the publication of classics (Karl Marx, Max Weber, Emile Durkheim, Talcott Parsons, to name a few). Is there a way to incorporate sociological insights to the question of culture with the Ostromian analysis?

I have three aims in this chapter: First, I want to underscore the fact that acknowledging the place of culture and incorporating insights from cultural theory is valuable and can often alert us to social mechanisms that we might ignore or pay less attention to if we are to ignore or not fully appreciate the epistemological reasons underpinning cultural analysis. Second, in order to understand how culture shapes social actions, order, and change, we need to incorporate three insights from cultural theory in our framework—the subject in question, the nature of rationality (rules that the subject is using to make distinctions beyond utility principles) that the subject is using, and the context in which the subject is rationalizing. Finally, to demonstrate that sociology has much to offer to the Ostroms and sociologists have much to learn from them. In particular, their focus on the rules of social interactions is an important area of not just framing empirical questions but also theory building.

This chapter has four broad sections. In the first section, I elaborate on how Elinor and Vincent Ostrom viewed culture and its role in how the commons and individuals emerge, participate, and exist as actors in society. Culture is predominantly discussed in relation to natural resources (e.g., forest, land, water, to suggest a few) or language which emerge as a social institution with embedded rules in a particular historical milieu which in turn governs social interactions. I highlight how key aspects of their conceptualization—context, orientation of action, and rule-ordered interactions—are related to culture. In particular, I show that the Ostroms primarily analyzed social contexts where language plays an important role such as media and communication. In other cases, culture takes on a more concrete form as products of human labor that can be consumed or exchanged (the case of intellectual property as cultural commons will be discussed later in this chapter).

In the second section, I will suggest that their conceptualization of rules and action situation(s) is particularly useful in incorporating insights from cultural theory. However, since cultural theorists understand the relationship between culture and rationality differently, we will need to expand on how they are connected. Here I show, alongside other cultural theorists, that cultural analysis and cultural theory do not reject the notion of rationality. On the contrary, culture and rationality are intimately related but this is not completely recognized or made explicit in the Ostroms.

In the third section, I will discuss how culture is closely connected to rationality and why this is important to acknowledge. Here I make explicit that when individuals rationalize based on culture, they are also informed by nonutilitarian criteria such as morality, emotions, and taste, to suggest a few important modes of rationalizing. In the final section, I demonstrate that even though culture derives its force from nonutilitarian sources, it works through the register of rules which in turn shapes social choices and actions. To that extent, there are important synergies between sociology and the Ostroms. I conclude by summarizing my key observations in the chapter. Furthermore, I suggest that there needs to be more in-depth and context-based studies in order to supplement the growing work on experiment-based findings.

CULTURE AS IS IN THE OSTROMS: CONTEXT, CHANGE, SOCIAL RELATIONS, AND EXPERIENCE

The Ostroms labored to make visible communities of shared experiences and member's ability to come together, cooperate, trust, and develop practical solutions to their existential and everyday problems. Through their work they underscored the place of *ideas* in how people make sense of their surroundings and made choices and decisions. Ideas, according to the Ostroms, are important in how people form judgments about fairness and justice; moreover, ideas are instrumental in solving big and small problems. Vincent Ostrom makes a clear connection between ideas and social action and order in the following quote: "The artefactual character of institutional arrangements turns on how ideas expressed through the language of rules are used to constitute patterns of human relationships. Playing football and watching football with an awareness of what is happening on the field of play depend on common knowledge and shared communities of understanding about the rules of the game and the enforcement of those rules in accordance with standards of fairness" (V. Ostrom 1997, 26). In this regard, culture plays an important role in bridging and mediating between ideas and social action. In the following section, I will explore key elements that the Ostroms emphasized regarding culture and tease out some aspects that need further development and critical engagement.

IDEAS, LANGUAGE (AS CULTURE), AND DEEDS

Largely influenced by John Dewey's work on pragmatism,[3] Vincent Ostrom expends much thought and writing on how ideas, language, and deeds are closely related. Language is seen as one of the most important cultural artifacts. It connects idea to deeds, but the nature of this connection is neither a given or permanent, notes Vincent Ostrom.

Language plays the dual role of transmission (of symbols, ideas, rules, etc.), and creativity and/or change. It is through learning and experience that language is passed on but the transmission of language does not happen passively. Instead, as it flows and filters through the interrelated gamut of institutions, structures, and participants, language transforms and, in turn, also changes what it touches. Vincent Ostrom (1997) notes, "Culture among Homo sapiens can broadly be conceptualized as that which is learned and derived from learning" (122). Unlike heritability of genetic or biological traits, the transfer and/or adaptation of culture is complex and the experiences the individuals have possess the potential to change culture in significant ways. Thus, institutions, learning, and experiences work as a sieve through which culture moves, recombines, and/or filters out as possibly different from what it was before, and the result may be something that is completely novel—a new cultural artifact.

Transmission of language plays a significant role in maintaining social ties and interactions by reinforcing boundaries, incorporating rules of accountability, devising rules of inclusion and exclusion, and engendering a sense of commonality. Vincent notes, "All human capital—all human productive capabilities – is tied up with the pragmatics of language and the way that languages function as a basis for common understanding, social accountability, and mutual trust in human communities" (Ostrom 1997, 51).

Apart from its functional role, language also proves to be a form of praxis—a powerful vector of change and a site where, Vincent Ostrom (V. Ostrom 1997, 92) suggests, we can expect new emergent orders and new rules of being and belonging. In this case, language is also the "means for constituting knowledge, organizing thought, arraying alternatives, ordering choice, and taking actions in arranging present means in appropriate ways to realize future apparent goods."

However, language is also a problematic cultural sphere. While language plays a functional role in society of organizing thought, orienting cognitive focus, the rules of grammar and speech make language a powerful medium and tool for interaction and sustaining human relations; it can, however, be extremely fragile and ambiguous. Much effort, in their analysis, is placed on critical analysis of how languages are manipulated, monopolized, centralized, and distorted. In particular, Vincent Ostrom (V. Ostrom 1997, 64–66) discusses how a new form of language—*Newspeak*—infiltrates our lives during the twentieth century: "Newspeak is the *separation* of a language of political discourse from the language of everyday life and the languages of the sciences and technologies" (66). The real tragedy here is not that we live a life surrounded my mirages. Instead, the real tragedy is that we think that we know and understand politics and how to be active citizens, but actually we barely understand political life because it is mediated by rules of language that orient us in particular ways. The nature of language of Newspeak and the rules that are instrumental in organizing it means that there will be "the corruption of language, the failure of communication, the loss of problem-solving capabilities, and the erosion of political and social order" (64). The separation of political discourse from everyday language and science adds to the ambiguity inherent in language systems and/or orders.[4]

Their focus on language, related institutions, learning, and evolution provides a dynamic and complex view of how cultural artifacts come to be key players in shaping social interaction. The distance between ideas and deeds, to some extent, can be measured by how language changes or stays the same. There, nuanced understanding of how language changes and of its frail nature underscores the fact that context (institution, other cultural orders, participants, and material conditions) significantly shapes which rules of language continue and which ones are modified.

COMMON POOL RESOURCES (CPRS), INSTITUTIONAL ANALYSIS AND DEVELOPMENT, AND CONTEXT OF CULTURAL COMMONS

Within the realm of CPR and IDA literature, there have been some attempts to study "cultural commons" (Hess and Ostrom 2003; Elinor Ostrom 2010). In observing the complex nature of cultural goods and its embedded nature, Elinor Ostrom notes, "We have learned that aspects of cultural environments can be thought of as 'cultural commons' because cultural products (for example, new knowledge or software) are often available to many users who do not have to pay the producer in order to use those products" (Elinor Ostrom 2010).

In cases such as production and distribution of academic knowledge and open source software (OSS), close attention is paid to taxonomy of rules that players devise in order to overcome problems of distribution and overuse. In particular, attention is given to the context in which these cultural goods (software codes or academic knowledge, for example) become CPRs, the interplay of other formal institutions such as law and policy, the number of actors involved, and the spatial and temporal dimensions within which rule-ordered relationships emerge, to suggest a few. One of the insights that Elinor Ostrom highlights is that in these cases the design principle of *excludability or exclusion principle* cannot work seamlessly. For example, recent development in technology means that academic knowledge that is produced can be made available for anyone and it might be very hard to use money as a way to exclude people from consuming knowledge that is published in online spaces. This means that these goods are now available to anyone to use and no obligation or sanction can be imposed on actors if they abuse these cultural products. One interesting finding from this area of research, Elinor Ostrom notes, is: "The incentives in this cultural commons (OSS) differ from the incentives in the cultural commons associated with discovery and publication of new scientific facts and relationships" (Elinor Ostrom 2010, 814). This reinforces their theoretical claim that "the structure of institutional arrangements that one finds in natural settings is, of course, far more complicated than the structure of any of the extremely simple games" (E. Ostrom 2015, 18), while at the same time showcasing that case studies and comparative analysis of cultural commons can illuminate rules and strategies that people use even in complex action arenas such as managing use and distribution of knowledge and innovation. But the insights from cultural commons also shows that the management of culture is driven, based on motivations and intentions that are different from the ones that are applicable with more concrete resources such as forest, fish, water, and so forth.

Despite making significant inroads and shifts in their analytical lens, their analysis of culture and the unit of observation remains narrow. Narrow is not to say that it's insignificant, put simply, analytical claims about the effect of culture on rule-ordered arrangements within certain action situations are mostly elaborated in the sphere of language and knowledge. While the realm of language, through which we can analyze the effects of culture on human action, is illuminating and productive, unfortunately, the other realms of culture such as social habits, interests, emotions, and so forth remain obscured or under analyzed. In particular, the silence around cultural practices is particularly conspicuous in Vincent Ostrom's (1997) writing, as he mentions the deep and complex interrelationship between ideas-language-deeds but never really opens up the discussion of how deeds can be seen as social practice rather than chains of singular decisions and choices made over time.

In the following section, I will elaborate on how culture is closely related to rationality. This deviation, or rather a return to the drawing board, is necessary in order to demonstrate two things. First, culture in itself is complex, but it's ability to shape social action is closely tied to how people think, imagine, and make distinctions. Unless there is a clear recognition of this fact, it is difficult to reconcile the place of culture in the Ostroms' work and the insights from cultural theory.

CULTURE, RATIONALITY, AND CULTURAL THEORY: A MISSED OPPORTUNITY?

Culture is a messy concept, and it is often challenging to conceptualize and place it amid other social processes. Too often it seems all encompassing, yet it says nothing specific. To illustrate, one of the most well-known definitions of culture was articulated by Edward Burnett Taylor. He observes, "Culture or civilization, taken in its wide ethnographic sense, is that *complex whole* which includes knowledge, belief, art, morals, law, custom, and any other capabilities and habits acquired by man as a member of society" (Edward Burnett Taylor 1871, I). While Taylor was not the first person to use the word culture, it was the manner in which this new avatar of culture was articulated—as encompassing a '*complex whole*' of disparate social artifacts, capabilities, and habits—that gave culture a new scholarly purchase and empirical rigor. While this definition encompasses a myriad of different things, it says little about how they come to matter. To put this differently, what gives culture the force to shape social behavior and action?

In this section, I will argue that at the heart of cultural theory there is a need to understand how is it that human beings are not necessarily rational beings or aspire to be one but are in fact rationalizing beings (Sahlins 1976;

Laguna 1949; Singleton 2017). Culture, to this extent, enables and shapes how human beings make judgments and distinctions, when confronted with choices and decisions. It derives its force not just from the places where utilitarian rationality derives its force—in cost and benefit calculations and incentive structures. In regards to culture, it derives its force from a different form of rationality that emerges in the context of emotions, feelings, experiences, and passions. Culture reproduces, constraints, and engenders social action not just because it can have a tangible existence but because it is part of our psyche and manifests in how we think and feel about our everyday lives. Vincent Ostrom suggests, "The Mind's Eye . . . refers to the organization of human cognition as constituted by languages, experiences, thoughts, feelings, habits, and associations, some of which may be quite invisible to the retina and inaccessible to other sensory organs" (V. Ostrom 1997, 33). Despite this very important connection between culture and how humans rationalize, there is little discussion in the Ostroms on how culture works as form of rationality. Hence, in this section I will show how cultural theory has been concerned with rationality with the aim to show that culture impacts decision-making in important ways, not only as an artifact that is part of our everyday lives, but also because of how important it is in shaping who human beings are and modes in which they interact and relate to each other.

AGAINST THE PERSISTENCE OF NORMS AND INHERITABILITY OF RATIONALITY

While the Taylorian conceptualization is helpful in making some key distinctions between cultural forms along the lines of tangible versus intangible, or observable versus nonobservable, its ability to say something about where culture comes from, where it is located, and how it derives its legitimacy is narrowly developed. Moreover, the Taylorian perspective on cultural change and diffusion has been heavily criticized by scholars for holding on firm to an evolutionary perspective, purporting heritability of cultural traits and norms, and using Western social formations, structures, and institutions as normative ideals that other societies need to move toward. Scholars in anthropology, feminism, and sociology have rigorously argued for a move away from the Taylorian evolutionary perspective and devise theoretical agendas that challenge simple dichotomies (e.g., civilized vs. primitive cultures, Western vs. non-Western cultures, first-world vs. third-world cultures, white vs. black cultures, men vs. women, citizens vs. aliens, to suggest a few) (Abu-Lughod 2008). Significantly, sociologists, such as Emile Durkheim, Max Weber, and Talcott Parsons, alert us to how neither cultures are a coherent system of ideas, meanings, beliefs, and symbols nor are they stable, as people tend to make decisions and choices that are not normative (Eisenstadt 1992). Culture's ability to affect behavior is not because it is blindly accepted by people; culture is instrumental because it orients our thoughts and ideas, but this happens at the intersection of various other forces and social relations. Thus, simple explanations around heritability of culture or loss of culture holds little value in developing theory or explaining social phenomenon because empirically neither of these facts about culture holds true.

CULTURE, RELATIONAL RATIONALITY, AND REFLEXIVITY

Perhaps one of the most productive but contested development in thinking about the culture–rationality nexus, argued for thus far, comes from a group of scholars (often referred to as structuralist or the French structuralists) who have reinvigorated epistemological concerns in Karl Marx's work (reproduction of inequality, resistance and agency, material/economic basis of social reality and decision-making, bourgeois rationality, to suggest a few) and its variants (often referend to Marxism) by incorporating insights from the works of Claude Lévi-Strauss (Sahlins 1976). These developments, alongside others, brought into question the primacy of Marxist explanation of how economic/material conditions of production and existence shape ideas. As a consequence, scholars began discussing the nature of relationship between the economic/material base and the superstructure (the realm of ideas, passions and interest) rather than assuming that the economic and/material base in-it-self affects ideas and belief (see, Sahlins 1976).[5] In particular, there has been an important shift in understanding how culture becomes effective in determining social action via symbols, meanings, schemas, and ideas (Sahlins 1976; Geertz 1973; Bourdieu 1984; Laguna 1949). These scholars aimed to demonstrate, among other things, the persistence and efficacy of a different form of rationality beyond the utilitarian perspective which stems from material conditions of human existence. This group of work looked to diverse social institutions and forms of social interactions (language, art, music, love, to suggest a few) in order to reconceptualize rationality beyond the realm of utility maximization (as conceptualized by rational choice theorists) or decisions based on economic costs and benefits (Eisenstadt 1992).

Extending and arguing against the former theoretical developments were sociologists, mostly in the twentieth century, who were quick to note the changes in social structures and institutions in war and postwar societies. In particular, nation-sates, organizations, firms, and interest groups were becoming key players in shaping developmental work and agendas, cities and suburbia, technology, employment, migration, education, to name a few.

These developments called for the incorporation of new insights, theoretical modifications, and reconceptualization of the classics within the field. For example, and pertinent to this discussion, how to think about culture as a whole in the light of myriads of structural changes at a rapid rate but on different scales and rates. Lash and Urry have observed that there is no unifying, static, and enduring norm within the capitalistic system(s) that structures it in determinate ways irrespective of context, space, or time (Lash and Urry 1988). Theoretical validity of Marxist economic analysis came into question and scholars diverged in their explanations as they grappled with real material and institutional changes.

One set of explanations and further refinements regarding culture and rationality was inspired by Max Weber's work (Weber [1930] 2005). His works on the economy, law, and religion have been extremely generative. In particular, his nuanced and descriptive incorporation of meta-analysis of the societies and social institutions alongside the analysis of smaller, powerful interest groups which struggle over material resources (money, land, and wealth, to suggest a few) and nonmaterial resources (influence, prestige, and dignity, to suggest a few) to "get things done" accelerated the move away from analyzing large system to analyzing context-based decision-making and embedded rationalities that guide social actions. The shift away from understanding society as a social totality based on class relation and changes in economic process (as suggested by Karl Marx) to specifics of the context (society, religion, and law) and intersubjective interactions (temporal and spatial) within which decisions and choices are made by actors became an urgent matter of empirical discovery and not an a priori given.

One implication for cultural theory, in this watershed moment, was to consider the realm of meanings that emerge at an interactional level rather than assuming that meanings are static and inherited without mutation. The other implication for cultural theorists was to acknowledge that subjects, in their own right, mattered as they bring to social interactions their own set of experiences, beliefs, superstitions, bodies, language. Thus, it is important to address who this subject is, where it comes from and how the subject thinks and feels.[6] The implication of using Max Weber in cultural theory was also to acknowledge that despite the primacy of interactional space where meanings emerge it was crucial to see that these interactions are in *relation to other interactions, subjects, and institutions*. Thus, while social interactions and subjectivities could alter the meanings and belief system but only to an extent that the field of social action allowed (Bourdieu 1984).

This form of relational rationality is particularly important; people often make decisions based on judgments not only in a certain context (bounded rationality[7]), but these judgments and decisions emerge at an intersection of other competing and/or acquiesce rationalities. William H. Sewell (Sewell 1992) notes, "In a great variety of times and places, structures are in fact dual: how historical agents' thoughts, motives, and intentions are constituted by cultures and social institutions into which they are born, how these cultures and institutions are reproduced by structurally shaped and constrained actions of those agents, but also how, in certain circumstances, the agents can (or are forced to) improvise or innovate in structurally shaped ways that reconfigure the very structure that constituted them" (5). Ongoing support for this argument also comes from another group of scholars—system analysts. These scholars have argued for a plural rationality approach (Grauer, Thompson, and Wierzbicki 1984; Singleton 2017).

In the following section, I will explain how the Ostroms and sociology can inform each other by acknowledging that rules are a constituent part of culture but these rules are not a priori; they emerge in a context of relational rationality.

A POSSIBLE SYNERGY? RULES, VALUES, AND RELATIONAL RATIONALITY

Benedict E. Singleton (2017) suggests that one of the reasons that we find Ostromian framework limited in its ability to speak about culture is because it relies heavily on a very specific form of rationality whose theoretical legitimacy and underlying assumptions must be questioned in the light of the recent developments in cultural theory. Singleton notes, "Basing Ostrom's design principles upon an economically rational choice-based framework has pragmatic advantages, but entailed a model of the individual separate from the social" (Singleton 2017, 1001). While I do not entirely agree with Singleton's criticism of the fact that the Ostroms saw the individual separate from the social, I do believe that Singleton's call to include cultural theory is important. But what does it mean to include culture and cultural analysis within the Ostromian framework?

Empirically, the Ostromians focused on rule-ordered arrangements or institutions. Vincent Ostrom (1997) notes, "All action situations occur within a context that has reference to rules and rule-ordered arrangements, which need specification" (151). In cultural sociology, rules have also come to occupy an indispensable position. Anthony Giddens (1979) notes that culture needs to be seen as a social structure that is made up of rules that guide and orient action. Giddens defines structure as "rules and resources, recursively implicated in the reproduction of social systems. Structure exists only in memory traces, the organic basis of human knowledgeability, and as instantiated in action" (Giddens 1984, 377). This definition is consistent with the core argument in this chapter thus far: that there is a close connection between culture and rationality. Furthermore, it is in this definition that we see a clear articulation of the key operational unit of social structure (such as culture)—rules and resources. This is where insights from the Ostroms meet cultural theory in sociology, that is, in the realm of rules.

The focus on rules and rule-ordered arrangements frees their framework to incorporate different sources and forms of rules that might govern or affect how individuals think and make decisions. Their analysis of rules is further enriched by the thought that is given to the context in which these rule-ordered arrangements are realized. Yes, context matters and specifying its characteristics is crucial, but it is their focus on rules and the subsequent rule-ordered arrangements that emerge, I suggest, align their theoretical agenda closely to other disciples who also concern themselves with culture.

Using Ann Swidler's (1986) conceptualization of "culture as a tool kit," I show that the Ostroms and Swidler were conceptualizing culture and its place in structuring human action in similar ways. Here I focus on two interrelated dimensions: (1) value-oriented action versus norm-oriented actions and (2) action situation, action orientation, and relational rationality.

VALUE-ORIENTED ACTIONS VS. NORM-ORIENTED ACTIONS

In sociology, there is a healthy debate as to how culture (in all its manifestations) influences action. According to conventional theories (e.g., Talcott Parsons), culture is the realm of values that orients social actions. In these theories, each society or collective has its own set of universal values that they cherish; there is value consensus (a latent moral compact) around which these values are crucial for societies to function well. Rewards and punishments are put in place in order to check behavior. Social institutions are encumbered with the task of transferring these values through socialization and learning, and the individual, like a sponge, internalizes these values and behaves accordingly. These are referred to here as value-oriented actions.

However, more recent reconceptualizations of culture argue against value-oriented actions. Swidler notes, "Parsonian values are abstract, general, and immanent in social systems . . . he does not treat values as concrete symbolic elements (like doctrines, rituals, or myths) which have histories and can actually be studied" (Swidler 1986, 274). In this conceptualization, values remain unchanged and uncontested. A bigger concern for Swidler (1986) is to not reduce the individual to "cultural dopes" who are not reflexive about their circumstances and the values that they are confronted with.

Swidler goes on to note that in studies that document and analyze delinquency among working-class youths, it is often observed that they do not reject the values around education and success (as the Parsonian paradigm would predict). In fact, they often value education and the opportunities that education can provide to them, in most cases, as much as a middle-class individual does (there is "value congruency" in this case). Neither do they reject these values and adopt oppositional cultural practices. Often times, the effect of culture on social action cannot be explained based on dominant values that are in place. Swidler reverses the value-action equation—"Action is not determined by one's values. Rather action and values are organized to take advantage of cultural competencies" (275). In her reformulation, culture comes to the fore and becomes a site for further investigation. Thus, engendering myriads of different empirical questions: Which types of culture are relevant to a particular action situation? Where do we find these cultures? The answer to these questions is twofold—the actors involved and the nature of problem that they want to solve (values are suspended or are now seen as an emergent phenomenon rather than pregiven universals).

In the case of juvenile delinquents, there now emerges a third explanation which elaborates on how individual actions are not necessarily affected by universal values (acceptance or rejection of education). Instead, youths from deprived neighborhoods build on skills, dispositions, and habits that they already have and choose unpredictable lines of action such as choosing group loyalty vis-à-vis individual achievement (Swidler 1986, 277). This type of analysis moves us away from the trap of over "socialized subject" explanations but neither does it fall into the "methodological individualism" trap as the tools and resources that these actors mobilize are relational. Here we see that "culture influences action . . . by shaping a repertoire or 'tool kit' of skills, and styles from which people construct 'strategies of action.'" (273). Culture's impact is not that of direct causality but it is the mobilization and transformation of various social rules and institutions in order to solve problems. The context in which a particular assemblage is activated remains pertinent but never a pregiven.

How similar or different are the Ostroms with regard to values versus norm orientation actions? I suggest, quite similar. First, because the Ostroms begin by privileging the notion of action situations and not value orientation, they avoid the problem of only looking at the effect of culture as effects of dominant values on social actions. In fact, their research agenda aims to understand how individuals work with one another to solve the problems that they face. Elinor Ostrom notes, "When individuals genuinely participate in the crafting of multiple layers of rules, some of that crafting will occur using pen and paper. Much of it, however, will occur as problem-solving individuals interact trying to figure out how to do a better job in the future than they have done in the past" (Ostrom 2009, 19). Here, the art and the practice of crafting multiple layers of rules can be seen as a site where culture could have played and important causal role. As I have shown earlier, with regards to Swidler's (1986) argument, culture, and associated values and norms, is not pregiven normative schemas and scripts that we all need to follow and conform to. Culture can be seen as emergent social orders with embedded rules that participants mobilize as response to a problem situation. "Culture's causal significance [is] not in defining ends of action, but providing cultural components that are used to construct strategies of action," argues Swidler (1986, 273).

The Ostroms have extensively analyzed how language, communication, and information can affect social action. However, because Swidler (1986) rescues culture from the domain of predetermined norms, we can now conceptualize and incorporate material and nonmaterial objects into our cultural explanation. The impetus to incorporate the realm of mythologies, beliefs, and emotions as cultural factors comes from Weber's observation on the role of the nonmaterial in determining social action.

> Not ideas, but material and ideal interest, directly govern men's conduct. Yet very frequently the "world images" that have been created by "ideas" have like a switchmen, determined the tracks along which action has been pushed by the dynamic interest. (1946, 280)

Within the Ostromian framework, we could incorporate moral rules that underpin certain design principles. Similarly, cultural artifacts such as mythology, religion, and stories can also be effectively incorporated. Additionally, rules are often acted by and enforced by individuals in an action situation. We could raise pertinent questions about how and why certain rules (loyalty) were used and implemented by certain people. One strategy here could be to try and understand how different actors with different backgrounds mobilize different assemblages of action strategies and delve deeper into how they use culture in order to rationalize and institutionalize these rules.

ACTION SITUATION, ACTION ORIENTATION, AND RELATIONAL RATIONALITY

> *The rule-ordered relationships that are constitutive of human organization function as soft constraints that are themselves subject to choice.*
>
> —Vincent Ostrom [1973] 2008, 3

In many respects, Swidler and the Ostroms tried to move away and challenge the typical conceptualization of what constitutes action. Swidler notes that we have to move "away from the notion that people choose their actions one at a time according to their interests or values" (Swidler 1986, 276). Swidler suggests that in a single action situation people mobilize a myriad of "symbols, stories, rituals and world-views which people may use in varying configurations" (273). These strategies however are oriented toward something—solving a problem.

The focal concern of Elinor Ostrom's book, *Understanding Institutional Diversity* (2009), is that "the holon called an action arena in which two holons—participants[8] and an action situation—interact as they are affected by exogenous variables . . . and produce outcomes that in turn affect the participants and the action situation" (13). Similarly, Vincent Ostorm (1997) notes: "All action situations also occur in a context in which it is necessary to specify the common knowledge, the shared community of understanding, and the identities that exist among those acting with reference to others in any given action situation" (1997, 151). In both these conceptualizations, action situations are a complex of disparate structures, objects, and activities.

Equally important here is the appreciation of what these activities are oriented to. The answer to this question is a few things—to the future, to another actor, to objects, or to a problem situation (Ostrom 1997, 151; Swidler 1986, 273; Weber 1976). The nature of orientation of action is an important factor in understanding why and how culture can have a significant effect on social action, alongside other variables. First, understating orientation of actives can give us an important insight into existential and practical concerns that actors may have. In the case of cultural commons, as discussed earlier, consumers abusing (by not paying for the use) and overusing cultural products such as knowledge or software codes may not be considered a problem situation at all. In fact, if the commons take on a more future-oriented and risk-taking stance, then these breeches may be seen as opportunities (learning from feedback from the users) rather than as a problem that needs solving.

CULTURE, RELATIONAL RATIONALITY, AND LOOKING FORWARD

What does it mean to live in a democratic society? Unfortunately, that puzzle is bound up with questions that are not easily resolved and that ultimately turn on mysteries about the nature of life and existence that cannot be resolved in a definitive way.

—Vincent Ostrom (1997)

The realm of culture and how it impacts social actions is one such mystery. Culture is often a messy area to study. Culture enhances and enriches human freedoms and agency, but it also appears as a social space that can be easily taken away, controlled, and manipulated. In many respects, culture is delicate, elusive, and oftentimes resistant to simple operationalizations. But, these are the qualities that place much urgency upon us to study it, document it and analyze its various manifestations and internal workings.

The Ostromian intellectual endeavor envisions the role of culture in their work in a crucial way. Using insights from cultural theory in sociology, and other disciplines within the broad umbrella of humanities, we can come to appreciate how the Ostroms did not singularly burden the individual to engender and foster agency and effect change against the tide of history. Nor do they completely negate or ignore that norms, values, and culture, which have historically evolved, instituted can lead to change and enhance individual agency, under specific conditions. One important way to look at culture is to conceptualize it as a social structure that shapes how people rationalize. In this regard, how culture informs rule formation and which then become the basis of social interaction, thinking, and exchange, and fear, power are all fundamental to understanding how people come together to solve problems.

A necessary corollary to this discussion is the incorporation of different research tools. Apart from conducting experiments where various decision-based games yield insights into how people make choices, it is important to triangulate these with insights from fieldwork, interview, content analysis, to suggest a few. Tools that provide us with "thick descriptions" (Geertz 1973) of the contexts, the individuals involved, ideas, symbols, and the cultural practices valued and displayed by the actors can only enrich our understanding of how and why people decide to come together. But, we have to be more reflexive about what causal role does culture play in shaping social action (Swidler 1986) as culture is not just elusive but also mercurial.

In meditating on their ideas and analytics, I join Vincent Ostrom in his endeavor not to provide solutions but to engender curiosity, thought, and questions. As he eloquently acknowledges, "Unfortunately, as a dweller in Plato's Cave, I cannot see the direct light of Truth. I can only hope to pursue this inquiry through an intellectual struggle with others who concern themselves with the sciences of human affairs in ways that contribute to 'the mass of those ideas which constitute their character of mind' among peoples in democratic societies and comprise 'the moral and intellectual conditions' of democratic peoples" (Ostrom 1997, 29). There is much to be learned from their holistic and dynamic approach and their vision of social life through the lens of the commons.

NOTES

1. One important exception is the lecture by Elinor Ostrom (2011) that discusses the role of culture in managing resources.

2. This chapter presents itself with a difficult challenge. In doing so, it is but a small attempt to bring together some key works of the Ostroms on culture.

3. Some of the works of John Dewey that Vincent Ostrom is referencing here are, *The Public and Its Problems* (1927), *Logic: The Theory of Inquiry* (1938), and *The Problems of Men* (1946).

4. Also see Elinor Ostrom's discussion on policies as metaphors (Ostrom [1990] 2017, 22–23) as examples of how policy-language and legal-language purport to state things clearly but they are merely "oversimplified idealized institutions" (22).

5. In observing the close and complex relationship between material causes and symbolic systems, Sahlins (1976) notes, "The so-called material causes must be, in that capacity, the product of a symbolic system whose character it is our task to investigate; for without the mediation of this cultural scheme, no adequate relation between a given material condition and a specific cultural form can ever be specified" (Sahlins 1976, 65).

6. Please note that the turn to relational subjectivities was also critical for Karl Marx as he tried to understand how the bourgeois economy succeeded in maintaining an unequal relationship with the proletariat.

7. Simon Herbert (1997, 88) on bounded rationality: "To assert that behavior in organizations is boundedly rational does not imply that the behavior is always directed toward realizing the organization's goals. Individuals also strive rationally to advance their own personal goals, which may not be wholly concordant with organizational goals, and often even run counter to them. Moreover, individuals and groups in organizations often strive for power to realize their own goals and their own views of what the organization should be. To understand organizations, we must include all of these forms and objectives of rationality in our picture. We must include human selfishness and struggles for power."

8. It is worthwhile to mediate on the nuances of how both Vincent and Elinor Ostrom conceptualize participants. In the first instance it seems simple, but there are inherent complexities, sophistications, and conceptual and operational voids; ironically, these issues also make the application of this definition pliable. Thus, we are not restricted by the question of who and how many; participants could be individuals, collectives, groups, organizations, the nation-state, and so forth. The use of the word "participants" is open to interpretation. Specifying how many of these participants actually participate in an action arena is also an empirical question. Thus, the researcher is tasked with either taking the time and effort to elaborate on the issues of who and why these actors were chosen and not the other. This strategy is quite freeing as it allows for reconceptualization of social interactions not within the confines of specific social institutions such as family, schools, and so forth, although these institutions do remain part of their analysis.

REFERENCES

Abu-Lughod, Lila. 2008. "Writing Against Culture." In *The Cultural Geography Reader*, edited by Timothy S. Oakes and Patricia L. Price, 50–59. New York: Routledge.

Aligica, P.D., and P.J. Boettke. 2009. *Challenging Institutional Analysis and Development: The Bloomington School*. London: Routledge.

Bourdieu, Pierre. 1984. *Distinction: A Social Critique of The Judgement of Taste*. Cambridge: Harvard University Press.

Eisenstadt, S.N. 1992. "The Order-Maintaining and Order-Transforming Dimensions of Culture." In *The Theory of Culture*, 64–87. Berkeley: University of California Press.

Geertz, Clifford. 1973. "Thick Description: Toward an Interpretive Theory of Culture." In *The Interpretation of Cultures: Selected Essays*, edited by Clifford Geertz, 3–30. New York: Basic Books.

Giddens, Anthony. 1979. *Central Problems in Social Theory: Action, Structure, and Contradiction in Social Analysis*. Berkeley: University of California Press.

———. 1984. *The Constitution of Society: Outline of the Theory of Structuration*. Berkeley: University of California Press.

Grauer, M., M. Thompson, and A.P. Wierzbicki. 1984. "Preface." Plural rationality and interactive decision processes: Proceedings of an IIASA (International Institute for Applied Systems Analysis) Summer Study on Plural Rationality and Interactive Decision Processes, Sopron, Hungary 1985.

Hess, Charlotte, and Elinor Ostrom. 2003. "Ideas, Artifacts, and Facilities: Information as a Common-Pool Resource." *Law and Contemporary Problems* 66 (1): 111–146.

Laguna, Grace A. de. 1949. "Culture and Rationality." *American Anthropologist* 51 (3): 379–391.

Lash, Scott, and John Urry. 1988. *The End of Organized Capitalism*. Gerrards Cross, UK: Polity Press.

Megyesi, Boldizsár, and Károly Mike. 2016. "Organising Collective Reputation: An Ostromian Perspective." *International Journal of the Commons* 10 (2): 1082–1099. https://doi.org/http://doi.org/10.18352/ijc.657.

Ostrom, Elinor. 2010. "The Institutional Analysis and Development Framework and the Commons." *Cornell Law Review* 95 (4): 807–816.

———. 2015. *Governing the Commons*. Cambridge: Cambridge University Press.

Ostrom, Vincent. [1973] 2008. "The Crisis of Confidence." In *The Intellectual Crisis in American Public Administration*, edited by Vincent Ostrom, 1–19. Tuscaloosa: University of Alabama Press.

———. 1997. *The Meaning of Democracy and the Vulnerability of Democracies: A Response to Tocqueville's Challenge*. Ann Arbor: University of Michigan Press.

Ostrom, Vincent, and Elinor Ostrom. 1997. "Culture: Frameworks, Theories, and Models." In *Culture Matters: Essays in Honor of Aaron Widavsky*, edited by Richard J. Ellis and Michael Thompson, 79–88. Boulder, CO: Westview Press.

Powell, W.W., and P.J. DiMaggio. 1991. *The New Institutionalism in Organizational Analysis*. Chicago: University of Chicago Press.

Sahlins, Marshall David. 1976. *Culture and Practical Reason*. Chicago: University of Chicago Press.

Sewell, William H. 1992. "A Theory of Structure: Duality, Agency, and Transformation." *American Journal of Sociology* 98 (1): 1–29. http://www.jstor.org/stable/2781191.

Simon, Herbert. A. 1997. *A Study of Decision-making Processes in Administrative Organizations*, 4th ed. New York: The Free Press.

Singleton, Benedict E. 2017. "What's Missing from Ostrom? Combining Principles with the Theory of Sociocultural Viability." *Environmental Politics* 26 (6): 994–1014.

Swidler, Ann. 1986. "Culture in Action: Symbols and Strategies." *American Sociological Review* 51: 273–286.

Weber, Max. [1930] 2005. *The Protestant Ethic and the Spirit of Capitalism*. New York: Routledge.

Chapter 3

Social Services as Impure Public Goods

Ostromian Lessons for their Provision in Contemporary Welfare States[1]

Roland Fritz

INTRODUCTION AND RESEARCH QUESTIONS

Welfare states[2] presently are—and have been so almost since their inception—exposed to a variety of criticisms that cast doubt on their long-term efficacy to solve, or at least ameliorate, social problems. Despite high (and growing) rates of spending,[3] ever-expanding scope of welfare state programs,[4] and high support among the general population of Western countries (for instance, Mau 2001), most welfare states continually fall short of achieving their ultimate goals: the abolition, or—as some argue—merely even the reduction of poverty and inequality (Wagner [1998] 2019, 95f). Welfare state reform thus seems to be an ever-topical issue—a fact that is well reflected in a growing literature on the problems of overexpanding social problems and the various difficulties of downsizing or reforming existing welfare states (Jensen, Arndt and Lee 2018). While advocates of programs and measures of the welfare state often describe those as inadequate and demand an expansion of the various practice, there are of course a certain number of critics of the modern welfare state who would rather advocate a reduction of social policy and a withdrawal of the state from this area in order to achieve better policy outcomes. It need not be said that these debates have a tendency to easily turn from academic discussions on economic policy into fully (day-to-day) political debates. Questions of the latter kind are not dealt with here.

I nevertheless plan to add to the various debates, not by offering concrete policy advice on how welfare states should be reformed, but by discussing the nature of some of the goods provided in welfare states in the light of the familiar typology of private-, club-, and public goods as well as common pool resources (CPRs), whom I will oftentimes also refer to as impure public goods. With respect to this, we do not deal with the welfare state in its entirety, but focus on the provision of social services. These comprise services such as child- or elderly care, active labor market policies, reintegration services for former convicts or drug addicts, help for migrants, and debt counseling—all services that aim to alleviate or solve perceived social problems. Further down, a more concise definition and a precise demarcation from other elements of modern welfare states will be provided. I also wish to point out that this chapter will explicitly not deal with other, more commonly known aspects of the welfare state such as redistributive programs or social insurance. While discussing the nature of those welfare state programs might also be valuable, I omit such endeavors here and wish to concentrate my efforts solely on social services.

The chapter does not give concrete policy advice, but aims to improve outcomes by providing a clear framework for thinking about the goods being "exchanged" on "markets" for social services. Throughout the chapter, I will be building the argument that social services should be considered as having similar properties—and thus also problems with respect to their provision and use—as CPRs. With respect to this, the work of Elinor Ostrom in particular will be of paramount importance. This should also allow conclusions to be drawn as to which policy responses are appropriate in relation to potential reforms of the provision of social services. For reasons of better intelligibility, I will occasionally illustrate certain points by examples from the elderly care and childcare sector in Germany.[5]

In order to set the stage for the further line of argumentation, the next section briefly introduces the concept of the typology of goods and reviews literature that attempts to understand social services as public goods. Then I lay out in which sense the public goods theory about social services is deficient and build my own account of viewing social services as CPRs by demonstrating their nonexcludability (given contemporary value-systems in many Western countries) and rivalry of consumption. In order to do this, I make use of the literature of public attitudes originating from welfare state research and theories as well as empirical evidence about nonprice rationing mechanisms. I then discuss Elinor Ostrom's writings about making CPR systems sustainable and resilient and apply her insights on the matter of social services. The following section discusses how accepting the common pool nature of social services might lead to improved policy outcomes and highlight a few potential real-world implications. The last section concludes.

SOCIAL SERVICES AND THE TYPOLOGY OF GOODS

Systematizing and classifying the nature of the goods traded on markets is a very foundational practice in economics. Only by thinking clearly about which characteristics the goods exchanged on various markets have will one be able to offer coherent explanations of the processes unfolding on various markets. For this reason, the most common way of classifying goods is briefly discussed here. Furthermore, a short account of contemporary social services provision is given and the particularities of these services are highlighted. In order to make the point of this chapter more understandable, it will also be necessary to refer to one further way of interpreting the types of goods that exist on markets for social goods: That of social services as a public good.

The Typology of Goods

The most familiar attempt to classify goods is according to the two dimensions of excludability and rivalry of consumption. Rivalry here refers to whether the consumption of a good or service by one party necessarily diminishes the ability of other parties to consume the same good or service, while excludability points to how easy it is to preclude noncontributors from the consumption of the good or service. Combining these two dimensions, the standard account describes four distinct types of goods emerging from this dichotomy: private goods, club goods, allmende goods (also referred to as CPRs or impure public goods) as well as public goods.[6] It also needs to be pointed out that the classification of goods into these four categories is obviously not a fixed scheme, but much rather takes place along a continuum, in which a single good or service can seldom be assigned unconditionally to any category, but much rather display these characteristics varying in degree only (Aligica and Boettke 2009, 40, as well as Ostrom and Ostrom 1965).

With respect to this, private goods are defined by both excludability and rivalry of consumption and comprise the vast majority of goods and services that individuals typically consume on a daily basis. With club goods, exclusion can easily be conducted, while rivalry typically is not a strong property of club goods, especially with regards to the marginal user/consumer of the good. In case of severe congestion, rivalry can still reemerge for these kinds of goods, for example, on a highway during rush hour. Pure public goods refer to goods that are both nonexcludable and nonrivalrous, in which case the relevant literature frequently states the necessity of governmental intervention in order to supply the good in question, given that providers of a good can typically not charge or exclude potential consumers once the good is provided. National defense or measures taken to improve air quality serve as standard examples here. CPRs or impure public goods are also deemed mostly nonexcludable, but suffer from the additional problem that their consumption must largely be seen as rivalrous. High sea fishing grounds or irrigation systems (as an example of a man-made CPR) constitute most common examples. Overuse is often thought to be a recurrent problem of CPRs, a topic that will be dealt with in detail in the following chapter.

Social Services

Given that the chapter will apply the typology of goods onto the provision of social services, this section attempts to give a brief overview of the definition and the provision of social services in contemporary Western welfare states. Social services may be defined as services that attempt to overcome or ameliorate social problems, to offer help in situations of distress suffered by individuals, groups, or communities or try to circumvent them by preventive measures (Cremer, Goldschmidt, and Höfer 2013, 7; Weyrich 2011; Bäcker et al. 2010, 505). The fields generally counted as falling within the domain of social services are: child and youth welfare services, family assistance, help for elderly persons, health services, labor market activation policies, help for persons with disabilities, help for people with migratory background, and help in difficult situations such as drug addiction, indebtedness, and homelessness. In that sense, social services comprise both services that are highly specific to particular and rare problems but also certain services that most people will consume at some point or another in their lives (Cremer, Goldschmidt, and Höfer 2013, 10). Social Services have to be distinguished from other, more general elements of welfare states, such as redistributive transfers or forced insurance schemes. While many users of social services also obtain transfer payments (e.g., in the case of acute poverty or temporary unemployment), these transfer- or insurance-related measures need to be distinguished from "active" attempts to reintegrate them on the labor market via labor market polices, the latter of which clearly falls into the realm of social services. We also can distinguish social services from other programs of the welfare state by referring to the service characteristics of the former—while social insurance or social security programs entail the transfer of some resources from one group to another, social services are concrete, observable services performed for a person. Only the financing of these services is, under conditions of many jurisdictions, relegated to the welfare state and its institutions (Le Grand 1991 and 2007).

Economically, social services are interesting for a couple of reasons: Firstly, the areas which social services pertain to usually have highly emotional backdrops and the success of their provision means a lot in terms of the future life chances of the consumers of these services. Unlike the goods and services traded in conventional markets, social services thus have a strong tendency to be evaluated not only in terms of the supply and demand framework characteristics of usual economic analysis, but also for all sorts of normative, institutional, and cultural aspects to enter the analysis (Cremer, Goldschmidt, and Höfer 2013, for a detailed application of the principles at work in the health sector Arrow 1963). Among these, as we shall see later in more detail, a general tendency not to accept the exclusion of nonpaying individuals from access to the services in question will be one of the most important particularities here. Therefore, questions of social services perfectly lend themselves to be viewed not only from an economic angle but to bring interdisciplinary perspectives to the scene as well. Moreover, this also means that "contextual" approaches to economics will generally be in a better position to explain the processes unfolding on these markets and to come up with policy advice concerning their design than the usual "isolating" approach (Goldschmidt, Grimmer-Solem, and Zweynert 2016). Secondly, and for our purpose perhaps even more importantly, the provision of social services usually takes place not only on ordinary markets, but in complicated and diverse arrangements that span wide varieties of provisions such as quasi-markets (Bartlett and Le Grand 1993, for a critique of service provision via quasi-markets, see Boettke, Coyne and Leeson 2011), public-private partnerships (Esping-Andersen 1996), heavily regulated markets, as well as genuine markets. The provision of social services is, at least in Western welfare states, seldom completely exempt of government interference, but can—and oftentimes is—still be facilitated via market mechanisms (Shera 1996 and Blöchinger 2008).[7]

Only the financing of the services in question is oftentimes relegated to government, while the provision can be taken over by public-private partnerships, nonprofit organizations, or even for-profit companies, leading to complex interrelationships between consumers, providers, and government institutions (Tynkkynen et al. 2013). All the particularities of these markets make social services a highly interesting arena for economic inquiry. However, the complexity of the services involved and the multiple entities involved in their provision have also led to quite differing views about the nature of the goods involved. The following two paragraphs review two of the most prominent attempts at interpretation: social services as public goods and as club goods.

Social Services as Public Goods

The notion of social services as "public goods" is not only relevant from the perspective of theoretical economics. Also, in public discourse the idea of the services provided in welfare states as goods with public character has a certain significance, even though this use is not dealt with here.[8] However, attempts are also being made within economic theory to classify the welfare state as a collection of goods with public character. Here the fundamental private nature is not disputed by many, but it is pointed out that nonexcludability is a very strong political postulate, which should not be ignored in the formation of economic theory. Since public opinion has an extremely strong effect on the design of social policy, and in most places the exclusion of the genuinely needy from access to social services is regarded as undesirable, the exclusion principle must ultimately be regarded as inapplicable for social services.

Cremer, Goldschmidt, and Höfer (2013), for instance, formulate an approach of that sort building on Musgrave's (1959) theory of merit goods, thereby defining social services as goods that might, if demanded for them would be left entirely to people operating in private market, not be demanded in an amount optimal for overall societal welfare. Just like people might not provide their children with a socially optimal amount of education (a classic example of a merit good-inspired market failure situation), they might also not see the need to save for their own care after having reached old age. Similarly, a person just released from prison or a refugee recently embarked in a country will seldom have the resources necessary to purchase (re-)integrative services, or an alcoholic on withdrawal—given the particularities of his condition—will perhaps find it difficult to finance the necessary medicinal and psychological treatment herself. Cremer, Goldschmidt, and Höfer (2013) argue that, because many people in contemporary welfare democracies would implicitly agree with the nonexclusion of potential nonpayers from these merit goods, the classification of social services in the typology of goods yields surprising results: while they actually agree with the proposition that many social services actually are private goods along the dimensions of excludability and rivalry of the goods in question, they hold that both aspects—and hence the privateness of social services—are deliberately repealed. By not accepting the exclusion principle for noncontributors, societies would regularly actively choose to transform social services from private into public goods (Cremer, Goldschmidt, and Höfer 2013, 63–67).

By providing access to social services (either via their provision directly by state institutions or via quasi-market mechanisms such as vouchers or personal budgets), it shall be ensured that adequate consumption of the goods in question takes place, thereby also satisfying the societal demand for nonexcludability of these services.

However, in their attempt to classify social services, they do not pay adequate attention to the second dimension of public goods, namely the nonrivalry of consumption. The authors do not go to great length to confirm their point: it is simply assumed that, because excludability cannot be assumed to be operating in any meaningful way for these goods, the ascription of "public goods" is justified. Just because political action is used to render excludability unnecessary, it does not automatically follow that scarcity per se—and thus rivalry in consumption—is abolished together with it, as will be shown further down. However, in the notion of social services as public goods, this aspect is not considered in any meaningful way.

SOCIAL SERVICES AS IMPURE PUBLIC GOODS

Not much has been written on the topic of social services as CPRs—the closest parallels are found in a (modest) literature attempting to apply the commons-literature on redistributive programs on the welfare state. With regards to this, Thomson (1996) discusses welfare state failure in New Zealand and bleak prospects for the maintenance of current provision levels in the future, ends up finding the reason for the persistent underfunding in the common-like nature of social policy arrangement, and proposes shifts in the incentive structures to minimize the problem. Jakee and Turner (2002) apply a similar reasoning onto the welfare budgets needed to keep welfare states going, the proverbial "fiscal commons," but also discuss behavioral difficulties associated with boundedly rational human actions in CPR situations. The analogy between social services and CPRs is not a perfect one, but it is certainly conceivable that similar forces are operating in the two domains. The following sections discuss reasons for why the provision of social services can be assumed—under conditions of many welfare states in advanced economies—to be nonexcludable and rivalrous. Special emphasis will hereby be paid to distinguish between the services themselves, the claims/rights to access them on the part of the citizenry and the budgets that fund them.

Nonexcludability

The discussion of the approach of Cremer, Goldschmidt, and Höfer (2013) in a previous chapter has already briefly indicated as to why nonexcludability can be assumed for access to many social services. The findings are by no means based on the inherent properties of social services, but exclusively on the social valuation and social attribution of these goods by the majority of members of society. In other words, the classification of goods is not independent of what and how people think about them.[9] If people strongly believe in nonexcludability, then a certain degree of nonexcludability must probably be assumed to be real and will lead to real-world consequences.[10] This also shows Ostroms' insight that the nature of goods is usually not an "ontological given," but that "institutional arrangements have an effect on the degree of choice and accordingly on the way the nature of goods is perceived and their production organized" (Ostrom and Ostrom 1965, 80 in Aligicia and Boettke 2009, 40). Similarly, Vincent Ostrom also hints at[11] "the basic presupposition . . . that human beings, to some significant degree, create their own social reality. Order in human societies is constituted by concepts and beliefs that human beings share and hold in common with one another. Customs, laws, or rules more generally, are used to order relationships with one another and with events of the world in which live. Seen from this perspective, human beings are the 'artificers' who create their own social reality" (Ostrom [1973] 2008: xxvi).

This insight can in a certain sense also be transferred to social services whose nonexcludability decisively does not originate from the goods themselves, but merely from the attribution by social valuations. This strong degree of nonexcludability for social services can best be illustrated by some opinion polls (Svallfors 2010). Given that social services are subsumed as a part of welfare states more generally, the opinion polls listed here will oftentimes refer to welfare states, broadly speaking. With respect to this, it is not difficult to show that the welfare state as an institution is virtually undisputed in most places.[12] In no country is the welfare state itself open to discussion. However, there are naturally individual areas of welfare states which, in relative terms, have less approval in some places, such as highly progressive taxation or extreme redistribution mechanisms (Busemeyer and Garritzmann 2017b).

Shifting the focus to areas that resemble social services to a larger degree, we find that public attitudes about education spending among citizens of the European Union (EU) are such that spending cuts for universities are much more likely to be accepted than those for elementary education (Busemeyer and Garritzmann 2017a, 384)—which can be interpreted as a nonexcludability declaration for basic school education, while the same cannot be maintained for tertiary education—clearly a state of affairs that is reflected also on the policy level in most countries. Furthermore, Mischke (2014) explains the evolution of family polices in Europe and finds that changing family models and societal valuations about what constitutes a "proper" family have been the main drivers of the resulting policy changes. Kananen, Taylor-Gooby and Larsen (2006) show that even in times of general expenditure cuts for social policy purposes it is possible to open up completely new fields of social support, as long as the social demand for it is large enough. The findings remain consistent when the matter is viewed from a much wider angle: Busemeyer, Goerres, and Weschle (2009) compare a large number of welfare states around the globe and conclude that cultural attitudes are everywhere a reliable predictor of the scope and extent of social programs. Likewise, Goerres and Tepe (2010) find that attitudes toward childcare in contemporary OECD countries are decisively not formed according to self-interest and personal gain, but instead are formed almost exclusively on the basis of general social norms and cultural convictions, thereby suggesting that nonexcludability might in fact be assumed for other social services as well.

While this is of course not an exhaustive description of the factors influencing the progression of social policies and other factors do certainly play an important role, it nevertheless underlines the distinct importance of public attitudes on the provision of social services. We thus think that by presenting evidence for the strong cultural determination of social policies, the criterion of nonexcludability can be accepted for social services provided in modern societies. Besides the opinion polls cited, the intended aims of many organizations providing social services underscore this particular interpretation.[13] All in all, accepting the nonexclusionary nature of social service provision already shows why the club good approach presented earlier shall not be used to classify social services. In the next paragraph, I turn to the question of whether rivalry of consumption shall also be considered an important characteristic of social services, thereby demonstrating that the public good narrative is also afflicted with severe problems.

Rivalry of Consumption/Subtractability of Use

The public goods approach presented earlier considers the provision of social services to be nonrivalrous. This means that, although the underlying goods and services are in principle scarce and their provision is often associated with a considerable effort, their transfer to the care of the welfare state miraculously renders unimportant any consideration of rivalry, even scarcity in principle. The issue is not even discussed in detail and it is apparently simply assumed that the obligation on the part of state authorities not to allow the exclusion principle to be applied will, as it were, also—without much effort—render the problem of underlying scarcity obsolete.

We would like to reject this idea here and explain that rivalry in consumption is a fundamental characteristic of social services. One illustration can be found in the health sector, where—especially in social democratic states that offer their citizenry "universal" health care without imposing costs directly at the moment of consumption—the official insistence on the principle of nonexclusion leads to the use of alternative, often nonprice rationing mechanisms (Parish 1981). When exclusion is not possible on monetary terms, overcrowding of the relevant providing institutions (such as doctor's practices, hospitals and care homes) not being able to cope with the inflow of patients/people in need of care will be prevented by alternative mechanisms, for example the use of personal contacts and relationships, or the giving or promising of personal gifts to decision-makers in the bureaucracies concerned (Iversen and Siciliani 2012; Frech III and Lee 1987; Alderman 1987). This category also includes recourse to private offers to address the problem at hand (Breyer 1995). For some social services, the rivalry of consumption is not even limited to the underlying budget and the raising of the necessary funds, but simply to the real shortage of skilled labor that could provide the services demanded in the first place. Examples of this are the prevailing shortage of skilled care- and nursing-workers in Germany despite repeated efforts to attract additional workforce from abroad (Deutsche Welle 2018) and the shortage of kindergarten- and day care-facilities for children, where the practice of not applying the exclusion principle clearly meets reality.[14] Overall, it can therefore be seen that in addition to strong tendencies toward nonexcludability for social services, a certain rivalry in consumption must also be assumed. While this rivalry is not permitted to manifest itself in the allocation of goods according to willingness to pay, it still shows up in the alternative, nonprice rationing mechanisms described and, thus, entails consequences for the optimal provision of social services. I would argue that it is this characteristic that chiefly distinguishes the public good approach from the common pool approach presented and advocated here. It explains why the most influential characterizations of socials services as public goods continually and, even more so policy implementations built up on it, continuously fall short in reality. Even though many people might believe that their fellow citizens ought not to be excluded from social services, it does not follow that access to those is abundant.

Social Services as Impure Public Goods

It is worth pondering where exactly the elements of nonexcludability and rivalry for social service provision stem from. The notion that goods can change their nature due to interpretation of the actors involved or via societal pressures will not hold for, for instance, fisheries: if large amounts of people were to develop the conviction that high-seas fishing grounds are in fact excludable, this would not change anything about the fact that those would remain CPRs. However, what seems to change the situation with respect to social services becomes apparent when we divide the good "social services" in three components: (a) the good itself, namely the physical provision of social services, which could still be best described as a private good; (b) the claim/right to it, which is derived from political action guaranteeing the financing of various social services for everyone and is ultimately rooted in the societal conviction that exclusion with respect to social services is not desirable; and finally, (c) the public budgets that fund the provision of social services, from which exclusion is made impossible by the claims/rights discussed under (b), but which nevertheless are vulnerable to depletion, rivalry, and subtractability of use.[15]

Figure 3.1 summarizes the account presented here: the originally private good of social services is attempted to be transformed into a public good by the acceptance of universal claims onto those services but ultimately bounces "back" to a CPR due to the need to exclude (either groups of people from access altogether or everyone from certain aspects of social services), in order to remain within the realm of the budget allocated for their provision or, more

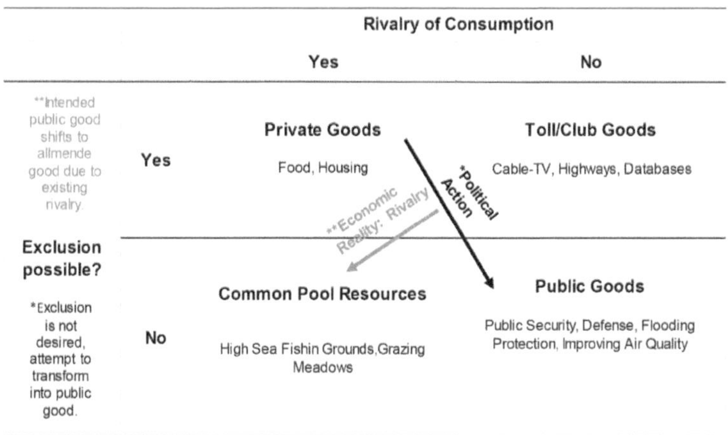

Figure 3.1 Social Services Shifting from Public to Allmende Good due to Rivalry of Consumption Existing Despite Societal Nonacceptance of Exclusion.

generally, not to engage in nonjustifiable spending for social services. Hence, we can describe the dilemma of the provision of social services in modern welfare states as one of a continuous oscillating movement between the one of public and impure public goods. While the transformation of an initially private good or service to a public good is intended to be facilitated in welfare states, the transformation falls short of its objective and has the intended public goods swinging back to the level of a common pool resource. It is with respect to this that the not-so-frequently used but highly accurate term of an "impure public good" shows its full beauty and descriptive force—while we would perhaps like social service provision to be treated as a public good, (fiscal) reality thwarts our plans and renders the potential public good impure. The next section will briefly state the main properties of CPRs or impure public goods and, drawing mostly on the contributions of Elinor Ostrom, suggest institutional arrangements for their sustainable usage.

COMMON POOL RESOURCES, THEIR DURABILITY, AND THE SAMARITAN'S DILEMMA

As this chapter aims to define social services as impure public goods, this section will briefly introduce, building mostly on the work of Elinor Ostrom, ways in which their governance can best be facilitated. Because of their characteristics, the incentives for their overuse are ever present: Given that it is hard to exclude potential appropriators from using a CPR and their consumption is generally rivalrous, these resources are prone to the problem of overuse and—in the worst case—complete depletion of the resource. Typically, CPR goods are thought of consisting of a stock of the resource in question, which in turn provides a limited amount of harvestable output, a so-called flow variable. While the flow of a CPR can be extracted and made usable to human consumption without problems, the stock will have to remain intact in order to also supply future users of the resources with adequate flows suitable for consumption (Ostrom [1990] 2017, 30). Because of their potentially fragile nature and the incentives present for their overuse, CPRs have been (and still quite often are) often seen as being subjected to the "tragedy of the commons" (Hardin 1968), according to which CPRs will necessarily and without exemption be overused. The overuse of CPRs in the natural world has a clear parallel with respect to our example of social service provision under conditions of socially nonaccepted exclusion of noncontributors: the Samaritan's dilemma. Introduced by Buchanan (1975), it models the interaction between a potential donor (the Samaritan) and a prospective recipient alongside the dimensions of "Work/No Work" (recipient) and "Donate / Not Donate" on the part of the Samaritan. While the latter would prefer the potential recipient to work and thus to be independent of his aid, his utility function might be shaped in such a way as to always prefer to donate if the relevant alternative is the recipient potentially suffering in the absence of help. If the recipient is aware of the Samaritan's preference, the situation lends itself to being exploited by recipients who prefer a steady inflow of Samaritan aid at the cost of no work to a (potentially higher) income derived from labor markets.[16] The stock–flow discussion thus also has a clear analogy in the realm of social service provision. In the sense that the budget available for social service provision can be kept in check and "Samaritans" are not discouraged by an ever-rising number of needy recipients, the "stock" of a budget suitable for alleviating the social problems of the genuinely needy will be preserved.

While the Samaritan's dilemma, in its initial formulation, is strictly theoretical, it has been found to be operating to some degree in real-life situations (Ostrom 2011; Raschky and Schwindt 2009; Pedersen 2001). Even though it seems as if the problems raised by the Samaritan's dilemma mostly pertain to redistributive programs of the welfare state, the provision of social services can also be affected by Samaritans being overly generous, thereby being taken advantage of by unnecessarily high numbers of needy recipients. The following discussion of Elinor Ostrom's design principles will thus always have to be viewed as responses to overcoming the tragedy of the commons and preventing society-wide Samaritan's dilemmas (Ostrom 1996). Naturally, E. Ostrom writes solely about ways in which the tragedy of the commons when she deals with physical CPRs and reserves discussions of the Samaritan's dilemma to policy-problems occurring in development (Gibson et al. 2005). However, there clearly seems to be a parallel between these two dilemmas, as this chapter implicitly tries to show, in the nonexcludability of access to a natural resource and the Samaritan's reluctance to stop supporting a needy recipient.

Ostrom on Common Pool Resources

Originally, policymakers were thought to be confined to two options for overcoming the problem of overused CPRs: either the privatization of the resource in question or, alternatively, heavy governmental involvement in the form of regulation or even the socialization of the resource system in question. Elinor Ostrom's work was crucial in breaking up this notion and bringing into discussion alternative ways in which CPRs could be made more durable, by highlighting that the "tragedy of the commons" and other overly pessimistic theories such as the prisoner's dilemma (Dawes 1973) or Olson's "logic of collective action" (Olson 1965) ultimately rest on severely under-complex hypothesis about human action and motivation. By rejecting all too simple models of self-interest and the gloomy predictions drawn from them, Ostrom attempted to base the study of CPRs on a different and more solid footing. In order to do this, she refused to draw far-ranging policy conclusions from "models as metaphors" (Ostrom [1990] 2017, 24) all too easily and instead advocated and actively pursued the empirical investigation of CPRs existing in the real world. The CPRs examined by her range from fisheries in Sri Lanka, Nova Scotia, and Turkey to grazing grounds in the Swiss mountains, groundwater basins in California, and irrigation systems in southern Spain and the Philippines. Ostrom's insight suggest that the supposed "tragedy of the commons" might not be unavoidable after all: the problems that result from the combination of subtractability of use and rivalry of consumption can, under certain conditions, indeed be overcome and do not subject users of CPRs to eternal struggles and chronic overuse of the common pool resource they wish to use. Having studied CPRs worldwide, Ostrom felt confident to formulate "a set of seven design principles that characterize all of these robust CPR institutions," which would "help . . . to account for the success of these institutions in sustaining the CPRs and gaining the compliance of generation after generation of appropriators to the rules in use" (Ostrom [1990] 2017, 89–90). According to Ostrom, the seven design principles necessary for this were (Ostrom [1990] 2017, 90):

1) Clearly defined boundaries of the CPR
2) Congruence between appropriation and provision rules and local conditions
3) Collective choice arrangements to modify the rules
4) Monitoring of appropriators

5) Graduated sanctions in case of rule breaking
6) Conflict resolution mechanisms
7) Minimal recognition of rights to organize on the part of governments

For CPRs that are not autonomous on their own, but are embedded in larger systems (such as financing- and provision mechanisms for certain services in welfare states, which are themselves embedded in the larger structure of a government), she added the criterion of (8) "nested enterprises," which should allow for the implementation of the other design principles in this more complex structure on many layers (Ostrom [1990] 2017, 103f). This would, in our case, pertain to a federal structure for the provision of social services or to agencies active in the financing and provision of social services to hold independence of the federal government. The next section will apply these design principles onto the matter of social service provision in welfare states and inquire which ones can be seen as being fulfilled and with respect to which policy changes might be called for.

IMPROVING SOCIAL POLICY BY REALIZING ITS COMMON POOL NATURE

For Elinor as well as for Vincent Ostrom, clear demarcation of types of goods was not an end in itself, but a prerequisite for establishing coherent policy prescriptions (Aligica and Boettke 2009, 116). While they have over their careers engaged in numerous attempts to study in detail the nature of various goods and resources, their attention has scarcely been put onto matters of social policies more generally. However, it is not the case that these matters were altogether unimportant to them: Vincent Ostrom's work on the meaning of democracy and the vulnerability of democracies clearly states that a country's policy choices with respect to social policies can have long-lasting effects on economic prosperity and—perhaps even more importantly—the long-term viability of free social orders (Ostrom [1997] 2009). He placed special emphasis on the cultural effects of overarching welfare policies and stressed the importance and significant meaning of citizens coming together voluntarily in order to discuss, vote on, and craft the sociopolitical institutions of their society. By relegating questions of poor relief, health care, provision for old age—and presumably also social services—to central bureaucracies and not taking responsibility for their own affairs, societies run the risk of long-term social decay and the neglect of their political institutions as well as their moral imaginations (Ostrom [1997] 2009). In that regard, the project undertaken here of contextualizing the nature of social services within the typology of goods can be seen as a valuable—and highly relevant—exercise.

Given that, in an Ostromian framework, the purpose of social science is—in the last respect—always the application of scientific insights onto real-world problems and the finding of solutions to social problems, the preceding discussion shall in the following be made fruitful to concrete policy advice. In order to do this, I will discuss Elinor Ostrom's design principles presented above and their applicability will be at the center of the discussion. The Bloomington School's ultimate task of "free[ing] our institutional and political imagination" (Aligica and Boettke 2009, 141) would certainly find few areas of social reality as needy of this modification as the welfare state.

Solutions to Problems of Social Service Provision

Because neither "government intervention" nor "privatization"—as the historically most widely applied ways of trying to overcome the tragedy of the commons—promise much success for a satisfactory reform of social service provision, a close look at the approach of using Elinor Ostrom's design principles considerable merit here. Thus, the postulate that the CPR, that is, the provision and financing of social services, could be preserved and its operation improved by the invoking of Elinor Ostrom's design principles and their application onto the matter will occupy us for the remainder of the chapter. The ultimate goal would be to offer practical solution for making presently existing welfare states sustainable, resilient (Tarko 2017, 103–37), and more responsive to the people they are deemed to be serving (Aligica 2016). Thus, the following paragraphs will apply these principles onto the provision of social services, ask whether the Ostromian conditions for successful provision are met, discuss potential problems for the provision of social services, and offer some tentative suggestions for remedies. I will start with two design principles that I see as being mostly in place with respect to the provision of social services and then shift the discussion to those where I find considerable deviations from Ostrom's principles.

Boundaries of Access to Social Services

It is not difficult to define at a given moment the social services that can be obtained in a welfare state. More important will be, however, the question of how these boundaries change over time. To give an example: While the question of state provision or financing of care services was not even raised fifty years ago, it is common practice today—at least in European welfare states. This same effect can be shown to exist for many other areas of social service provision. This means that the problem of the boundaries of state involvement in welfare states is not a static but a dynamic one. The same informal cultural mechanisms that influence the exclusion criterion of social services at a given point in time also have a major impact on the areas to which the said exclusion criterion may no longer be applied in the future. A clear boundary or definitive criterion for what constitutes a "legitimate" provision of a given social service will thus be hard to get hold off, at least over longer periods of time. In the short run, however, it is absolutely no problem to define where access to a social service begins or ends and given that I would conclude that this design principle does not pose a severe obstacle to social service provision in welfare states.

Congruence between Appropriation and Provision Rules and Local Conditions

With regard to this design principle, the greatest relevance can probably be seen in correctly determining the carrying capacity (Jakee and Turner 2002, 496), that is the sustainable financing of the corresponding programs. Jakee and Turner see two different problems with regard to this: first, the financing of social services is subject to "soft budget constraints" (Kornai 1986, 3), which is why the financing of social services was and is not always tied to budgetary limits (for the recent instances of this with regards to nursing care insurance in Germany, see Aerzteblatt 2018). Here, however, demographic change processes could lead to a "hardening" of the budget constraint in the not-too-distant future. Moreover, it must be assumed that in many Western welfare states the upper threshold of the possible corridor for tax rates might already have been reached and that resistance can be expected in the event of future increases in taxes to finance social services. Similar considerations can also be made in some places with regard to the possibilities for further government debt. Secondly, Jakee and Turner (2002, 497) point out that in many places the inflows and outflows into the fiscal commons of social service systems have reached such a scale and complexity that neither politicians nor policy experts—not to mention the users of the services—can get a good overview of the extent of the underlying CPR. The overview becomes even more difficult if future developments—for example, to estimate future funding requirements for the financing of care services—are also to be taken into account. However problematic these outlooks seem to be, I would still argue that the underlying problems can potentially be resolved. In the case of care insurance in Germany for instance, the demographic outlook automatically leads to rising rates on the part of contributors to the budget (BPB 2014); while this might not be a perfect adaptation to the challenges ahead, it still demonstrates that congruence between appropriation and provision rules and the particularities social service provision in welfare states can be facilitated.

Thus far, I have suggested that some design principles might be—at least partially—fulfilled with regards to social service provision. I will now shift to those where I see greater potential for them of not being fulfilled and where consequently a less-than-optimal and potentially unsustainable management of the underlying CPR needs to be feared. It will become apparent that this pertains mostly to those design principles that pertain to the ways in which the collective choice about the organization of the CPR are made and how the procedures within it are to be monitored and administered.

Collective Choice Arrangements and Conflict Resolution Mechanisms

While in democratic welfare states a certain civic participation can be localized through participation in elections, it must nevertheless be stated that the influence of the individual citizen on the design of concrete policy measures is likely to be relatively small. This is due to the sizeable political distance to the decision-making centers for social policy matters, as well as to the vastly larger group sizes that contemporary welfare states cater to. A rather simple takeaway to solving this problem would be to split the respective supply systems into smaller geographical units (Sellers and Lindström 2015). However, this is decisively not the direction in which contemporary social service provision seems to be moving; much rather, international organizations such as the ILO, the UN, and—in the European context—the EU are attempting to come up with and implement principles for social policies to be unified over jurisdictions and its administration centralized (Holden 2017; Kelly 2011; ILO Global Flagship Program 2019; Gerhards et al. 2014). Thus, one would have to predict that also the future realization of this particular design principle does not seem all too likely at this point. The same criticism would hold for conflict resolution mechanisms, which—according to Ostrom ([1990] 2017, 100)—should be available rapidly and at low cost to appropriators. While, again, the political arena of modern welfare states facilitates some function of this design principle, it is of course a far cry from the potential that relatively small and somewhat homogeneous groups of appropriators can have to solve conflict in the CPRs described by E. Ostrom.

Monitoring and Sanctioning

Similar conclusions can be drawn with regard to effective monitoring. While social security systems can easily be designed in such a way that corresponding violations of the directives can be identified and sanctioned, the difficulty is probably more in ensuring that (a) violations of the rules are defined so precisely that they can also be proven in daily practice, (b) monitoring techniques that span entire societies can be developed, and (c) the members of society responsible for monitoring—with regard to social services these are politicians and bureaucrats—have a sufficient interest in enforcing the sanctions. Jakee and Turner (2002, 499–502) point to the difficulty of the first point and, with regard to the last one, show with Buchanan (1967) that this desired behavior cannot be easily assumed. While I do not wish to belittle the public choice problems that questions of the welfare state are inherently confronted with[17] and the difficulties of properly defining the rules in a complex welfare state, I would still posit that the difficulties of effective monitoring discussed under (b) pose the greatest challenge in this regard. While the mechanisms used to monitor the behavior of a small-scale community concentrated in a relatively limited geographic area can easily be facilitated by the appropriators themselves, extending the scope of the impure public good in questions to millions and millions of people necessarily requires monitoring to be delegated to agents that might not have the same interest and ability to effectively pursue their tasks.

Minimal Recognition of Rights to Organize

Correspondingly, I would also state a less-than-perfect congruity between this design principle and the reality of social service provision. While it is certainly possible—in most cases[18]—for individuals to make their own arrangements for certain social services (if they can afford to), it is under most conditions not possible for them to correspondingly withdraw from the financing mechanisms for the collective provision of these services for other members of society. Thus, even though the formal recognition of citizen's rights to self-organize to provide social service is mostly not curtailed, the prevailing financial incentives make it unlikely that these rights will be acted upon by the majority of the populace—by making the opt-out option with regards to social services undesirable, welfare states practically make this design principle of the Ostromian account not fulfilled.

Summing up, we can see that while the design principles that pertain to the definition of the boundaries of CPR and the appropriation rules can be seen as fulfilled for social service provision, it is rather those design principles that deal with the importance of collective choice mechanisms, monitoring, sanctioning, and rights to self-organization that must be seen as found wanting. It is thus apparent that the takeaway from this realization lies in an appeal to strengthening those areas in which the Ostromian design principles seem to apply the least.

While I am not going to engage in concrete policy proposals and even a thorough discussion of potential responses to the mismatch between the design principles and the reality of social service provision is beyond the scope of this chapter, the following lines shall play with some ideas of how service provision can be made more robust vis-à-vis the described shortcomings.

Interestingly, potential remedies for the shortcomings in the application of the design principles can be found in other works of Elinor and Vincent Ostrom. Especially their insights about the polycentric nature of—apart from a manifold of other social phenomena—what they came to call "the public economy" can serve as a useful starting point here. Realizing that "(t)he public economy need not be an exclusive government monopoly" (Ostrom and Ostrom [1977] 2002, 75), the Ostroms set the base for a polycentric view on service provision (also see Ostrom [1972] 2002). While social service provision, as I have previously laid out, is already being financed and provided in a way not completely foreign to the "public economy" approach developed by the Ostroms, the pendulum could still be shifted further away from governments with respect to social service provision. The characteristics of polycentric systems, namely that "there exist many decision-making centres, formally independent of each other" (Ostrom 1991, 223), are certainly an idea that could potentially be fruitfully applied to social service provision as well. Or, as Elinor Ostrom had put it in her Nobel Prize Speech: "Moving away from the presumption that the government must solve all common-pool resource problems while recognizing the important role of governments is a big step forward" (Ostrom 2010: 197). The big step with respect to social service provision would be to realize that governments, while they might continue to be important players in the financing of social services, ought to realize that their capacities to manage and oversee social security system in complex modern societies are necessarily limited.

Similarly, Ostromian insights from the Metropolitan Governance Debate can be applied to social services, which in turn might also be defined very differently. The most striking finding of E. Ostrom's investigations with respect to this surely is the insight that higher degrees of "professionalization" on the part of service providers do not necessarily lead to greater satisfaction for service users. This effect was most pronounced with the provision of policing services, for which increased specialization actually lead to worse results. Police officers, who might have gotten excellent training and were well equipped in terms of their technical capacities but had no grounding in or relation to the community they were serving in, produced worse results (Ostrom, Parks, and Whitaker 1978; Boettke, Palagashvili and Lemke 2013). Consequently, professionalism and the optimal background for effective provision would also need to be viewed in a differentiated way with regards to social services. While it is certainly important that providers of social services be professional in the sense that they are able to perform their tasks well, perhaps not enough attention is being paid to the inherently human element of social service provision and the fact that it might be more important to stress those elements than insisting on ever-greater specialization and professionalization in those fields.

All in all, what has been said leads to the conclusion that the remedy to the deviations observed between the design principles and social service provision could be remedied by taking steps toward a more participatory welfare state (Delsen 2016), which would attempt to search for polycentric solutions not only for the provision of social services, but for a host of other welfare policies as well. Additionally, the role of community and localized service provision could be strengthened.

CONCLUSION

I have tried to show in this chapter that social service provision in modern welfare states has characteristics that resemble a CPR or an impure public good. The contrary definition and practical treatment of social services as "public goods" regularly leads to problems. In particular, the assumption that in the provision of social services—after their financing and guarantee of provision by state institutions—the rivalry in consumption can be ignored must be regarded as mistaken—rivalry of consumption still manifests itself, although perhaps along different avenues than merely prices. At the same time, the problem of the principle of exclusion being inapplicable because of social and cultural beliefs about social services must also be accepted—nonpaying but needy persons cannot simply be excluded from access to care, health, or education. Having demonstrated this impure public good character of social services, the chapter then applied Ostrom's design principles for sustainable CPRs onto matters of social service provision and found that mostly design principles that speak to the self-organizational and monitoring collective choice capacities of the "appropriators" (i.e., service users and taxpayers) seem not to be fulfilled.

In my view, two major takeaways follow from what was discussed here: first of all, it would be important—both for the economists analyzing and for the politicians making decisions about the provision of social services—to assess the nature of social service provision correctly. If the fundamental nature of social services as goods, whose properties are very similar to those of CPRs, is correctly recognized, the effects of economic and social policy decisions in this respect will be better assessed. As for practical proposals, the chapter has argued that a more participatory version of the welfare state and social service provision within it would help to remedy some of the shortcomings associated with it. While I have refrained from discussing concrete policy responses to narrowly defined real-world problems,[19] I have challenged the reader to rethink policy responses to social service provision along Ostromian lines. These would call for a greater citizen participation in the design and provision of social services and more plurality in the institutional structures used for their financing. Additionally, citizens shall be enabled and encouraged to, as far as possible, devise their own solutions to social problems. While these proposals certainly do not serve as a panacea (Ostrom, Janssen, and Anderies 2007) against problems experienced with social service provision, I would hope that the thoughts laid out here could serve as the starting point for further inquiries into the nature of the goods and services offered in welfare states.

NOTES

1. This chapter is the fruit of the research sequence of the 2018–2019 Adam Smith Fellowship. Hence, my deepest thanks go to the Mercatus Center at George Mason University for enabling this wonderful fellowship format to happen in the first place as well as for the generous intellectual and financial support throughout the year. A few people there deserve special praise: Courtney Dunn and Peter Lipsey for organizing the Adam Smith Program with such enormous professionalism as well as Bobbi Herzberg, Brian Kogelmann, and Peter Boettke for giving their precious time to oversee our group over the academic year and helping this chapter take shape with their comments and reports. Equally important were the numerous discussions (both during and apart from the official sessions) with my colleagues in our "research track group," without which I would understand many issues about the Ostroms, political economy, and life in general considerably less. Thank you guys! Furthermore, my colleagues at the University of Siegen made helpful comments, both on the concept of the chapter in October 2018 and on the first draft in June 2019. I would especially like to thank my adviser Nils Goldschmidt for his valuable insight concerning the oscillating movement taking place from public to impure public goods with respect to social services. I do not thank him however for putting so much additional work on my desk throughout the year that the finalization of the project seemed to be in jeopardy at times! I would additionally like to thank Julia C. Cremer for going over the manuscript in July 2019 in order to—courageously—adapt the format and edit out my numerous spelling and typing mistakes. I do of course take full responsibility for the ones that remained despite her best efforts.

2. Defined as mechanisms to "enhance the welfare of people who (a) are weak and vulnerable, largely by providing social care, (b) are poor, largely through redistributive income transfers, or (c) are neither vulnerable nor poor, by organizing cash benefits to privies insurance and consumption smoothing, and by providing medical insurance and school education." (Barr 2012, 7).

3. For data for Europe, see Eurostat 2018, for the US OECD 2018.

4. Especially the expansion of regulatory practices is notable here (Hollcombe and Boudreaux 2015).

5. These sectors represent typical examples of social services and perfectly capture the intricate relationships between public opinion, financing needs, private service provision, and public financing that is the topic of this chapter. However, I would not want to be misunderstood in as much as the framework for understanding social

services developed in this chapter should just as much be valid for other types of social services and should also apply in other places than Germany. It just so happens that I am most familiar with these aspects of the German market for social services and hence chose to use these areas for my illustrations. Given the local character of many of the debates about social services, it was unavoidable to cite some sources in German in order to illustrate some points. I hope that this does not cause the reader too much inconvenience.

6. My account skips the complexity of the process necessary to arrive at the classification of these four types of goods. Originally, it was customary to only distinguish between private and public goods (cf. the original dichotomy by Samuelson, 1954), with Buchanan, 1965, first bringing club goods into the discussion. Ostrom and Ostrom [1977], 2002, then was instrumental in broadening the classification by introducing "common pool resources" or impure public goods into the discussion. By "doubling the types of goods" (Ostrom 2010, 412), social science thus had a more powerful analytical toolkit at hand.

7. See also the Ostromian point that "the *production* of goods and services needs to be distinguished from their *provision* at public expense" (Ostrom, Tiebout, and Warren 1961, 36).

8. These are statements according to which certain goods or services—mostly provided by state institutions—have a public character because their adequate provision is in the "public interest." Typical services of this kind are, for example, the provision of public transport, infrastructure, or schooling. For an example of this practice, cf. Kratzwald 2018. Leaving aside question about how difficult it can be to come up even with an approximation of that the "public interest" would be, we do not consider this type of literature here due to the improper use of the term "public good." It bears notice however that a better understanding of what and should be considered as public good is certainly also among the secondary aims of the chapter.

9. Interestingly enough, one could refer to similarities in my approach to subjectivist approaches to economics in general, and in particular to the Austrian school. Consider, for instance, Carl Menger 1871 on the nature of value: "Value is thus nothing inherent in goods, no property of them, nor an independent thing existing by itself. It is a judgment economizing men make about the importance of the goods at their disposal for the maintenance of their live and well-being" (Menger [1871] (1976), 120f). While the analogy must of course remain somewhat imperfect and this subjectivist strand is by now firmly accepted in all of economics while thinking about social services in a similar way must seem rather obscure to many at this point, the quote is intended to illustrate how many "facts" that we as human beings experience on a daily basis are rooted in influencing forces completely unknown to us. Just like the task of the subjectivist economist can be seen as identifying the forces that propel prices to move up and down in line with changing valuations and knowledge on the part of market participants (Hayek 1937, 1945), my task can be seen as uncovering societal valuations of the need for a nonexclusionary social service provision and elaborating on the consequences that seem to follow from this.

10. This finding also reminds of the famous theorem ascribed to the American sociologist William Isaac Thomas: "If men define situations as real, they are real in

their consequences" (Thomas 1928). As such, "the definition of a situation" (Thomas 2002: 104) will have vast influence on the outcomes that can be expected from what is sometimes seen as an objective manifestation of the situation. Just like the fairy Tinker Bell in the play "Peter Pan" is brought back from death by the sheer belief of the audience, so social services can be rendered nonexcludable if enough members of a polity do indeed interpret the matter to be like this. (For illustrations of the "Tinker-bell-effect" in other domains of the social sciences, see Paris 1997 and Stewart 2004.)

11. He does this writing about the German tradition of "Ordnungsökonomik," for the support of which he was quite well known (Aligica, Lewis, and Storr 2017).

12. Cf. For instance Busemeyer and Neimanns 2017, even though it is also clear here that the approval of individual programs of the welfare state can fluctuate considerably due to the social positioning.

13. See for instance the organizational motto of "Caritas," the most important provider of social services in Germany: "Not sehen und handeln!"—"When you see poverty, act upon it!" (Caritas 2019).

14. Even though the central government guarantees access to day care services for every child below three, in practice there are around 200,000 day care spots missing (Deutsche Welle 2016).

15. The insight that the same resource can be classified as multiple types of goods does not originate with me, but has—for instance—clearly been worked out for groundwater basins by Elinor Ostrom (Tarko 2017, 79ff. as well as Gibson et al. 2005), where the *quantity* of water can be seen as a common pool resource, whereas the *quality* of the water stock displays public goods character.

16. On this, also see the Ostroms on the free-rider problem (Ostrom and Ostrom 1977 (2002), 81).

17. For, in my opinion, still the best overview on the matter, see Wagner [1998]2019.

18. Note that, for example, education, which is not included in most definition of social services but whose provision mechanism are similar under conditions of most Western welfare states, some countries do not even allow citizens to withdraw their children from state-run or certified schools, thereby rendering homeschooling illegal (for an overview of the situation regarding this in Germany, see Deutsche Welle 2019).

19. The Ostroms themselves would probably have liked my chapter more had I done this!

REFERENCES

Aerzteblatt. 2018. "Bundeszuschuss muss Pflegeversicherung stützen." *Aerzteblatt*, November 26, 2018. https://www.aerzteblatt.de/nachrichten/99415/Bundeszuschuss-muss-Pflegeversicherung-stuetzen.

Alderman, Harold. 1987. "Allocation of Goods through Non-price Mechanisms: Evidence on Distribution by Willingness to Wait." *Journal of Development Economics* 25 (1): 105–124.

Aligica, Paul D. 2016. "Neither Market nor State Domain: Nonprofits From the Ostrom's Theoretical Perspective." *Nonprofit and Voluntary Sector Quarterly* 45 (45): 435–605.

Aligica, Paul D., and Peter J. Boettke. 2009. *Challenging Institutional Analysis and Development: The Bloomington School*. New York: Routledge.

Aligica, Paul D., P. Lewis, and V.H. Storr. 2017. "Austrian Economics and the Bloomington School: An Introduction and Overview." In *The Austrian and Bloomington Schools of Political Economy*, edited by P.D. Aligica, P. Lewis, and V.H. Storr, ix–xxi. Bingley, UK: Emerald Insight Publishing.

Arrow, Kenneth. 1963. "Uncertainty and the Welfare Economics of Medical Care." *The American Economic Review* 53 (5): 941–73.

Bäcker, Gerhard, Gerhard Naegele, Reinhard Bispinck, Klaus Hofemann, and Jennifer Neubauer. 2010. *Sozialpolitik und soziale Lage in Deutschland*. Wiesbaden, Germany: VS Verlag für Sozialwissenschaften.

Barr, Nicholas. 2012. *Economics of the Welfare State*. Oxford: Oxford University Press.

Bartlett, William, and Julian Le Grand. 1993. "The Theory of Quasi-Markets." In *Quasi-Markets and Social Policy*, edited by W. Bartlett and J. Le Grand, 13–34. London: Palgrave MacMillan.

Beito, David T. 2000. *From Mutual Aid to the Welfare State: Fraternal Societies and Social Services, 1890-1967*. Chapel Hill: The University of North Carolina Press.

Blöchinger, Jansjörg. 2008. "Market Mechanisms in Public Service Provision." OECD Economics Department Working Papers, August 4, 2019. https://www.oecd-ilibrary.org/economics/market-mechanisms-in-public-service-provision_241001625762.

Boettke, Peter J., Christopher J. Coyne, and Peter T. Leeson. 2011. "Quasimarket Failure." *Public Choice* 149 (1–2): 209–224.

Boettke, Peter J., Liya Palagashvili, and Jayme Lemke. 2013. "Riding in Cars with Boys: Elinor Ostrom's Adventures with the Police." *Journal of Institutional Economics* 9 (4): 407–425.

BPB. 2014. "Zukünftige Finanzierungsmodelle für die Pflegeversicherung." BPB-Bundeszentrale für politische Bildung, September 1, 2014. http://www.bpb.de/politik/innenpolitik/gesundheitspolitik/72843/ezukuenftige-finanzierungsmodelle.

Breyer, Hans. 1995. "The Political Economy of Rationing in Social Health Insurance." *Journal of Population Economics* 8 (2): 137–148.

Buchanan, James. 1965. "An Economic Theory of Clubs." *Economica* 32 (125): 1–14.

———. 1967. *Public Finance in Democratic Process: Fiscal Institutions and Individual Choice*. Chapel Hill: University of North Carolina Press.

———. 1975. "The Samaritan's Dilemma." In *Altruism, Morality, and Economic Theory*, edited by E. Phelps, 71–85. New York: Russel Sage.

Busemeyer, M.R., A. Goerres, and S. Weschle. 2009. "Attitudes towards Redistributive Spending in an Era of Demographic Ageing: The Rival Pressures from Age and Income in 14 OECD Countries." *Journal of European Social Policy* 19 (3): 195–212.

Busemeyer, M.R., and E. Neimanns 2017. "Conflictive Preferences towards Social Investments and Transfers in Mature Welfare States: The Cases of Unemployment

Benefits and Childcare Provision." *Journal of European Social Policy* 27 (3): 249–66.

Busemeyer, M.R., and J.L. Garritzmann. 2017a. "Academic, Vocational, or General? An Analysis of Public Opinion towards Education Policies with Evidence from a New Comparative Survey." *Journal of European Social Policy* 27 (4): 373–386.

———. 2017b. "Public Opinion on Policy and Budgetary Trade-Offs in European Welfare States: Evidence from a New Comparative Survey." *Journal of European Public Policy* 24 (6): 871–89.

Caritas. 2019. "Official Website." July 30, 2019. https://www.caritas.de/.

Cremer, Georg, Nils Goldschmidt, and Sven Höfer. 2013. *Soziale Dienstleistungen. Ökonomie, Recht, Politik*. Tübingen: Mohr Siebeck.

Dawes, Robin M. 1973. "The Commons Dilemma Game: An N-Person Mixed Motive Game with a Dominating Strategy for Defection." *ORI Research Bulletin* 13: 1–12.

Delsen, Lei. 2016. "The Realization of the Participation Society: Welfare State Reform in the Netherlands: 2010-2015." Nijmegen Creating Knowledge for Society Series, August 2016.

Deutsche Welle. 2016. "Germany Needs more than 200,000 Day Care Spots." December 30, 2016. https://www.dw.com/en/report-germany-needs-more-than-200000-day-care-spots/a-36956739.

———. 2018. "'Who Will Look after Us?' — Germany's Ailing Elderly Care System." July 16, 2018. https://www.dw.com/en/who-will-look-after-us-germanys-ailing-elderly-care-system/a-44702143.

———. 2019. "European Court Rules against German Homeschooling Family." January 10, 2019. https://www.dw.com/en/european-court-rules-against-german-homeschooling-family/a-47021333.

Esping-Andersen, Gøsta. 1996. *Welfare States in Transition: National Adaption to Global Economies*. London: Sage.

Eurostat. 2018. "Government Expenditure on Social Protection in European Countries." Accessed March 10, 2018. https://ec.europa.eu/eurostat/statistics-explained/index.php/Government_expenditure_on_social_protection#Evolution_of_.27expenditure_on_social_protection.27.

Frech III, H.E., and William C. Lee. 1987. "The Welfare Cost of Rationing –By-Queuing across Markets: Theory and Evidence from the U.S. Gasoline Crisis." *The Quarterly Journal of Economics* 102 (1): 97–108.

Gerhards, Jürgen, and Silke Hans. 2014. "Explaining Citizens' Participation in a Transnational European Public Sphere." *Comparative Sociology* 13 (6): 667–691.

Gibson, Clark C., Krister P. Andersson, Elinor Ostrom, and Sujai Shivakumar. 2005. *The Samaritan's Dilemma: The Political Economy of Development Aid*. Oxford: Oxford University Press.

Gibson, Clark C., Margaret A. McKean, and Elinor Ostrom. 2000. *People and Forests: Communities, Institutions, and Governance*. Cambridge, MA: MIT Press.

Goerres, A., and M. Tepe. 2010. "Age-based Self-interest, Intergenerational Solidarity and the Welfare State: A Comparative Analysis of Older People's Attitudes towards Public Childcare in 12 OECD Countries." *European Journal of Political Research* 49 (6): 818–851.

Goldschmidt, Nils, Erik Grimmer-Solem, and Joachim Zweynert. 2016. "On the Purpose and Aims of the Journal of Contextual Economics." *Journal of Contextual Economics* 136 (1): 1–14.

Hardin, Garrett. 1968. "The Tragedy of the Commons." *Science* 162: 1243–8.

Holden, Chris. 2017. "Global Social Policy: An Application of Welfare State Theory." *Journal of International and Comparative Social Policy* 34 (1): 40–57.

Hayek, Friedrich A. 1937. "Economics and Knowledge." *Economica* 4 (13): 33–54.

———. 1945. "The Use of Knowledge in Society." *The American Economic Review* 35 (4): 519–530.

Hollcombe, Randall G., and Christopher J. Boudreaux. 2015. "Regulation and Corruption." *Public Choice* 164 (1): 75–85.

ILO Global Flagship Program. 2019. July 31, 2019. https://www.social-protection.org/gimi/gess/Flagship.action.

Iversen, Tor, and Luigi Siciliani. 2012. "Non-price Rationing and Waiting Times." In *The Oxford Handbook of Health Economics,* edited by S. Glied and P.S. Smith, 649–670. Oxford: Oxford University Press.

Jensen, Carsten, Christoph Arndt, and Songhui Lee. 2018. "Policy Instruments and Welfare State Reform." *Journal of European Social Policy* 28 (2): 161–176.

Jakee, Keith and Stephen Turner. 2002. "The Welfare State as a Fiscal Commons: Problems of Incentives Versus Problems of Cognition." *Public Finance Review* 30 (6): 481–508.

Kananen, J., P. Taylor-Gooby, and T.P. Larsen. 2006. "Public Attitudes and New Social Risk Forms." In *The Politics of Post-Industrial Welfare States: Adapting Post-war Social Policies to New Social Risks*, edited by A. Klaus and G. Bonoli, 83–99. New York: Routledge.

Kelly, James P. 2001. "Building the Global Welfare State: The United Nations as Community Organizer." *Engage* 12 (1): 62–67.

Kornai, Janos. 1986. "The Soft Budget Constraint." *Kyklos* 39 (1): 3–30.

Kratzwald, Brigitte. 2018. "Rethinking the Social Welfare State in Light of the Commons." Accessed March 10, 2019. http://wealthofthecommons.org/essay/rethinking-social-welfare-state-light-commons.

Le Grand, Julian. 1991. "Markets and Social Policy." *The Economic Journal* 101 (408): 1256–1267.

———. 2007. *The Other Invisible Hand: Delivering Public Services through Choice and Competition.* Princeton: Princeton University Press.

Mau, Steffen. 2001. "Patterns of Popular Support for the Welfare State: A Comparison of the United Kingdom and Germany." *WZB Discussion Paper* No. FS III: 01–40.

Menger, Carl. [1871] 1976. *Principles of Economics.* Arlington, VA: Institute for Humane Studies.

Mischke, M. 2014. *Public Attitudes Towards Family Policies in Europe. Linking Institutional Context and Public Opinion.* Wiesbaden, Germany: Springer VS.

Musgrave, Richard A. 1959. *The Theory of Public Finance.* New York: McGraw Hill.

OECD. 2018. "Social Spending." *OECD.* Accessed March 10, 2018. https://data.oecd.org/socialexp/social-spending.htm.

Olson, Mancur. 1965. *The Logic of Collective Action: Public Goods and the Theory of Groups.* Cambridge: Harvard University Press.

Ostrom, Elinor. 1986. "An Agenda for the Study of Institutions." *Public Choice* 48 (1): 3–25.

———. [1990] 2017. *Governing the Commons: The Evolution of Institutions for Collective Action*. Cambridge: Cambridge University Press.

———. 1996. "Crossing the Great Divide: Coproduction, Synergy and Development." *World Development* 24 (6): 1073–87.

———. 2010. "Beyond Markets and States: Polycentric Governance of Complex Economic Systems." *The American Economic Review* 100 (3): 641–72.

———. 2011. "Overcoming the Samaritan's Dilemma in Development Aid." *Revue d'Économie du Développement* 19: 5–18.

Ostrom, Elinor, Marco A. Janssen, and John M. Anderies. 2007. "Going beyond Panaceas." *PNAS* 104 (39): 15176–15178.

Ostrom, Elinor, Roger B. Parks, and Gordon P. Whitaker. 1978. *Patterns of Metropolitan Policing*. Cambridge: Ballinger.

Ostrom, Vincent. [1972] 2002. "Polycentricity." In *Polycentricity and Local Public Economies: Readings from the Workshop in Political Theory and Policy Analysis*, edited by M.D. McGinnis, 52–74 and 119–38. Ann Arbor: The University of Michigan Press.

———. [1973] 2008. *The Intellectual Crisis in American Public Administration*. Tuscaloosa: The University of Alabama Press.

———. 1991. "Polycentricity: The Structural Basis of Self-Governing Systems." In *The Meaning of American Federalism: Constituting a Self-Governing Society*, edited by V. Ostrom, 223–44. San Franciso: ICS Press.

———. [1997] 2009. *The Meaning of Democracy and the Vulnerability of Democracies: A Response to Tocqueville's Challenge*. Ann Arbor: University of Michigan Press.

Ostrom, Vincent, Charles M. Tiebout, and R. Warren. 1961. "The Organization of Government in Metropolitan Areas: A Theoretical Inquiry." *American Political Science Review* 55 (December): 831–42.

Ostrom, Vincent, and Elinor Ostrom. [1977] 2002. "Public Goods and Public Choices." In *Polycentricitiy and Local Public Economies: Readings from the Workshop in Political Theory and Policy Analysis*, edited by M.D. McGinnis, 75–105. Ann Arbor: The University of Michigan Press.

Paris, D.C. 1997. "School Reform: Too Much Talk, Too Little Action." *Forum for Applied Research and Public Policy* 12 (3): 46–56.

Parish, Ross. 1981. *Economic Analysis of Non-Price Rationing with Particular Reference to Petrol*. Canberra: Australian Government Publishing Service.

Pedersen, Karl R. 2001. "The Samaritan's Dilemma and the Effectiveness of Development Aid." *International Tax and Public Finance* 8 (5): 693–703.

Raschky, Paul A., and Manijeh Schwindt. 2009. "Aid, Natural Disasters and the Samaritan's Dilemma." *The World Bank Policy Research Working Paper* 4952.

Samuelson, Paul. 1954. "The Pure Theory of Public Expenditure." *Review of Economics and Statistics* 36: 387–389.

Shera, Wes. 1996. "Market Mechanisms and Consumer Involvement in the Delivery of Mental Health Services: A UK-US Comparison." *Journal of Sociology & Social Welfare* 23 (1): 13–22.

Stewart, Cameron. 2004. "The Rule of Law and the Tinkerbell Effect: Theoretical Consideration, Criticisms, and Justifications for the Rule of Law." *Macquarie Law Journal* 4: 135–164.

Svallfors, Stefan. 2010. "Public Attitudes." In *The Oxford Handbook of the Welfare State*, ed. F.G. Castels, S. Leibfried, J. Lewis, H. Obinger, and C. Pierson. Oxford: Oxford University Press.

Tarko, Vlad. 2017. *Elinor Ostrom: An Intellectual Biography*. London: Rowman & Littlefield.

Thomas, William I. 1928. "The Methodology of Behavior Study." In *The Child in America: Behavior Problems and Programs*, authored by Thomas William, 553–76. New York: Alfred A. Knopf.

———. 2002. "The Definition of the Situation." In *Self, Symbols, and Society: Classic Readings in Social Psychology*, edited by N. Rousseau, 103–15. New York: Rowman & Littlefield.

Thomson, David. 1996. *Selfish Generations? How Welfare States Grow Old*. Cambridge: White Horse Press.

Tynkkynen, Liina-Kaisa, Ilmo Keskimäki, and Juhani Lehto. 2013. "Purchaser-Provider Splits in Health Care: The Case of Finland." *Health Policy* 111 (3): 221 –225.

Wagner, Richard E. [1998] 2019. *To Promote the General Welfare: Market Processes vs. Political Transfers*. Arlington, VA: Mercatus Center at George Mason University.

Weyrich, Karl-Heinz. 2011. "Soziale Dienste." In *Fachlexikon der sozialen Arbeit* 7, 788–90. Baden-Baden, Germany: Nomos.

Part II

APPLICATIONS OF POLYCENTRICITY

Chapter 4

Polycentric Party Governance

Competition, Federalism, and the Production of Political Leadership in American Politics

Nicholas F. Jacobs

Great leaders are not just born; they climb the ranks of power, maneuver around political obstacles, and attract mass support in a governing system defined by rules, procedure, and institutional norms. Leadership is produced, and in the United States, as with most constitutional republics, political leadership develops within a highly institutionalized form of organized party competition. Party organizations structure coalition formation, and ambitious leaders that desire to control governing institutions, such as the presidency, must first build political support within a party. Parties, like the formal constitutional offices being sought, are also governed by rules, and those rules change the behavior and strategies of those seeking leadership positions. Rules within the party also determine whether the organization is able to produce leaders who can build majority coalitions in various political jurisdictions and win elections among the general electorate. And rules govern the extent to which leaders, once in control of various institutions, respond to public demands and incorporate the concerns of potential political adversaries.

While most modern republics have party system, the American party system is unique for its abundant polycentricity. The system, while comprised of just two major parties, nevertheless contains multiple, independent centers of competing authority. There is no single Democratic or Republican party, but, rather, hundreds of smaller entities within each umbrella organization, each defined by their own rules and sets of relationships to one another. As a result of America's federated constitutional order, party organizations compete for office at a variety of different scales. Democrats and Republicans organize themselves and compete for offices at a local level—within various cities and counties—at the state level, and, finally, at a national level. These organizations respond to one another and establish procedures to manage the considerable overlap in political jurisdiction. They share resources and collectively develop the capacity to produce viable candidacies and win elections. Consequently, as Vincent Ostrom (1972) noticed, "polycentricity in the selection of political leadership and in the organization of political coalitions [has been a] condition for the maintenance of an enforceable system of constitutional law and for the maintenance of a lawful public order." Polycentricity in the production of political leadership increases the degree of citizen choice over potential political leaders, and it increases the likelihood that empowered officials respond to the popular demands of the opposing party.

While the American party system meets certain definitional criteria of polycentricity, this chapter describes its variation over the course of American political development. Over the past 180 years, the party system has developed in at least three distinct phases. Initially, party organizations were highly decentralized and fragmented. At the turn of the twentieth century, internal reforms restructured both major parties that continued to disperse authority, but increased the amount of overlap between organizations of different scale. Within the last fifty years, however, further reforms have centralized the decision-making powers of each organization, making each party more organizationally cohesive. While each era still exhibits the characteristics of polycentric order, I argue that both parties have increasingly failed to produce satisfactory levels of choice, or diffuse leadership authority to such an extent as necessary for the maintenance of other polycentric institutional arrangements, such as constitutional federalism.

By applying the concept of polycentricity to the structure and reform of the American party system, this chapter offers several insights on the institutional nature of political competition and the Ostrom's study of institutional diversity.

First, extant work on party organization and institutional choice often views parties as essential institutional arenas for overcoming collective action problems in debates about public goods. Yet, parties produce goods in their own right, which are essential to political life in the United States. Parties produce candidates for office, positions on important issues, and resources for campaigns. Most important, parties produce political leadership. Polycentricity matters for the study of party organizations because it allows us to better understand the production of political leadership as defined by the rules, procedures, and norms that govern debate over issues within the party, especially in the selection of candidates for office (E. Ostrom 1986). Those rules alter how institutions of different scale respond to citizen demands and then channel information back to participants in the organization. Rules change across different jurisdictions and across time. Those changes alter the interdependence of various elements within the party system and, ultimately, the efficient production of political leadership. Whether parties can efficiently produce leadership in a polycentric order depends on whether rule-making and rule-enforcing can be organized across multiple, overlapping political jurisdictions, each vested with some degree of independence (Polanyi 1951).

Second, if proponents of "stronger parties" suggest that there is too much conflict as a result of America's complicated party structure, while proponents of "weaker parties" claim that the nationalization of both parties fuels divisive partisan rancor, polycentrism offers an alternative that places these two poles in balance. Using the framework of polycentricity, we can evaluate whether a party system is a viable method of organizing the production of political leadership if it "can resolve conflict and maintain competition within appropriate bounds" (Ostrom et al. 1961, 838). Parties structure political conflict, and because they involve many citizens in that structure, reforming parties alter the ways in which individuals consider their own interests and the relation of their interests to their fellow citizens. As Vincent Ostrom (1987) recognizes, "The occurrence of conflict" is "recognized as inviting inquiry about the nature of the contending relationships, and the conditions where those interests might become complementary to one another within a larger community of interests" (163). As such, in producing political leadership, political parties represent the interests of partisans within a specific political jurisdiction. And so, a party's competitive impulses must be balanced against a need to resolve disagreements over those interests internally, among co-partisans, and externally, among all citizens in the general electorate.

Balancing conflict with competition, political parties can organize disparate political beliefs in a constitutional system, so long as citizens possess choice among competent leaders within a given political jurisdiction. As I show below, the United States is a revealing case about the development and transformation of polycentric institutional orders when considering the amount of choice its citizens have. Polycentricity, as both the Ostroms stress, does not simply mean more people making decisions, but rather the presence of more independent centers of decision-making authority that operate with their own distinctive logics. Paradoxically, the current era of party competition in the United States is less polycentric than previous eras, even as more people have become involved in the selection of party nominees. More democracy might not always be desirable if, as I argue, the people involved, such as party activists, all think and behave in a similar way. Under such conditions, democratizing reforms make the system susceptible to simple majoritarian rules, ease coalition formation, and facilitate the domination of governing institutions, usurping constitutional restraints.

Finally, if we can conclude that less citizen choice over potential leaders is debilitating, we can look to institutional reforms that would allow us to capture the benefits from duplication and overlapping organizational forms within a party. To be sure, we must apply other criteria to evaluate the produced efficiencies as normatively good or bad, and those criteria exist outside the analytical model and description of that system as presented here (McGinnis and Ostrom 2012). Nevertheless, parties produce political leaders and optimal performance is defined by vigorous competition across a diverse set of political jurisdictions. The production of political leadership matters for decisions made elsewhere in the constitutional system, and we can consider how polycentric organization in the production of political leadership matters for other decision-making processes outside of electoral processes, such as the diffusion of policymaking responsibility across governments of different size in a federal system.

This chapter proceeds as follows. First, I elaborate on the applicability of polycentricity to the production of political leadership. For most readers, this association might seem strange, since leadership seems inherently unlike other types of tangible goods studied under the Ostrom's framework. I argue that the Ostrom's nuanced, multifaceted view of economic goods is particularly well suited to the study of politics and to those who become political leaders. I also claim that citizen choice is desirable, that polycentric party systems are capable of providing citizens choice, and that the United States party system is abundantly polycentric, even if we can imagine alternative systems that might contain even more robust degrees of polycentricity, such as a multiparty system, or a system that contains no political parties at all. However, drawing on previous research, and in extending Vincent Ostrom's own historical observations, I conclude that more polycentricity is not always desirable in the production of political leadership.

The next section presents a measure of citizen choice over political leaders as a way of denoting different degrees of polycentricity in American political development. While there are numerous potential measures of citizen choice, this chapter considers how partisan segregation—the concentration of co-partisans across discrete political jurisdictions—relates to different degrees of polycentricity in the history of the American party system. Segregation indicates a failure of party organizations to produce viable political competition across overlapping jurisdictions. For any election, a high degree of segregation demonstrates that one party dominated in a geographic area, which comports with a reduction in choice that citizens had over potential political leaders. Using county-level election returns, I show that there are three distinguishable eras of partisan segregation in the United States between 1840 and 2016. I focus on US presidential elections and document how these three eras were brought about by traceable reforms in the organizational rules that altered the relative degree of polycentricity in both parties.

This chapter concludes with a set of observations about the relationship between polycentric party governance, the nationalization of American politics, and the transformation of constitutional federalism as a result of party reform. Polycentric party governance does not matter just for ensuring that citizens have options in the voting booth. Party organization can also reinforce certain constitutional restraints that protect the vitality of state and local government, and American federalism.

THE ECONOMIC NATURE OF PARTISANSHIP AND POLITICAL LEADERSHIP

Parties are institutions, governed by specific rules, norms, and procedures that affect the outcomes they produce. As institutions, parties impose order on collective action dilemmas facing fellow partisans within government (Shepsle 1979). For instance, within a voting body and absent party organization, there is high probability that on each vote taken, an individual legislator might find themselves on the losing end of the vote, with little to show for their efforts (Weingast 1979). Consequently, absent parties, there might be little incentive for fellow partisans to cooperate in the legislature over the long run, which might produce "chaos" as partisans endlessly cycle through various majoritarian outcomes (McKelvey 1976; Riker 1980). Party organizations allow rational, self-serving members to achieve their personal goals, while also creating a Pareto-superior outcome in legislative negotiations (Olson 1965; Axelrod 1984). The presence of a public goods dilemma helps to explain the rise of party organizations (Shepsle 1986) and, within a constitutional system defined by a first-past-the-post, winner-take-all system, why a stable two-party system emerges in equilibrium conditions (Aldrich 2011, 1997; Cox 1997).

Parties not only provide an institutional context that allows legislators to more efficiently produce policy in line with their electoral needs. Parties also produce candidates, and, in the process, they produce a variety of other goods that might be arrayed on the public-private spectrum. Parties help the average voter decide, reducing information costs during election season, increasing the likelihood that they will vote (Green et al. 2002; Popkin 1991). In a system where there is viable competition between at least two parties, citizens benefit from pressures that increase accountability in elections (Erikson et al. 1989; Burnham 1970) and inform parties of position changes in mass electorate attitudes (Jenkins 2000; Sundquist 1983). Parties as organizations also provide goods and services during campaigns and offer expertise, experience, and resources that benefit candidates who are members of a party (Rosenstone and Hansen 1993). Party labels advantage certain candidates running for office, providing ambitious office seekers with a tangible benefit if they can secure a party endorsement (Jacobson and Carson 2015). To be sure, none of these outcomes are strictly public. There is a degree of excludability, in that various rules govern who can and who cannot run as a partisan (e.g., primaries, caucuses, conventions). In most elections, only one candidate benefits from a party label, and parties exercise some veto authority on who can use, or consume, that label. And, at a certain point, the consumption of other benefits—money, staff, advertisement space—precludes another candidate's usage. Additionally, parties produce these goods, even though public entities provide venues for their provision, and even though public laws impinge on the organizational rules responsible for governing nomination and general election processes.

Political parties also produce leaders. In one sense, political leadership is an input into various organizational patterns that produce other goods. This is the dominant perspective taken by most institutional analyses of party coalition formation and management (Smith 2007). In another sense, however, political leadership is itself a public good. Leaders represent territorially defined jurisdictions and the people within them. Nonresidents are unable to vote for leaders of a jurisdiction that they do not live in, thereby satisfying the excludability principle; and the amount of representation a leader can provide is nonrivalrous among those within a jurisdiction. However, in other aspects, political leadership sits in between the private and public, reifying a key insight of the Ostrom's that rarely are goods that are thought to be public, in fact, public (Ostrom and Ostrom, 1977). Elected leaders serve dual roles, representing a constituency whose members jointly benefit from the nonsubtractable act of representation whether they voted for the member or not, while also representing a subset of that constituency, comprised of fellow partisans who can choose to be members or leave the party. In addition, while nonresidents and noncitizens are excluded from the production process through formal, legal prohibitions on voting, leadership is not entirely excludable. As Jane Mansbridge (2003) has recently argued, representatives often serve as "surrogates" for citizens with no electoral connection.[1] Individuals outside of the formal jurisdiction can even participate in their selection if electoral rules do not prohibit, for example, outside funding or other types of electioneering support.

Neither public, nor private, political leadership must be studied as an institutionally determined good because of its intricate relation to other types of processes and outcomes that govern the production and consumption of public goods. "Polycentricity," Vincent Ostrom (1972) argues, "in the essential structure of government is a necessary, but insufficient condition for the maintenance of an enforceable system of constitutional law," because there is always the "possibility that a single dominant coalition will be able to control all essential decision structures for its advantage." However, he continues, "so long as voters have a choice among candidates, severe constraints will be placed upon the discretion which politicians can exercise over the conduct of government" (15).

THE STRUCTURE OF INSTITUTIONAL ARRANGEMENTS IN A FEDERATED PARTY SYSTEM

Election laws and "electoral machinery"—to use Ostrom's term—operate in conjunction to create an institutional framework that can provide citizens a choice in the selection of political leadership.

Changes to law create new incentives for those running for office, which affect the substance and quantity of leadership in a political system. For example, legal reforms often make it more difficult for a single party to dominate the constitutional institutions of government, because law might provide for a more expansive set of interests in the electorate: in the United States, mass enfranchisement of property-less, white males in the 1840s, the extension of the suffrage to women in 1920, and the creation of federal voting rights protections on behalf of racial minorities in the 1960s all altered the strategy of the two parties seeking control of constitutional offices (Keyssar 2009). These formal changes can be at the level of ordinary politics (decrees by the legislature) or involve more foundational transformations of the constitutional rules governing the relationship among institutions, party, and candidates.

Changes to the organization of parties themselves also matter. For political elites seeking office, political parties behave as any voluntary collectivity. However, as Vincent Ostrom (1994) recognizes, parties are unique because the good sought by the association is intricately braided into the larger constitutional structure anchored by routine and public elections. For example, as electoral constituencies grew larger throughout the 1800s, it became more difficult for candidates to develop personal relationships with voters. Candidates for office, therefore, faced new incentives to join together as slates of candidates, decreasing information costs on voters, absent any underlying change in the law. Over time, as the advantages of slating grew, those seeking office dedicated greater resources for organizing candidate access to ballots. Needing resources, organizations sought to take control of as many governmental offices as possible. As a result, political machines developed with a "boss" at the top. Consequently, by the turn of the twentieth century, boss rule had become the "basic threat to constitutional principles of separation of powers with checks and balances. A boss's control is facilitated by secrecy; and it is in his interest to minimize his exposure to public scrutiny" (V. Ostrom 1987, 183–184). In the early twentieth century, state constitutions underwent a drastic period of constitutional reform to take those developments in mass party organization into account. Formal constitutional changes included the adoption of the citizen referendum and initiative, which limited the mediating effect of party organization on citizen choice. Additional procedures, such as the recall of elected officials, further limited the ability of party bosses to dominate all centers of authority in a subnational government (Dinan 2006). According to Ostrom (1994), "With the introduction of systems of primary elections, which allowed any dissident to challenge the candidates offered by party leaders, and other electoral reforms, contestation was reestablished in electoral processes and strategies of dominance were sharply constrained" (240). In other words, rule changes within the party organization altered the potential for a single dominant strategy to prevail, thereby changing governing outcomes and the logic of the constitutional or legal order.

Party organizations structure the behavior of political elites outside a specific jurisdiction as well, because in most representative systems, multiple candidates for office run for multiple offices in multiple jurisdictions at the same time. This adds a degree of complexity to the institutional design of a mass party system. This order is already polycentric insofar as there is no hierarchical command structure dictating what each center of power must do. There is no rule, for example, mandating that a party must run a candidate in every political jurisdiction in order to win office, or that a party must recruit a certain candidate for contested races.

In federal constitutional systems, there is an additional component in the creation and selection of political leadership: the boundaries of various constituencies have vastly different scales, and representatives' constituencies overlap. Parties form and run candidates for office in each of these jurisdictions. Moreover, each individual party is composed of smaller organizations that are geographically dispersed and which function autonomously. Traditionally, these smaller organizations within the larger party organization have corresponded with the formal units of political authority in the American federal system, namely states and incorporated municipalities. Defined by different scales of formal organization, the decisions reached by each unit are not fixed a priori to the politics that takes place within them. There is no command or enforcement structure at the highest levels of authority that dictate what a state or local party organization must do. Yet, in providing participants with multiple points of access in a network of organizations that share jurisdiction, the decisions reached in one necessarily affect the decisions reached in another (E. Ostrom 1972). The interdependence created by rational self-interest among fellow partisans and disparate degrees of power comprise a polycentric organization defined by mutual self-adjustment between and within party organizations. As a result, various degrees of polycentricity alter the substance and quality of political leadership available for citizens to choose.

Parties become more or less polycentric as a result of the rules that govern the various aspects of production within the party. As it relates to the creation of political leadership, the rules that matter are the ones that govern the selection, or nomination, of various nominees, none more important than the party's presidential candidate. First, rules determine how a winner is selected. In both the Republican and Democratic Party contests for the presidential nomination, the winner is whomever wins the greatest number votes cast by delegates at the presidential nomination convention. Rules determine how those delegates are won; in modern times, both parties allocate delegates to the various states in proportion to the state's population and the party's vote share in the previous presidential election. Rules determine how those delegates are then awarded to the contenders within the states. At the broadest level, state parties choose whether to hold primaries or caucuses, or some other method of awarding delegates, and those rules determine who participates in the selection of delegates. Additionally, state parties can choose to award all their delegates to the victorious contender (winner-takes-all) or divide them proportionately; proportionality can be strict (percentage of votes for the same percent of delegates) or heavily irregular (the plurality winner gets a majority, with a few token delegates given to runners-up). Finally, rules govern the timing of the selection process in setting the dates of various contests; changing the date advantages some participants over others.

Any number of rules combinations can fragment or centralize authority in the selection of candidates. And the degree of fragmentation or centralization in the selection of candidates will alter the extent to which a party's nominee will have mass appeal or, alternatively, depend on a narrower electoral constituency.

CRITERIA FOR THE EFFICIENT PRODUCTION OF VIABLE ELECTORAL COMPETITION

Political parties compete with one another under a set of electoral rules. Constituent units within a party also compete with one another under a set of organizational rules. At various times in American political history, the competition between and among various units in a party system has been characterized by an abundance of polycentricity. Under such conditions, "Inequalities in the authority of 'rulers' [party elites] and the 'ruled' [citizens] are purposely constrained and limited so that 'rulers" can also be subject to a 'rule' of law and be required to serve the 'ruled'" (V. Ostrom 1972, 4). At other moments, the relationship among constituent units is more aptly defined by features of monocentricity. Under such conditions, party elites have exercised a degree of control far removed from the influence of the average citizen. As described above, this characterization applies to organization of local politics in the late nineteenth century. The degree of polycentricity is affected by the rules that change the incentives of political elites to respond to the interests of citizens, as well as the faction that constitutes the "elite" or "rulers" in the first place.

Parties are efficient producers of political leadership insofar as they provide a viable choice over candidates for as many citizens as possible. Viable choice does not mean, however, that the most efficient polycentric party system is the one that produces the greatest number of candidates for a particular office. Within a single organization, it is in the party's rational interest to run only one candidate for each available office within a jurisdiction. Otherwise, an organization risks splitting its supporters over multiple candidates, reducing the chance that its preferred candidate ultimately wins. Likewise, candidates for office and elected representatives benefit from a single-candidacy system in order to constrain ambitious actors, whose individual goals of seeking higher office might prevent a collective goal of maintaining a majority (Rhode 1979). This incentive structure is independent of the relative degrees of fragmentation and overlap within a single organization. Or, in other words, polycentric and monocentric party organizations both face similar constraints in running a single candidate for each available office.

Likewise, while it might be the case that a party system is more polycentric if it contains more than two parties, it is not always the case that such high levels of polycentricity are desirable or necessary in order to produce viable competition and offer citizens satisfactory levels of choice over potential leaders. If maximizing citizen choice is the optimal outcome for a polycentric system, it would seem, on first consideration, that the most efficient system should produce an abundance of candidates for each office. A multiparty system that contains more than two options—as many proportional systems do—might very well be more polycentric, insofar as multiple parties running for a single office better reflects a larger number of independent decision-making centers that possess overlapping jurisdiction. However, higher amounts of polycentricity are only desirable when the relationships incentivized under such organizational patterns correspond to "theoretically specified conditions for efficient performance" (V. Ostrom 1972, 2). Such considerations about this aspect of polycentricity require empirical comparative analysis of differing institutional systems, as well as normative considerations regarding the act of representation in the first place. Having more than two parties might mean that citizens can select a candidate who more closely represents their preference for government activity, but it might also make it more difficult to assemble coalitions within the government to enact those preferences. Likewise, a multitude of party organizations might proliferate to the point where little interdependency exists between units of various scales. For example, regional parties might be able to compete in small, localized jurisdictions, but unable to attract support at larger scales. A high degree of polycentricity might exist within smaller jurisdictions, but not at the largest. There is greater choice, but less overlap between units. To that extent, party systems with more than two parties may not meet minimum definitional standards of polycentric ordering.

In either case, the American mass party system remains distinct because it is dominated by two parties that compete for office at various units of scale. The two-party system is a result of electoral rules, since, for the clear majority of offices in the United States, the candidate who wins the greatest number of votes wins. The first-past-the-post, or winner-takes-all, method encourages the formation of two, broad-based parties, who each try to amass a simple majority (Downs 1957). Two parties regularly contest seats in jurisdictions of different scale, and, as a result of stable election rules, respond to one another in calculated manner. Since 1840, two parties have dominated American politics in the largest jurisdiction, as measured by competition over the country's only office with a national constituency, the American presidency. Moreover, in the United States, there has been no major change in the *electoral* rules that determine relative degrees of polycentricity in an institutionally induced two-party system. Winning candidates must always win the most votes, and reforms to encourage run-off voting, ranked-choice selection, or proportional vote share have failed to become law in a significant number of jurisdictions until very recently.

This remarkable degree of stability in the electoral rules provides an interesting case, where the most important rules affecting the degree of polycentricity in the American party system have been the rules parties impose of themselves in the selection of candidates. Formal electoral rules matter, but have largely existed independent of the decisions made within the parties over who chooses candidates for office. Likewise, the collective action dilemmas facing ambitious candidates are seemingly fixed, and the constitutional structure establishing elected offices at various scales of political authority has been enduring.

PRODUCING POLITICAL LEADERSHIP IN US PRESIDENTIAL ELECTIONS, 1840–2016

Parties are efficient producers of political leadership when they provide a viable choice of candidates for various offices of varying scale. Efficiency in the production of political leadership is revealed by high degrees of competitiveness across political jurisdictions of differing scale. While there are thousands of elected offices in the United States at the local, state, and national levels, it is commonly recognized that both parties dedicate the greatest amount of resources and energy to the nomination and election of presidential candidates (Truman 1967). The overall degree of efficiency in the two-party system is a function of both parties and their ability to compete for thousands of offices across the country, but the degree of competition for the presidency reveals much about the party system's overall responsiveness in the creation of political candidates who can win in multiple jurisdictions.[2]

While we often reference geographic distributions of voter returns to make sense of partisan support, there are several measurement issues that make it difficult to account for variation in competitiveness across territorially defined units of analysis that vary in size. Reliance on state-level data often masks deep social, economic, and political divisions within states and often leads to ecologically fallacious findings of voter support that conflict with individual-level behavioral accounts (Gelman 2009). County returns provide a more granular way of assessing partisan support, but counties, like states, substantially vary in population size, making most county-to-county comparisons nefariously misleading: in 2016, Donald Trump, for example, won 2,621 counties to Clinton's 490 counties, while receiving almost three million fewer votes nationwide. More to the point, the total number of ballots cast in a given election is, in itself, a reflection of the voting rules that encourage voter turnout and party mobilization.

For any election, there is some underlying distribution of support dependent on electoral rules (e.g., winner-takes-all), the campaign environment (e.g., the economy), and the electioneering activities of the parties themselves. When parties are purely competitive across different geographies—when they produce viable leaders that can gain support in diverse and overlapping constituencies—that support is evenly distributed across jurisdictions. However, when the distribution of votes is unequally dispersed across different geographies, some underlying inefficiency is operative. When parties inefficiently produce political leadership, in other words, there exist discrepancies from the expected value of support for any one election.[3] When party support deviates from the expected value in a subnational political jurisdiction, we are measuring the degree of partisan segregation in any one election.

Measures of geographic competitiveness or partisan concentration are attempts to capture the spatial distribution of Democrats and Republicans, at a particular level of analysis, with more precise geographic units best approximating the day-to-day interaction between and among partisans. One of the most common ways in which scholars measure different degrees of segregation in social settings is to rely on an "exposure index" (Jacobs 2013; Frankenberg and Lee 2003). An exposure index for a particular year gives us the expected value of how many Democratic voters, that is, the typical Democratic voter (or Republican voter), would live around in her or his county, if there was no inefficiency in the production of viable political leadership. Partisan exposure is, in effect, an average of every county's partisan vote share in the United States weighted by the number of partisan voters in that county:[4]

Partisan Exposure Index

$$\theta_{Year} = \frac{\sum_{i}^{N}\left[\left(\textit{Two-Party Vote Share}_i\right) * \left(\textit{Total Votes for Party}_i\right)\right]}{\sum_{i}^{N} \textit{Total Votes for Party}_i}$$

County Discrepancy from Exposure Index

$$\textit{Party Vote Share}_i - \theta_{Year}$$

* Where the unit, *i,* is the individual county.

If there were no inefficiencies in the creation of viable political leaders, we would expect the exposure index for each county to equal the national vote share of each candidate—that is to say that the percentage of Democratic voters in each county is the same as the percentage of the population that voted for the Democrat. The exposure index for a given year diverges from the national vote share when the typical Democratic voter lives in a county with a greater or lesser percentage of Democratic voters than what an equalized distribution would entail. For example, in 2016, the typical Republican voter in 2016 lived in a county where a majority, 52.27 percent, of voters also supported the Republican candidate, while the typical Democratic voter in 2016 lived in a county where a majority, 54.06 percent, of voters chose the Democrat. However, the Democratic candidate in 2016, Hillary Clinton, received just 48.06 percent of the national vote, and the Republican candidate, Donald Trump, received 45.93 percent of the national vote. The exposure index reveals that both parties inefficiently produced a choice for president in that both Democratic and Republican voters experienced higher degrees of intra-partisan exposure in their respective counties—by about six percentage points—than if we were to take every voter in the country and distribute them evenly across each county. Trump and Clinton, in other words, were not appealing to voters in many jurisdictions and were not viable contenders in many jurisdictions. Figures 4.1 and 4.2 map the discrepancy from the expected value and reveal that the geographic malapportionment of voters was also highly associated with regional variation in candidate support.[5]

What matters in measuring geographic competitiveness is the discrepancy from the national vote share (the expected value, given no inefficiencies), and the typical experience of the average Democratic voter and average Republican voter, as measured by the exposure index. By measuring county-level

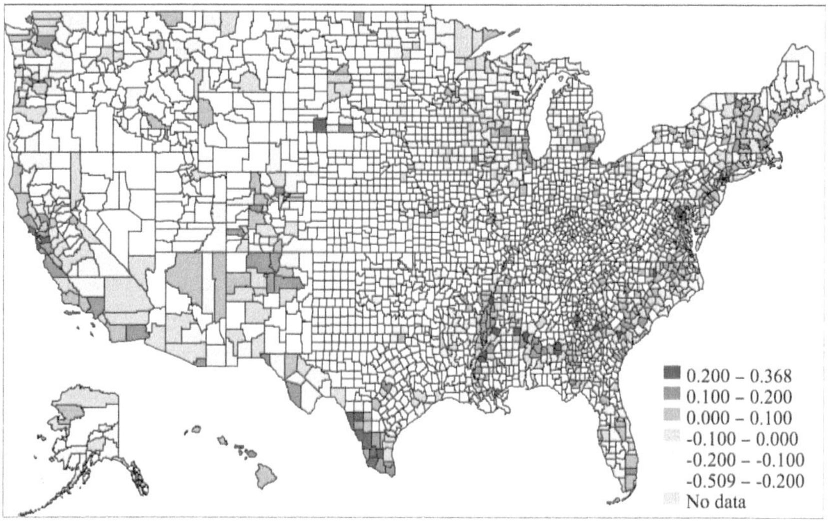

Figure 4.1 Democrat–Democrat Exposure in the 2016 US Presidential Election. Election Data from Dave Leip, *Atlas of US Presidential Elections*, Accessed through the University of Virginia Data Services Center. Last Updated, May 22, 2017.

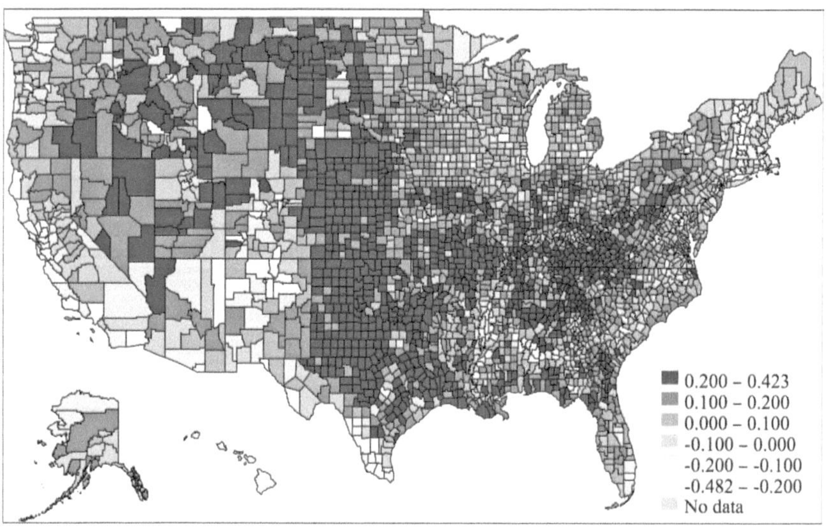

Figure 4.2 Republican–Republican Exposure in the 2016 US Presidential Election. Election Data from Dave Leip, *Atlas of US Presidential Elections*, Accessed through the University of Virginia Data Services Center. Last Updated, May 22, 2017.

exposure, I am measuring the efficient production of political leadership for the most nationalized office within the most localized political unit.

While this measure gives us the average partisan composition of counties, weighted by the number of partisans in each county, it is still somewhat imprecise. For example, a 50 percent exposure index for Democrats exposed to other Democrats could emerge from two possible distributions: either in a country in which all counties were 50 percent Democratic or in a country in which half the counties were 10 percent Democratic and the other half 90 percent Democratic, assuming the counties were of equal populations. The implications for understanding the production of political leadership would be very different in these two scenarios.

Therefore, we can use the exposure index and the county-by-county measures of discrepancy to classify counties by how concentrated they are. Once categorized, we can sum the number of votes that each candidate from either party drew from those concentrated counties. That number indicates the proportion of the party's overall support that depended on voters living in places where residents overwhelmingly voted for the same party. This measure also smooths out fluctuations from election year to election year, and also demonstrates how the geographic concentration of voters contributed to each party's overall electoral support. Any number of justifiable thresholds exist for establishing categories for comparison. I classify counties as concentrated when the discrepancy from the year's exposure index exceeds twenty percentage points.

Together, these measures collectively give us the level of intra-partisan exposure (concentration of like-minded voters in a county for a given year), the percentage of all voters living in geographically concentrated counties, and the degree to which both parties failed to produce candidates that were competitive and responsive to citizen demands. Both indicators measure inefficient production of political leadership in a polycentric system, insofar as both reflect changes in how competitive the party system is in a given year across multiple jurisdictions comprising a national electorate. These measures also rely on an important assumption: partisan segregation is the result of decisions made by the party *and* decisions made by individuals about where they want to live. It is the case that liberals and conservatives often live in different communities, because they value different ways of living (Bishop 2009). However, the supply of political messages given by candidates and parties also matters for how individuals identify their communal distinctions. The measure used here captures people moving to different communities as well as variation in both parties' ability to appeal to those various types of communities in the country.

In the past forty-six US presidential elections, there has been remarkable variation in the efficiency of the party system to produce viable political

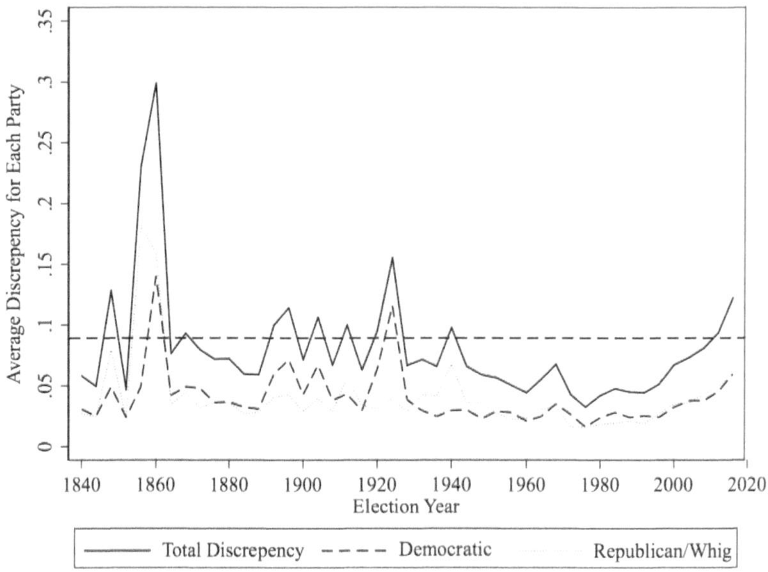

Figure 4.3 Average Deviation from Expected Vote, Democratic and Republican Vote Share. Pre-1972 Election Data: Jerome Clubb, William Flanigan, and, Nancy H Zingale. "Electoral Data for Counties in the United States: Presidential and Congressional Races, 1840–1972." Ann Arbor, MI: *Interuniversity Consortium for Political and Social Research* [distributor], 2006-11-13. https://doi.org/10.3886/ICPSR08611.v1. Post-1972 election Data: Dave Leip, *Atlas of US Presidential Elections*, Accessed through the University of Virginia Data Services Center. Last Updated, May 22, 2017.

leaders who can compete across multiple jurisdictions. On average, most presidential elections return a discrepancy of about 0.08 (dotted horizontal line, figure 4.3). Or, in other words, voters lived in counties where there were approximately four percentage points more fellow partisans than we might expect if there was no geographic stratification. However, in many years, the total discrepancy from the expected value was drastically higher. The 1860 presidential election produced Democratic and Republican coalitions that were highly segregated. The average Democratic voter in that election lived in a county where there were nearly 30 percent more co-partisans than there should have been. The Republican candidate, Abraham Lincoln, simply did not compete in those counties, and nearly 5 percent of his total vote share came from places that were geographically concentrated, or comprised primarily, with Republican voters (figure 4.4).

Other elections, however, reveal starkly different patterns in geographic support. Both the election of 1976 and of 1980 were highly efficient to the extent that neither candidate from either party depended on a specific region or type of place for support. In 1980, for example, the average voter for

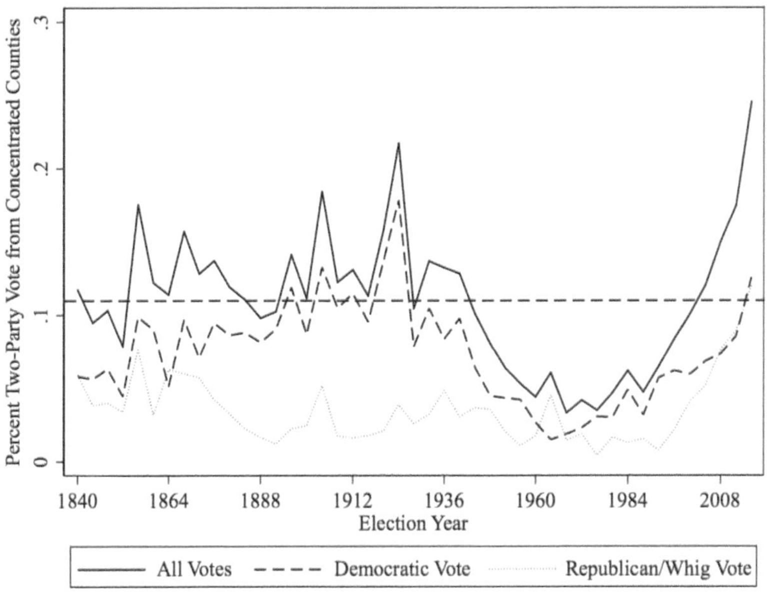

Figure 4.4 Percent of Party Vote Share Coming from Concentrated Counties. Pre-1972 Election Data: Jerome Clubb, William Flanigan, and, Nancy H Zingale. "Electoral Data for Counties in the United States: Presidential and Congressional Races, 1840–1972." Ann Arbor, MI: *Interuniversity Consortium for Political and Social Research* [distributor], 2006-11-13. https://doi.org/10.3886/ICPSR08611.v1. Post–1972 Election Data: Dave Leip, *Atlas of US Presidential Elections*, Accessed through the University of Virginia Data Services Center. Last Updated, May 22, 2017.

Ronald Reagan lived in a county comprised with the expected number of Reagan voters and the expected number of voters for Reagan's Democratic opponent, Jimmy Carter (figure 4.3). Likewise, the Republican Party did not rely on places that were overwhelmingly filled with Republican supporters; it drew voters from across the country (figure 4.4). The system provided viable choice in multiple jurisdictions, and, even though Reagan walloped Carter in the general election, we can still say that voters had a choice between two viable candidates, given these patterns.

Considering the past 176 years collectively, the data suggest three distinct eras in production of viable political leadership, or geographically diffuse competition: a period between 1840 and 1920 defined by intermittent cycles of efficient and inefficient production of presidential nominees; a period between 1920 and 1996 marked by relatively high degrees of efficiency and intra-jurisdictional competition; and finally, our current era, which has seen increasing inefficiency and greater concentration of party vote share. Each of these three eras is distinct for the different rules governing party organization and the nomination of candidates in the party. As reviewed above, the rules, norms, and procedures are what make the party system, as a whole, more or less polycentric. There has always been a degree of polycentricity in the American party system, but overtime the relationship between constituent organizations within the two major parties has changed. Those changes are responsible, at least in part, for the broad patterns in the efficient production of political leadership graphed in figures 4.3 and 4.4.

PURE FRAGMENTATION AND MINIMAL OVERLAP: 1840–1920

The period between 1840 and 1920 saw an average discrepancy in the creation of presidential nominees of 0.09—slightly above average for the entire time series, but minimally so. The distinguishing feature of this period is the high degree of variation between years. In some election years, both parties were able to produce candidates whose geographic appeal was broad. In others, neither party produced candidates who garnered widespread appeal. In those off years, citizens lacked worthwhile choice in most jurisdictions. This variation is a function of the party rules governing the selection of presidential nominees. Dominated by party "bosses" and absent much public input, the system's overall efficiency fluctuated because it was too decentralized.

The time series begins in 1840 because this is when most scholars date the start of the modern two-party system in the United States. Prior to 1840, there was organized competition in elections, but by the mid-1820s, partisanship in the United States had reached a low ebb. The 1824 presidential election was the upshot of this premodern, monocentric political organization. Four distinct personalities who each represented a different section of the country split the vote. Unable to amass a majority of electors in the Electoral College, organized party politics gave way to unorganized, petty rivalry that threatened to destabilize the still fragile project of nation-building. The original Electoral College was premised on the belief that state leaders would identify promising presidential aspirants and then select the eventual winner independent of debates taking place in other state delegations. This would ensure that the president would be someone of national repute, and whose temperament and policy positions were attractive across multiple states (Ceaser 1979). The pre-1840 party system warped the incentives electors faced and, instead, encouraged presidential aspirants to campaign for office, but only among a small set of elected leaders in Washington, DC.

The modern, post-1840 mass party system emerged from these failings and resulted in two broad-based parties who regularly go in and out of power. The system is a conscious creation—the work of political entrepreneurs who recognized the institutional benefits of organized party competition. Martin Van Buren—then a junior senator from New York—was the most aggressive in organizing the first, enduring national party. Pragmatic and theoretical, he convinced fellow national leaders that organized party leadership was necessary to thwart off excessive centralization and demagogic politics that plagued national elections in the 1820s. Throwing his support to Andrew Jackson in 1828 and again in 1832, Van Buren took the lessons he learned from New York state politics, and established the new "Democratic Party" as an important link between national leaders and the people. So successful was the Van Buren-Jackson creation in building a broad, multiregional coalition of support, that their opponents replicated their new organization. Led by Adams and Senator Henry Clay, the Whig party emerged to combat the Jacksonian Democrats.

While there were important policy differences between the two parties, they shared similar organizational patterns and applied similar rules governing the selection of candidates for local, state, and national offices. The Whig and Democratic parties were both national, insofar as they competed in each part of the country. However, their national appeal followed from the creation of independent state party organizations. Within the various states, authority for selecting candidates and distributing patronage was further fragmented. Local party organizations became schools for political leadership, and created new enduring, national identities out of grassroots organizations. The principal mechanism that bound local partisans together was in the selection of statewide office holders. Likewise, the principal way that state partisans in one area of the country cultivated relationships with state partisans in another area was through the selection of national candidates, none more important than nomination of the party nominee for president every four years.

The quadrennial presidential nomination contests hosted by each party were, in effect, the only semblance of a national organization binding partisans together across a disparate landscape. Delegations of state officials, selected by nomination processes, would convene in their respective states that stemmed from complicated organizational arrangements of various local party leaders. Implicit in the idea of the national convention was that delegates sprang directly from the rank and file. State and local political leaders, with strong ties to the voters, thus became the principal intermediaries—or brokers—of presidential politics. The eventual nominee had to amass support at the convention from a set of delegations independently selected from one another, and who often disagreed on fundamental political issues. Popular generals and uncontroversial "dark horse" candidates routinely emerged as consensus candidates after days—if not weeks—of arduous convention brokering and successive balloting. In some years, this process led to party leaders getting it "right"—selecting a candidate who could amass a large enough national coalition to achieve victory and viably compete in multiple jurisdictions. In other years, internal squabbles and personal politicking produced candidates whose geographic support was highly concentrated.

Ultimately, one issue proved so vexing that this method proved unable to broker agreement in the selection of national leaders: slavery. By the mid-1850s, the Whig Party collapsed over the issue, while the Democratic Party was torn asunder internally by its vacillation. The Republican Party and its unified stance that there should be no extension of slavery into the territories reinvigorated party competition. But the issue of slavery was so clearly sectional that neither the Democrats nor the Republicans could produce a viable political leader. The 1850s witnessed an increasing degree of sectionalism in the presidential vote share, culminating in the election of Lincoln in 1860. Lincoln's demonstrated statesmanship aside, the outbreak of Civil War following his election is the ultimate testament to how frail the system of decentralized presidential selection had become. Almost half the country rejected Lincoln and neither party produced a viable political leader who could command national unity. However, while the Civil War put an end to the slavery issue that broke organized party competition in 1860, both parties remerged after the war and maintained their prewar organizational structure. As before, presidential candidates often emerged who were weak, unknown, and everybody's third or fourth choice. This was a consequence—as before—of highly fragmented authority in the selection of national delegates. Once again, some years the parties got it right and produced viable candidates; in other years, presidential contests were marked by high degrees of geographic concentration.

The selection system and the process of quadrennial nomination conventions reinforced the dispersion of governing authority in the United States throughout this period. This era of organized party competition was not just distinct because authority for choosing delegates was highly fragmented, but the overlap between different political jurisdictions was strongly curtailed. Political leaders in more expansive jurisdictions owed their political fortunes to local party officials and faced little incentive to curtail or check their power. Local, state, and national governing prerogatives were clearly defined, and little duplication in governing activity existed. Citizen choice and recourse to appeal were sparse in between elections. Corruption, misuse of funds, and government favoritism were rampant. Appeals to higher levels of political authority routinely fell on deaf ears, even when an opposing political party possessed power. After all, elected officials in both parties depended on this decentralized framework for their next election, and neither faced a strong imperative to disrupt the status quo that had sent them to the statehouse or Washington.

This was the age of machine politics, nurtured by the organization of party organizations. In fragmenting authority and cementing minimal overlap in jurisdiction for government service, it is a highly decentralized form of polycentric order. It left a trivial record in the creation of viable political leaders and, instead, encouraged widespread government corruption within state and local governments. Both parties benefited from the widespread system of patronage politics, government contracts, and institutional rules that structured the electorate in their favor. By the end of the nineteenth century, both the Democrats and the Republicans were engaged in hotly contested and highly mobilized campaigns, but the party system was driven by partisan maneuvers that maintained a system of graft, electoral fraud, and limited government accountability. This "spoils system" was critical to the ability of parties to secure financial resources and to mobilize support all the way down to the local precinct. Neither party had any real incentive to challenge the prevailing order that maintained strong, decentralized party organizations (Lee 2016).

FRAGMENTATION OF AUTHORITY AND OVERLAPPING JURISDICTION: 1920–1996

Industrialization and urbanization only raised the stakes for partisan control of governing institutions, but it also spawned a political movement that succeeded in dismantling the decentralized system of nineteenth-century parties. While the goal of this "Progressive Movement" was the complete centralization and nationalization of party organizations, the result of their efforts produced a highly polycentric order of intra- and interparty competition. Both parties maintained their state and local organizations, which produced competitive pressures within each party to nominate candidates that had broad geographic support. Yet, reforms such as the public primary, made former state and local leaders more responsive to the national public mood. Neither as centralized as it would become, or as decentralized as it once was, this chaotic system of local parties, national electorates, and simplified nomination rules increased citizen choice.

The Progressive Movement that arose in response to the party system's insularity and corruption offered a set of varying—and often incompatible—critiques. As noted by Vincent Ostrom (1973), many of the most prominent intellectuals, including Woodrow Wilson, condemned the fragmentation of political authority present in the US Constitution and sought to replace it with a more hierarchical administrative structure to more fully deploy national regulatory power. In addition to building new administrative structures, the Progressives—including Wilson—also sought to destroy the vital institutions that seemingly buttressed local autonomy. No institution was more critical in this regard than the political party.

Curiously, then, Ostrom and Wilson share a certain disdain for the organization of the mass party system in the late nineteenth and early twentieth century. But, whereas Ostrom felt that party government supplanted the original logic contained within the separation of powers—allowing an organization to take monopoly control over the levers of local governing authority—Wilson argued the reverse. Parties were necessary, but they too had to be hierarchical. "There must," Wilson (1908) wrote, "be an exterior organization, voluntarily formed and independent of the law, whose object it shall be to bind them together in some sort of harmony and cooperation" (207). However, Wilson added, "we have come within sight of the end of the merely nationalizing process. . . . Party organization is no longer needed for the mere rudimentary task of holding the machinery together or giving it the sustenance of some common object, some single cooperative motive. The time is at hand when we can with safety examine the network of party in its detail and change its structure without imperilling [*sic*] its strength. . . . We must see to it that it is made responsible" (Ibid., 220).

The Progressive clarion call to make party government "responsible" brought about the second era of party competition in American political development. Responsibility, as Wilson suggests above, meant maintaining party strength, but reforming the organization to put that strength in service to national political objectives. Instead of local party bosses, Progressives championed a new vision of strong, ideological leadership. Where the previous party system rewarded the wheeling and dealing skills of backroom negotiation and coalition management, the new system would ensure that only those who could personally mobilize and inspire the mass public would get the vote.

Yet, like most political developments, the Progressive assault on party organizations was never fully completed. Wholesale reform required some support from the prevailing status quo, and party bosses never faced enough political pressure to dismantle the institutional apparatus that kept their positions secure. No state experimented with the boldest reforms, such as referenda on court decisions. And, Wilson's own panacea—a national presidential primary held on a single day—was never seriously considered. Rather, Progressive reform gradually eroded the party establishment for the first half of the twentieth century. Franklin D. Roosevelt continued and accelerated the trajectory of party centralization. However, Roosevelt was also never all powerful. Even with staggering majorities in the legislature, his fellow Democrats routinely rolled important votes and led the charge against his most aggressive proposals to centralize control over the Democratic Party—none more potentially transformative than his failed purge campaign in the 1938 midterm elections (Milkis 1993).

While FDR accomplished much in defining the new form of partisanship, so decentralized did parties remain that leading progressives of the post-FDR era still craved party reform. Led by a team of prominent political scientists, the American Political Science Association (APSA) issued a comprehensive report in 1950 on the need to establish a "more responsible two-party system" (Committee on Political Parties 1950). Committee members called for an "honestly prepared," politically achievable party platform to be written at National conventions—a process that was dominated by the presidential nominee taking center stage every four years. Additionally, the committee suggested that state delegations within the convention be proportioned by the party's share of the presidential vote within each state—a principle that strengthened the national character of the parties and its dependence on presidential elections.

Like Wilson's calls for action, this academic report did not mandate change. Yet, the 1950 APSA study did portend a future of party reform that would take place over the next few decades. Both the Republican and the Democratic parties gradually reformed the system of presidential nomination in line with the APSA recommendations to make them more open and accessible to the average voter. Throughout the 1950s and 1960s, it was still necessary for aspiring candidates to have experienced convention brokers to wrangle the necessary delegate counts for nominations and most states still choose their delegations to the national convention with guarantee that they would honor the result of informal primary elections. Nevertheless, both parties were changing. By 1964, the Republican Party had "democratized" to the extent that party leaders proved unable to stop the nomination of Barry Goldwater. Yet, in 1968, the Democratic Party establishment remained so influential that it unleashed a wrath of protest when convention leaders selected Vice President Hubert Humphrey (who had not even competed in a presidential primary) as their presidential nominee in Chicago—a city still run by a machine boss, Richard Daley. The system was a mix of centralizing and decentralizing impulses. It was polycentric.

The period of party competition sketched here was one of rapid change. Yet, in the production of viable political contenders for the presidency, the party system was relatively efficient. For several decades, the Democratic and Republican candidates for office continuously drew support from varied jurisdictions throughout the country. The notable exception was in 1940—FDR's final reelection under a Democratic Party label that had become dependent on presidential pronouncement. Even with the mass disenfranchisement of African American voters in the Southern states and the effective monopoly the Democratic Party exercised on Southern politics, both presidential candidates drew support from a variety of regions and competed with one another across the country, offering citizens choice, and creating responsive leaders.

Candidates for the presidency ran for office and the new democratizing features of the selection process sent clearer signals to party elites as to what the American voter wanted. Yet, candidates still needed establishment support, and regional diversity was protected from strict majority voting because each party maintained certain convention rules. Delegates at both conventions for presidential nominees, for example, were malapportioned, and favored smaller states, thereby ensuring widespread geographic appeal. With time, both the Republican and Democratic party came to rely on fewer heavily or intensely concentrated counties for their support—a trend that escalated in the mid-1960s with the extension of federal voting rights protections. By 1976, neither party could lay claim to a specific monopoly on any one area of the country. Presidential candidates may have varied in substance and personality, but they all had mass appeal.

MINIMAL FRAGMENTATION AND MAXIMIZING OVERLAP: 1996–PRESENT

The tumult unleashed by the 1968 Democratic National Convention ushered in the next, and current, era of party competition. Over the course of two decades, both the Republican and the Democratic Party establishment routinely bowed to the pressures of party activists and insurgent leaders. Party reform had a common objective: the empowering of "the people," that is, the social movement organizations that transformed the meaning of partisanship during the late 1960s and 1970s. On the left, these movements were legacies of 1960s protest from African Americans, feminists, environmentalists, and immigration rights activists. On the right, counterprotesters proved just as well-organized, and with the rapid rise of the new evangelical movement, conservative activists soon found common cause with the "religious right." Changes to the media environment augmented the reforms of campaign finance and delegate selection that made the modern system more candidate-centered and media-driven. By 1996, the scope of reform had become so great and ambitious politicians had learned the new game so well that the totality of change finally gave way to a system of party competition that centralized decision-making authority for presidential candidates and increased the degree of geographic concentration in each party's constituency. The system became more inefficient and less polycentric.

Following the violence from the 1968 Democratic National Convention—not to mention Humphrey's loss to Richard Nixon in the general election—Democratic Party leaders responded to activist demands to transform selection rules. The resulting 1971–1972 McGovern-Fraser Commission amounted to a "quiet revolution" in American politics (Shafer 1983). The

Commission extended, and ultimately codified two, somewhat competing objectives of liberal activism that continued into the 1970s: "participatory democracy" as expressed in popular primaries or caucuses; and the inclusion of groups previously denied access to the political process, namely African-Americans, women, and the young. The enactment of these reforms deprived party leaders of the power they had exercised since the early part of the nineteenth century to select delegates to the national convention, the place and time when the party—in its traditional form—actually came into being to engage in the important work of writing a platform and selecting the party's presidential candidates. The Republican Party, which had once been at the vanguard of reform, found itself in the position of following the Democrat Party's lead and adopted much of McGovern-Fraser's recommendations.[6]

Changes to campaign finance law in 1974 and again in 2002 further pushed partisanship beyond the party. Under the 1974 Federal Elections Campaign Act, a Democratic Congress sought to limit both campaign donations and expenditures—in effect, making it more difficult to raise and spend money. A new core campaign institution arose from this framework, Political Action Committees (PACs), which codified a place for "independent" groups. When the Supreme Court struck down limitations on campaign expenditures in *Buckley v. Valeo* (1976), candidates were now free to spend unlimited amounts of money, albeit under a set of rules that made it more difficult for them to raise funds from individuals. PACs filled the place of the traditional donor who tended to have close ties to the party. Then, under the 2002 Bipartisan Campaign Finance Reform Act, Congress further restricted direct contributions to parties, further advancing the candidate-centered nature of elections. No longer dependent on parties for their contributions, candidates became more beholden to those groups and individuals outside the parties who could raise the massive funds necessary to run increasingly expensive campaigns (La Raja 2008; Samples 2006).

Supporters of campaign finance and delegate selection reforms claimed that it would give new voice to the common citizen. Yet, as Morton Keller (2007) recognizes, "the voices of newly empowered groups turned out to be not *vox populi* but activists whose claims as spokesmen lacked verification by elections and opinion polls." And, as a result, "the policy agenda came to be defined less by the parties, with the tempering effect they usually brought, and more by leading voices of the new regime: the media, advocacy groups, judges, lawyers and law professors, academic experts and foundations, bureaucrats, presidential and congressional staffers" (246). Diminishing the influence of traditional party organizations and leaders did not level the playing field. Rather, it shifted power to those who personal constituencies were narrower and had more in common with one another than the general electorate.

The result of this process is evidenced by the accelerating trend of partisan concentration in the selection of presidential candidates. Beholden to party activists and primary voters, traditional party "leaders" lost their influence in the production of viable political leadership. Instead, primary voters supplanted the old rules to dominate the production of presidential candidates who, as a result, have limited appeal to voters across a variety of geographic contexts. Substantively, those contexts dictate much about what the eventual nominees promise. Since 1996, one candidate has spoken for the coastal United States and the major urban judications within those several states, while another has claimed to represent everywhere else. There is little overlap in the type of jurisdiction in which presidential nominees succeed and the types of voters they attract. Having concentrated the authority for selecting nominees in the hands of a homogeneous, activist base, the system is less polycentric, even though the number of individuals involved is greater.

This paradoxical outcome—having more voters and less polycentrism—is resolved by taking note of the rational incentives that structure the creation of political leaders in the new system, compared to the older system. In simplest terms, establishment figures, party leaders, and "bosses" do not have the same political imperative as the modern activist and primary voter. Both relish power and use that power to maintain that power. But when authority is fragmented, and no one leader can exercise monopolistic control in producing nominees for office, the second best outcome is to keep authority fragmented, decision-making dispersed, and nationalist outcomes respective of the autonomy exercised within the constituent parts. When authority is centralized, and a single coalition of like-minded individuals can dominate the selection process, or the construction of political leadership, they are able to pursue their strategy of first resort successfully and completely. This creates leaders who are attractive to a small group, but fail to compete successfully in different jurisdictions.

The most recent US presidential election in 2016 demonstrates how various aspects of the selection process allow for a single coalition to dominate, thereby creating nominees who cannot viably compete in the general election. In 2016, the Republican Party awarded 2,285 pledged delegates to the winners of various state primary contests and caucuses.[7] By "pledged," these delegates agreed to vote for a specific candidate on the first round of balloting at the national convention. Individual states determined whether these delegates were allocated on a winner-takes-all basis or were awarded proportionate to a contender's vote share. States also choose what rule determines proportionality and when they hold the nomination contest. These rules are related, since of the nineteen states that allocate delegates on a winner-takes-all rule, thirteen hold their contests near the end of the selection process (after April 1st). As a result of these rules, the victorious candidate, Donald Trump, won

64.9 percent of all delegates to the Republican National Convention with only 44.0 percent of votes cast in his favor. If we consider the point in the nomination process where just half of all delegates had been awarded, the resulting outcome is equally as perverse. By March 15, Trump had earned 49.9 percent of all delegates, but had earned just 36.7 percent of the vote. Moreover, by that point, Trump had failed to secure a majority of votes in any single state contest, and yet he commanded a practical majority of delegates. Under the modern system, the rules centralized authority for creating the candidate, even when a unified consensus failed to emerge.

FEDERALISM, POLYCENTRICITY, AND PARTY GOVERNMENT IN AMERICA

Partisanship is an inescapable feature of political life in most constitutional democracies. On the one hand, there are those who argue that parties are problematic because they are too *centralized.* Dominated by two major parties, the modern system offers little choice to voters on Election Day (Mann and Ornstein 2012; Fiorina 2009). On the other hand, many argue that political parties are too *decentralized.* Unable to send clear messages to voters or enact programmatic change once in office, neither party can be held "responsible" by the electorate (Muirhead 2014; Schattschneider 1960).

The solution might not be one of greater party centralization or greater party decentralization. Recent trends in party centralization—motivated largely by empowering activist, single-issue groups—suggest that voters have less choice in the general election as a result. However, during the period of decentralized party competition, voters often lacked choice because party leaders faced little incentive to adequately respond to citizen demands. There is a middle option—an option realized in the twentieth century that contained elements of centralized and decentralized decision-making. When both parties organized themselves so as to maximize the number independent centers of authority that competed for the party's nomination, they efficiently produced viable candidacies year after year. This was a polycentric order.

Beyond producing candidates whom voters regularly find satisfactory, the production of political leadership has important residual effects. The changing geographic nature of the victorious candidate's constituency matters for very specific aspects of presidential policymaking. A Democrat who depends on the support of coastal, urban jurisdictions will pursue different policies than a Republican who wins with the support of suburban and rural voters. Parties represent and the representation they provide is an essential service to the functioning of self-governing systems. But partisanship can also be debilitating. Competition can escalate to the point of ideological intransigence, increasing the likelihood that governing institutions become irresponsive. Unable to resolve meaningful conflict, party competition can provide fewer choices to voters and lead to unsatisfactory outcomes in the production of various public goods.

More fundamentally, partisan segregation matters for the overall structure of the American constitutional system and the endurance of important constitutional relationships. In the United States, the party system is especially vital for structuring federated political relationships, or the balance of power between the local, state, and federal governments. American political parties, because of their fragmented or federal organization, create incentives for actors in one area of America's constitutional order to respect the guarantees of other centers of power. Parties provide benefits to those seeking election, but in doing so establish an underlying set of rules that change the incentives for party members who routinely define the contours of governmental power in a polycentric system (Truman 1985). Indeed, the structure and organization of party organizations might matter more than its ideological substance, since, as Derthick (2001) recognizes, "a review of American history would show that the positions of leading politicians and the major political parties on the question of centralization versus decentralization have often been determined largely by expediency" (3).

Parties are, therefore, essential institutions for making aspects of constitutional polycentricity—separation of powers, federalism, bicameralism—work (Wildavsky 1985). If leaders of party organizations have power to determine who gets to run and benefit from the party organization, then members face incentives to be loyal partisans, curry favor with those leaders, and coordinate strategy with other members in the organization. If leaders are geographically and constitutionally dispersed—holding power at different levels of the constitutional order in different parts of the country—incentives for respecting the constitutional guarantees of each office are further encouraged under the assumption that leaders want to protect the governmental autonomy of the units they control. Polycentric parties, in other words, help to nourish polycentric governance.

Governance in modern American politics is hardly polycentric. Instead, as I have written elsewhere, it reflects the transcendence of "executive-centered partisanship," whereby parties increasingly rely on presidential candidates to mobilize the base, recruit other candidates, raise funds, and establish party doctrine. Consequently, once in office, presidents face little incentive to negotiate with Congress, maintain constitutional limits on executive power, or respect the governing prerogatives of local and state government (Jacobs et al. 2019). Recovering constitutional principles, such as federalism, is a lofty endeavor. However, reforming nomination rules for presidential party candidates to encourage greater geographic diversity in electoral support is a bit more definite. "Every system of polycentric ordering is potentially vulnerable to circumstances where some achieve dominance at the cost of others," Ostrom writes. "A self-governing people need to understand when failures occur and how to reform their systems of order" (240). The sharp rise in partisan segregation showcases our collective failure to maintain polycentric party governance. It is time to reform the reforms and restore some degree of institutional autonomy to parties and party leadership.

NOTES

1. Mansbridge recognizes that there is a long history of considering these types of informal representative relationships, beginning with Edmund Burke's notion of "virtual representation." See: Edmund Burke. 1792. "A Letter to Sir Hercules Langrishe, January 3." In *The Best of Burke: Selected Writings and Speeches of Edmund Burke*, edited by Peter J. Stanlis. Washington DC: Regnery Publishing, Inc., 1963.

2. To be sure, there are multiple empirical indicators of efficient political leadership. One might alternatively consider the number of uncontested seats for political office in different governments, or citizen responses to a variety of public opinion polls. As Ostrom and Ostrom (1977) note, "Since public goods are difficult to package or unitize they are also difficult to measure . . . the task of measuring performance in the production of public goods will not yield to simple calculations. Performance measurement depends instead upon estimates in which indicators or proxy measures are used as estimates of performance. By utilizing multiple indicators, weak measure of performance can be developed even though direct measures of output are not feasible" (79).

3. Most pundits use "margin of victory" or the arithmetic difference between the two-party vote share to measure competitiveness. However, using county-level, two-party vote share is problematic for assessing party competitiveness for at least two distinct reasons. First, in a year where a significant proportion of the electorate voted for a third party, some ballots simply do not enter the equation in considering just the two-party vote share, which can artificially inflate the margin of victory for any single election. Second, vote share in a particular year is fixed to specific candidates on the ballot. While presidential nominees certainly define and reshape the images of the two major parties, the distribution of votes within a given year is dependent, at least in part, on that candidate's personality and likeability, in addition to broader trends that matter for citizen vote choice, such as the economy. Both parties may produce viable candidates that create competitive elections across multiple jurisdictions, even if one candidate wins a much larger share of the vote. The overwhelming success of a single candidate does not mean that the party system, as a whole, failed to produce viable options for responsive political leaders in a given year. See: Samuel J. Abrams and Morris P. Fiorina. 2012. "'The Big Sort' That Wasn't: A Skeptical Reexamination." *PS: Political Science and Politics* 45 (2): 203–210.

4. The emphasis on "exposure" is slightly different than how other scholars using a related index have sought to measure county variation. Exposure here measures partisan similarity in a county and the deviation from a national norm, not the percentage of partisans who would have to move out of their current county of residence. See, for example, Philip A. Klinkner. 2004. "Red and Blue Scare: The Continuing Diversity of the American Electoral Landscape." *The Forum 2* (2).

5. *Source*: Post-1972 election data is derived from the total number of votes, per candidate on the Ballot. Data compiled by Dave Leip, *Atlas of U.S. Presidential Elections*, accessed through the University of Virginia Data Services Center. Last Updated, May 22, 2017. Pre-1972 data is compiled by Jerome Clubb, William Flanigan, and Nancy H. Zingale. "Electoral Data for Counties in the United States: Presidential and Congressional Races, 1840-1972." Ann Arbor: Interuniversity Consortium for Political and Social Research [distributor], November 13, 2006. https://doi.org/10.3886/ICPSR08611.v1.

6. The one change the Republican Party chose to forgo arguably democratized the GOP further. Unlike the Democratic selection process, there are no "superdelegates" representing party elites and elected officials. The establishment of superdelegates was one way that McGovern-Fraser sought to maintain a degree of establishment control over the party. In 2018, the Democratic Party officially stripped superdelegates of their voting powers, except in the unlikely event of a contested election.

7. The following calculations are derived from author-compiled data taken from *Politico's* live primary tracker. URL: https://www.politico.com/mapdata-2016/2016-election/primary/results/map/president/.

REFERENCES

Aldrich, John D. 1997. "The Study of Party Politics in the Twenty-First Century." *Election Law Journal* 6 (2): 209–219.

———. 2011. *Why Parties? A Second Look.* Chicago: University of Chicago Press.

Axelrod, Robert M. 1970. *Conflict of Interest: A Theory of Divergent Goals with Application to Politics.* Chicago: Markham.

Bishop, Bill. 2009. *The Big Sort: Why the Clustering of America Is Tearing Us Apart.* Boston: Mariner Books/Houghton Mifflin Harcourt.

Burnham, Walter D. 1970. *Critical Elections and the Mainsprings of American Politics.* New York: Norton.

Ceaser, James W. 1979. *Presidential Selection: Theory and Development.* Princeton: Princeton University Press.

Committee on Political Parties, American Political Science Association. 1950. "Toward A More Responsible Two-Party System." *The American Political Science Review* 54 (1): 1–96.

Cox, Gary W. 1997. *Making Votes Count: Strategic Coordination in the World's Electoral Systems.* New York: Cambridge University Press.

Derthick, Martha. 2001. *Keeping the Compound Republic: Essays on American Federalism.* Washington DC: Brookings Institution Press.

Dinan, John J. 2006. *The American State Constitutional Tradition.* Lawrence: University Press of Kansas.

Downs, Anthony. 1957. *An Economic Theory of Democracy.* New York: Harper and Row.

Erikson, Robert S., Michael B. Mackuen, and James A. Stimson. 2002. *The Macro Polity.* New York: Cambridge University Press.

Fiorina, Morris P., with Samuel Abrams. 2009. *Disconnect: The Breakdown of Representation in American Politics.* Norman: University of Oklahoma Press.

Frankenberg, Erica, and Chungmei Lee. 2003. "Charter Schools and Race: A Lost Opportunity for Integrated Education." *Education Policy Analysis Archives* 11 (32): 1–48.

Gelman, Andrew. 2009. *Red State, Blue State, Rich State, Poor State: Why Americans Vote the Way They Do.* Princeton: Princeton University Press.

Green, Donald, Bradley Palmquist, and Eric Schickler. 2004. *Partisan Hearts and Minds: Political Parties and the Social Identities of Voters.* New Haven, CT: Yale University Press.

Jacobs, Nicholas. 2013. "Racial, Economic, and Linguistic Segregation: Analyzing Market Supports in the District of Columbia's Public Charter Schools." *Journal of Education and Urban Society* 45 (1): 120–141.

Jacobs, Nicholas F., Desmond King, and Sidney M. Milkis. 2019. "Building a Conservative State: Partisan Polarization and the Redeployment of Administrative Power." *Perspectives on Politics* 17 (2): 453–469.

Jacobson, Gary C., and Jamie L. Carson. 2015. *The Politics of Congressional Elections* (9th edition). New York: Rowman and Littlefield Publishers.

Jenkins, Jeffery. 2000. "Examining the Robustness of Ideological Voting: Evidence from the Confederate House of Representatives." *American Journal of Political Science* 44 (4): 811–822.

Keller, Morton. 2007. *America's Three Regimes: A New Political History.* Oxford: Oxford University Press.

Keyssar, Alexander. 2009. *The Right to Vote: The Contested History of Democracy in the United States* (rev. edition). New York: Basic Books.

La Raja, Raymond J. 2008. *Small Change: Money, Political Parties, and Campaign Finance Reform.* Ann Arbor: The University of Michigan Press.

Lee, Frances. 2016. "Patronage, Logrolls, and 'Polarization': Congressional Parties of the Gilded Age, 1876–1896." *Studies in American Political Development* 30 (2): 116–127.

Mann, Thomas, and Norman Ornstein. 2012. *It's Even Worse Than It Looks: How the American Constitutional System Collided with the New Politics of Extremism.* New York: Basic Books.

Mansbridge, Jane. 2003. "Rethinking Representation." *The American Political Science Review* 97 (4): 515–528.

McGinnis, Michael D., and Elinor Ostrom. 2012. "Reflections on Vincent Ostrom, Public Administration, and Polycentricity." *Public Administration Review* 72 (1): 15–25.

McKelvey, Richard D. 1976. "Intrasitivities in Multi-dimensional Voting Models and Some Implications for Agenda Control." *Journal of Economic Theory* 18 (3): 472–482.

Milks, Sidney M. 1993. *The President and the Parties: The Transformation of the American Party System since the New Deal.* New York: Oxford University Press.
Muirhead, Russell. 2014. *The Promise of Party in a Polarized Age.* Cambridge: Harvard University Press.
Olson, Mancur, Jr. 1965. *The Logic of Collective Action.* Cambridge: Harvard University Press.
Ostrom, Elinor. 1972. "Metropolitan Reform: Propositions Derived from Two Traditions." *Social Science Quarterly* 53 (3): 474–493.
———. 1986. "An Agenda for the Study of Institutions." *Public Choice* 48 (1): 3–25.
Ostrom, Vincent. 1972. "Polycentricity." Paper prepared for delivery at the 1972 Annual Meeting of the American Political Science Association, Washington Hilton Hotel, Washington DC, September 5–9.
———. 1973. *The Intellectual Crisis in American Public Administration.* Tuscaloosa: The University of Alabama Press.
———. 1987. *The Political Theory of a Compound Republic: Designing the American Experiment* (2nd ed.). Lincoln: University of Nebraska Press.
———. 1994. *The Meaning of American Federalism.* San Francisco: Institute for Contemporary Studies.
Ostrom, Vincent, Charles M. Tiebout, and Robert Warren. 1961. "The Organization of Government in Metropolitan Areas: A Theoretical Inquiry." *The American Political Science Review* 55 (3): 831–842
Ostrom, Vincent, and Elinor Ostrom. 1977. "Public Goods and Public Choices." In *Alternatives for Delivering Public Services: Toward Improved Performance*, edited by E.S. Savas, 7–49. Boulder, CO: Westview Press.
Polanyi, Mihály. 1951. *The Logic of Liberty.* Routledge and Kegan Paul.
Popkin, Samuel L. 1991. *The Reasoning Voter: Communication and Persuasion in Presidential Campaigns.* Chicago: University of Chicago Press.
Rhode, David W. 1979. "Risk-Bearing and Progressive Ambition: The Case of the United States House of Representatives." *American Journal of Political Science* 23 (1): 1–26.
———. 1980. "Implications from the Disequilibrium of Majority Rule for the Study of Institutions." *American Political Science Review* 74 (3): 432–46.
Riker, William H. 1980. "Implications from the Disequilibrium of Majority Rule for the Study of Institutions." *American Political Science Review* 74 (2): 432–446.
Rosenstone, Steven J., and John Hansen. 1993. *Mobilization, Participation, and Democracy in America.* New York: Pearson.
Samples, Jonathan. 2006. *The Fallacy of Campaign Finance Reform.* Chicago: The University of Chicago Press
Schattschneider, E.E. 1960. *The Semisovereign People.* New York: Holt, Reinhard and Winston.
Shafer, Byron. 1983. *Quiet Revolution: The Struggle for the Democratic Party and the Shaping of Post-Reform Politics.* New York: Russell Sage Foundation.
Shepsle, Kenneth A. 1979. "Institutional Arrangements and Equilibrium in Multidimensional Voting Models." *American Journal of Political Science* 23 (1): 27–59.

———. 1986. "Institutional Equilibrium and Equilibrium Institutions." In *Political Science: The Science of Politics*, edited by Herbert F. Weisberg, 51–82. New York: Agathon Press.

Smith, Steven S. 2007. *Party Influence in Congress*. New York: Cambridge University Press.

Sundquist, James L. 1983. *Dynamics of the Party System: Alignment and Realignment of Political Parties in the United States* (2nd ed.). Washington DC: Brookings Institution Press.

Truman, David. 1967. "Federalism and the Party System." In *American Federalism in Perspective*, edited by Aaron Wildavsky, 81–109. New York: Little, Brown, and Company.

———. 1985. "Party Reform, Party Atrophy, and Constitutional Change: Some Reflections." *Political Science Quarterly* 99 (4): 637–655.

Weingast, Barry R. 1979. "A Rational Choice Perspective on Congressional Norms." *American Journal of Political Science* 23 (2): 245–262.

Wildavsky, Aaron. 1985. "Federalism Means Inequality." *Society* 22 (6): 42–49.

Wilson, Woodrow. 1908. *Constitutional Government in the United States*. New York: Columbia University Press.

Chapter 5

Governing the (Banking) Commons

Polycentric Solutions to Bank Runs

Pablo Paniagua Prieto

The 2007–2008 financial crisis has led macroeconomists to reconsider some fundamental ideas about monetary institutions and banking stability (Beckworth 2012; Sumner 2012; Paniagua 2016). The recent experiences with business cycles and the Great Recession have led some economists to put monetary institutions in general, and central banking arrangements in particular, under institutional scrutiny (Hetzel 2012; Sumner 2012). These institutional concerns have largely come from the passive, or even negative, role that central banks, particularly the Federal Reserve, played while managing the housing boom and in exacerbating the early stages of the 2007–2008 recession (Beckworth 2012; Selgin, Lastrapes, and White 2012).

Despite these critical apprehensions about the passive (and distortive) role of central banks, as well as the Fed's contractionary monetary policies at the early stages of the financial crisis, most economists now recognize the important role that the Fed played later for providing additional liquidity to the system when the financial system experienced a panic (Bullard 2010). Indeed, as Bullard (2010, 156) has commented, one of the greatest lessons that economists have gained from the crisis is "about the Fed's role as lender of last resort on a grand scale. . . . The Fed's ability to act decisively in a crisis through its lender-of-last-resort (LOLR) function far outstrips previous conventional wisdom." Paradoxically, it means that most economists now recognize the importance of central banks as providing the services of liquidity and "lender-of-last-resort" services to the banking system in order to avoid panics; however, they do so without questioning why the system entered a financial panic in the first place (Hetzel 2012; Sumner 2012). A positive outcome of the post–Great Recession literature is that questions about how to best deal with banking panics, with bank runs, and how to institutionally attain a robust banking system have once again risen to notoriety (Salter 2016).

Alas, institutional analysis concerning different banking arrangements, and attention to the "institutional details" that make monetary institutions robust or fragile are one of the most pressing, yet highly disregarded, subfields of monetary policy and banking scholarship.

Yet, despite the advances in the post-recession literature, not much research has focused on any fundamental and institutional questions derived from the empirical evidence concerning central banks' poor performances (Selgin, Lastrapes, and White 2012); research has also ignored analyzing the recent unfortunate results of central banks in managing the macroeconomy (Hetzel 2012). In other words, considering the statistical evidence and the recent poor track record of central banks (Selgin, Lastrapes, and White 2012), the disregarded question concerns the institutional and inherent need for central banks in order to achieve a resilient and stable banking system (Schwartz 1993; Paniagua 2016).

Hence, despite the growing number of criticisms of our current institutional state of affair in money and banking, few scholars have seriously engaged with the more fundamental question: Ultimately, are central banks necessary? (Schwartz 1993). The present macroeconomic consensus and policy perspective on financial stability and bank runs are persistently narrow and monocentric (Salter and Tarko 2018). What is missing in the postcrisis literature on banking stability is a more fundamental questioning about the institutional need for monocentric-only solutions, such as central banks, in order to attain a robust and stable banking order (Paniagua 2017). The banking literature is also conceptually trapped within the false dichotomy broadly identified by the Ostroms between "Leviathan" and "anarchy"; in other words, they disregard the possibility of a social and self-governing order that potentially exists in between these two polar ends (E. Ostrom 2010). Consequently, the banking literature lacks the proper conceptual tools for understanding institutional diversity and polycentricity in banking; thus, we find few banking scholars thinking positively about banking governance and bank runs *without* necessarily thinking also about monocentric forms of financial government.

The present chapter argues that a polycentric system can better provide crucial banking services—such as safeguarding from bank runs and emergency liquidity—than a monocentric system. Goodhart's (1988) *The Evolution of Central Banks* established that central banks are institutionally necessary, and that they evolved naturally, to provide banking services such as economizing on reserves and surveying bank members. These "natural" evolutionary claims of central banking have been deeply questioned, for example by Paniagua (2017). Goodhart, and most contemporary banking scholars, have contended that what makes central banks ultimately indispensable are their unconstrained capacities to create money in order to solve banking panics. The need to govern bank runs *must* incorporate the institutionalization of a "lender of last resort" to allow the expansion of liquidity. Goodhart claims that providing these services must be delivered by a single and dominant center of decision-making. This chapter explores these monocentric claims, examining them throughout the work of the Ostroms on polycentricity and self-governance.

By borrowing from the Ostroms, this chapter argues that polycentric banking systems would not need a single and dominant center for providing LOLR services; rather, they would develop a polycentric and overlapping system of institutions and contracts that achieve *both* severely lessening the possibility of systemic panics in the first place (ex ante functions) and providing also crucial banking, reputational, and liquidity services whenever needed (ex post functions). By arguing that polycentric systems can deal with governing bank runs and provide LOLR services, this chapter contributes to the literature on alternative monetary institutions. Ultimately, understanding the capacity of polycentric systems in effectively self-governing the banking reputation commons and bank runs will also challenge Goodhart's "Gargantuan claims" concerning the inherent need for a monocentric banking system in order to manage panics.

First, this chapter explores Goodhart's institutional justifications for central banks and the arguments employed by the banking literature for the inherent need of monocentric structures in governing bank runs. Second, it reviews relevant Ostromian insights on polycentricity and institutional diversity, relating them also to polycentric banking. Third, it analyzes the role that clearinghouses play *within* polycentric banking systems and how they contribute to self-governance and the coproduction of confidence. Fourth and finally, it presents necessary historical evidence concerning how polycentric banking systems have provided crucial governance and monitoring banking functions to govern bank runs. There is a concluding section.

THE GOVERNANCE OF BANK RUNS AS INSTITUTIONAL JUSTIFICATIONS FOR CENTRAL BANKS

Goodhart's (1988) *The Evolution of Central Banks* established that central banks are institutionally necessary and theoretically justified. Moreover, he argues that they have evolved naturally, as to provide a crucial bundle of banking services such as economizing on reserves, financial stability, and the surveillance and regulation of its bank members. Goodhart (1988) proposes that central banks evolved institutionally and gradually from commercial proto-central banks as the natural outcome of banking systems' inherent economies of reserve holdings. In this seminal book, he provides both historical and theoretical arguments to sustain his claims. However, these "inevitable" and "natural" institutional-evolutionary claims of central banking and the claims concerning their inherent institutional necessity have been questioned both theoretically and historically, such as by Dowd (1994), Paniagua (2017), and Selgin and White (1999).

Nevertheless, in responding to Paniagua (2017), Goodhart has restated his arguments, stating that what makes central banks *ultimately necessary* is their unconstrained capacities to create a great deal of extra money (liquidity) in order to solve banking panics and ameliorate bank runs. Goodhart contends that the need to govern bank runs must incorporate the institutionalization of a liquidity "safety valve," or an uncompetitive (nonprofit making) "lender of last resort" within the banking system, in order to allow the expansion of massive additional liquidity when required, and when illiquid banks are under financial distress.

Goodhart (1988) admits that competitive alternative institutions and decentralized (nonmonocentric) systems can indeed provide *some* crucial banking services such as internal regulation, monitoring bank members, and the netting and clearing of reserves (as Paniagua [2017] argues); however, he also suggests that those decentralized and polycentric banking orders are unable to promptly, and at will, create a great deal of extra money in the quantities and to the scale that central banks can. Consequently, he argues, *non*monocentric banking systems are unable to provide massive liquidity services, and thus are also incapable of successfully governing systemic banking panics. As seen by the financial panic and events of 2008–2009, the resolution of banking panics and bank runs requires a great deal of extra money (Bullard 2010; Gorton 2010). Nevertheless, Goodhart continues to claim that voluntary banking associations and private self-interested banks are unable to cooperatively provide those services and *at the scale* required to curtail bank runs and panics. At the very least, Goodhart further contends that the need to deal with banking panics must incorporate the institutionalization of a nonprofit-seeking, hierarchical, and massive "safety valve" for the expansion of liquidity to banks when required.

Importantly, it is assumed above that both competitive and private banks, as well as groups of them in clearinghouses, lack the incentives, coordination capacities, long-term vision, and the capacities to overcome collective action problems—during times of a banking panic—and thus unable to overcome the tragedy of the banking commons (Goodhart 1987). In other words, narrow and self-interested banks will have the immediate incentives to *not* contribute to *collective solvency* and liquidity; they will refrain from lending to each other and, as a result, threaten the interbank liquidity and overall solvency of the system. In their own narrow and self-interested quest for survival and liquidity, banks will make a rational, yet long-term inefficient, use of resources during panics by hoarding money and negligently allowing other banks to fall into insolvency, which would exacerbate the tragedy for all banks, including themselves (Gorton 1988).

Consequently, the resolution of banking panics requires strong coordination, leadership, overcoming short-term private and commercial interests, and a great deal of extra money or liquidity (Gorton 1988). Nevertheless, these are exactly the banking services and group coordination that Goodhart contends clearinghouses and private banks *cannot provide* together in times of distress, and at the scale, that central banks can. Goodhart maintains that the provision of these crucial kind of cooperative and collective banking services (e.g., collective action to confront the sudden and massive expansion of liquidity in times of stress, and the governance of bank runs) must be delivered by a single (noncompetitive and government appointed) dominant center for monetary decision-making.

Accordingly, Goodhart's institutional justification for central banking, or for a monocentric organization in banking, ultimately relies on two points. First, it rests on correctly recognizing an economic need for providing *both* crucial liquidity or LOLR services, and also the need to govern the reputational banking commons as to manage bank runs. Second, on the rather questionable assumption that alternative *non*monocentric or polycentric arrangements in banking are *incapable* of providing those crucial LOLR services, meaning they are also unable to robustly maintain banking governance, uphold joint confidence, and manage bank runs.

As suggested by the banking literature, bank depositors may not be equipped with specialized and accurate knowledge, nor prompt information to be able to distinguish between the behavior and soundness of the banking industry's individual members (Bordo 1990; Gorton 1988). Thus, in the face of severe information asymmetries, opacity, and search costs, depositors and investors basically use collective or generalized reputation in order to judge an individual firm or a bank. Because of those information asymmetries, depositors simply use narrow information that is revealed about a few specific banks in order to evaluate the soundness of other banks (Yue and Ingram 2012). As a result, a financial shock that affects a few banks can have *larger spillover effects* and damage the confidence in the entire banking system (Goodhart 1988). If an illiquid but *solvent* bank cannot quickly and successfully distinguish itself from the insolvent and distressed banks in the system, then the reputational commons problem arises, which would then exacerbate the financial panic throughout the entire banking system (Gorton 1988).

Negative reputation spillovers from insolvent banks during panics are what ignite indiscriminate bank runs (Bordo 1990; Diamond and Dybvig 1983). Consequently, it makes sense to interpret financial crises, such as the panic of 2008, as essentially informational or reputational problems (Gorton 2010), or as systemic challenges to correctly governing the joint production of banking confidence (Gorton and Mullineaux 1987). Hence, the severity and magnitude of indiscriminate bank runs are largely dependable upon financial information available and the existence and maintenance of systemic banking confidence (Gorton 1988). Consequently, the crucial collective challenge of governing the "reputation and confidence banking commons" lies at the core of both: the emergence of indiscriminate bank runs and hence a subsequent need for an LOLR agency (Gorton 1988, 2010).

Under such a potential systemic panic situation, the banking "reputation (confidence) commons" problem arises because banks under the LOLR theory are assumed to be unable to collectively manage the system's informational, reputational, and liquidity commons (Yue and Ingram 2012). Thus, sound (but illiquid) banks are assumed to be *unable* to collectively and confidently signal to markets, and to communicate credibly also to bank depositors the actual differences between insolvent and solvent banks in the system (Goodhart 1987, 1988). They are assumed to be incapable of conveying the long-term soundness and viability of potentially illiquid banks to markets, which comprises sensitive information for depositors that would have been required in order to subside indiscriminate bank runs and to reestablish confidence in the banking system (Goodhart 1987; Gorton 1988). In other words, "the effects of negative spillover on market confidence created a 'reputation commons' for banks during times of panic" (Yue and Ingram 2012, 3). Thus, the reputation and economic viability of banks during financial shocks are affected by factors and relevant information *beyond* their narrow and individual control (Gorton and Mullineaux 1987). In consequence, the "interdependence of organization and industry reputations creates a challenging problem of [an intangible reputational and confidence] commons" (Yue and Ingram 2012, 23).

Essentially, the LOLR literature critically assumes that profit-seeking banks are unable to collaborate and jointly manage the production of collective reputation, the governance of confidence, and the correct provision of information diffusion mechanisms for banks, which are required to govern bank runs. The joint reputation of sound management, transparency in banks' balance sheets, and low systemic risk are "intangible commons" because banks share illiquidity and insolvency penalties and risks, as well as the long-term rewards associated with the collective reputation and soundness of the banking system as a whole (Yue and Ingram 2012).

Indeed, if we consider the classification of the types of goods (V. Ostrom and E. Ostrom 1977), then the problems of generating and preserving banking joint confidence and the challenges of preserving a banking group's reputation—to avoid indiscriminate bank runs—more closely resembles a problem of governing intangible "commons" or "common-pool resources" (CPRs) than managing a public good. This is mainly due to *rivalry in consumption* that affects the shared reputation capital of all banks (Yue and Ingram 2012). If one bank is unsound, is insolvent, and has mismanaged its financial activities, it in turn degrades the reputation capital of the group and the other banks can no longer enjoy the system's collective reputation capital and sound confidence. Thus, if a few insolvent and mismanaged banks degrade the image and undermine the reputation capital of the group, then *less* reputation capital is left for other sound banks to manage and to use accordingly to subside indiscriminate bank runs.

Interpreted in this Ostromian manner, the systemic problem of bank runs relates to a banking self-governance challenge, and to an *intangible reputational commons problem.* Put differently, a collective banking challenge concerns "how a group of principals [e.g., banks] who are in an interdependent situation can organize and govern themselves to obtain continuing joint benefits when all face temptations to free ride, shirk, or otherwise act opportunistically" (E. Ostrom 1990, 29). The broad task of this chapter is to extend the Ostroms' framework of institutional analysis and self-governance to the banking literature in order to analyze how systems of self-governance and polycentricity could be applied in banking to overcome the collective challenge of bank runs without a definitive center of financial power.

It is important to recognize that the Ostroms did not explicitly use the ideas of polycentricity and self-governance in the banking literature, nor more broadly in macroeconomics. They did, however, acknowledge that institutional analysis and the concept of polycentricity could be successfully applied to numerous challenging situations in which groups of individuals *seem* to be "trapped" in settings resembling the tragedy of the commons, but were able to overcome them through collaboration and endogenous rules (E. Ostrom 2010). Moreover, V. Ostrom (1991) recognized that polycentricity seems to be the "structural basis of [resilient] self-governing systems." In other words, successful cases of self-governance and groups overcoming several challenges related to collective action problems or the tragedy of the commons seem to be strongly associated with the groups' capacity of properly using the principles of polycentricity and endogenous rule formation to overcome collective challenges through institutional creativity and consent (Aligica and Boettke 2009; E. Ostrom 2005). Following, if banking scholars are concerned about the potential self-governing capacities of banks as voluntary groups and their actual collective capacities to move away from the reputational "tragedy" of the banking commons, then banking theorists should also be concerned about how the principles of polycentricity could also apply to banking regimes and financial governance. It seems appropriate to extend the Ostroms' oeuvre toward new avenues of research, such as the institutional possibility of polycentric banking systems to govern bank runs (Paniagua 2017; Salter and Tarko 2018). Such novel banking extensions and new applications of the Ostroms' existent polycentric framework will be this chapter's main contribution.

As hinted at earlier, regrettably the LOLR literature still holds a "Hardinian" view regarding the capacity of private banks to self-maintain the reputational commons and, thus, to subside a banking panic. This pessimistic "Hardinian" view is sustained upon the assumption that the mere presence of self-interest, opportunism, and competitive relations among banks will be enough to permanently undermine the willingness and capacity of banks to cooperate (Goodhart 1987, 1988). Thus, the LOLR theory, similar to the monocentric theory of governance in political science and echoing the underlying setting of the tragedy of the commons, also seeks to "invoke an image of helpless individuals caught in an inexorable process of destroying their own resources" (E. Ostrom 1990, 8). Put differently, the proponents for monocentric solutions for bank runs make institutional claims based on the crucial assumption that local actors and commercial banks would not be able to negotiate or bargain their way around inefficiencies or collective challenges, no matter how hard they try.

To conclude, the LOLR theory obtains the negative and system-wide outcome of an undistinguishable and general bank run; it does so by impinging on the crucial, yet questionable, assumption that private banks are unable to *self-govern* the "intangible" reputation and confidence commons, thus making them incapable of collectively ameliorating "the negative spillover effect on market confidence during bank panics" (Yue and Ingram 2012, 1). Thus, similar to the Hardinian vision of the social order that E. Ostrom challenged in political science, the theory on bank runs seems to be also "undertaken with a presumption that individuals cannot organize themselves and always need to be organized by external authorities" (E. Ostrom 1990, 25).

The Ostroms' work shows that other sources of governance might exist beyond requiring a single and dominant center for decision-making. Yet, similar to the Hobbesian view that the social order *cannot* exist without a definitive center of power, macroeconomists have always considered that banking stability requires a single and dominant center for providing banking governance (Goodhart 1988). This "Gargantuan" and monocentric banking stability assumption echoes what E. Ostrom broadly identified as the "fundamental presumptions about the nature of governments as external authorities governing over societies" (E. Ostrom 1990, 18). The alternative proposed here is to instead think about the institutional possibilities for self-governance under polycentric forms of banking.

POLYCENTRIC BANKING AND THE OSTROMS' PRINCIPLES OF POLYCENTRICITY

Bank runs are negative outcomes that arise from being *unable* to collectively govern an intangible and reputational commons challenge (Yue and Ingram 2012). Nevertheless, and following E. Ostrom (1990) insights about collective challenges, the fact that banks' survival largely depends on the reputation of the industry as a whole should create strong private interests for protecting mutual welfare, which in turn should motivate banks to collaborate in order to manage the commons. Similar to what E. Ostrom (2005, 2010) argued regarding local governance, the need for monocentric solutions to govern bank runs and the reputational commons could be avoided and potentially overcome through self-governance within a polycentric banking system that allows for institutional diversity and cooperation among banks.

Theories of polycentric governance have been more consistently developed and successfully applied within the context of governing *tangible* CPRs and also applied to local or ecological communities facing collective dilemmas (Aligica and Boettke 2009; E. Ostrom 1990, 2010). The Ostroms did not apply the principles of polycentricity and self-governance to *intangible* or reputational commons problems, nor to the theory of banking stability and bank runs. However, since indiscriminate bank runs, financial panics, and the need for LOLR services are closely related to cooperative and social challenges of reliably delivering forms of governance and public goods (Bordo 1990), and with collectively governing an intangible and reputational *commons* in banking (the joint production of banking confidence) (Gorton and Mullineaux 1987; Yue and Ingram 2012), the principles of polycentricity, self-governance, and institutional diversity could be fruitfully extended to financial stability and the theory of bank runs (Paniagua 2017; Salter and Tarko 2018). Indeed, as V. Ostrom suggested, the "principles of polycentricity need to be extended through the whole system of human affairs. This applies to public economies as well as to market economies, . . . in short, to all of the conditions of life" (V. Ostrom 1991, 243). Hence, this section draws a theoretical connection between the Ostroms' general principles of polycentricity and banking institutional diversity and financial self-governance. It does so to argue that the Ostroms' general principles of polycentricity are applicable to some cooperative and competitive forms of banking.

It is important to delineate what it is meant by a polycentric system, and particularly a polycentric system of banking. This chapter's Ostromian approach to understanding alternative (*non*monocentric) forms of banking governance is built upon the Ostroms' notion of polycentric governance (e.g., V. Ostrom 1991). A polycentric system of governance is one that is comprised of many heterogeneous—both collaborative and competitive—decision centers (or nodes), in which

> citizens are able to organize not just one but multiple governing authorities at different scales. . . . Each unit exercises considerable independence to make and enforce rules within a circumscribed domain of authority. . . . In a polycentric system, some units are general-purpose governments while others may be highly specialized. . . . In a polycentric system the users of each common-pool resource would have some authority to make at least some of the rules. (E. Ostrom 2005, 283)

Additionally, within polycentric systems, "cooperation is conditional [among the small scale units], involving a certain degree of conflict, as well as entry and exit from larger associations" (Tarko 2017, 66). Thus, "to the extent that these political jurisdictions take each other into account in competitive relationships, enter into contractual and cooperative relationships, or turn to central mechanisms to resolve conflict, they may exhibit coherent, consistent, and predictable patterns of behavior and may be said to function as a 'system'" (V. Ostrom 1991, 223). For the Ostroms, polycentricity develops as a nonhierarchical, institutional, and cultural framework that allows for cooperation and coexistence of multiple decision centers holding different objectives and principles. Such a nonhierarchical framework therefore contains an evolutionary process of competition, cooperation, and contestation among those diverse viewpoints and governing principles of the coexisting decision centers (Aligica and Boettke 2009).

Put differently, the concept of polycentricity refers to a governance or a social system that possesses many decision centers (individuals, associations, civil society, institutions, etc.) having autonomous yet limited and constrained prerogatives, while such decision centers also simultaneously compete and cooperate under an overarching system of rules (V. Ostrom 1972). However, as the Ostroms noticed, such a system is neither chaotic nor entirely fragmented, as the decision nodes display ordered, overlapping, and cooperative relationships among themselves that persist through time (V. Ostrom 1991). Indeed, spontaneous patterns of collaboration and competition stemming from consent comprise a fundamental feature of polycentricity that allows the systems to attain adaptability, self-organization, spontaneity, and "emergent order" properties. In other words, "patterns of organization within a polycentric system will be self-generating or self-organizing in the sense that individuals will have incentives to create or institute appropriate patterns of ordered relationships" (V. Ostrom 1972, 8).

It is important to recognize that "the existence of a predominantly polycentric political system need not preclude elements of monocentricity from existing in such a system" (V. Ostrom 1972, 3). This suggests that some elements of command and vertical organization might still exist within a predominantly decentralized and polycentric system. Yet, importantly, under a polycentric system *no* single decision center has an ultimate monopoly over the legitimate use of force and coercion; moreover, the rule of law or an overarching system of constitutional rules constrains the centers. Polycentric systems are ultimately constitutional and rule-of-law-oriented type of systems (V. Ostrom 1991).

Further specifying the concept of polycentricity, V. Ostrom (1971) acknowledged that the "spontaneity," beneficial emergent properties, and the self-organizing tendencies of a polycentric system are conditioned on three specific institutional conditions or properties at different levels. "Such conditions must be met before . . . a polycentric . . . system becomes a technically-feasible, empirical possibility" (V. Ostrom 1971, 8). The first condition is the freedom of association and thus the entry and exit within a particular social or economic system. Individuals and organizations must be able to establish new and contestable decision centers, public economies, and collaborative arrangements. The freedom of association, contestability, and disassociation ensure that entities' spontaneous collaborations will morph into an adaptable polycentric order (V. Ostrom 1971, 7).

The second condition relates to the existence and enforcement of general and abstract rules of conduct or procedures, "which provide the legal framework for a polycentric order" (V. Ostrom 1971, 8). The third relates to a level of organization pertaining to "the formulation and revision of the basic rules of conduct which provide the framework for any particular polycentric order" (V. Ostrom 1971, 8). The idea is that individuals and entities cannot only (dis)associate freely; they can also change and adapt the general and abstract rules of conduct in an orderly and procedural manner. In sum, the Ostroms' polycentricity is a complex system of overlapping powers, checks and balances, incentives, rules, and institutional diversity combined with a complex network of dynamic (cooperative and competitive) relationships among multilevel units (Tarko 2017).

At this point, we can recognize that the properties of polycentricity suggest that not all decentralized, competitive, fragmented, and lightly regulated banking systems are necessarily polycentric systems (Paniagua 2017). One of the defining features is that the local decision centers that together form an overall order, which are at the same time independent enough to make and enforce local rules, are also governed and guided at the preconstitutional level by an *overarching set of rules* or meta-procedures (E. Ostrom 2005; V. Ostrom 1991). This overarching set of rules should attempt to guide the incentives of the decision centers and nodes, so that their individual actions and local rules at the post-constitutional level will contribute to (and align with) desirable social goals (E. Ostrom 1990). The existence of general procedures and the overarching system of rules does *not* mean that the many decision centers share all their types of procedures and local rules for their action situations.

"Patterns and regularities which occur under an illusion of chaos may involve an order of complexity that is counterintuitive" (V. Ostrom 1972, 23). In this banking context, the desirable social goal and overarching objective is to govern bank runs and the reputational banking commons in order to attain banking stability and achieve the sustainability of banking businesses activities (Bordo 1990). In most polycentric systems, local agents operating *inside* the overall social system usually enforce the overarching rules. Therefore, they are endogenously enforced and locally administered through: mutually agreed procedures for decentralized monitoring and patterns of accountability, well-defined schemes of graduated sanctioning to guide and enforce compliant behavior, and dynamic systems of checks and balances among the different units (E. Ostrom 1990, 70–74, 2010). The decision centers and nodes within a polycentric order can have overlapping jurisdictions, and thus do not need to be territorial or geographically defined (E. Ostrom 2010).

Consequently, the delineated general properties of polycentricity suggest that polycentric banking systems are neither unregulated nor anarchic financial arrangements. They are different from speculative forms of "wildcat" banking that are unregulated, unorganized, and uncooperative; moreover, these "anarchic systems" lack the general properties delineated above and thus cannot be said to function as an *orderly* "system" (Paniagua 2017; Salter and Tarko 2018; V. Ostrom 1991).

Instead, polycentricity in banking occurs when there are coexistent and competing banking groups within cooperative interactive networks comprised of a wide range of banks, financial institutions, and banking associations (or clearinghouses) that possess different kinds of ends, rules, business models, and goals (such as maximizing banking profit, increasing banking resilience, improving banks' reputation, etc.). Moreover, a polycentric banking system is characterized by the presence of freedom of association and disassociation; banks have the freedom of entry and exit from different banking associations or clubs (clearinghouses). Under such a banking system, banks and banking organizations must be able to freely establish: new and contestable decision centers, bank branches, and more complex collaborative arrangements, if deemed necessary (Paniagua 2017). Hence, there are (a) no legal or governmental boundaries on entry and exit from the banking industry; (b) no restrictions on banks forming clearinghouses, and (c) no restrictions on competing to offer notes and money issuance and other financial services.

Importantly, under a polycentric banking system *no* single bank or banking association has a residuary or ultimate monopoly over the services of notes and money issuance activities, or over the legitimate use of financial, banking, and regulatory powers. The contestable banking nodes, banking clubs, and bank branches are not constrained by monocentric central banks, but rather by banking competition, legal contracts established between banks and their customers, the rule of law, and by an overarching system of constitutional rules (Salter and Tarko 2018). Whenever these banking and institutional features are present, we can contend that such a financial system indeed possesses the general features of a polycentric system. A paradigmatic example of these polycentric properties in banking can be found in the 1716 to 1845 competitive banking period in Scotland (Goodspeed 2016; White 1995 [1984]). They can also be partially found in the contestable clearinghouses episodes in Massachusetts and New York during the nineteenth century, as well as in several others banking systems throughout history (see Dowd 1994; Paniagua 2017; Timberlake 1984).

Finally, considering the Ostromian polycentric characteristics, a polycentric banking system is an overlapping and cooperative system that broadly retains three important systemic features. First, local banking actors *endogenously* create local banking regulation, monitoring, and sanctioning. In this way, the banking units and/or associations (such as clearinghouses) exercise what E. Ostrom identifies as the required "independence to make and enforce rules within a circumscribed domain of authority" (E. Ostrom 2005, 283). Within a polycentric banking system, there are many legitimate generators and enforcers of banking rules, such as banking clubs, banking associations, and clearinghouses (Yue and Ingram 2012). Second, cooperation, contestability, and competition among different banking units and associations are *not* mutually exclusive; instead, they coexist in predictable patterns of banking and legal interactions. The banking units could also replicate a very important feature identified by the Ostroms in other polycentric regimes: the subunits (e.g., banks) might "enter into contractual and cooperative relationships, or turn to central mechanisms to resolve conflict" (V. Ostrom 1991, 223). Hence, private banks could establish ordered and coherent (cooperative and competitive) relationships with each other that persist through time (e.g., clearing and netting arrangements, shared rules and banking processes, and interbank lending procedures). Third and finally, given their higher degrees of contractual and procedural agreements, cooperation, and coordination, the network of competing banks might be defined as what V. Ostrom described as a "system"; meaning that they "exhibit coherent, consistent, and predictable patterns of behavior and may be said to function as a 'system'" (ibid, 223). Thus, private banks in a polycentric system establish competing and collaborative centers of "banking power" at different organizational levels. For instance, financial power could lie in—and be distributed among—unit banking structures, systems of branch banking with their headquarters, interbanking networks for clearing and lending, and finally—if deemed necessary—among contestable clearinghouses.

Following, it is relevant to ask, how are these three core properties and systemic features of polycentricity generated and encouraged *in practice* within a polycentric banking system? The most significant collaborative institution, or broad "banking unit," in this regard is forming a contestable network of "banking clubs" or a system of contestable clearinghouses; these are multiple governing and competing authorities at different scales and with *circumscribed* domains of authority (Paniagua 2017). Clearinghouses could align the overarching self-governance system of banking rules to the private incentives of banks (endogenous rules are considered useful by bank members). These will be explored in depth in the following sections through historical evidence illustrating their main governing mechanisms. Importantly, the potential capacity of polycentric banking systems in correctly building resilient forms of banking self-governance and effective systems of self-regulation could potentially challenge Goodhart's (1987, 1988) institutional justifications for the necessity of central banks to attain banking stability.

INTERBANK CLEARINGHOUSES: THE FOUNDATIONS FOR A SELF-GOVERNING BANKING SYSTEM

The interbank clearinghouse system can be conceived as an evolving and voluntary mechanism for governing banking organizations' behavior and for self-regulating their financial practices. Clearinghouses can also be understood as local community-based "banking clubs" and as self-regulatory programs among private and commercial banking organizations. Originally, clearinghouses were endogenously designed by private banks under competitive forms of banking systems, in order to minimize interbank redemption and clearing costs (Dowd 1994). Usually, clearinghouses were city-based "banking clubs" and voluntary forms of association within a close-knit banking community (Yue and Ingram 2012). Under a polycentric and competitive system, profit-seeking banks have incentives to collaborate to a certain degree in order to establish regular clearing patterns and predictable banking procedures. These serve to help them clear and net bank liabilities against each other (or offset the value of multiple positions or payments due to be exchanged between interbank parties) in a quicker and cheaper way than otherwise. In Cosean terms, the establishment of clearinghouses has generally been the rational and collective intention of *lowering* transaction costs for banks, and thus to jointly *mitigate* the management and organizational problem of the complex, costly, and time-consuming note redemption process between them (Dowd 1994). Banks that initially settled and cleared liabilities only bilaterally eventually found that establishing a clearinghouse was economically beneficial for all of them; this is because it allows netting and clearing interbank liabilities and interbank debt positions quicker and multilaterally, hence economizing on time as well as organizational and transaction costs.

The crucial functions of a clearinghouse can be broken down into two broad categories: clearing liabilities and banking self-regulation (or financial governance) (Cannon 1910; Dowd 1994). To fulfill its first and original function, the clearinghouse provides centralized clearing and netting services for all of its bank members over notes, drafts, checks, and bills of exchange. To fulfill its second function, it establishes also internal rules, norms, sanctions, and banking procedures for controlling and monitoring its members. This second function is crucial since its provision collectively ameliorates the banking reputation commons problem, which exacerbates bank runs.

It is important to recognize that the clearing and netting function (lowering transaction costs for banks) historically *preceded* the other regulatory, liquidity, and monitoring functions. Nevertheless, those original and previous cooperative experiences of multilateral clearing created the social conditions (trust) and cooperative foundations from which self-regulation could take root (Yue and Ingram 2012). In other words, once clearinghouses evolve to a level of performing more professional and institutionalized multilateral clearing, bank members realize that they could also use such an arena of collaboration and trust for other more complex and additional banking activities such as self-regulation. This is because they could collectively reap further economies of scale and extra benefits if clearinghouses offered also additional services, such as collecting and disseminating relevant banking information, enforcing minimum quality and banking standards—such as leverage and capital rations—or working as a counterparty and center coordinator for interbank credit and liquidity allocation ("credit intermediary"); these additional services would ultimately facilitate low transaction cost emergency lending among solvent bank members during times of stress (Salter and Tarko 2018).

Put differently, clearinghouses or "bank clubs" could be interpreted as successful voluntary mechanisms for efficiently providing crucial banking services and self-governance. As such, they could be potentially successful at solving the challenges of the intangible banking reputation commons and banking panics, mainly through dual roles: first as ex post coordinators and facilitators of interbank emergency lending, like interbank "liquidity intermediaries," and second (more importantly), through the ex ante effective provision of crucial informational, reputational, and governance functions. It is mainly through providing these latter functions that clearinghouses are able to effectively solve ex ante the banking reputation commons challenge—thus ameliorating bank runs before they can even materialize. Importantly, clearinghouses provide these governance services in the form of club goods (V. Ostrom and E. Ostrom 1977), meaning that these services are accessible *only* to clearinghouse members. Therefore, free riders, noncompliant banks, and noncontributors to the reputational banking commons are excluded from the banking club. This scenario of exclusion also avoids negative reputational spillovers that can ignite bank runs.

Furthermore, being part of a respectable and self-regulated "banking club" works as a confidence and reputational device. It also acts as a valuable signaling mechanism for banks to ease the concerns and doubts of creditors, depositors, and financial markets regarding their solvency and liquidity conditions. This organization allows for clear and swift financial information sharing, and for disseminating relevant epistemic resources among the network's different banking nodes, such as to clearinghouses, between bank members of a single clearinghouse, and among creditors and depositors. In addition to clearly transmitting banking information among the network, this *joint production* of confidence and a sound and collective reputation help to overcome banking's inherent reputational opacity and asymmetric information problems plaguing the financial relationships among banks and between banks and depositors. Clear information diffusion and banking signaling mechanisms help to overcome the problem of negative reputational spillovers (reputational externalities) during bank panics; in turn, this reduces the overall risk of indiscriminate and chaotic bank runs among bank members.

Moreover, imposing sound regulation and credible discipline among banks work as reassurance mechanisms, good signaling strategies, and information diffusion mechanisms. Through them, investors and depositors can gain confidence regarding the banks' soundness, and on the banking group as a whole, which reassures them that banks are solvent as a single banking cluster. This greatly lowers the threat of an undistinguishable financial panic among banks. Clearinghouse membership therefore provides a form of "banking certificate," a signal of quality, or a "badge of honor" to bank members. This allows them to show markets and depositors that they abide by both sound self-imposed rules of banking management and prudential financial procedures co-established with the clearinghouse.

Additionally, clearinghouses are able to generate and disseminate accurate information about banks to markets by constantly assessing and monitoring their financial activities, balance sheets, and collateral (Gorton and Mullineaux 1987). Clearinghouses' assessments, monitoring, and epistemic properties are particularly relevant for ameliorating indiscriminate bank runs during financial stress; this is because one of the most important collective challenges that banks face is to quickly and accurately differentiate between sound and unsound banks in order to discover and communicate which banks are in liquidity and/or solvency danger (Gorton 1988). In short, a clearinghouse-validated status and membership work as a sort of signaling strategy to generate confidence in banks' management, or as a clear *epistemic signal* (or epistemic shortcut) about the soundness of their management and liquidity conditions that banks can easily use to swiftly convey this information back to customers and depositors.

The fact that such relevant—clearinghouse generated—banking information is distributed in a simple, transparent, and democratic manner allows depositors to simultaneously have access to the same information, and in a credible manner, avoiding information inconsistencies, unwarranted rumors, and uncertainty from spreading across the system. This allows depositors to more quickly judge different banks and avoid indiscriminate bank runs due to a lack of detailed and reliable information about them (Gorton and Mullineaux 1987). Maintaining clearinghouse membership thus provides a clear and discernible *reputational boundary*, or a "confidence firewall," and a distinguishable mechanism for sorting between sound (but potentially illiquid) bank members from unsound and poorly managed *non*member banks. Membership and its signaling thus decreases systemic contagion and negative spillover effects since it reduces uncertainty and a lack of clear financial information that usually exacerbate banking panics (Gorton 1988, 2010).

Moreover, clearinghouses' *raisons d'être* and entire profitability ultimately reside in providing decent "club goods" type of valuable services to banks. This helps maintain a strong image of quality and a banking reputation commons through time. Clearinghouse's managers have strong incentives to protect the group from bad banking practices, risky strategies, and from a bad reputation that could damage the group image. Thus, they have strong incentives (and "skin in the game") to monitor and protect the group from "bad (banking) apples" either within the group or that want to become a part of it just to free ride on its reputation capital (Dowd 1994; Yue and Ingram 2012). Clearinghouses have strong vested interests to safeguard the group reputation because their own survival and economic viability is entirely at stake if the "reputation commons" of the banking group is degraded, or if depositors and creditors question its soundness (Gorton and Mullineaux 1987).

Consequently, a direct threat to its reputation (a threat to its own economic survival) generates strong incentives for the clearinghouse to monitor and treat unsound and mismanaged bank members accordingly. This entails implementing strong and graduated sanctions on imprudent banks. These sanctions act as a signal to customers regarding the specific riskiness of the irresponsible and insolvent banks. Another complementary approach would also be to temporarily suspend bank members from using the "club's services." Ultimately, if deemed necessary, the clearinghouse would expel unsound banks from the club, negating them from emergency liquidity services, thus allowing them to fail outside the club.

Importantly, a polycentric system that engages in the coproduction of confidence and information helps to provide an ex ante (or before the fact) robust micro-prudential form of governing bank runs and panics before they even materialize. This makes an ex post and emergency need for actual LOLR and liquidity interventions far less necessary to save bank members in distress (Gorton and Mullineaux 1987). Regarding LOLR services, generating accurate financial information alongside clear reputational boundaries greatly lessens the negative spillover effects of a single bank failure. This reduces the probability that the failure of mismanaged banks would "contaminate" other sound, but potentially illiquid, banks in the network. A prudent clearinghouse "quality certificate" and the membership signal provide a strong reputational and informational "banking-quality firewall" that quickly distinguishes banks and protects sound banks from contagion and negative reputation spillover effects from insolvent and unsound banks.

The "reputational and informational firewalls" and "quality sorting" processes allow unsound and insolvent banks to potentially fail *outside* clearinghouses' "firewalls," while also protect sound bank members from negative reputational spillovers and unwarranted liquidity drains that could trigger chaotic bank runs (Gorton and Mullineaux 1987). Indeed, unsound "members were expelled from clearinghouse membership for failure to repay [emergency] loan certificates after the panic had clearly ended and their failure would result in weaker externality effects" (Gorton and Mullineaux 1987, 464). These micro-prudential and sorting mechanisms greatly lower the entire banking system's overall emergency liquidity needs, since more and accurate information about specific banks and their quality sorting help customers and depositors to *not* indiscriminately run on all banks simultaneously, which lowers concomitantly the systemic need for massive liquidity across the entire network. In other words, there is a potential redistribution and reallocation (recycling) of both deposits and liquidity from unsound and insolvent banks to sound banks ("flight to banking quality"), *rather* than a systemic and indistinguishable liquidity drain and overall chaotic deposit withdrawals throughout the system (Hetzel 2012).

Thus, the presence of clear resource (reputational banking commons) boundaries and the signaling and informational diffusion mechanisms for reputational differentiation and bank-quality sorting *during* bank failures allow the system to deal with isolated bank runs and panics in an orderly and predictable manner (Goodspeed 2016). It also allows them to do so without necessarily engaging in massive provisions of additional ex post interbank lending and emergency liquidity. Conceivably, some minor *inner*-clearinghouse liquidity might be necessary for a few solvent, but illiquid, bank members in times of stress; however, the need for system-wide, indiscriminate, and massive amounts of liquidity to all banks will be substantially reduced (perhaps even entirely eliminated) through the complementary and reputational "informational firewall" and "bank-quality sorting" ex ante processes (Gorton and Mullineaux 1987).

Accordingly, the actual LOLR services and the liquidity "safety valve" that is required in a polycentric banking systems can be *substantially smaller* whenever compared to monocentric arrangements; due to the fact that the need for dealing with panics through the ex post expansion of liquidity is here complemented, and largely sustained instead, by the ex ante correct management of the "reputation banking commons," and through clear information diffusion mechanisms and reputational boundaries. Therefore, the presence of the other aforementioned complementary banking governance and regulatory services provided ex ante by voluntary banking groups and branch banking networks substantially reduce the actual need for ex post LOLR emergency liquidity services.

Consequently, the success and efficacy of polycentric banking systems in governing bank runs resides not merely in clearinghouses' ex post capacities to provide emergency liquidity. As argued in this chapter, a "multi-layered" or "nested" form of correctly governing the "banking (reputational) commons" challenge makes the subsequent emergency liquidity and interbank "safety valve" aspects of the LOLR bundle of services much less necessary. Hence, a polycentric system would largely govern bank runs in a decentralized, micro-prudential, and ex ante manner, without requiring the institutionalization of a monocentric and definitive center for liquidity and LOLR services to subside financial panics.

To conclude, a polycentric banking system largely solves the problem of bank runs by transforming the previous Hardinian setting of the banking confidence commons and the reputational capital "open to all" (to both sound and unsound banks) into the restricted provision of a limited bundle of reputational and governance functions, under an institutional form of excludable banking "clubs." Through clear reputational boundaries and "informational firewalls," a contestable network of clearinghouses prevents rumors and perceived insolvency of a few banks from cascading into a full-blown banking panic. As such, polycentric banking systems lower the actual need for massive ex post last resort emergency lending. In such a nested and polycentric manner, the problem of bank runs is alternatively governed, not through the ex post and monocentric production of massive liquidity, but rather through both the correct governance of the "reputational banking commons" and a polycentric creation of endogenous and prudential rules for robust banking self-governance. Indeed, such polycentric banking systems have successfully governed both the banking reputational commons and bank runs *in practice*, without the need for a monocentric and definitive center of financial power, as the historical evidence in the following section illustrates.

CLEARINGHOUSE GOVERNANCE FUNCTIONS AND HISTORICAL EVIDENCE OF BANKING SELF-GOVERNANCE

Clearinghouses' capacities to ex ante govern the reputation banking commons reside in their ability to provide an important "bundle" of banking services and a set of governance functions such as the following: exclusion strategies (clear boundaries for excluding unsound banks and noncontributors to the reputational banking commons), the creation and maintenance of regulatory and minimum quality standards (e.g., capital requirements) enforced through bank members' local monitoring (banking inspections), and graduated sanctions to noncompliant members (Dowd 1994; Yue and Ingram 2012). This creates a wide set of formal mechanisms that enforce, punish, and monitor in order to prevent (or at least greatly discourage) any one bank from "misbehaving"; it also discourages free riding on existent banking confidence, reputation capital, or sound management stemming from the coproduction between compliant members within the association (Salter and Tarko 2018).

The institutional properties and aforementioned governance functions are *not* merely theoretical conjectures devoid of empirical content or historical evidence; contrarily, they have been the real practices and institutional properties throughout history that self-governed and polycentric banking arrangements have employed to deal with the reputational banking commons (Goodspeed 2016; White 1995 [1984]). Thus, I will here briefly provide some historical evidence that illuminates how self-organized banking arrangements have successfully provided crucial governance functions and regulatory banking services in order to govern together the problem of bank runs, both ex ante and ex post the actual need for emergency liquidity services (meaning both before and after the actual materialization of systemic bank runs).

To prevent moral hazard, clearinghouses can encourage bank members to maintain minimum quality standards, such as requiring a high level of reserves (or well-defined capital ratios) and then constantly monitor and enforce such sound behavior and best practices (Lake 1947). Indeed, the New York Clearing House Association (NYCHA), which was the first clearinghouse in the United States and established in 1853, "closely monitored the balance sheets of member banks and required them to report their condition every week. Moreover, the clearing house had the authority to audit members' books at any moment, which it could do in response to rumors about the state of a particular member" (Yue and Ingram 2012, 17). US clearinghouses, such as the NYCHA, were founded voluntary and had special committees in charge of member admissions. Also, new members had to be approved by the majority of existing members (Cannon 1910). Roughly between 1853 and 1914, clearinghouses in the United States not only closely monitored member banks' balance sheets and required them to report their financial conditions weekly, but they also had the authority to audit and scrutinize their books and financial ratios at any moment (Gilpin and Wallace 1904; Gorton and Mullineaux 1987).

More specifically, the NYCHA utilized voluntary and regulatory tools such as reserve requirements, deposit rate ceilings, and random bank examinations to incentivize and control how bank member institutions chose to behave (Gorton and Mullineaux 1987). The NYCHA included a number of different institutional aspects that provided screening, sanctioning, and monitoring services. For example, they required

> that member institutions satisfy an admissions test (based on certification of adequate capital), pay an admission fee, and submit to periodic exams (audits) by the clearinghouse. Members who failed to satisfy CBCH [Commercial-Bank Clearinghouses] regulations were subject to disciplinary actions (fines) and, for extreme violations, could be expelled. . . . The ability of the CBCH to audit a member's books (to measure quality) at any moment provided strong incentives for prudent behavior by each bank. (Gorton and Mullineaux 1987, 461)

The NYCHA would quickly investigate rumors concerning the financial states and liquidity positions of particular member banks under pressure. They would audit the banks in question and publish the results, making the minutes available and transparent to the public (Gorton and Mullineaux 1987). Throughout history, clearinghouses have thus played the role of both generating and transmitting relevant and accurate information about banks' behavior and financial positions to the public and depositors; by doing so, they also reduced unwarranted financial rumors and informational asymmetries that can ignite indiscriminate bank runs.

The success and advantages of the NYCHA were such that in less than a decade a large number of new and local clearinghouses were voluntary established throughout the United States, such as in Buffalo, New York, and Sioux City, among several others around the country (Cannon 1910). Before the Federal Reserve System was established in late 1913, there were more than 200 city-based clearinghouses in the United States alone, forming a kind of contestable—albeit imperfect—network of clearinghouses and competitive banking (Timberlake 1984; Yue and Ingram 2012).

The success of US clearinghouses in governing the reputation banking commons and in regulating their members have been further corroborated by the recent historical and statistical findings of Yue, Luo, and Ingram (2009). These scholars find that the NYCHA drastically reduced the operational risk of banks and the failure rate of member banks by 56 percent. They also find that NYCHA members were relatively more prudent and avoided highly risky financial operations. They confirmed that the NYCHA was successful at imposing self-regulation and in organizing cooperative ad hoc arrangements. Additionally, and echoing E. Ostrom's (1990, 2005) findings, the "effectiveness of the private institution [the NYCHA] hinges on its nature as a local organization that includes a relatively small number of homogeneous and densely-connected banks. Localism enables strong monitoring and enforcement mechanisms that are critical to solve the problem of collective action" (Yue, Luo, and Ingram 2009, 1). Conclusively, their statistical results showed that

> the overall bank failure rate is lower when the NYCHA was the sole market order maintaining institution, even compared with the relative stable period after the Great Depression. . . . Our results suggest that cooperation among banks themselves is not only an effective way to prevent bank failures but may achieve better monitoring. (Yue, Luo, and Ingram 2009, 5)

Finally, the welfare and overall systemic implications of the NYCHA were substantial. The survival benefits did not only remain solely with NYCHA members, but spread to all Manhattan commercial banks. The efforts of the NYCHA in rescuing its members in distress and in dampening waves of banking panics stabilized financial markets and allowed the entire population of commercial banks to flourish (Cannon 1910). The overall failure rate of this banking population during the clearinghouse self-regulatory period was significantly lower than in the previous period without clearinghouses, which had no endogenous regulation (Yue and Ingram 2012). Thus, the banking population in Manhattan thrived under the presence of clearinghouses. The number of commercial banks located in Manhattan increased from 51 in 1853 (when the NYCHA was established), to nearly 100 banks in 1913. Hence, it is not surprising that the NYCHA was considered "a most important and beneficial part in the general economic health of the nation" (Gilpin and Wallace 1904, 5).

Clearinghouses have been neither accidental nor minor institutional outcomes throughout history; on the contrary, the emergence of contestable clearinghouses has been the most likely outcome in most banking systems that have allowed the financial freedom of banking association (banking self-governance) as well as allowed entry and exit within the banking system (Paniagua 2017; White 1989). In this sense, clearinghouses have been established regularly throughout history (Dowd 1994; Lake 1947). Some of these banking systems have possessed some of the crucial polycentric and competitive features described in the previous sections (Paniagua 2017). Consequently, under a polycentric banking system that promotes both freedom of banking association and competitive entry and exit, "eventually all the banks within an economy will be connected through one or a small number of clearinghouses . . . the histories of the best-known early clearinghouses, in London, Edinburgh, and New York, all conform to this general pattern" (White 1989, 231). Additional and paradigmatic examples of contestable networks of clearinghouses, networks of interbanking cooperation, and systems of banking self-regulation can also be found in the Suffolk Banking System in New England between 1824 and 1858 (Lake 1947; Trivoli 1979). The same goes also for the eighteenth-century competitive Scottish banking system from 1716 until 1845 (Goodspeed 2016; White 1995 [1984]).

In sum, so far there is abundant circumstantial evidence showing how competitive clearinghouses can effectively self-regulate and monitor its members (Dowd 1994). Governance, monitoring, and reputational functions help ex ante to accurately govern the potential challenges of indiscriminate bank runs via micro-prudential banking measures such as the accurate provision of self-regulation, the maintenance and enforcement of strong quality standards, and the correct diffusion of relevant banking information. This bundle of ex ante governance banking functions makes far less necessary the actual need for ex post LOLR and emergency liquidity services. In what follows, I review some additional historical evidence of how clearinghouses have complementary also governed ex post the problem of indiscriminate bank runs when they indeed materialize, with particular attention to the NYCHA.

The success of the NYCHA in mitigating ex post banking panics was largely the result of an interbank system of loan certificates. The clearinghouse loan certificate was a new security created by the NYCHA in 1857 (Gorton and Mullineaux 1987). These clearinghouse loan certificates were issued only in emergencies on the basis of loans made to bank members by the clearinghouse policy committee (Timberlake 1984).

During the panic of 1857, the NYCHA organized a voluntary emergency loan committee. It issued fixed interest loan certificates to commercial banks, which could be borrowed by a financially distressed (illiquid) bank member if backed by sound collateral (Yue, Luo, and Ingram 2009). Illiquid member banks could use the loan certificates in the interbank clearing and netting processes, instead of using directly cash and currency, which freed liquidity and cash to be used alternatively for depositors' claims and demands for currency (Gorton and Mullineaux 1987). So clearinghouses' loan certificates served as a *temporary liquidity medium* to transfer cash away from sound and liquid banks in surplus, toward illiquid or financially distressed banks to help them survive banking panics or sudden periods of illiquidity and deposit claims (Timberlake 1984). Borrowing bank members were charged interest rates varying from 6 to 10 percent, and they were also required to present acceptable collateral to be discounted by the clearinghouse (Gorton and Mullineaux 1987, 463). These loan certificates served mainly as *temporizing devices* promoting the efficient reallocation and recycling of transitory liquidity and elasticity throughout the banking system (Timberlake 1984, 9). They were then promptly extracted (withdrawn) from the banking system when the panic and the sudden demand for liquidity ceased (Cannon 1910). As banking panics and rumors subsided, the loan certificates were retired from the system as banks redeemed their collateral securities (Timberlake 1984).

The fact that illiquid borrowing bank members paid lending banks interest rates encouraged reserve-abundant bank members to "share" their liquidity and concomitantly discouraged reserve-deficient banks from borrowing more frequently than necessary (Yue and Ingram 2012). Hence, the clearinghouse system "provided a selective incentive for banks to contribute to collective solvency, and to refrain from threatening that solvency. Serving as a credit intermediary [coordinator], the clearing house enabled a more efficient use of resources [liquidity] during panics, when banks [usually] hoarded money" (Yue and Ingram 2012, 16). Throughout this clearinghouse credit coordination procedure, "banks with stronger reserve positions loaned to those who felt deficient in reserves—a procedure that anticipated the contemporary federal funds market" (Timberlake 1984, 4). Hence, in this ex post manner, the NYCHA served as a factual, ad hoc, and private lender of last resort whenever necessary (Timberlake 1984, 8).

After the first issue of clearinghouse loan certificates during the panic of 1857, they were issued in every subsequent financial panic up until 1914 (Gorton and Mullineaux 1987). The certificates became prominent throughout the US clearinghouses due to their successful employment in subsiding the tide of banking panics and indiscriminate bank runs (Yue, Luo, and Ingram 2009). Specifically, before the establishment of the Federal Reserve System in late 1913, the NYCHA issued loan certificates eight times during financial panics, without losing even a single dollar in the rescuing process (Gilpin and Wallace 1904).

The NYCHA's lender of last resort practices became prominent, and most local clearinghouses around the United States began to imitate them. Moreover, this system allowed NYCHA member banks to have *lower* failure rates, as compared to unregulated nonmember banks, because of their collective reduced probabilities of indiscriminate bank runs (Yue, Luo, and Ingram 2009). During banking panics, the NYCHA operated a vertical and small-scale capital market that allocated liquidity and financial resources by nonmarket, hierarchical (albeit private) means in order to safeguard the reputational banking commons and for private banks' collective benefit. When financial panics subsided, the clearinghouse reverted toward its more horizontal and limited organizational structure (Gorton and Mullineaux 1987, 466).

Consequently, US clearinghouses in general, and the NYCHA in particular, clearly possessed a great deal of (delegated) control over bank members in times of financial panics. They also substantially "regulated" banks' behavior during acute banking panics (Gorton and Mullineaux 1987, 464). Despite NYCHA only rescuing its own bank members in distress, its credible efforts at dampening waves of banking panics also generated positive reputational externalities throughout the banking system and generally throughout financial markets, allowing the entire New York commercial banking population to flourish (Yue and Ingram 2012). This evidences that contestable networks of clearinghouses have been an important cooperative and bottom-up element in polycentric banking systems in successfully self-governing the challenges of bank runs and the reputational banking commons. Indeed, Cannon (1910) concluded that the loan certificates were "one of the finest examples the country has ever seen of the ability of the people when left to themselves to devise impromptu measures for their own relief" (Cannon 1910, 96).

Finally, it is relevant to acknowledge that this aforementioned and specific way of dealing ex post with banking panics is not the only way polycentric forms of banking can successfully govern the threat of indiscriminate bank runs when they materialize. Throughout history, clearinghouse systems have never operated alone (isolated), nor within an institutional and financial "vacuum" (Dowd 1994; Paniagua 2017). As E. Ostrom's (2010, 653) "design principles" suggest, the general efficacy and resilience of polycentric systems at self-governing collective challenges depend also on nested enterprises and broader sets of legal and political institutions that support them. Consequently, resilient "governance activities are organized in multiple nested layers" (E. Ostrom 2010, 653). Similarly, in regards to polycentric banking and clearinghouses, their effectiveness at self-governing bank runs *partly* depends also on a wider set of nested and overlapping banking activities, banking contracts, legal procedures, and other complementary legal and economic institutions (Paniagua 2017; Salter and Tarko 2018).

For example, different polycentric banking arrangements have utilized a combination of decentralized measures and services to deal with bank runs in a more multifaceted and polycentric (nested) manner. For instance, the eighteenth-century Scottish banking system at various times utilized a complementary set of ex post tools such as option clauses (temporary banking suspensions of deposit convertibility), enforceable legal systems of both liquidation procedures and of unlimited liability (or of extended liability regimes) for banking shareholders, and clearinghouse arrangements in order to coordinate interbank lending and emergency financial transactions to threatened banks (Goodspeed 2016; White 1995 [1984]).

All of these alternative banking measures and services have usually been historically provided concomitantly, at different institutional scales, and in a decentralized-nested manner; this importantly reduces also (perhaps even entirely excludes) the institutional need for a strong and monocentric provision of ex post LOLR liquidity services (Goodspeed 2016; Gorton and Mullineaux 1987). Actually, extended and unlimited liability regimes of banks' shareholders "are ways to 'bail-in' funds. This solves the same problem as a lender of last resort, but without the problems of moral hazard" (Salter and Tarko 2018, 10). In other words, in addition to the aforementioned legal and liquidation processes, these alternative, ex post, and contractual run-proofing devices greatly complement the other ex ante LOLR monitoring and regulatory services that polycentric banking regimes provide at different levels of complexity. Consequently, this polycentric and nested manner of providing heterogeneous, yet complementary, ex ante and ex post aspects of the LOLR bundle of services make it far less necessary to have a single and dominant institutionalized center providing large amounts of last resort liquidity and emergency lending.

CONCLUDING REMARKS

It has been argued that contestable clearinghouses could be able to successfully govern bank runs and liquidity shortages since they provide information about bank members and group confidence, as well as govern the reputational commons by various explored governance functions—delivered in the form of *club goods*. This prevents the insolvency of a few banks from spreading into a systemic and chaotic banking panic. In parallel to the reviewed historical evidence on banking and clearinghouses, the polycentric banking properties and measures explained in this chapter suggest that (contra Goodhart) self-regulation and nonmonocentric forms of banking could solve problems related to informational asymmetries, the coproduction of confidence, and the "reputational banking commons" that lie at the core of self-fulfilling banking panics (Diamond and Dybvig 1983).

Consequently, this chapter has also argued that polycentric forms of banking could be capable of governing bank runs and providing LOLR services without necessarily relying on a single dominant center for monetary decision-making. Thus, cooperative and nonmonocentric forms of providing those crucial banking services and governance could be feasible and effective within competitive banking structures that promote the general principles of polycentricity as outlined by V. Ostrom (1972, 1991).

Finally, this chapter has argued that polycentric banking systems could be effective and resilient at managing and self-governing the banking reputational commons. It had formed these arguments with historical evidence reviewing the crucial role of clearinghouses and other complementary banking and legal tools that have effectively subsided waves of panics and bank runs. By borrowing from the Ostroms' self-governing vision about the social order, this chapter has contended that central banks could be neither essential nor preferable to polycentric alternatives for overcoming bank runs and other crucial banking challenges (Paniagua 2017). Moreover, the plausible polycentric provision of LOLR services and governance (regulatory) activities, organized in multiple and nested levels, indicate that banking stability could be achieved without a definite center of banking power and without governments providing also deposit insurance or acting as lenders of last resort. The historical evidence and the Ostroms' oeuvre suggest that central banks are far from being the only institutional arrangement that can govern successfully collective banking challenges and attain banking stability.

REFERENCES

Aligica, P.D., and P.J. Boettke. 2009. *Challenging Institutional Analysis and Development: The Bloomington School*. New York: Routledge.

Beckworth, D., ed. 2012. *Boom and Bust Banking: The Causes and Cures of the Great Recession*. Oakland: Independent Institute.

Bordo, M. 1990. "The Lender of Last Resort: Alternative Views and Historical Experience." Federal Reserve Bank of Richmond *Economic Review* 76 (1): 18–29.

Bullard, J. 2010. "Three Lessons for Monetary Policy from the Panic of 2008." Federal Reserve Bank of St. Louis *Review*, 92 (3): 155–163.

Cannon, J. 1910. *Clearing Houses*. U.S. National Monetary Commission. Washington: Government Printing Office.

Diamond, D.W., and P.H. Dybvig. 1983. "Bank Runs, Deposit Insurance, and Liquidity." *Journal of Political Economy* 91 (3): 401–419.

Dowd, K. 1994. "Competitive Banking, Banker's Clubs, and Bank Regulation." *Journal of Money, Credit, and Banking* 26 (2): 289–308.

Gilpin, W., and H. Wallace. 1904. *New York Clearing House Association, 1854-1906*. Whitefish, MT: Kessinger Publishing.

Goodhart, C. 1987. "Why do Banks need a Central Bank?" *Oxford Economic Papers* 39: 75–89.

———. 1988. *The Evolution of Central Banks*. Cambridge: MIT University Press.

Goodspeed, T. 2016. *Legislating Instability: Adam Smith, Free Banking, and the Financial Crisis of 1772*. Cambridge: Harvard University Press.

Gorton, G. 1988. "Banking Panics and Business Cycles." *Oxford Economic Papers* 40 (4): 751–781.

———. 2010. *Slapped by the Invisible Hand: The Panic of 2007*. New York: Oxford University Press.

Gorton, G., and D.J. Mullineaux. 1987. "The Joint Production of Confidence: Endogenous Regulation and Nineteenth Century Commercial-Bank Clearinghouses." *Journal of Money, Credit, and Banking* 19 (4): 457–468.

Hetzel, R. 2012. *The Great Recession: Market Failure or Policy Failure?* Cambridge: Cambridge University Press.

Lake, W. 1947. "The End of the Suffolk System." *Journal of Economic History* 7: 182–207.

Ostrom, E. 1990. *Governing the Commons: The Evolution of Institutions for Collective Action*. Cambridge: Cambridge University Press.

———. 2005. *Understanding Institutional Diversity*. Princeton: Princeton University Press.

———. 2010. "Beyond Markets and States: Polycentric Governance of Complex Economic Systems." *American Economic Review* 100 (3): 641–672.

Ostrom, V. 1972. "Polycentricity." Workshop Working Paper Series No. 2204, Workshop in Political Theory and Policy Analysis, Presented at the Annual Meeting of the American Political Science Association, September 5–9.

———. 1991. "Polycentricity: The Structural Basis of Self-Governing Systems." In *The Meaning of American Federalism: Constituting a Self-Governing Society*, edited by Vincent Ostrom, 223–244. San Francisco: ICS Press.

Ostrom, V., and E. Ostrom. 1977. "Public Goods and Public Choices." Published in *Alternatives for Delivering Public Services: Toward Improved Performance*, edited by E.S. Savas, 7–49. Boulder, CO: Westview Press.

Paniagua, P. 2016. "The Stability Properties of Monetary Constitutions." *Journal des Economistes et des Etudes Humaines* 22 (2): 113–138.

———. 2017. "The Institutional Rationale of Central Banking Reconsidered." *Constitutional Political Economy* 28 (3): 231–256.

Salter, A. 2016. "Robust Political Economy and the Lender of Last Resort." *Journal of Financial Services Research* 50 (1): 1–27.

Salter, A., and V. Tarko. 2018. "Governing the Banking System: An Assessment of Resilience Based on Elinor Ostrom's Design Principles." *Journal of Institutional Economics* 15 (3): 505–519.

Schwartz, A.J. 1993. "Are Central Banks Necessary?" *Critical Review* 7 (2–3): 355–370.

Selgin, G., and L.H. White. 1999. "A Fiscal Theory of Government's Role in Money." *Economic Inquiry* 3 (1): 154–165.

Selgin, G., W.D. Lastrapes, and L.H. White. 2012. "Has the Feed been a Failure?" *Journal of Macroeconomics* 34 (3): 569–596.

Sumner, S. 2012. "How Nominal GDP Targeting Could Have Prevented the Crash of 2008." Published in *Boom and Bust Banking: The Causes and Cures of the Great Recession*, edited by David Beckworth. Oakland: Independent Institute.

Tarko, V. 2017. *Elinor Ostrom: An Intellectual Biography*. New York: Rowman and Littlefield International.

Timberlake, R.H. Jr. 1984. "The Central Banking Role of Clearinghouse Associations." *Journal of Money, Credit, and Banking* 16 (1): 1–16.

Trivoli, G. 1979. *The Suffolk Bank: A Study of a Free-Enterprise Clearing System*. London: The Adam Smith Institute.

White, L.H. [1984] 1995. *Free Banking in Britain: Theory, Experience, and Debate, 1800-1845* (2nd edition). London: Institute of Economic Affairs.

———. 1989. *Competition and Currency: Essays on Free Banking and Money*. New York: New York University Press.

Yue, L., J. Luo, and P. Ingram. 2009. "The Strength of a Weak Institution: Clearing House, Federal Reserve, and Manhattan Banks." *Best Paper Proceedings of the Academy of Management Meeting*. Chicago.

Yue, L., and P. Ingram. 2012. "Industry Self-regulation as a Solution to the Reputation Commons Problem: The Case of the New York Clearing House Association." Published in *The Oxford Handbook of Corporate Reputation,* edited by Pollock and Barnett. Oxford: Oxford University Press.

Chapter 6

The Political Economy of the European Union

An Exploration of EU Institutions and Governance from the Perspective of Polycentrism

Jan P. Vogler

Elinor and Vincent Ostrom have made many significant contributions to political economy, including Elinor's famous work on the "tragedy of the commons" (Ostrom 1990, 1999).[1] However, this chapter focuses on another key aspect of their work: the theory of *polycentric governance* (Ostrom 1972, 2009, 2010a, 2010b; Ostrom, Tiebout, and Warren 1961). I apply this framework to the European Union (EU)—a case that has received relatively little attention from theorists of polycentrism. Accordingly, the key research question is: To what extent does Ostromian polycentrism allow us to appropriately describe, categorize, and analyze the EU's institutions and governance?

Originally, polycentrism was developed to evaluate the provision of public goods in metropolitan areas, that is, conglomerates of towns and cities that are economically and socially interdependent (Ostrom, Tiebout, and Warren 1961; McGinnis 1999; Aligica and Tarko 2012, 240–244). However, its insights may go far beyond the local and regional levels. Indeed, considering the significant horizontal and vertical decentralization of decision-making authority in the EU, its structures have several features that echo polycentric principles. Consisting of a large number of member states, political power is distributed in several ways.[2] First, the authority of central EU institutions is dispersed among multiple entities, many of which represent the interests of lower-level governmental units ("subunits"). Second, the provision of public goods and services takes place at different administrative levels—including central EU institutions as well as national, regional, and local governments.

Additionally, responsibilities are often overlapping between political entities (Benz 2015; Trondal 2010; Wessels 2003). Similarly, significant externalities and spillover effects from political, social, and economic developments create incentives for formal and informal regulatory collaboration across borders, including in areas in which supranational solutions are not feasible (Boin, Ekengren, and Rhinard 2013, Ch. 4; Eberlein and Grande 2005). Finally, despite frequent claims that the EU is an overly centralized system, many critical decisions are taken in a deliberative process (Puetter 2012, 2014), in which individual member states (and sometimes even regional governments) have joint influence on the outcome. The European Council—a hybrid institution that connects subunits and centralized structures—exemplifies the principles of collaboration, coordination, and deliberation across multiple levels.

This chapter discusses the above claims in detail and illustrates them with reference to two specific cases. It is structured as follows. First, to establish a background against which we can compare polycentrism, I provide an overview of the literature on EU governance. Then, I introduce the Ostromian theory of polycentric governance. Based on this framework, the EU's institutional structures are evaluated. In my discussion, I argue that polycentrism is an appropriate analytical tool for describing European institutions. In the following sections, I analyze two specific cases of governance "in action," namely the EU's responses to (1) the European sovereign debt crisis 2010–2012 and (2) the refugee crisis 2015–2016. I chose these major political-economic challenges because in comparable, extreme situations, decision-making power in governance systems is often centralized. Accordingly, one of my goals is to assess if polycentric governance was maintained. Indeed, I find that, in both crises, it was only a mix of decentralized *and* centralized policy initiatives that ultimately provided effective responses to the unfolding situation, highlighting the polycentric character of EU governance. Finally, I discuss both theoretical and practical aspects of "leaving a polycentric system," referring primarily to Brexit. Similar to metropolitan areas, significant social and economic interdependence between subunits in polycentric systems makes leaving very costly for any one of them.

THE LITERATURE ON EUROPEAN GOVERNANCE AND THE UTILITY OF A POLYCENTRIC PERSPECTIVE

Several important theories of EU governance exist. Hooghe and Marks' theory of multilevel governance already closely resembles aspects of the Ostromian perspective (Hooghe and Marks 2001; Marks, Hooghe, and Blank 1996). They analyze the EU's complex, multitiered system of decision-making and the influence of subnational units within it. From their perspective, considering significant economic and social interdependence across units, such a multitiered decision-making structure becomes necessary to effectively address political challenges. Hooghe and Marks also generally illustrate how political authority is reallocated away from national governments to supranational entities and to regional/local governments.[3] Thus, they are concerned with the reallocation of political power and the reasons behind these developments. Interestingly, while the earlier works of Hooghe and Marks on European integration do not include specific references to the insights of the Ostroms, some articles they published later on the general issue of multilevel governance directly take the Ostromian account of polycentrism into consideration (Hooghe and Marks 2003). This circumstance highlights the potential utility of polycentrism with respect to the EU.

Other contributions on EU governance that have parallels to the framework of polycentric governance include the following: an edited volume by Sabel and Zeitlin (2010) on "experimentalist governance" (the recursive development, comparison, and sharing of best practices in policymaking and implementation)[4]; an article by Börzel (2010) on the coexistence of multiple distinct forms of governance in the EU, ranging from market organization to hierarchical structures; a book by Héritier, Knill, and Mingers (2011) on the bidirectional influence of states and the EU in the policymaking process; a collection of essays on innovative multilevel governance in different substantive areas (Tömmel and Verdun 2009); and contributions by Gerstenberg and Sabel (2002) as well as Cohen and Sabel (1997) that develop the idea of "directly-deliberative polyarchy"—with a focus on local learning, self-governance, and policy experimentation in the EU.[5] However, none of these contributions is built on the Ostromian framework of polycentrism. This is also true for Von Bogdandy (2000) and Jachtenfuchs (1995), although they use the term "polycentric" when describing the EU.[6]

In light of the vast existing literature on EU governance and integration, which additional benefits could a perspective based on polycentric theory provide? First and foremost, given the framework's known utility in terms of analyzing governance structures in metropolitan areas, the perspective of polycentrism may provide a highly useful background against which to evaluate the EU's effectiveness at delivering public goods, managing internal administrative relations, and responding to major political-economic challenges. The theory is particularly strong at assessing complex, overlapping political authority structures as well as multitiered decision-making processes, making it potentially highly suitable for a comprehensive analysis of the EU's system of governance. Its theoretical openness in terms of accounting for vast array of governmental and nongovernmental actors means that it enjoys a greater flexibility than several existing EU theories that are centered on—or restricted to—specific types of entities.[7] Moreover, its partial focus on (economic) *efficiency* in the delivery of public goods and other aspects of governance also clearly distinguishes it from most other EU-centered theories, where this aspect only plays a negligible role.[8] Finally, the analysis presented in this chapter could also help to refine and expand the *original* Ostromian theoretical framework in a way that it becomes more broadly applicable to different types of political-economic systems, meaning a contribution to the creation of an overarching governance theory.

Similar to the argument presented here, a recent volume by van Zeben and Bobić (2019) attempts to apply polycentrism to the EU. In multiple chapters, different authors analyze subsidiarity, the internal market, and access to justice in the EU among a number of topics. There are three ways in which the chapter at hand distinguishes itself from this previous contribution. First, this chapter represents a more concise application of polycentric governance theory to the EU than a book-length volume. Second, the set of criteria developed here has overlaps with—but also several differences to—the framework laid out by van Zeben and Bobić (2019, esp. 27).[9] Accordingly, I evaluate a slightly different range of principles. Finally, the contribution at hand has a significant emphasis on polycentric governance "in action," analyzing the EU's response to two major political-economic, as well as Brexit—topics that are not as prominently featured in the volume by van Zeben and Bobić.

How is it possible to think of the EU as a polycentric system (i.e., one with many decision-making centers and overlapping authorities), if there are numerous EU opponents who claim that it is the exact opposite? Indeed, by its critics, the EU is often characterized as a giant and unresponsive bureaucratic apparatus that concentrates enormous decision-making power in central institutions and negates national and local self-determination.[10] For instance, British journalist McKinstry (2016) calls the EU "a federalist monster that will not stop until nations are abolished." Similarly, Bakshian (2016) suggests that the EU has "a single giant bureaucracy and an imposed-from-above social model."

There are multiple responses to these perspectives. First, the EU actually has a comparatively small bureaucracy, which is highly effective considering its size. For instance, in direct comparison with the US federal civil service, the number of EU bureaucrats is marginal.[11] Second, De Bruycker (2019) shows that European policies are very responsive to public opinion when there is a high level of politicization.[12] Furthermore, I will show throughout this chapter that national, regional, and local governments either retain substantial decision-making authority or even gain influence on central EU processes and institutions. This is true with respect to both the supply of public goods and addressing larger political-economic challenges. Accordingly, the claim that the EU is a giant and unresponsive bureaucratic apparatus—aiming to impose its centralized will on the member states—is at best misleading and at worst entirely inaccurate.[13]

THE THEORY OF POLYCENTRISM

The term "polycentric" had already been used by a number of scholars before Elinor and Vincent Ostrom began to develop their framework. However, the Ostroms made a major contribution in advancing the term's theoretical utility by establishing systematic criteria and applying them to practical challenges of metropolitan governance. If the Ostromian framework of polycentric governance had to be condensed into a single sentence, the tentative summary by Aligica and Tarko (2012, 237) is useful. They define a polycentric system as one "of many decision centers having limited and autonomous prerogatives and operating under an overarching set of rules."

While this definition is a good starting point, for this chapter I would like to lay out six separate and specific criteria of polycentric political-economic systems that are based on several key contributions by the Ostroms (Ostrom 1972, 2009, 2010a, 2010b; Ostrom, Tiebout, and Warren 1961).[14] Following these works, six essential features related to polycentric systems of governance can be identified:

1. They consist of multiple political-administrative units, facing both *shared* and *individual* (economic, social, and environmental) conditions and challenges.
2. Each of these political units has some degree of autonomous decision-making power.
3. There are overlapping responsibilities and authorities between the administrative units (often mirroring issues and challenges which can spill over between them due to economic, social, or environmental interdependence).
4. All units operate under a shared framework of rules.
5. There is no single, unified chief executive, which has the ultimate political authority.
6. The governance of some issues is pooled at the central level, while the governance of other issues remains decentralized. The pooling versus decentralization of responsibilities is primarily guided by the criteria of (1) responsiveness toward citizens and (2) efficiency concerns.

The opposite of a polycentric system of governance is a political system "with a single dominant center for making decisions" (Ostrom, Tiebout, and Warren 1961, 831), meaning the highest possible level of centralization. In such a system, the power of the executive branch is unified in one institution.

Additionally, nonpolycentric (or *monocentric*) systems can be characterized by (strictly) hierarchical relationships between the upper and lower units of government, with a top-down system of decision-making (cf. Ostrom, Tiebout, and Warren 1961, esp. 837–838). In a perfect hierarchical command system, higher-level political units are able to *overrule* decisions taken by subunits, even if the latter have some discretionary power in a specific policy area.

One key disadvantage of fully monocentric political-economic systems is that, regardless of efficiency and responsiveness concerns, they unify and centralize all decision-making authority in a single political entity. While there might be certain aspects of governance that can be efficiently executed at the highest administrative level, it is unlikely that *all* aspects of governance are most efficiently organized by a single central authority.

How can we distinguish polycentrism from federalism? First, "federalism" is a broader and less theoretically dense term, primarily describing the existence of multiple layers of government. While federal systems can be polycentric in character, they are not necessarily so. For example, in federal systems, there could theoretically be a single, unified chief executive at the central level. Furthermore, the pooling versus decentralization of responsibilities for providing public goods may not be guided by efficiency or responsiveness concerns. Accordingly, the concept of polycentrism shares some similarities with federalism but simultaneously goes far beyond it.

To summarize, polycentric systems have a number of key characteristics. Most importantly, multiple political-administrative entities—operating under a shared framework of rules—have autonomous decision-making power, overlapping responsibilities and authorities, without being subject to a hierarchical command structure. Even though there may be a chief executive, this chief executive should not concentrate political power in a single institution. The delegation of responsibility to the central level is guided by the principles of responsiveness toward citizens and efficiency.

IS THE EU A POLYCENTRIC SYSTEM? AN ANALYSIS OF INSTITUTIONAL STRUCTURES AND THE DIVISION OF POLITICAL AUTHORITY

The EU's Core Executive and Legislative Institutions

Considering their significance, a discussion of the EU's core executive and legislative institutions at the central level may be the best point of departure for an institutional analysis against the background of polycentric theory. These institutions are the following:

1. The European Council consists of the heads of state or government. It is at the very center of the institutional framework and has authority over the broad trajectory of the political union as a whole. However, it is usually not focused on the practical implementation of the broad goals that it sets (McCormick 2014, 76–79; Olsen and McCormick, 2018, Ch. 9).
2. The European Commission leads the European civil service and has the responsibility to turn the Council's decisions into concrete policy proposals (McCormick 2014, 7984; Olsen and McCormick 2018, Ch). Even though it typically does not set broad policy goals, its power in policy development and implementation is substantial.[15]
3. The European Parliament is the lower house of the EU's legislature and consists of directly elected representatives from all member countries. Among others, they approve or reject the policy proposals of the Commission (McCormick 2014, 87–90; Olsen and McCormick 2018, Ch. 7).
4. The Council of the EU can be seen as the upper house of the EU's legislature and consists of ministers from the EU member states. The Council of the EU, too, is involved in the Union's legislative process (McCormick 2014, 84–87; Olsen and McCormick 2018, Ch. 6).

Considering that there are multiple different institutions that share political power at the EU's central level—especially the European Council and the Commission (as a form of *dual executive*)—we cannot speak of a single or unified chief executive. Instead, from a horizontal perspective, multiple centers of decision-making authority and administration exist within the executive branch of European governance; and they have both unique and shared responsibilities (McCormick 2014, 94–95; Trondal 2010). While the European Council determines the EU's broad trajectory, the Commission has much more leeway over the practical implementation of these decisions. Thus, there is effective practical decentralization in decision-making authority among multiple political entities.[16]

Furthermore, the central EU institutions are also not in a perfect hierarchical relationship with national governments. Instead, there is a delicate balance of power between national governments and EU institutions. This balance of power is best reflected by the European Council, which allows individual member states to directly voice their interests at the central level and will be discussed in more detail below.

The Centralized Governance of Economic Exchange and Other Policy Areas

Critics of the EU may claim that the consolidation of certain functions at the central level violates the ideals of polycentrism, but these arguments deserve further scrutiny. First, as shown above, even at the central level, decision-making power is dispersed among multiple units and not concentrated in a single political entity. Moreover, the EU primarily organizes markets, economic exchange, and other issues of strong transnational character[17] (such as agricultural and environmental policy) at the central level (Olsen and McCormick 2018, Ch. 12, 14).[18]

Do these circumstances necessarily violate the principles of polycentrism? One can argue that the centralized organization of certain aspects of European governance—first and foremost internal and external relationships of economic exchange (Spolaore 2015, 14–15)—does not directly contradict polycentrism. Indeed, as Ostrom, Tiebout, and Warren (1961, 837–838) write, some aspects of governance may be most appropriately organized at the central level. Specifically, Ostrom and Ostrom (1977, 18) state that, in order to have a flourishing market economy, "nonmarket decision-making arrangements" are necessary and governments should provide the foundations for economic activity, "including a common medium of exchange, common weights and measures, roads, and so forth." In a similar fashion, by organizing market exchange at the central level, the EU allows for common standards in these and other economic institutions. This centralized organization enables the free movement of goods, services, capital, and labor across national boundaries, which leads to a closer-to-optimal geographic allocation of productive assets and human capital.

Moreover, Spolaore (2015) suggests that the centralization of governmental authorities can have two positive effects: (1) the exploitation of economies of scale and (2) the internalization of (cross-unit) externalities.[19] Both advantages directly speak to the important efficiency criterion of polycentrism. Accordingly, the unification of decision-making power in certain areas does not necessarily contradict polycentrism. On the contrary, the Ostroms consider centralization appropriate in certain areas and even *essential* to the optimal functioning of market exchange.

It is important to note that even the politicians and bureaucrats who work for the central EU institutions generally represent their country's national interest to some extent. For instance, as a study by van Esch and de Jong (2019) shows, even in one of the most coherent epistemic communities of the EU—the central bankers of the European Central Bank (ECB)—national culture was more dominant than EU socialization when it came to decision-making in the European sovereign debt crisis.

The European Council as a Carrier of Polycentric Principles

From the perspective of polycentric governance, the European Council deserves special attention. Formally, it is an organization at the central (EU) level and participates in the governance of the EU as a whole. However, it consists of the heads of state and government of the subunits (individual member states). Accordingly, the members clearly have a representative function, and can voice the interests of the political subunits they lead.

Moreover, the modus operandi of the European Council is usually deliberative and its members generally attempt to find the widest political consensus (Puetter 2012, 2014). This method of governing is the opposite of hierarchical top-down processes, in which a unified chief executive makes decisions without the participation of or regard to the interests of subunits. Additionally, the European Council's rotating presidency gives even the governments of smaller EU states possibilities to influence the policy agenda and steer central policies in a specific direction (Bunse 2009).

In short, the European Council embodies key principles of polycentric governance for two primary reasons. First, it allows for the active representation of the subunits' political interests. Moreover, its internal decision-making processes are not hierarchical, but instead deliberative and focused on the achievement of the widest possible consensus.[20]

The Role of Regional and Local Governments in the EU

According to the Ostroms, in the ideal polycentric system, local and regional governments retain influence over policy areas that are most efficiently organized by them. This also allows them to uphold the ideal of local self-governance. Therefore, we must ask: Do local governments lose a substantial amount of their responsibilities in the provision of public goods and/or political power through European integration?

This is not necessarily the case, because EU integration usually leads to the delegation of power away from *national* governments and *national* parliaments to EU institutions (Auel and Höing 2014, 1184; Hooghe and Marks 2003; Jensen, Koop, and Tatham 2014).[21] It is much less common for subnational governments to give up authority over aspects of governance that had been under local or regional control. The policy areas over which the EU has gained authority are typically those over which individual local entities did not have influence in the first place, meaning that integration has not severely reduced their political autonomy.

Furthermore, the pooling of some resources and responsibilities at the central level does not mean that lower-level governments are in a direct hierarchical relationship with central EU institutions, which would mean a severe loss of relative power. On the contrary, Hooghe and Marks (2001) argue that, in many countries, regional governments have actually *gained* relative political power through the EU integration process.[22] Not only might the process have weakened the relative power of national governments, but subnational governments have gained a multiplicity of channels to influence policies.

Additionally, through the allocation of financial aid as part of EU cohesion policy, regional and local governments have enjoyed administrative power over substantial amounts of incoming funds, which may have led to increases in local state capacity (Charasz and Vogler 2019). All in all, the dominant perspective in EU studies is that regional and local actors have not significantly diminished in political power through European integration, but they might have actually gained influence.

Considering the Ostroms' emphasis on varying local conditions in polycentric systems (Ostrom 1972; Ostrom, Tiebout, and Warren 1961), they would likely agree that it makes sense for many responsibilities to remain in the hands of regional and local governments. Indeed, the EU is a community of extremely heterogeneous local conditions, especially different languages and cultures. Many additional factors, including climate, wealth, geography, expectations toward public services,[23] and so on differ vastly across Europe. If the EU had to deal with all of these challenges at the central level—where the aggregation and use of information is most likely imperfect (c.f. Hayek 1945; Ostrom, Tiebout, and Warren 1961, 837–838; Rodrik 2007, Ch. 5)—its central institutions would be completely overloaded. Furthermore, national governments have the responsibility of implementing EU-wide policies, giving them limited (but helpful) discretion in concrete execution and timing.

Polycentrism	European Union
Multiple political-administrative units, with *shared* and *individual* conditions/challenges	28 EU member states (+ regional & local governments), shared and individual conditions/challenges
Political units have some degree of autonomous decision-making power	Member states retain decision-making power in many policy areas, subnational governments often gain additional political power
Overlapping responsibilities and authorities between the administrative units	Significant overlaps in authority through (1) deliberative intergovernmental bodies, (2) cross-border policy coordination
Shared framework of rules	Shared general framework of policy-making + common rules in many other areas (e.g., economic exchange)
No single, unified chief executive with ultimate political authority	Significant dispersion of political power among several political entities + strong representation of subunits
Mix of pooling versus decentralization of responsibilities, based on efficiency/responsiveness	Policies organized at multiple levels: Central level most concerned with policy areas with cross-border spillovers or greatest benefits of centralization (economy, environment)

Figure 6.1 Features of Polycentric Systems of Governance and the EU.

Summary

My analysis of various aspects of the EU's institutional structures suggests that they indeed mirror fundamental polycentric principles. They are (1) characterized by significant horizontal and vertical decentralization of political power, (2) do not constitute a perfect hierarchical command relationship between the center and lower-level units, (3) pool responsibilities primarily in areas where it is appropriate to do so (given the criteria laid out by the Ostroms), (4) provide national governments with strong representation in the deliberative body of the European Council, and (5) operate under a shared framework of rules, but also leave significant autonomy for the provision of public services in the hands of local and regional governments (which each face vastly different social and economic conditions). Accordingly, the EU's institutional framework can generally be described and analyzed from the perspective of polycentrism. Figure 6.1 provides an additional systematic comparison of the characteristics of the EU.

POLYCENTRIC GOVERNANCE "IN ACTION" (I): THE SOVEREIGN DEBT CRISIS AND THE EU'S RESPONSE, 2010–2012

While an analysis of the EU's institutional framework can provide crucial insights regarding its compatibility with polycentrism, any such examination should be complemented by an investigation of the polycentric system "in action," that is, when facing a concrete major problem that might be solved through coordination among different entities. With respect to polycentric systems, an analysis of crisis responses would be particularly interesting because a typical reaction to crises is the centralization of decision-making power (Raudla et al. 2015).[24] Therefore, such a study can give us insights into whether at least some aspects of polycentric governance are maintained in critical situations. Ultimately, crises could also lead to the disintegration—or failure—of polycentric systems (Schimmelfennig 2018b, 969–970). Accordingly, they offer suitable testing grounds for these systems' resilience.

Because of their significance, two historical situations appear particularly appropriate for such an analysis: (1) the European sovereign debt crisis 2010–2012 and (2) the refugee crisis 2015–2016. In accordance with polycentrism, I will pay most attention to the interplay between subunits and central actors and institutions. Are policies initiated by *different* actors, that is, a mixture of subunits and central actors? Is decision-making in crises entirely centralized or is it dispersed among multiple entities at different levels of the EU's administrative hierarchy?

Background of the Sovereign Debt Crisis

The global financial crisis started in 2007–2008 and led to the collapse of major banks by severely restricting liquidity on financial markets around the world (Brunnermeier 2009). These conditions made it increasingly difficult for many governments to refinance their debt and thereby revealed that their overall debt levels were unsustainable. With their economies facing a prolonged downturn, the ability of a number of European governments to repay their creditors came into doubt as well.[25] Given economic interdependence and the common currency of European Monetary Union (EMU) member countries, the bankruptcy of a single state could have triggered negative and uncontrollable spillover effects, including a breakdown of the entire Eurozone (Biermann et al. 2019, 251; Buti and Carnot 2012, 905; De Grauwe 2013b, esp. 163–164; Lane 2012; Mody and Sandri 2012; Verdun 2015, 223–224; Schimmelfennig 2018b, 975, 983; Wasserfallen et al. 2019, 5).

Decentralized Decision-Making: Policy Initiatives of Subunits

When the described events took place, the EU had no formal mechanisms to address a problem of this unprecedented magnitude (Gocaj and Meunier 2013, 240–242; Niemann and Ioannou 2015, 203; Schimmelfennig 2018b, 970, 976; Verdun 2015, 219). This made quick innovation—a possible strength of polycentric systems—imperative. Different actors can formulate distinct policy proposals, some of which might be more effective than others at addressing the effects of the crisis.

It is important to note that a significant economic asymmetry exists between the member states of the Eurozone. The Northern and Western European states—particularly Germany—have more robust economies, which were less severely affected by the financial crisis (Finke and Bailer 2019, 110–111; Ioannou, Leblond, and Niemann 2015, 165; Laffan 2017; Schimmelfennig 2015, 182–185, 2018b, 977–978). Moreover, their public finances were more balanced, with a smaller debt-to-GDP ratio, especially compared to Greece—the state that would experience the most significant problems (Buti and Carnot 2012; OECD 2019).[26]

However, the worsening financial situations of several Southern European economies put increasing pressure on the Northern and Western Eurozone members to support the struggling members. Although Germany had been hesitant to intervene in the severe crisis of the Greek economy—initially treating it as a Greek domestic matter (Bulmer 2014, 1253)—when the crisis intensified, the German government began to assume a leadership role.[27] As one of the initial steps, in March 2010, Germany and France issued a joint statement that proposed to complement IMF financing for struggling

European economies with bilateral loans. Subsequently, the European finance ministers made a similar public proposal (Gocaj and Meunier 2013, 241–242).

However, this could ultimately not stabilize financial markets and the situation in May 2010 deteriorated to the point that further action needed to be taken urgently (Gocaj and Meunier 2013, 243–244). With Germany and France having the greatest influence on the process, representatives of the EU member states came together in the European Council to decide on a practical solution. The result of those meetings was the creation of a new financial entity in May/June 2010: the European Financial Stability Facility (EFSF) (Finke and Bailer 2019; Gocaj and Meunier 2013; Niemann and Ioannou 2015; Verdun 2015). Its purpose was to give European countries with economic difficulties access to financial markets. To perform this function, the EFSF itself could borrow money—backed up with financial guarantees at the level of €440 billion—and transfer funds to member states in need (Boin, Ekengren, and Rhinard 2013, 127; Verdun 2015, 226). The guarantees came from the more stable European economies (Biermann et al. 2019, 251–252), with the biggest absolute guarantors being Germany and France and the highest per capita guarantees coming from Luxembourg.

The EFSF was under strict supervision by individual member countries, particularly (as indicated above) the key contributors Germany and France, and should primarily be seen as an intergovernmental institution, not an EU-level institution (Gocaj and Meunier 2013, 245–247; Niemann and Ioannou 2015, 209). The importance of the member states is underscored by the fact that the EFSF (and an increase in its lending capacity) required the approval of national parliaments (Closa and Maatsch 2014).[28]

Although initially successful at containing the worst consequences of the crisis, because of the EFSF's ad hoc and short-term character, a longer-term, more institutionalized solution seemed desirable. Consequently, in 2011, the European Stability Mechanism (ESM) was created and eventually took over the responsibilities of the EFSF. The ESM had a higher lending capacity and was intended to be a long-term institutionalized solution (Boin, Ekengren, and Rhinard 2013, 128; Gocaj and Meunier 2013, 247–248; Ioannou, Leblond, and Niemann 2015, 160; Niemann and Ioannou 2015).[29]

Despite the EFSF's ad hoc and short-term character, it succeeded in its primary objective of stabilizing the financial situation of several struggling economies and preventing major spillovers to the rest of the Eurozone. Even though a long and rocky way to recovery followed, Greece and other threatened economies were eventually able to overcome the perilous situation they had faced in 2010.

As we would expect from a polycentric system, at several points during the crisis, individual member states and the European Council coordinated with the ECB and the Commission, for example in terms of providing support to Greece (Gocaj and Meunier 2013, 241). This vertical coordination between political entities at different levels of the hierarchy is a cornerstone of polycentric governance "in action."

Centralized Decision-Making: Policy Initiatives of Supranational Institutions

Polycentric systems often do not only consist of subunits. Instead, following polycentrism, we would expect that some responsibilities—in cases in which this can be efficiently organized—are located at the central level (Ostrom, Tiebout, and Warren 1961, 837–838). In the case of the Eurozone, because it is a common currency area, the key responsibilities for setting monetary policy are necessarily found in a centralized institution. In the EMU's case, this central institution is the ECB.

When the sovereign debt crisis accelerated in 2010, policy initiatives were not limited to the individual member states or the hybrid institution of the European Council. For instance, the Commission suggested to create its own stabilization fund, which would have had the ability to sell bonds financially backed by Eurozone members (Gocaj and Meunier 2013, 243). Even though this proposal did not materialize, it shows that initiatives come from many different actors in the EU's governance structure.[30] Moreover, the Commission did successfully initiate the first in a series of fiscal rule reforms: the so-called six-pack, a collection of six policies aimed at facilitating long-term budgetary stability (Ioannou, Leblond, and Niemann 2015, 160–162; Laffan and Schlosser 2016; Menz and Smith 2013, 197–198; Schild 2013, 31; Verdun 2015, 220, 228–229).

Most importantly, Europe's Central Bank—the ECB—engaged in a wide variety of measures aimed at restoring bank liquidity and allowing struggling governments to refinance their debt (Trichet, 2010). For example, the ECB lowered interest rates, promoted the idea of a banking union (to stabilize European banks), and even bought government bonds (Lane 2012; Niemann and Ioannou 2015, 210–211). The ECB's most decisive step was taken in September 2012, when it announced that it would provide unlimited financial support to struggling Eurozone economies.[31] While this action had been unprecedented and caused concern among some European leaders, the ECB's unique move helped to swiftly stabilize the situation on the financial markets (De Grauwe 2013a). These centralized mechanisms provided substantial help, but ultimately only the *combination* with initiatives by individual member states and the European Council (in the form of the EFSF and the ESM) could address the crisis in a comprehensive form.

In general, when analyzing the European sovereign debt crisis, we observe polycentric governance "in action." The centralized institution of the ECB was able to address some aspects of the crisis, but only cooperation and coordination with and among the subunits (especially the creation of the EFSF) were able to stabilize the situation more comprehensively. No single side of EU governance—neither national governments nor the Commission—was able to handle all aspects of the crisis alone (cf. Finke and Bailer 2019, 130). Thus, polycentric governance was possible and indeed *necessary*. While the recovery from the sovereign debt crisis took many years, the E(M)U eventually stabilized and established a comprehensive regulatory framework aimed at preventing similar crises (Biermann et al. 2019, esp. 250; Boin, Ekengren, and Rhinard 2013, 128; Börzel and Risse 2018, 83–84; Finke and Bailer 2019, 110; Schimmelfennig 2018b, 970, 979–980; Târlea et al. 2019, 25).[32] This underscores that the crisis was not only a challenge to but also an *opportunity* for the advancement of joint economic governance (Tosun, Wetzel and Zapryanova 2014).

In addition to reworking the conditions of the Stability and Growth Pact (SGP) and further intergovernmental agreements regarding economic stability, an important part of the process that followed was the establishment of a banking union (Ioannou, Leblond, and Niemann 2015, 160–164; Laffan and Schlosser 2016). According to Nielsen and Smeets (2018), this was a collaborative process that involved the joint efforts of both supranational institutions and national governments—as one would expect from a polycentric system.[33]

There are many additional aspects of polycentric economic governance in the EU that could be explored in the future. In particular, new studies could consider the level of public support that EU institutions and policies receive. In this respect, the work by Kuhn and Stoeckel (2014) highlights differences between support for EU economic governance and European integration more broadly.

Does Crisis Leadership by Individual Subunits Violate the Principles of Polycentric Governance?

One might argue that the financial crisis was not a case of polycentric governance because Germany—a single subunit—played such an important role in terms of policy initiatives (Bulmer 2014; Bulmer and Paterson 2013; Laffan 2017, 140). However, there are several arguments in favor of the utility of a polycentric perspective:

1. Even though Germany's initiative and financial contribution were crucial to solving the crisis, it depended on the cooperation of several other

European states, most importantly France, in coordinating the response and stemming the financial burden of stabilization (Degner and Leuffen 2019; Schild 2013; Schoeller 2018).

2. Similarly, without the decisive actions by the ECB—a key central institution—the crisis might have intensified (or at a minimum continued).
3. From a long-term perspective, only the active cooperation of national governments most heavily affected by the crisis can bring a sustainable solution and prevent similar future situations. For example, part of the EU's support for Greece were required structural reforms that can only be implemented at the national level.[34]

Accordingly, while Germany might have played a leadership role, only coordination and collaboration across different levels of the EU's institutional hierarchy could effectively address the crisis. No single subunit would be able to solve a crisis of this magnitude on its own. Furthermore, none of the criteria about polycentric systems of governance laid out above were violated by the actions taken in the European sovereign debt crisis. Even in "perfect" polycentric systems of governance, individual subunits may play a more prominent role because they might be affected by conditions to a completely different extent and may also have vastly different institutional or economic capabilities. These asymmetries are a core aspect of metropolitan areas as well, meaning that by no means do they contradict polycentrism.

POLYCENTRIC GOVERNANCE "IN ACTION" (II): THE REFUGEE CRISIS AND THE EU'S RESPONSE 2015–2016

Background of the Refugee Crisis

The combination of the Arab Spring, which started in late 2010, and the Syrian Civil War, which started in 2011, created strong incentives for a large number of people in North Africa and the Middle East to seek a better life in Europe. In 2015, there was an escalation of refugee flows, resulting in numerous humanitarian disasters, especially in the Mediterranean, which put enormous pressures on the EU to find a coordinated policy response (Buonanno 2017; Carrera et al. 2015, 1; Niemann and Zaun 2018, 3–4; Schimmelfennig 2018b, 975–976).

Decentralized Decision-Making: Policy Initiatives and Actions of Subunits

Because of the disproportionately high burden placed on Southern European countries by the massive migrant flows that reached new heights in 2015

(Buonanno 2017, 113; Schimmelfennig 2018b, 976–978), we would expect them to act early to address the crisis. Indeed, following a major humanitarian disaster in the Mediterranean in April 2015, Italian prime minister Matteo Renzi demanded an emergency EU summit (BBC 2015). Moreover, the acceptance of migrants by EU member states had been completely voluntary up to this point. But the governments of the Northern and Western European states knew that, for many migrants, their country would be the final destination (Schimmelfennig 2018b, 978). Therefore, German Chancellor Angela Merkel proposed to distribute refugees among member countries—potentially in accordance with a quota system, assigning a specific share of refugees to each country. She asked for cooperation and compliance of other member states with this proposal. However, resistance against the proposal quickly came from Britain and several Eastern European countries (The Guardian 2015b; Zaun 2018).

Initiatives like these came from subunits because the central EU institutions faced criticism that they had not dealt with the situation sufficiently up to this point (Washington Post 2015). At first glance, the fact that the political leaders of subunits took these initiatives could seem like a weakness of the EU's system of governance. But from a theoretical perspective, the possibility for subunits to initiate policymaking is a key strength of polycentric organization. In line with Ostromian polycentrism, some subunits may face individual challenges and conditions. Their greater awareness of local or regional circumstances makes them a much better point for initiating policy than central institutions that may not fully comprehend the situation "on the ground."

The result of these calls for action was an emergency summit of the European Council on April 23, 2015 (Carrera et al. 2015, 2–3), which led to a declaration that read in part: "We have . . . decided to strengthen our presence at sea, to fight the traffickers, to prevent illegal migration flows and to reinforce internal solidarity and responsibility" (European Council 2015). Beyond this formal declaration, factual support in the form of more funding was provided to several initiatives, specifically an additional €120 million in emergency funding for border patrols. Furthermore, subunits of the EU governance structure—the governments of Germany, Ireland, and the United Kingdom—sent (military) ships to the Mediterranean to support sea patrol missions (Reuters 2015; The Guardian 2015a).

This episode clearly illustrates the *interplay* between the subunits and governance structures at the central level. While individual member states initiated the process and called for the emergency summit, this summit took place in the European Council. Moreover, it is important to recall that—considering its composition (with the leaders of all subunits being represented there) and the blocking power of subunits—the European Council is a hybrid institution between a completely centralized and a decentralized decision-making mechanism. Finally, the practical implementation, which followed the meeting, was partially organized by central institutions and partially implemented by subunits.

Additional steps were taken later in 2015. For instance, in October, European leaders agreed to set up camps for 100,000 refugees (*New York Times* 2015b). This helped to further stabilize the situation in countries that did not have adequate facilities to house the large number of incoming migrants.

Beyond these policies passed at the central level, several measures were also implemented by individual subunits. Given the struggles that EU border states had with the large number of migrants, the German government decided on August 25, 2015, to no longer send Syrian refugees back to the first EU country they had entered (Deutsche Welle 2017; Niemann and Zaun 2018, 4). Furthermore, on September 4, 2015, Germany began to accept refugees from Hungary (Deutsche Welle 2017). Although minor by themselves, these individual steps constituted additional measures toward addressing the crisis in a comprehensive form.

Centralized Decision-Making: Policy Initiatives of Supranational Institutions

On April 20, 2015, around the time when individual member states began to call for action, the Commission, too, proposed a ten-point plan to address the crisis. Most importantly, it advanced the idea of reinforcing border and sea patrols (European Commission 2015c). In mid-May, this initial plan was complemented by a more comprehensive agenda authored by the European Commission (2015b).[35] Among others, this agenda included proposals for targeting smuggler networks, relocating incoming refugees, and cooperation with countries outside of the EU. But the members of the Commission knew that they could not solve the problem by themselves. Instead, as indicated in the previous section, the cooperation of subunit leaders was needed to comprehensively address the crisis.[36]

Ultimately, even further internal EU measures, such as the establishment of emergency hotspots in the most severely affected areas, did not fully succeed in dealing with the massive inflows of migrants (Niemann and Zaun 2018, 5–8). As a large number of Syrian refugees came through Turkey before entering Europe, the EU needed Turkey's cooperation. Thus, in October 2015, the EU and Turkey created a joint action plan to deal with the migration crisis (Buonanno 2017, 120; European Commission 2015a; Deutsche Welle 2017). Most importantly, on March 18, 2016, the two political entities agreed on the following: Turkey offered to host a large number of migrants and the EU provided financial aid for housing and supporting them (Biermann et al.

2019, 259; Buonanno 2017, 120–121; Deutsche Welle 2018; Niemann and Zaun 2018, 8–9; Rygiel, Baban, and Ilcan 2016).[37]

In general, in the refugee crisis, too, we observe an interplay and interdependence between central institutions and subunits, which is a key feature of polycentrism. The crisis could not be solved by entities at one level alone, but instead required the initiative and actions of multiple entities. No side—whether central institutions or the subunits—was able to impose its will on the other, and the subunits have to find cooperative solutions. Accordingly, while the EU's response to the refugee crisis certainly was not flawless, the analysis at hand provides further support for the perspective that the EU is a polycentric system.

Problems of Polycentric Governance in the Refugee Crisis—Systemic Flaws?

Despite the general successes described above, the polycentric governance of the EU in response to the migrant crisis was not flawless. There were many internal frictions between the subunits themselves as well as between central structures and subunits (cf. Scipioni 2018; Niemann and Zaun 2018).[38]

The most important problem might have been that, from the beginning, many Eastern European countries were against taking in refugees through a formal quota system, even though they were asked to host only a relatively small number compared to some other states (*New York Times* 2015a; Niemann and Zaun 2018, 6–7; Zaun 2018). There were several possible reasons for this position. In 2015–2016, many governments in Eastern Europe were headed by populist right-wing parties, which are often strongly opposed to immigration (Börzel and Risse 2018, esp. 100–101). Additionally, many Eastern European states faced low "migratory pressures," making them less interested in finding a common political solution (Biermann et al. 2019; Zaun 2018).

As this example shows, the polycentric system of EU governance often relies on the voluntary cooperation of individual member states.[39] Considering the absence of solidarity by several Eastern European states, the system of formal quotas had to be abandoned eventually. Instead, as requested by the Visegrad Group (consisting of Poland, Hungary, Czechia, and Slovakia), a "system" of so-called flexible solidarity was implemented, which simply refers to a distribution based entirely on voluntary cooperation by member states (EURACTIV 2016). This meant that an important aspect of the EU's goals was not achieved: The institutionalization of sharing responsibilities among the member states was insufficient (Scipioni 2018; Zaun 2018).[40]

In light of these circumstances, it appcars that polycentric governance was not entirely effective. However, it can be argued that the observed problems were not necessarily a failure of polycentric governance because there might not have been any other viable course of action. Specifically, if some form of coercion had been used in the distribution of refugees, it could also have led to a further escalation of the refugee crisis, resulting in a major *political* (constitutional) crisis of the EU itself. Even though flexible solidarity meant disproportionate costs to some subunits—that is, those countries and regions that were willing or forced by circumstances to take in the refugees—there was not a complete lack of solidarity between EU member states. Instead, a large number of countries did eventually voluntarily participate.[41] While polycentric governance might have shortcomings, the EU experienced neither (1) a broader escalation of the crisis into a constitutional crisis nor (2) an overall failure in terms of addressing the refugee situation.

LEAVING A POLYCENTRIC SYSTEM? THEORETICAL CONSIDERATIONS AND THE PRACTICAL CASE OF BREXIT 2016–2019

Theoretical Considerations

A specific form of "exit" from a polycentric system finds attention in the work on polycentric governance: citizens exiting one subunit of a polycentric subsystem in order to move to another subunit that they perceive to provide superior public goods or services. This type of exit has been characterized as "vote with their feet" (Oakerson and Parks 1988; Ostrom 1972). However, another type of exit, namely the ability of *entire* political-economic subunits to leave a polycentric system, is not a prominent point of discussion in the original framework of polycentrism as developed by Elinor and Vincent Ostrom (Ostrom 1972, 2010a, 2010b; Ostrom, Tiebout, and Warren 1961).

The reason for why this may not have been prominently featured in the original works of the Ostroms is that metropolitan areas and their members are often strongly tied together through factual economic, social, and/or environmental interdependence (cf. Hewings and Parr 2007; Hewings, Okuyama, and Sonis 2001). Even towns that are at the (geographic) periphery of a metropolitan area may have multifaceted and deep social and economic ties to the center.[42]

Considering these circumstances of social and economic interdependence, two primary possibilities for "leaving" a polycentric system exist:

1. Leaving the formal system of governance, that is, cutting *political-administrative* ties to the other units, while maintaining *economic* and *social* interaction.

2. Leaving the system of governance *and* cutting social and economic ties, that is, (re-)establishing barriers to economic and social exchange with the other entities.

Depending on the degree of economic and social interaction, cutting all ties with a broader polycentric system (as in the second scenario) could inflict severe economic and/or social costs on the population of the leaving unit. Therefore, the first option of merely leaving the system of governance appears to be the option with fewer costs. But leaving the system of governance comes with other (potentially severe) downsides: The subunit that decides to leave no longer has the same level of influence on how economic and social interaction within the system is regulated. Even if a minor town or city in a large metropolitan area only has small influence on overall policy outcomes, completely leaving the polycentric system of governance will further reduce this influence to zero. In light of this discussion, it becomes clear that, in most polycentric systems of governance analyzed by the Ostroms (metropolitan areas), social and economic ties between units run so deep that the costs of exiting the system are prohibitive.

The Practical Case of Brexit 2016–2019

On June 23, 2016, a popular vote took place in the United Kingdom. The government asked its citizens if they wanted to leave or remain in the EU. Even though polls had predicted a slight victory of the "remain" camp, the "leave" camp ultimately won with a narrow margin (Bulmer and Quaglia 2018, 1089; Clarke et al. 2017; Gamble 2018, esp. 1215–1217).[43] As a consequence, since March 2017 there have been negotiations between the EU and the UK government regarding the conditions under which the United Kingdom will leave the EU's system of governance (Bulmer and Quaglia 2018; Gamble 2018). As of the time of this chapter's writing (July 2019), the negotiations have not been successfully completed yet—the United Kingdom's politicians are struggling internally with the specific conditions of the Brexit deal. Nevertheless, it is possible to consider the history of the matter up to this point.

Throughout the negotiations, major tensions arose regarding the issues of access to the European single market and the maintenance of freedom of movement for EU and UK citizens. The position of the United Kingdom's government under Prime Minister Theresa May evolved over time, but the government developed an interest in maintaining some form of access to the European market while reestablishing control over migration into Britain. This position was rejected by representatives of the EU who did not want to assign the same level of market access to nonmember states that did not fully participate in the other "European freedoms," especially the free movement of citizens (Bulmer and Quaglia 2018, 1092–1094; Gamble 2018, 1218–1222; Schimmelfennig 2018a, esp. 1166–1169).

These negotiations were difficult and full of tensions because restricting either the movement of goods or the movement of people would inflict severe economic and/or social costs on both the United Kingdom and the EU. While the United Kingdom was more willing to accept the (primarily) "social" costs of restricting freedom of movement, the EU was more willing to accept the (primarily) "economic" costs of excluding the United Kingdom from the common market (to maintain the integrity of the European freedoms) if no compromise could be reached.[44]

Overall, these problems mirror the issues that any subunit (in the form of a city or a town) would have when attempting to leave a metropolitan area. The United Kingdom has been a member of the European (Economic) Community since 1973 and nearly five decades of trade and the movement of people have created significant economic and social ties that cannot be cut easily. Thus, wide-ranging economic and social interdependence constitutes severe costs of a complete exit (cf. Gamble 2018, 1227–1228; Jensen and Snaith 2016, 1306–1307). The potentially most negative economic consequences for the United Kingdom could be in the area of financial services because Brexit might make other EU states increasingly attractive to actors from this sector (Howarth and Quaglia 2018).

Accordingly, in line with the previous theoretical discussion regarding the options for leaving a metropolitan area polycentric system, the United Kingdom has two possible courses of action for leaving the EU's polycentric system:

1. The United Kingdom can maintain existing economic and/or social arrangements (market access, mostly free movement of citizens) and merely leave the formal governance structures of the EU. This outcome would lead to some costs on the United Kingdom's part, because it would permanently undermine its ability to participate in the EU's system of governance.
2. Alternatively, the United Kingdom can leave the EU without an agreement (the so-called hard Brexit), meaning that barriers to trade and to the movement of people would immediately be reestablished. Given the level of economic (and social) interdependence between the EU and the United Kingdom, this course of action would likely inflict severe costs on the populations of both entities.

In short, even though metropolitan areas and supranational organizations are different in many respects, subunits may face similar challenges when attempting to *leave* them. Ultimately, the likely reason for why a polycentric system of governance was created (or joined) in the first place is the significant economic and social advantages associated with such a move. While the severe costs of leaving a polycentric system do not make exiting impossible, they make it an extremely costly course of action. A much less costly alternative may exist in the form of "differentiated integration," which refers to the selective participation in certain areas of common governance without being subject to all regulations or policies (Andersen and Sitter 2006; De Neve 2007; Schimmelfennig, Leuffen, and Rittberger 2015; Schimmelfennig and Winzen 2019).[45]

SUMMARY AND CONCLUSION

Elinor and Vincent Ostrom's framework of polycentric governance is a fundamentally important part of their contribution to political economy. Although its original focus was on metropolitan areas, many of its insights may be applicable to other types of systems. While the EU has sometimes been described as "polycentric" in the past (Jachtenfuchs 1995; Von Bogdandy 2000), few scholars have considered applying the Ostromian framework of polycentric governance to the EU—and the first such attempts have been very recent (van Zeben and Bobić 2019). Accordingly, in this chapter, I have laid out key criteria of Ostromian polycentrism and then evaluated the EU's institutional structures and governance against them. My finding is that the EU indeed has many characteristics that are compatible with polycentric governance, especially substantial vertical and horizontal decentralization of power. The European Council in particular has been found to echo several principles of polycentric governance due to its deliberative character.[46] The perspective of polycentrism has multiple strengths that jointly distinguish it from most other theories of EU governance: (1) its high level of suitability for the analysis of multitiered, complex institutional structures, (2) its theoretical openness and flexibility in terms of integrating many different actors, including nongovernmental entities,[47] and (3) its focus on the (economic) *efficiency* and *responsiveness* of public goods provision and political decision-making processes.

In addition, I have investigated polycentric governance "in action" by analyzing two different crises that the EU faced in the last decade: (1) the European sovereign debt crisis and (2) the refugee crisis. In both these crises—as one would expect from a polycentric system of governance—it was only a *combination* of initiatives by subunits (i.e., member states), hybrid institutions that represent actors at multiple levels (such as the European Council), and central institutions (such as the ECB and the Commission) that was able to comprehensively address the situation. Even though polycentric solutions were not perfect, the EU was mostly successful at containing the crises' negative consequences. In this respect, it is important to emphasize that—just like democracies—polycentric systems may sometimes be slow and produce outcomes that are not as comprehensive as in a completely centralized system. But there could also be advantages to slower, more deliberative processes, because they take the interests of all parties into account and often prevent outcomes that would completely contradict the interests of some subunits.

How can we go forward from here? Since this chapter has already demonstrated that polycentrism is an appropriate framework to analyze the EU's crisis governance, an ideal avenue for future research would be a comparative account of the explanatory power of polycentrism versus other established EU governance theories.

Last but not least, I have addressed the important topic of "leaving a polycentric system" because some students of polycentrism might believe that subunits should be able to freely leave a polycentric system at will. Qualifying this perspective, the key insight of my discussion is that, neither in the case of metropolitan areas—which were the initial object of analysis in the Ostroms' work—nor in the case of the EU/Brexit, leaving a polycentric system of governance comes without substantial and sometimes prohibitive costs to the affected subunit. This is visible in the difficulty of the Brexit negotiations.

Building upon this chapter, future contributions could explore the relationship between polycentrism and competitive governance (Breton 1998; Weingast 1995). The federal system of the United States is often considered a case that successfully combines elements of polycentric and competitive governance. In the EU, there certainly are some competitive pressures on national governments, too, but this competition might play out in a different way due to a higher degree of heterogeneity in languages, cultures, and socioeconomic conditions.

Moreover, in the future, the interplay of polycentric governance structures and electoral politics at the national and the European level could be analyzed. A study by Schneider (2013) on the Europeanization of national electoral politics would be a good starting point for such an endeavor. Another interesting question is how the internal polycentric structures of governance affect the EU's *external* relationships with its neighbors. Zaiotti (2007) already shows that the security culture of the EU has important implications for the relations with countries in its vicinity. Similarly, polycentric governance and the associated culture could affect these neighbors in unexpected ways.[48]

Finally, the essay by Scharpf (1988) about the possible downsides of involving subunits in central decision-making processes can be seen as contradicting some of the arguments made here.[49] A direct comparison of the merits of polycentrism versus Scharpf's framework would be of interest.

Thus, there are many possible ways in which future contributions can build upon this chapter and explore further aspects of polycentrism in the EU.

All in all, this chapter shows that arguments and findings from the theory of polycentric governance are by no means limited to metropolitan areas. Instead, the theory generated by the Ostroms may also serve as a framework for understanding and analyzing many other political-economic entities, including supranational forms of governance like the EU. Applications to a broad variety of additional political-economic systems should be considered in the future and could show us how much more explanatory power the theory of polycentric governance has.

NOTES

1. Helpful comments have been provided by Michael Bauer, Tanja Börzel, Mads Dagnis Jensen, Herbert Kitschelt, Gary Marks, Wayne Sandholtz, Frank Schimmelfennig, and Natascha Zaun. Moreover, I am grateful to the participants of seminars at the Adam Smith Fellowship research sequence.
2. An excellent overview of this topic is provided by Jensen, Koop, and Tatham (2014).
3. See also Jensen, Koop, and Tatham (2014).
4. On the closely related topic of learning in the EU, see Radaelli and Dunlop (2013).
5. The chapter by Gerstenberg and Sabel (2002) is included in a volume that deals with the general topic of "good governance" in the EU (Joerges and Dehousse, 2002). Further "classics" on EU governance more broadly are by Kohler-Koch and Eising (1999), Sandholtz and Sweet (1998), and Marks et al. (1996). Finally, on the political geography of the EU's legal governance, see Kelemen and Pavone (2018).
6. Moreover, several prominent theories of EU integration are related to issues of governance. Among them are (1) neofunctionalism (focused on economic interdependence and spillover effects) (Haas 1958; Rosamond 2005; Sandholtz and Sweet 2012; Sandholtz and Zysman 1989), (2) liberal intergovernmentalism (focused on the decisions of national governments) (Milward 1999; Moravcsik 1993, 2013), and (3) new institutionalism (focused on the creation, persistence, and path dependence of institutional arrangements) (Jupille and Caporaso 1999; Bulmer 1993; Bulmer 1998). For a recent overview of these theories, see Hooghe and Marks (2019).
7. This greater openness and flexibility may come at the price of less predictive power, however.
8. It is important to note that the claims of polycentric theory can be seen as—at least to some extent—contradicting arguments by Scharpf (1988) about how the participation of lower-level governments can lead to suboptimal policy outcomes. For recent work on the topic, see also Falkner (2011). From the perspective of polycentrism, however, the involvement of lower-level governments in decision-making processes can greatly improve the quality of policy outcomes by adjusting them to local needs and conditions.

9. For instance, van Zeben and Bobić (2019) place slightly more emphasis on self-governance, while this chapter places slightly more emphasis on interunit relationships and the division of power.

10. Ostrom, Tiebout, and Warren (1961, 831) would call such a system "gargantua."

11. While the US federal civil service has approximately 2.7 million employees (2013) (serving more than 300 million Americans) (US Office of Personnel Management (OPM), 2019), the EU central bureaucracy only has approximately 50,000 employees (2019) (serving more than 500 million Europeans) (European Union, 2019).

12. However, work by Pannico (2017) shows that national parties bear much responsibility for communicating EU-related issues to local populations.

13. Perceptions of the EU bureaucracy are often formed by heuristics—rather than precise knowledge or direct experiences with EU institutions (Vogler 2019a).

14. See also McGinnis (1999). The arguments made by Ostrom and Ostrom (1977) will also be relevant to my analysis.

15. For instance, Bauer and Becker (2014) show that the Commission plays a key role in the EU's economic governance. Moreover, on the Commission's hybrid character as a political, normative, *and* administrative body, see Grande and McCowan (2015).

16. Future contributions could provide a comparative analysis of bicameral governance in national settings and the EU's legislative process from the perspective of polycentrism. For example, the American system of governance has several parallels.

17. For instance, as Begg (2009) argues, the possibility of contagious financial crises puts demands on central EU institutions to provide supranational regulation in an area in which decentralized supervision alone may not be able to effectively contain spillover effects. See also Buti and Carnot (2012, 905–906).

18. For a historical overview of the EU's supranational responsibilities, see Börzel (2005).

19. It is important to note that Spolaore (2015) also points out that, the higher the degree of heterogeneity of preferences across subunits, the greater the trade-off between centralization (with its positive effects on the efficiency of governance) and decentralization.

20. It is important to note that these are only some aspects of governance compatible with polycentrism. As elaborated in the theoretical section, to meet all criteria of polycentric governance, several additional requirements have to be fulfilled.

21. For example, prior to European integration, economic regulation, monetary policies, product standards, and so on were typically organized at the national and not at the subnational level.

22. See also Marks, Hooghe, and Schakel (2008) and Jensen, Koop, and Tatham (2014).

23. For a discussion of the importance of such expectations, see Vogler (2019b).

24. For a critical discussion of this topic, see also 't Hart, Rosenthal and Kouzmin (1993).

25. This was visible in worsening credit ratings by major credit rating agencies (CRAs)—institutions on which many actors on financial markets rely and that played a major role in the crisis (Eijffinger 2012).

26. Two additional factors were constitutive of variation in the vulnerability to external financial shocks: (1) fundamental divergence in political-economic systems (Hall 2012, 2014; Johnston and Regan 2016) and (2) vast cross-country differences in the interconnectedness of financial sectors (Târlea et al. 2019).

27. On the underlying economic ideology of ordoliberalism and its consequences for economic governance, see Nedergaard and Snaith (2015).

28. On the general role of national parliaments in the EU, see Benz (2004) and Auel and Benz (2005).

29. On different national preferences regarding the ESM, see Finke and Bailer (2019, 123–126).

30. Despite this initiative by the Commission, Puetter (2012, 172–173) suggests that—relative to the European Council—the initial responses of the Commission were not very visible. Instead, the Commission's contribution took mostly place in the background. See also Boin, Ekengren, and Rhinard (2013, 126–127).

31. Previously, the ECB's president had already declared that they would do "whatever it takes" to calm financial markets (quoted in: Schimmelfennig 2018b, 985). See also Boin, Ekengren and Rhinard (2013, 2).

32. A critical perspective on whether the resulting regulatory framework is sufficient for this purpose is provided by Jones, Kelemen and Meunier (2016).

33. Similarly, Falkner (2016) also confirms that only a combined perspective—analyzing both interactions among national governments *and* the decisions of supranational institutions—can comprehensively explain postcrisis policymaking.

34. On the (hurdles to the) implementation of these policies, see Afonso, Zartaloudis, and Papadopoulos (2015) and Ladi (2014).

35. See also Buonanno (2017, 117).

36. It is important to note that key central institutions dealing with migration, such as Frontex (the European Border and Coast Guard Agency) and the European Asylum Support Office (EASO), were less politically powerful than their counterparts in economic governance, such as the ECB (Schimmelfennig 2018b, 970, 985). This also meant that the cooperation of subunits was of crucial importance.

37. Similar to the Eurozone crisis, Germany played an important role in the establishment of this agreement. Germany's dominant role has therefore also received criticism, with some perceiving it as "unilateral" in character (Zaun 2018, 56).

38. On the problems associated with the EU's response to the refugee crisis, see also Schimmelfennig (2018b, 980–982).

39. Nevertheless, the Commission—an institution that clearly represents the central level—began working on a policy proposal that would have led to fines for member states that refused to take in their quota of refugees (Deutsche Welle 2017).

40. On this issue, see also Carrera et al. (2015, 1).

41. On the general issue of solidarity in the EU, see also Trein (2019).

42. Even in cases in which commuters only constitute a weak link between a city center and suburbs, other cross-unit activities, such as consumer mobility or interfirm activity could be responsible for creating substantial economic interdependence (Shearmur and Motte 2009).

43. For a comparative perspective on the reasons for Brexit, see Carl, Dennison, and Evans (2019).

44. Note that there are also economic costs to restricting the movement of people, because labor (or human capital) is an important factor of production as well.

45. For a perspective on Brexit as a form of "differentiated disintegration," see Schimmelfennig (2018a).

46. While it is important to also highlight the hierarchical character of some EU governance processes as described by Börzel (2010), I have argued that polycentricity—and not hierarchy—is the *dominant* organizational principle structuring EU governance.

47. As indicated earlier, this strength may come at the cost of decreased predictive power.

48. For an overview of major contributions on EU foreign and security policy, see Krotz and Maher (2011).

49. See also Falkner (2011).

REFERENCES

Afonso, Alexandre, Sotirios Zartaloudis, and Yannis Papadopoulos. 2015. "How Party Linkages Shape Austerity Politics: Clientelism and Fiscal Adjustment in Greece and Portugal during the Eurozone Crisis." *Journal of European Public Policy* 22 (3): 315–334.

Aligica, Paul D., and Vlad Tarko. 2012. "Polycentricity: From Polanyi to Ostrom, and Beyond." *Governance* 25 (2): 237–262.

Andersen, Svein S., and Nick Sitter. 2006. "Differentiated Integration: What Is It and How Much Can the EU Accommodate?" *European Integration* 28 (4): 313–330.

Auel, Katrin, and Arthur Benz. 2005. "The Politics of Adaptation: The Europeanisation of National Parliamentary Systems." *The Journal of Legislative Studies* 11 (3–4): 372–393.

Auel, Katrin, and Oliver Höing. 2014. "Parliaments in the Euro Crisis: Can the Losers of Integration Still Fight Back?" *JCMS: Journal of Common Market Studies* 52 (6): 1184–1193.

Bakshian, Aram Jr. 2016. "Brexit: Bad for Europe, Good for Britain." Accessed July 11, 2019. https://nationalinterest.org/feature/brexit-bad-europe-good-britain-16729.

Bauer, Michael W. and Stefan Becker. 2014. "The Unexpected Winner of the Crisis: The European Commission's Strengthened Role in Economic Governance." *Journal of European Integration* 36 (3): 213–229.

BBC. 2015. "Mediterranean Migrant Deaths: EU Faces Renewed Pressure." Accessed March 24, 2019. https://www.bbc.com/news/world-europe-32376082.

Begg, Iain. 2009. "Regulation and Supervision of Financial Intermediaries in the EU: The Aftermath of the Financial Crisis." *JCMS: Journal of Common Market Studies* 47 (5):1107–1128.

Benz, Arthur. 2004. "Path-dependent Institutions and Strategic Veto Players: National Parliaments in the European Union." *West European Politics* 27 (5): 875–900.

———. 2015. "European Public Administration as a Multilevel Administration: A Conceptual Framework." In *The Palgrave Handbook of the European Administrative System*, edited by Michael Bauer and Jarle Trondal, 31–47. Houndmills/Basingstoke: Palgrave Macmillan.

Biermann, Felix, Nina Guérin, Stefan Jagdhuber, Berthold Rittberger, and Moritz Weiss. 2019. "Political (Non-) Reform in the Euro Crisis and the Refugee Crisis: A Liberal Intergovernmentalist Explanation." *Journal of European Public Policy* 26 (2): 246–266.

Boin, Arjen, Magnus Ekengren and Mark Rhinard. 2013. *The European Union as Crisis Manager: Patterns and Prospects*. Cambridge: Cambridge University Press.

Börzel, Tanja A. 2005. "Mind the Gap! European Integration between Level and Scope." *Journal of European Public Policy* 12 (2): 217–236.

———. 2010. "European Governance: Negotiation and Competition in the Shadow of Hierarchy." *JCMS: Journal of Common Market Studies* 48 (2): 191–219.

Börzel, Tanja A., and Thomas Risse. 2018. "From the Euro to the Schengen Crises: European Integration Theories, Politicization, and Identity Politics." *Journal of European Public Policy* 25 (1): 83–108.

Breton, Albert. 1998. *Competitive Governments: An Economic Theory of Politics and Public Finance*. Cambridge: Cambridge University Press.

Brunnermeier, Markus K. 2009. "Deciphering the Liquidity and Credit Crunch 2007-2008." *Journal of Economic Perspectives* 23 (1): 77–100.

Bulmer, Simon J. 1993. "The Governance of the European Union: A New Institutionalist Approach." *Journal of Public Policy* 13 (4): 351–380.

———. 1998. "New Institutionalism and the Governance of the Single European Market." *Journal of European Public Policy* 5 (3): 365–386.

———. 2014. "Germany and the Eurozone Crisis: Between Hegemony and Domestic Politics." *West European Politics* 37 (6): 1244–1263.

Bulmer, Simon, and William E. Paterson. 2013. "Germany as the EU's Reluctant Hegemon? Of Economic Strength and Political Constraints." *Journal of European Public Policy* 20 (10): 1387–1405.

Bulmer, Simon, and Lucia Quaglia. 2018. "The Politics and Economics of Brexit." *Journal of European Public Policy* 25 (8): 1089–1098.

Bunse, Simone. 2009. *Small States and EU Governance: Leadership through the Council Presidency*. Houndmills/Basingstoke: Palgrave Macmillan.

Buonanno, Laurie. 2017. "The European Migration Crisis." In *The European Union in Crisis*, edited by Desmond Dinan, Neill Nugent, and William E. Paterson, 100–129. London: Palgrave Macmillan.

Buti, Marco, and Nicolas Carnot. 2012. "The EMU Debt Crisis: Early Lessons and Reforms." *JCMS: Journal of Common Market Studies* 50 (6): 899–911.

Carl, Noah, James Dennison, and Geoffrey Evans. 2019. "European but not European Enough: An Explanation for Brexit." *European Union Politics* 20 (2): 282–304.

Carrera, Sergio, Steven Blockmans, Daniel Gros, and Elspeth Guild. 2015. "The EU's Response to the Refugee Crisis: Taking Stock and Setting Policy Priorities." *CEPS [Centre for European Policy Studies] Essay* (20/16).

Charasz, Paweł, and Jan P. Vogler. 2019. "The External and Internal Determinants of State Capacity: The Impact of EU Funding on Local Government Capabilities." Working Paper. Accessed July 30, 2019. http://www.janvogler.net/Determinants_State_Capacity.pdf.

Clarke, Harold D., Matthew J. Goodwin, Matthew Goodwin, and Paul Whiteley. 2017. *Brexit. Why Britain Voted to Leave the European Union*. Cambridge: Cambridge University Press.

Closa, Carlos, and Aleksandra Maatsch. 2014. "In a Spirit of Solidarity? Justifying the European Financial Stability Facility (EFSF) in National Parliamentary Debates." *JCMS: Journal of Common Market Studies* 52 (4): 826–842.

Cohen, Joshua, and Charles Sabel. 1997. "Directly-Deliberative Polyarchy." *European Law Journal* 3 (4): 313–342.

De Bruycker, Iskander. 2019. "Democratically Deficient, yet Responsive? How Politicization Facilitates Responsiveness in the European Union." *Journal of European Public Policy*, 1–19.

De Grauwe, Paul. 2013a. "The European Central Bank as Lender of Last Resort in the Government Bond Markets." *CESifo Economic Studies* 59 (3): 520–535.

———. 2013b. "The Political Economy of the Euro." *Annual Review of Political Science* 16: 153–170.

De Neve, Jan-Emmanuel. 2007. "The European Onion? How Differentiated Integration Is Reshaping the EU." *Journal of European Integration* 29 (4): 503–521.

Degner, Hanno, and Dirk Leuffen. 2019. "Franco-German Cooperation and the Rescuing of the Eurozone." *European Union Politics* 20 (1): 89–108.

Deutsche Welle. 2017. "Two Years since Germany Opened Its Borders to Refugees: A Chronology." Accessed March 24, 2019. https://www.dw.com/en/two-years-since-germany-opened-its-borders-to-refugees-a-chronology/a-40327634.

———. 2018. "The EU-Turkey Refugee Agreement: A Review." Accessed March 24, 2019. https://www.dw.com/en/the-eu-turkey-refugee-agreement-a-review/a-43028295.

Eberlein, Burkard, and Edgar Grande. 2005. "Beyond Delegation: Transnational Regulatory Regimes and the EU Regulatory State." *Journal of European Public Policy* 12 (1): 89–112.

Eijffinger, Sylvester C.W. 2012. "Rating Agencies: Role and Influence of their Sovereign Credit Risk Assessment in the Eurozone." *JCMS: Journal of Common Market Studies* 50 (6): 912–921.

EURACTIV. 2016. "'Flexible Solidarity' becomes New Tool in Response to Refugee Crisis." Accessed March 24, 2019. https://www.euractiv.com/section/justice-home-affairs/news/flexible-solidarity-becomes-new-tool-in-response-to-refugee-crisis/.

European Commission. 2015a. "EU-Turkey Joint Action Plan." Accessed July 19, 2019. http://europa.eu/rapid/press-release_MEMO-15-5860_en.htm.

———. 2015b. "European Agenda on Migration." Accessed March 24, 2019. https://ec.europa.eu/ home-affairs/what-we-do/policies/european-agenda-migration_en.

———. 2015c. "Joint Foreign and Home Affairs Council: Ten Point Action Plan on Migration." Accessed March 24, 2019. http://europa.eu/rapid/press-release IP-15-4813_en.htm.

European Council. 2015. "Special Meeting of the European Council, 23 April 2015 — Statement." Accessed March 24, 2019. https://www.consilium.europa.eu/en/press/press-releases/2015/04/23/special-euco-statement/.

European Union. 2019. "EU Administration – Staff, Languages and Location." Accessed July 11, 2019. https://europa.eu/european-union/about-eu/figures/administration-en.

Falkner, Gerda. 2011. *The EU's Decision Traps: Comparing Policies*. Oxford: Oxford University Press.

———. 2016. "The EU's Current Crisis and Its Policy Effects: Research Design and Comparative Findings." *Journal of European Integration* 38 (3): 219–235.

Finke, Daniel, and Stefanie Bailer. 2019. "Crisis Bargaining in the European Union: Formal Rules or Market Pressure?" *European Union Politics* 20 (1): 109–133.

Gamble, Andrew. 2018. "Taking Back Control: The Political Implications of Brexit." *Journal of European Public Policy* 25 (8): 1215–1232.

Gerstenberg, Oliver, and Charles F. Sabel. 2002. "Directly-Deliberative Polyarchy: An Institutional Ideal for Europe?" In *Good Governance in Europe's Integrated Market*, edited by Christian Joerges and Renaud Dehousse, 289–341. Oxford: Oxford University Press.

Gocaj, Ledina, and Sophie Meunier. 2013. "Time Will Tell: The EFSF, the ESM, and the Euro Crisis." *Journal of European Integration* 35 (3): 239–253.

Grande, Edgar, and Martina McCowan. 2015. "The Two Logics of Multilevel Administration in the EU." In *The Palgrave Handbook of the European Administrative System*, edited by Michael Bauer and Jarle Trondal, 48–65. Houndmills/Basingstoke: Palgrave Macmillan.

Haas, Ernst B. 1958. *The Uniting of Europe: Political, Social, and Economic Forces, 1950-1957*. Stanford: Stanford University Press.

Hall, Peter A. 2012. "The Economics and Politics of the Euro Crisis." *German Politics* 21 (4): 355–371.

———. 2014. "Varieties of Capitalism and the Euro Crisis." *West European Politics* 37 (6): 1223–1243.

Hayek, Friedrich August. 1945. "The Use of Knowledge in Society." *The American Economic Review* 35 (4): 519–530.

Héritier, Adrienne, Christoph Knill, and Susanne Mingers. 2011. *Ringing the Changes in Europe: Regulatory Competition and the Transformation of the State. Britain, France, Germany*. Berlin, Germany: Walter de Gruyter.

Hewings, Geoffrey J.D., and John B. Parr. 2007. "Spatial Interdependence in a Metropolitan Setting." *Spatial Economic Analysis* 2 (1): 7–22.

Hewings, Geoffrey J.D., Yasuhide Okuyama, and Michael Sonis. 2001. "Economic Interdependence within the Chicago Metropolitan Area: A Miyazawa Analysis." *Journal of Regional Science* 41 (2): 195–217.

Hooghe, Liesbet, and Gary Marks. 2001. *Multi-level Governance and European Integration*. London: Rowman & Littlefield.

———. 2003. "Unraveling the Central State, but How? Types of Multi-level Governance." *American Political Science Review* 97 (2): 233–243.

———. 2019. "Grand Theories of European Integration in the Twenty-First Century." *Journal of European Public Policy* 26 (8): 1113–1133.

Howarth, David, and Lucia Quaglia. 2018. "Brexit and the Battle for Financial Services."*Journal of European Public Policy* 25 (8): 1118–1136.

Ioannou, Demosthenes, Patrick Leblond, and Arne Niemann. 2015. "European Integration and the Crisis: Practice and Theory." *Journal of European Public Policy* 22 (2): 155–176.

Jachtenfuchs, Markus. 1995. "Theoretical Perspectives on European Governance." *European Law Journal* 1 (2): 115–133.

Jensen, Mads Dagnis, Christel Koop, and Michaël Tatham. 2014. "Coping with Power Dispersion? Autonomy, Co-ordination and Control in Multilevel Systems." *Journal of European Public Policy* 21 (9): 1237–1254.

Jensen, Mads Dagnis, and Holly Snaith. 2016. "When Politics Prevails: The Political Economy of a Brexit." *Journal of European Public Policy* 23 (9): 1302–1310.

Joerges, Christian, and Renaud Dehousse. 2002. *Good Governance in Europe's Integrated Market*. Oxford: Oxford University Press.

Johnston, Alison, and Aidan Regan. 2016. "European Monetary Integration and the Incompatibility of National Varieties of Capitalism." *JCMS: Journal of Common Market Studies* 54 (2): 318–336.

Jones, Erik, R. Daniel Kelemen, and Sophie Meunier. 2016. "Failing Forward? The Euro Crisis and the Incomplete Nature of European Integration." *Comparative Political Studies* 49 (7): 1010–1034.

Jupille, Joseph, and James A. Caporaso. 1999. "Institutionalism and the European Union: Beyond International Relations and Comparative Politics." *Annual Review of Political Science* 2 (1): 429–444.

Kelemen, R. Daniel, and Tommaso Pavone. 2018. "The Political Geography of Legal Integration: Visualizing Institutional Change in the European Union." *World Politics* 70 (3): 358–397.

Kohler-Koch, Beate, and Rainer Eising. 1999. *The Transformation of Governance in the European Union*. New York: Routledge.

Krotz, Ulrich, and Richard Maher. 2011. "International Relations Theory and the Rise of European Foreign and Security Policy." *World Politics* 63 (3): 548–579.

Kuhn, Theresa, and Florian Stoeckel. 2014. "When European Integration becomes Costly: The Euro Crisis and Public Support for European Economic Governance." *Journal of European Public Policy* 21 (4): 624–641.

Ladi, Stella. 2014. "Austerity Politics and Administrative Reform: The Eurozone Crisis and Its Impact upon Greek Public Administration." *Comparative European Politics* 12 (2): 184–208.

Laffan, Brigid. 2017. "The Eurozone in Crisis: Core–Periphery Dynamics." In *The European Union in Crisis*, edited by Desmond Dinan, Neill Nugent, and William E. Paterson, 131–147. London: Palgrave Macmillan.

Laffan, Brigid, and Pierre Schlosser. 2016. "Public Finances in Europe: Fortifying EU Economic Governance in the Shadow of the Crisis." *Journal of European Integration* 38 (3): 237–249.

Lane, Philip R. 2012. "The European Sovereign Debt Crisis." *Journal of Economic Perspectives* 26 (3): 49–68.

Marks, Gary, Fritz W. Scharpf, Philippe C. Schmitter, and Wolfgang Streeck. 1996. *Governance in the European Union*. London: Sage.

Marks, Gary, Liesbet Hooghe, and Arjan H. Schakel. 2008. "Patterns of Regional Authority." *Regional and Federal Studies* 18 (2–3): 167–181.

Marks, Gary, Liesbet Hooghe, and Kermit Blank. 1996. "European Integration from the 1980s: State-Centric v. Multi-level Governance." *JCMS: Journal of Common Market Studies* 34 (3): 341–378.

McCormick, John. 2014. *Understanding the European Union: A Concise Introduction*. Houndmills/Basingstoke: Palgrave.

McGinnis, Michael Dean. 1999. *Polycentricity and Local Public Economies: Readings from the Workshop in Political Theory and Policy Analysis*. Ann Arbor: University of Michigan Press.

McKinstry, Leo. 2016. "The EU has Revealed Its True Nature: A Federalist Monster that will not Stop until Nations Are Abolished." Accessed July 11, 2019. https://www.telegraph.co.uk/news/2016/04/07/the-eu-has-revealed-its-true-nature-a-federalist-monster-that-wi/.

Menz, Georg, and Mitchell P. Smith. 2013. "Kicking the Can Down the Road to More Europe? Salvaging the Euro and the Future of European Economic Governance." *Journal of European Integration* 35 (3): 195–206.

Milward, Alan. 1999. *The European Rescue of the Nation State*. New York: Routledge.

Mody, Ashoka, and Damiano Sandri. 2012. "The Eurozone Crisis: How Banks and Sovereigns Came to be Joined at the Hip." *Economic Policy* 27 (70): 199–230.

Moravcsik, Andrew. 1993. "Preferences and Power in the European Community: A Liberal Intergovernmentalist Approach." *JCMS: Journal of Common Market Studies* 31 (4): 473–524.

———. 2013. *The Choice for Europe: Social Purpose and State Power from Messina to Maastricht*. New York: Routledge.

Nedergaard, Peter, and Holly Snaith. 2015. "'As I Drifted on a River I Could not Control': The Unintended Ordoliberal Consequences of the Eurozone Crisis." *JCMS: Journal of Common Market Studies* 53 (5): 1094–1109.

New York Times. 2015a. "Eastern Bloc's Resistance to Refugees Highlights Europe's Cultural and Political Divisions." Accessed March 24, 2019. https://www.nytimes.com/2015/09/13/world/europe/eastern-europe-migrant-refugee-crisis.html.

———. 2015b. "European Leaders Look Again for a Unified Response to Migrant Crisis." Accessed March 24, 2019. https://www.nytimes.com/2015/10/26/world/europe/merkel-and-east-european-leaders-discuss-migrant-crisis-in-brussels.html.

Nielsen, Bodil, and Sandrino Smeets. 2018. "The Role of the EU Institutions in Establishing the Banking Union. Collaborative Leadership in the EMU Reform Process." *Journal of European Public Policy* 25 (9): 1233–1256.

Niemann, Arne, and Demosthenes Ioannou. 2015. "European Economic Integration in Times of Crisis: A Case of Neofunctionalism?" *Journal of European Public Policy* 22 (2): 196–218.

Niemann, Arne, and Natascha Zaun. 2018. "EU Refugee Policies and Politics in Times of Crisis: Theoretical and Empirical Perspectives." *JCMS: Journal of Common Market Studies* 56 (1): 3–22.

Oakerson, Ronald J., and Roger B. Parks. 1988. "Citizen Voice and Public Entrepreneurship: The Organizational Dynamic of a Complex Metropolitan County." *Publius: The Journal of Federalism* 18 (4): 91–112.

OECD. 2019. "OECD Data: General Government Debt." Accessed March 24, 2019. https://data.oecd.org/gga/general-government-debt.htm.

Olsen, Jonathan, and John McCormick. 2018. *The European Union: Politics and Policies*. New York: Routledge.

Ostrom, Elinor. 1972. "Metropolitan Reform: Propositions Derived from Two Traditions." *Social Science Quarterly* 53 (3): 474–493.

———. 1990. *Governing the Commons*. Cambridge: Cambridge University Press.

———. 1999. "Coping with Tragedies of the Commons." *Annual Review of Political Science* 2 (1): 493–535.

———. 2009. "A Polycentric Approach for Coping with Climate Change." *The World Bank, Policy Research Working Paper 5095.*

———. 2010a. "Beyond Markets and States: Polycentric Governance of Complex Economic Systems." *American Economic Review* 100 (3): 641–72.

———. 2010b. "Polycentric Systems for Coping with Collective Action and Global Environmental Change." *Global Environmental Change* 20 (4): 550–557.

Ostrom, Vincent, Charles M. Tiebout, and Robert Warren. 1961. "The Organization of Government in Metropolitan Areas: A Theoretical Inquiry." *American Political Science Review* 55 (4): 831–842.

Ostrom, Vincent, and Elinor Ostrom. 1977. "Public Goods and Public Choices." In *Alternatives for Delivering Public Services: Towards Improved Performance*, edited by E.S. Savas, 7–49. Boulder, CO: Westview Press.

Pannico, Roberto. 2017. "Is the European Union too Complicated? Citizens' Lack of Information and Party Cue Effectiveness." *European Union Politics* 18 (3): 424–446.

Puetter, Uwe. 2012. "Europe's Deliberative Intergovernmentalism: The Role of the Council and European Council in EU Economic Governance." *Journal of European Public Policy* 19 (2): 161–178.

———. 2014. *The European Council and the Council: New Intergovernmentalism and Institutional Change*. Oxford: Oxford University Press.

Radaelli, Claudio M., and Claire A. Dunlop. 2013. "Learning in the European Union: Theoretical Lenses and Meta-theory." *Journal of European Public Policy* 20 (6): 923–940.

Raudla, Ringa, James W. Douglas, Tiina Randma-Liiv, and Riin Savi. 2015. "The Impact of Fiscal Crisis on Decision-Making Processes in European Governments: Dynamics of a Centralization Cascade." *Public Administration Review* 75 (6): 842–852.

Reuters. 2015. "Shocked by Drowned Migrants, Europe Restores Rescue Mission." Accessed March 24, 2019. https://www.reuters.com/article/us-europe-migrants/shocked-by-drowned-migrants-europe-restores-rescue-mission-idUSKBN0NE1DY20150423.

Rodrik, Dani. 2007. *One Economics, Many Recipes: Globalization, Institutions, and Economic Growth*. Princeton: Princeton University Press.

Rosamond, Ben. 2005. "The Uniting of Europe and the Foundation of EU Studies: Revisiting the Neofunctionalism of Ernst B. Haas." *Journal of European Public Policy* 12 (2): 237–254.

Rygiel, Kim, Feyzi Baban, and Suzan Ilcan. 2016. "The Syrian Refugee Crisis: The EU-Turkey 'Deal' and Temporary Protection." *Global Social Policy* 16 (3): 315–320.

Sabel, Charles F., and Jonathan Zeitlin. 2010. *Experimentalist Governance in the European Union: Towards a New Architecture*. Oxford: Oxford University Press.

Sandholtz, Wayne, and Alec Stone Sweet. 1998. *European Integration and Supranational Governance*. Oxford: Oxford University Press.

———. 2012. "Neo-Functionalism and Supranational Governance." In *The Oxford Handbook of the European Union*, edited by Erik Jones, Anand Menon, and Stephen Weatherill, 18–33. Oxford: Oxford University Press.

Sandholtz, Wayne, and John Zysman. 1989. "1992: Recasting the European Bargain." *World Politics* 42 (1): 95–128.

Scharpf, Fritz W. 1988. "The Joint-Decision Trap: Lessons from German Federalism and European Integration." *Public Administration* 66 (3): 239–278.

Schild, Joachim. 2013. "Leadership in Hard Times: Germany, France, and the Management of the Eurozone Crisis." *German Politics and Society* 31 (1): 24–47.

Schimmelfennig, Frank. 2015. "Liberal Intergovernmentalism and the Euro Area Crisis." *Journal of European Public Policy* 22 (2): 177–195.

———. 2018a. "Brexit: Differentiated Disintegration in the European Union." *Journal of European Public Policy* 25 (8): 1154–1173.

———. 2018b. "European Integration (Theory) in Times of Crisis. A Comparison of the Euro and Schengen Crises." *Journal of European Public Policy* 25 (7): 969–989.

Schimmelfennig, Frank, Dirk Leuffen, and Berthold Rittberger. 2015. "The European Union as a System of Differentiated Integration: Interdependence, Politicization and Differentiation." *Journal of European Public Policy* 22 (6): 764–782.

Schimmelfennig, Frank, and Thomas Winzen. 2019. "Grand Theories, Differentiated Integration." *Journal of European Public Policy* 26 (8): 1–21.

Schneider, Christina J. 2013. "Globalizing Electoral Politics: Political Competence and Distributional Bargaining in the European Union." *World Politics* 65 (3): 452–490.

Schoeller, Magnus G. 2018. "The Rise and Fall of Merkozy: Franco-German Bilateralism as a Negotiation Strategy in Eurozone Crisis Management." *JCMS: Journal of Common Market Studies* 56 (5): 1019–1035.

Scipioni, Marco. 2018. "Failing Forward in EU Migration Policy? EU Integration after the 2015 Asylum and Migration Crisis." *Journal of European Public Policy* 25 (9): 1357–1375.

Shearmur, Richard, and Benjamin Motte. 2009. "Weak Ties that Bind: Do Commutes Bind Montreal's Central and Suburban Economies?" *Urban Affairs Review* 44 (4): 490–524.

Spolaore, Enrico. 2015. "The Political Economy of European Integration." *National Bureau of Economic Research, NBER Working Paper No. 21250.*

't Hart, Paul, Uriel Rosenthal, and Alexander Kouzmin. 1993. "Crisis Decision Making: The Centralization Thesis Revisited." *Administration & Society* 25 (1): 12–45.

Târlea, Silvana, Stefanie Bailer, Hanno Degner, Lisa M. Dellmuth, Dirk Leuffen, Magnus Lundgren, Jonas Tallberg, and Fabio Wasserfallen. 2019. "Explaining Governmental Preferences on Economic and Monetary Union Reform." *European Union Politics* 20 (1): 24–44.

The Guardian. 2015a. "European Leaders Pledge to Send Ships to Mediterranean to Pick Up Migrants." Accessed March 24, 2019. https://www.theguardian.com/world/2015/apr/23/european-leaders-pledge-ships-mediterranean-pick-up-migrants.

———. 2015b. "Germany Presses for Quota System for EU Migrant Distribution." Accessed March 24, 2019. https://www.theguardian.com/world/2015/apr/29/germany-quota-system-eu-migrant-distribution.

Tömmel, Ingeborg, and Amy Verdun. 2009. *Innovative governance in the European Union: The politics of multilevel Policymaking*. Lynne Rienner Publishers.

Tosun, Jale, Anne Wetzel, and Galina Zapryanova. 2014. "The EU in Crisis: Advancing the Debate." *Journal of European Integration* 36 (3): 195–211.

Trein, Philipp. 2019. "Federal Dynamics, Solidarity, and European Union Crisis Politics." *Journal of European Public Policy*, 1–18.

Trichet, Jean-Claude. 2010. "State of the Union: The Financial Crisis and the ECB's Response between 2007 and 2009." *JCMS: Journal of Common Market Studies* 48: 7–19.

Trondal, Jarle. 2010. *An Emergent European Executive Order*. Oxford: Oxford University Press.

U.S. Office of Personnel Management (OPM). 2019. "Federal Employment Reports: Employment and Trends – September 2013." Accessed July 11, 2019. https://www.opm.gov/policy-data-oversight/data-analysis-documentation/federal-employment-reports/employment-trends-data/2013/september/table-1/.

van Esch, Femke, and Eelke de Jong. 2019. "National Culture Trumps EU Socialization: The European Central Bankers' Views of the Euro Crisis." *Journal of European Public Policy* 26 (2): 169–187.

van Zeben, Josephine, and Ana Bobić. 2019. *Polycentricity in the European Union*. Cambridge: Cambridge University Press.

Verdun, Amy. 2015. "A Historical Institutionalist Explanation of the EU's Responses to the Euro Area Financial Crisis." *Journal of European Public Policy* 22 (2): 219–237.

Vogler, Jan P. 2019a. "Citizen Perceptions of Corruption and Trust in the EU Administration: The Application of Heuristics Based on Domestic Experience." Working Paper. Accessed July 30, 2019. http://www.janvogler.net/EU-Trust.pdf.

———. 2019b. "The Entanglement of Public Bureaucratic Institutions: Their Interactions with Society, Culture, Politics, and the Economy." In *Interdisciplinary Studies of the Political Order: New Applications of Public Choice Theory*, edited by Donald J. Boudreaux, Christopher J. Coyne, and Bobbi Herzberg, 99–129. New York: Rowman & Littlefield International.

Von Bogdandy, Armin. 2000. "The European Union as a Supranational Federation: A Conceptual Attempt in the Light of the Amsterdam Treaty." *Columbia Journal of European Law* 6: 27–54.

Washington Post. 2015. "Calls for Action in Europe after Migrant Disaster in Mediterranean." Accessed March 24, 2019. https://www.washingtonpost.com/world/calls-for-action-in-europe-after-migrant-disaster-in-mediterranean/2015/04/19/c7bc9040-e697-11e4-8581-633c536add4bstory.html.

Wasserfallen, Fabio, Dirk Leuffen, Zdenek Kudrna, and Hanno Degner. 2019. "Analysing European Union Decision-Making during the Eurozone Crisis with New Data." *European Union Politics* 20 (1): 3–23.

Weingast, Barry R. 1995. "The Economic Role of Political Institutions: Market-Preserving Federalism and Economic Development." *Journal of Law, Economics, & Organization* 11 (1): 1–31.

Wessels, Wolfgang. 2003. "Beamtengremien im EU-Mehrebenensystem—Fusion von Administrationen?" In *Europäische Integration*, edited by Markus Jachtenfuchs and Beate Kohler-Koch, 353–383. Wiesbaden, Germany: Springer.

Zaiotti, Ruben. 2007. "Of Friends and Fences: Europe's Neighbourhood Policy and the 'Gated Community Syndrome'." *European Integration* 29 (2): 143–162.

Zaun, Natascha. 2018. "States as Gatekeepers in EU Asylum Politics: Explaining the Nonadoption of a Refugee Quota System." *JCMS: Journal of Common Market Studies* 56 (1): 44–62.

Part III

RESOLVING COLLECTIVE ACTION PROBLEMS

Chapter 7

The Inmate's Dilemma

Prison Strikes as Repeated Games

Joanna Carroll

In less than half an hour thirty-eight people were dead: five corrections officers, four civilian employees, and twenty-nine inmates, all victims of police gunfire. On that September day in 1971, a blanket of tear gas dropped into D Yard of the Attica Correctional Facility incapacitating the 1,300 inmates who had taken control of the prison. Before the gas cleared, state troopers, sheriffs, and corrections officers alike stormed the yard and began shooting indiscriminately. In total, 128 people were shot during the melee, including hostages as well as inmates. In the hours after the state had regained control of the facility, police and corrections officers began torturing the surrendered inmates. Medical care was withheld from the gravely injured while officers poured salt and lime into gaping wounds and stuck fingers into the bullet holes riddling the men's bodies. Inmates were stripped naked and forced to walk a fifty-meter gauntlet of broken glass where officers beat them with axe handles and baseball bats. Reports surfaced of prisoners murdered by corrections officers after the initial take back. One such inmate was L. D. Barkley, a twenty-one-year-old who was at Attica for driving without a license. He was found dead of a gunshot to the back. In the end, the Attica Prison Uprising cost the state of New York $12 million in legal fees and its victims a lifetime of physical and psychological torment (Thompson 2016).

In the decades preceding the uprising, the US state and federal prison population had been on a steady rise. When state forces retook Attica, the US prions population had doubled since 1925 (Bureau of Justice Statistics 1982). Attica exemplified this trend. Built in 1931 to house roughly 1,600 inmates, by 1971 the penitentiary was 25 percent over its built capacity. This continued overcrowding exacerbated long-standing issues at the facility. Inmates were inadequately fed, receiving only $0.63 of food a day. They were given one shower a week and one roll of toilet paper a month. Water was limited to two quarts a day. The overcrowded facility was poorly ventilated with irregular and extreme temperatures. The prison doctors consistently ignored inmates' medical needs and refused to treat Puerto Rican inmates due to their inability to speak Spanish. All media and correspondence with the outside world were monitored and censored. Any letter to an inmate written in Spanish was thrown away. Inmates of color were given the worst-paying and most laborious jobs in the prison. Though no inmate worker fared well, receiving between only $0.06 and $2.90 per day of work. Rules were inconsistently enforced and inmates were frequently punished with keeplock, twenty-four-hours-a-day confinement in their cells, for indeterminate amounts of time (Thompson 2016).

While the Attica Uprising began as a violent riot, the initial chaos was short lived. By the end of the first day, inmates were able to restore an acceptable amount of order and began organizing. They set up a makeshift medical station to treat both inmates and hostages that had been injured in the riot. They put together a security team to keep hostages safe and maintain order among prisoners. They distributed food and water. What had begun as an unplanned violent riot was quickly turning into a well-organized prison strike. During the days inmates had control of the facility, they were able to publish a manifesto of demands, elect leaders, communicate with government officials, invite an observatory board into the prison, and keep all hostages safe. Of the twenty-seven demands listed in their manifesto at the top was legal representation during parole hearings, adequate medical facilities and staff, and adequate facilities for family visits. Other demands included ending the use of solitary confinement due to political beliefs and the legal prosecution of correctional officers for the use of cruel and unusual punishment. In the end, none of these demands were met (Thompson 2016).

Yet the mere fact that inmates were able to organize seems an incredible feat in and of itself. Using insights from the scholarship of Elinor Ostrom, this chapter discusses how inmates, a population that faces seemingly insurmountable barriers to cooperation, successfully engage in nonviolent collective action, specifically how prison inmates are able to engage in strikes. Strikes are different than riots, gang activities, mass escape attempts, and other notable collective actions seen in prisons. For this chapter, I conceptualize *prison strike* as a collective action on the part of prison inmates that meets three essential criteria: (1) It intends to create institutional change within the prison or prison system.[1] (2) Actions taken during a strike are intended to draw attention to the prisoners and their demanded changes. (3) The main tactics used in a strike are nonviolent in nature. Though violence can be used as a contingent strategy and the eventual presence of violence does not negate a collective action as a strike.

Collective action refers to a situation in which individuals cooperate to achieve an outcome that increases their status. Opportunities for collective action arise when individual actions are taken in interdependent situations (Ostrom 2010, 155). For decades, scholars have studied and modeled how individuals behave in interdependent situations. Specifically, scholars have studied what are termed "collective action problems." These problems arise when individual incentives are such that each person will choose to maximize individual benefits in lieu of the socially optimal outcome (Ostrom 1990, 2010). Perhaps the most notable model of collective action problems is called, ironically enough, the Prisoner's Dilemma.

In this stylized game, two criminals must decide to remain quiet (cooperate) or confess their crime (defect). If they both stay silent, they face a short prison sentence. If one confesses (defector) and the other stays silent (cooperator) the cooperator gets a hefty sentence and the defector is set free as part of a plea bargain. If they both confess, then they both go to jail for a moderate period of time. The dilemma arises because the preferred strategy for each criminal is to confess, regardless of what the other criminal does. Let's consider the position of prisoner A. If prisoner B remains silent, then Prisoner A prefers to confess, because under these circumstances they will face no jail time. If Prisoner B confesses, then Prisoner A still prefers to confess as they can reduce their sentence length by confessing. The prisoners face a collective action problem because even though the best outcome for the pair happens when both cooperate and remain silent, the rational actor will always choose to confess as it is the way to optimize their individual outcome regardless of what the other criminal does (Hardin 1982; Ostrom 1990).

Ostrom criticized the use of the Prisoners Dilemma as a general theory rather than a single model of collective action problems. While some collective action problems fit the Prisoner's Dilemma model and fail to achieve cooperation, history is rife with examples of people who succeed in organizing themselves and collectively acting. Part of Ostrom's scholarship was concerned with developing a generalizable theory that could explain the success and failure of a wide variety of collective actions. Her theory has two major components. First, she identified a set of structural variables that affect the likelihood of collective action. While these variables may not always have a straightforward effect on collective action, they are the most important situational factors to consider when evaluating the success or failure of overcoming collective action problems. Second, she uses the theory of bounded rationality, where institutional norms affect individual behavior, as her foundation of human behavior. The ability of individuals to gain trust and build reputations, abilities not granted by the structure of a Prisoner's

Dilemma, go a long way in explaining the achievement of collective action (Ostrom 1990, 2010).

In this chapter, I will outline the collective action problem faced by inmates and discuss the theoretical mechanisms through which their dilemma may be solved. I will then use an Ostromian framework to discuss why collective action problems are particularly difficult for inmates to overcome and how they are able to successfully strike anyway. I will end with a case study to illustrate my analysis and make concluding remarks.

COLLECTIVE ACTION AND THE INMATE'S DILEMMA

Collective action problems arise from social dilemmas. A social dilemma exists when the independent actions of individuals are taken in an interdependent situation and lead to a less-than-socially optimal outcome. To solve the social dilemma, collective action is needed. The issue then becomes how to move from a state of noncooperation to a state of cooperation. This is the collective action problem (Ostrom 1990, 2010).

In the case of prison strikes and other revolutionary activities, the collective action problem is typified by the payouts of participation and nonparticipation in the strike itself.[2] Recall that a strike is defined as a collective action that pursues institutional change of the prison or prison system. If an individual chooses to participate in the strike, they experience some costs, but have the potential to gain the benefits of the strike. If an individual chooses to not participate, they have no costs, but still have the potential to gain the benefits of the strike. This is a standard public goods game. Because no one can be easily excluded from the benefits, there is always the incentive to free ride. Since it is assumed that any one individual's participation in the strike has a near-zero effect on the success of the strike, a rational actor would choose to not participate (Tullock 1971; Lichbach 1998).

Then what explains the presence of a vast number of prison strikes and other rebellions throughout history? In *The Paradox of Revolution*, Gordon Tullock (1971) posits that the public good benefits of a strike play an inconsequential role in the individual's decision to participate. When deciding, individuals will be interested in the net benefits of participation, which amount to the personal (not public) benefit an individual will receive from participating in the strike minus the costs of participation. He offers few insights into the benefits of participation that are relevant to the context of inmate strikes. He glibly uses the term "E" to represent entertainment value that rebels may get from participating in rebellion. He also acknowledges that some individuals may be rewarded with high-ranking government positions for their part in the overthrow of one regime and the institution of a new one.

Inmates do not strike in the hope that they will become the warden of the prison. Inmates strike in order to get the warden to concede some demand that will benefit a typically substantial number of prisoners. This is evidenced by the demands made by strikers over the decades. The Attica Manifesto, the list of demands made by the striking prisoners, spoke of facility and staff changes as well as revisions to rules and the proper enforcement of formal rules. Inmates in San Quentin State Prison created a similar list of demands during strikes in the late 1960s that were later adopted by inmates in Folsom State Prison during their massive strike in 1970 (Burger 2014). In the year prior to the Attica Uprising, there was another large strike at the nearby Auburn Correctional Facility a few hours west in upstate New York. Demands from prisoners in that strike had a similar tone. Inmates demanded more Spanish-speaking staff, better medical treatment, and improvement to parole proceedings, among other things (Thompson 2016). More modern strikes levy similar demands (Chen 2010; Wheaton 2010; Anderson 2014; IWOC 2016; Brown 2018; ACLU 2019).

It seems that beyond the institutional changes sought by the strike, which are public to varying degrees, the personal benefits to participation are largely psychological. In addition to the reforms demanded in these manifestos, there is a clear sense of desire to simply engage in the defiant act of the strike. The Attica and Folsom Manifestos are rife with frequent references to inmates as "men" and "human beings" while demanding to receive treatment commensurate with those titles (Thompson 2016; San Francisco Bay Review 2018). A press release ahead of a 2016 national prison work stoppage echoed this sentiment in the statement, "We will not only demand the end to prison slavery, we will end it ourselves by ceasing to be slaves (IWOC 2016)." The theme of personal identity and expressions of liberty, as will be discussed later in this chapter, are a major talking point of strike leaders. Indeed, Tullock (1995) later abandoned his measure of entertainment as a benefit to rebellion preferring Morris Silver's (1974) measure of "psychic income," though acknowledging that as of yet there was no formal measure of that effect.

Timur Kuran (1991) offers one formalized construct of these psychological impacts in the framework of preference falsification. Kuran contends that an individual's decision to participate in activities like a strike will depend primarily on the trade-offs between external and internal payoffs. As noted above, external benefits, in the form of rewards for participation are likely to be small for inmates who stand to gain little more than some admiration from their fellow prisoners. On the other hand, external costs, in the form of punishment, are likely to be high as evidenced in the Attica example. This leads us to consider the internal rewards.

Preference falsification occurs when the public actions of an individual do not match their private preferences. Say for instance an individual prefers a strike, but is aware that engaging in a strike could result in injury or death. They may falsify their private preference for the strike by presenting a public preference for no strike or merely not expressing their support. This falsification creates an internal discomfort as the individual sacrifices their integrity and personal autonomy. Thus, inmates may experience internal benefits to engaging in a strike by way of expressing their private preferences (Kuran 1991).

In addition to this personal discomfort, preference falsification also helps shape public opinion (Kuran 1995). In the perspective of Ostrom's scholarship, this process is akin to norm building (Ostrom 2010). An individual may falsify their preferences to gain some utility from publicly aligning their preferences closely with public opinion (Kuran 1995). This building of norms sets public preferences on a path that can be difficult to break. If the norm of behavior is to act opportunistically, then there is little incentive for someone to act cooperatively as they have few reasons to believe that others will cooperate with them. If, for instance, an inmate has a private preference for cooperation, but sees the rampant opportunistic behavior of the prison society, he will likely falsify this preference in public as history and experience have told him that the costs of expression are high. This will in turn affect the public opinion around cooperation and other individual's preference falsification decisions (Ostrom 1990; Kuran 1995).

Thus, there becomes an issue of credible commitment. When opportunistic behavior becomes a norm, it is difficult to build trust and solidify long-enduring commitments to cooperation (Ostrom 1990, 1995). To illustrate the dynamic between public opinion and private preferences, Kuran develops a concept called the revolutionary threshold. This is the point where the internal discomforts of preference falsification outweigh the external costs associated with publicly stating your private preferences. This threshold is conceptualized as a level of public support for a collective action that is needed for an individual's internal/external payoff calculation to induce participation. There are two ways to induce individual participation within this framework. First, increase the amount of public support for the collective action. The logic here being that as public support grows the external costs of participation decrease and the external benefits increase. Second, increase the individual's preference for the collective action, which in turn decreases the amount of public support needed to induce participation (Kuran 1991).

The social norms, public opinions, costs, and benefits are all part of the context of the social dilemma and resulting collective action problem. Context is an important consideration for the success of achieving cooperation (Ostrom 1990; Ostrom 2000, 2010). There are reasons to believe that the context of prison strikes makes the collective action problem for inmates more difficult to overcome. In the next section, I will discuss the unique context of the prison system and how it enhances barriers to collective action.

COLLECTIVE ACTION AND THE TOTALITY OF PRISONS

The prison system exerts an enormous amount of control over the lives of inmates. It applies control far beyond that levied by any oppressive regime on the average noninstitutionalized citizen. Within an institutional framework, this control is commonly referred to as totality. All institutions levy some control over individuals via rules and norms. All institutions vary in their levels of control. The term "total institution" is used to describe those that exhibit high levels of totality by exercising near-total control over individuals (Wallace 1971). People within total institutions are isolated physically from outside communities. Communication between them and the outside world is strictly controlled or completely prohibited. In prison, this isolation extends to personal liberties and rights.

In the broader US society, individuals exercise numerous rights and liberties. In prison, you are stripped of all but the most basic rights (Legal Information Institute 2019) and access to those remaining rights are frequently hampered (Hager 2016; Thompson 2016, 2018). You can no longer choose who you live with. You cannot decide when to eat or bathe. Inmates no longer have a right to privacy or property, save a few essential items. This is especially meaningful to prisoners because not only are they involuntarily restricted by the rules of the prison, but are isolated from their rights as American citizens. In all but two states prisoners are not allowed to vote while in prison (Timm 2018). First Amendment rights are also restricted as prisons are allowed to censor information that they deem harmful (Hager 2016). Prisoners have no say in the creation of formal prison rules, and those rules are imposed upon them without adequate recourse (Calavita and Jenness 2015). This isolation from the outside world and civil rights is perpetuated by the internalization of processes within the prison.

Prior to 1998, the primary formal recourse available to prisoners was to bring a federal civil suit against the prison. These suits were so commonplace that in 1995 they made up approximately 19 percent of all federal civil cases on the docket. Going through the courts was a long, cumbersome, tricky, and often unsuccessful process with only about 1 percent of cases decided in favor of the inmate. In 1994, when the Republican Party won a majority in Congress, they promised tort reform and the prisoner litigation system was front and center to that promise. To support the effort, the National Association of American Attorneys General (NAAAG) compiled a list of what they deemed "frivolous" lawsuits filed by inmates. The NAAAG representations of these lawsuits were quickly found to be fallacious depictions of the actual complaints levied in the suits. Regardless, Senators Orin Hatch and Robert Dole used these examples and the backed-up federal docket to introduce, galvanize support for, and pass the Prison Litigation Reform Act (PLRA), 42 U.S.C. § 1997e (Calavita and Jenness 2015).

The PLRA completely changed the face of the prisoner complaint system. Most notably, it internalized and further individualized the system. Judicial intervention in prison management was restricted. Prisoners were no longer allowed to sue for mental or emotional damages unless some physical injury was present, even if the damage resulted in physical symptoms. For instance, under the PLRA, damages awarded in the suit against a Massachusetts prison, where a guard was found guilty of putting the barrel of a cocked gun in a prisoner's mouth as retaliation for a rumored affair between the prisoner and the guard's wife, are no longer allowed. Most importantly, though, the PLRA required that inmates exhaust all available administrative remedies before they were allowed to bring a federal case against a prison, giving states broad discretion to set these administrative remedies and their processes (Calavita and Jenness 2015).

The internalization of the grievance process created by the PLRA was not just a way to get inmate grievances off the dockets, but was a way to decollectivize complaints. When handled internally, complaints become more about individual interests and needs rather than collective rights. The internal officials handling grievances are not motivated by protecting prisoner rights. They are motivated to keep the internal operations of the prison smooth. The handling of these matters internally also curtails social impact by circumventing the legal system which would create public precedent of grievances (Calavita and Jenness 2015; Edwards 1979). Evidence suggests that this internalization has worked to at least some degree. California prisoners report high levels of feeling that if they play by the rules and follow the internal grievance process, they will find recourse, even when less than 1 percent of all grievances are granted in full (Calavita and Jenness 2015).

Another by-product of the internalization of total institutions is the creation of new societies and individuals building a new sense of identity within the context of those societies (Denzin 1968). Namely, the population within prisons is a concentration of individuals who have been deemed unfit for life in broader society. These individuals are then exposed to extreme amounts of deprivation and high levels of control. Though the paradox of prisons seems to be that while they exercise an extreme amount of control over prisoners, they simultaneously fail to keep control of inmates, allowing violence and chaos to rule. This encourages social factions to form and deepen as prisoners seek out alternative forms of governance and protection (Skarbek 2014). Prison guards often have limited resources, training, and experience, but are put in charge of large groups of potentially violent felons. Guards frequently do not enforce formal behavioral rules they find overly burdensome to enforce. These can be menial rules like failing to cite an inmate for possessing contraband or more serious rules like failing to intervene when an inmate is attacked by another inmate. They also selectively or arbitrarily enforce other rules handing out citations to prisoners for the most minor and mundane of infractions one day and not the next or specifically targeting one group of prisoners over others for frequent punishment (Sykes 1955; Hassine 2004; Calavita and Jenness 2015; Thompson 2016).

Thus, informal norms and social groupings form to bring some measure of order to prisoners' lives (Sykes 1955; Hassine 2004; Skarbek 2014). The formal rules and social norms, as well as their enforcement mechanisms, combine to form the "working rules" (for a recent and complete discussion of these topics, see Cole 2017) that control the everyday movement and actions of individuals (Ostrom 2005). Lines get drawn between groups according to race and religion. Gangs begin forming to act as physical protection as well as economic units. Since prisons are often places of extreme distrust, disorder, and violence, a prisoners' ability to align themselves with a particular group can be essential to survival and security (Hassine 2004; Skarbek 2014). Prisoners who do not belong to a gang often must be willing to engage in violent behavior in order to protect themselves and their property as they get minimal protection from the prison system itself (Hassine 2004). An inmate of Graterford Prison in Pennsylvania, named Omar, describes this system as a Dodge City craps game. He asserts, "All the staff do is sit back and let the men here tear each other apart. . . . Tell me why, with all the guards, guns, locks, gates, walls, and money they still can't stop what's going on" (Hassine 2004, 76).

Other major contributors to the formation of prison societies and social groupings are the heterogeneity of prisoners, their preferences, and the frequent in and out migration. There is a strong belief among theorists that the more heterogeneous a group the more difficult cooperation becomes. Heterogeneity of participants has the potential to impede collective action by increasing transaction costs and conflicts over the distribution of benefits (Ostrom 2010). For inmates, the length of sentences poses a major obstacle as it is likely to alter individuals' preferences for engaging in a strike as well as the makeup of the prison community as a whole across time. Engagement in a strike could affect an inmate's eligibility for parole or, if they are accused of committing a crime during the strike, could add time onto their sentence. This means those with shorter sentences have greater incentives to simply "do a good piece."

There is also heterogeneity in preferences for the potential strike benefits. While Tullock (1971, 1995) contended that the public goods nature was effectively meaningless in the rebel's personal calculation of whether to engage in protest, he did not consider that public goods vary in both their subtractability and excludability. Thus, some individuals may gain more benefit from the public good than others and have vastly different preferences for the different types of institutional changes being demanded (Lichbach 1998). For instance, institutional change of the parole system will exclude individuals who are ineligible for parole. Improvements to the solitary confinement policies are going to have higher payoffs for those currently in solitary confinement or those most likely to be sent there, even though technically all inmates would benefit. There is also the potential that individual preferences for these various institutional changes could be altered by the spreading of ideology by strike leaders (Lichbach 1995). If leaders are able to successfully convince inmates that the institutional changes which do not directly impact them will bring other benefits, particularly through the expression of liberty and power, they may be able to alter the revolutionary threshold of some prisoners (Kuran 1991)

Inmates must also deal with the uncontrollable population changes in their communities. Ostrom (2010) asserts that major in and out migration pose a threat to sustained collective action. This can be particularly acute for prisoners. Some inmates are there for life, while others may only be there for a few years before they are eligible for parole or their initial sentence is fulfilled. Inmates are also frequently moved between prisons, an issue discussed in more depth shortly. So not only do prisoners have to contend with an uncontrollable flow of inmates into the prison, but they have to contend with the outflow as well. As people move in and out, issues with information and trust among the broader inmate population manifest and exacerbate (Hassine 2004).

In short, the internalization of processes and rules, the inconsistent enforcement of formal rules, and the development of prison norms, as well as the heterogeneity among prisoners serves to keep inmates individualized, insecure, and divided along strong social factions. This simply amplifies the incentives to act individually and opportunistically, a major barrier to cooperation. The consistent and overt uses of control by the prisons add to this disconnectedness and pose additional barriers to collective action. The degree of control can vary between and within prisons, though. Minimum security prisons will exhibit less control than maximum security prisons. Certain cell blocks within a prison will be more restrictive than others. All standard cell blocks will, in turn, be less restrictive than the solitary confinement units. Regardless, there are two major forms of overt control that prisons exercise over inmates that make strikes particularly difficult: control over location and control over communication.

The most salient control a prison wields over inmates is the segregation of prisoners within the prison walls from broader society. It is, however, the control over where they are allowed to be within the prison that has, perhaps, the most implications for the ability of inmates to strike. Each prison has a security level ranging from minimum to maximum security. What distinguishes these prisons is the freedom of movement that inmates experience inside. Minimum security prisons are typically dormitory style, that is, no locked cells, with prisoners free to move about a large portion of the prison campus at their leisure. Staffing is minimal and there are few, if any, barriers around the campus itself. Maximum security prisons, on the other hand, employ cell blocks where inmates are confined within a locked cell during most of their days. They are allowed out at scheduled intervals for food, recreation, and job duties. These campuses are surrounded by fences or walls and often include a gun tower, where armed guards keep watch. The level of control and the violent nature of the individuals kept in these prisons also requires a large amount of staff (Federal Bureau of Prisons).

In addition to the average amount of control dictated by the security level of the prison, officials often use location control to impede collective action among prisoners. Prison officials, from administrators to guards, are extremely interested in keeping prisoners from engaging in nearly all forms of collective action, whether that be gang formation, political organizations, riots, or strikes. Inmates who are thought to be participating in these activities are often moved in an attempt to hamper their organizational efforts (Lavender 2014; Berger 2014; Wallace-Wells 2014; Thompson 2016). One prominent tactic is to transfer troublesome prisoners to different prisons. In the late 1960s, prisoners in San Quentin B Block began staging several small demonstrations, including the destruction of property. In an effort to stave off the spread of these demonstrations to the rest of the prison, participating inmates were dispersed throughout the prison and the leaders were sent to different prisons (Berger 2014).

The use of Secure Housing Units, or SHU (pronounced like shoe), is also common. SHU consists of cement cells, usually around 8 x 10 feet, where a lone individual is kept nearly all day, only let out for an hour of solitary recreation time, medical treatments, and visitations. There is no formal legal process that determines who gets placed in SHU, though some states may restrict its use. These are disciplinary decisions made within the prison administration and are not subject to the rigors of the court of law. The amount of time spent in SHU is also determined at the prison administration level and prisoners have no control over how long they spend there. Some individuals spend decades in the SHU. Officially, these units are often reserved for gang leaders and particularly violent inmates who officials believe pose a significant threat to the larger prison population. Sometimes SHU is used as a punishment for infractions committed by inmates, though these tend to be shorter sentences (Wallace-Wells 2014; Camon 2016). The use of SHU, or its sister facility Administrative Segregation (AdSeg), is another way of using internalized processes to individualize and decollectivize the experience of inmates.

The vast amount of internal control over communication levied by prison poses another significant barrier. In 2014, an unofficial announcement had made its way out of the St. Clair Correctional Facility in Melville, Alabama. Prisoners were about to strike. A week after the announcement, there had been no signs of an impending strike. Rumors began spreading that the leader of that strike had been placed in solitary confinement. More rumors that prison officials threatened others with the same fate and stirred religious tensions between Christians and Muslims to ensure noncooperation also surfaced. When asked about these rumors by a journalist, the warden of St. Clair, Carter Davenport, responded, "I'm able to tell you a lot of things, sir, I'm just not going to tell you anything" (Lavender 2014).

Such appears to be the status quo with communication in and out of prisons. Prisons control whom with, when, and for how long inmates can have communication. There are frequent issues of getting information about prisons strikes to the general population because prison officials control nearly all information that comes out of prisons. Members of the public are not allowed to simply walk around a prison whenever they would like. Government officials must arrange visits and get approval from prison officials to get access (Thompson 2016, 2018). If prisoners were indeed in the midst of a strike, prison officials would need only deny it and the public would have no easy way to verify their statements. Phone calls, letters, internet access, and visitations are monitored closely, given and taken away as privileges. This ability of prisons to control visitations was upheld in the Supreme Court case *Overton v. Bazzetta*, #02-94, 539 US 126 (2003), which stated that prisons could limit or deny visitation to inmates if the restriction rationally related to prison management.

Another recent practice in prisons with implication for effective communication is the use of video visitations, where inmates communicate with the outside world using some form of video chat. As of 2014, roughly 500 correctional facilities had some form of video visitation system. Initially, this may seem to ease communication between prisoners and the outside, but where in-person visits are free, video visitations cost up to $1.50 per minute. It is also a common practice, particularly in county jails, to eliminate in-person visits all together once a video visitation system is in place. Additionally, there are frequent issues with the technology used for these visitations (Rabuy and Wagner 2015). While video visitations themselves may contribute minorly to overall restrictions on communication in and out of prisons, it illustrates the legal precedent that communication with the outside world is a privilege granted by internal prison processes and those internal processes can be severely limiting.

The ability to communicate with the outside world is essential for strikes. The success of a strike at achieving institutional change is largely dependent on outside forces putting pressure on lawmakers and prison officials. The purpose of a strike is to bring attention to the plight of inmates and create institutional change. The broader legal, political, and social system are a part of the prison institution and integral to change. The less plausible connection with the outside world seems, the less plausible success seems and the lower the incentive to strike will be (Lichbach 1998).

Prison officials also attempt to keep tight control on communication within the prison itself. Communication between strike participants is necessary to ensure successful execution. As will be discussed more in depth later, the need for communicating ideologies and information is key for overcoming collective action problems. Additionally, information about what actions are to be taken and when have to be decided and disseminated. However, any prisoners caught engaging in communication about such activities can face disciplinary action. In the months before the Attica Uprising, a small group of inmates sent a list of demands known as the July Manifesto to the commissioner. The document circulated among prisoners in Attica, but reports surfaced that inmates found with a copy were given sixty days in solitary confinement (Thompson 2016). Moving prisoners around, isolating them to their cells or SHU, and limiting their access to communication with the outside world are all ways to inhibit the transmission of these communications. There are numerous claims of prisoners being moved to the SHU, AdSeg, or other prisons in an attempt to segregate them and cut off communication (Chen 2010; Berger 2014; Lavender 2014; Wallace-Wells 2014; Dilawar 2018).

THE GAMES PRISONERS PLAY

Given the totality of prisons and the incentives faced by potential strikers, the inmate's dilemma may be more difficult than other collective action problems. Yet there is a rich history of inmate strikes in the United States and around the world. Clearly, these individuals are occasionally able to overcome their challenges and achieve collective action. Ostrom (1990, 2005, 2010) proposes a set of structural factors that make successful collective action more likely including, but not limited to, the subtractability of benefits, number of participants, how individuals are linked, and whether individuals have free entry and exit options. An examination of Ostrom's factors reveals three primary mechanisms that allow prisoners to overcome their vast obstacles and successfully create a strike: strike leaders, communication innovation, and game repetition.

Strike Leaders and the Prisoner Class

Inmates are able to overcome issues of heterogeneity in race, religion, gang membership, and so on with the help of strike leaders. Strike leaders are those that hold high preferences for the strike itself (Ostrom 2010). These individuals can also be thought of as those whose revolutionary threshold is very low, meaning that not participating in a strike would bring them immense psychological discomfort (Kuran 1991). Strike leaders have an extreme preference for the collective action of strikes. They are often political radicals self-schooled in both political ideologies and histories of revolution. Many strike leaders study political and philosophical texts, reading authors such as Mao Zedong, Karl Marx, W. E. B. Du Bois, Naomi Wolf, Howard Zinn, and Michel Foucault. The biography of Bobby Sands, IRA member, MP, and prisoner who starved himself to death in a Northern Ireland political prison, is also popular among strike leaders (Jackson 1994; Berger 2014; Wallace-Wells 2014; Thompson 2016).

Both the Attica and Folsom manifestos were rife with radical political language. Attica organizers proclaimed their constitutional rights to assembly and legal representation multiple times in their manifesto. Folsom organizers called the California prison system a "fascist concentration camp of modern America." More modern strikers have similar political tones. A letter released announcing the 2016 Texas Prison Work Stoppage was a scathing criticism of the economic exploitation and human rights violations happening within prisons, going so far as to call Rick Perry, then governor of Texas, a serial killer (Speri 2016). This political activism stands in stark contrast with the average prisoner's desire to just "do good time." The incentive to simply not make waves, be a "good" prisoner, and just finish out your time is strong. Calavita and Jenness (2015) found that even in the face of disorganized, inconsistent, and unfair practices within the prison system prisoners still held some measure of confidence in rule following, that as long as you followed the rules you would be alright.

It is, however, these engagements with political radicalism that seem to allow prison strikers to overcome most problems of heterogeneity. Those with the dedication and preference for strikes are able to create solidarity among many prisoners by revealing and appealing to their collective identity as prisoners. They are able to communicate a sense that previous social factions either are completely made up and perpetuated by the prison system or, at the very least, are not as important as their commonality as prisoners. To put it another way, they found solidarity in their common enemy: the prison. Not only that, they are able to instill a sense of righteousness, hold the act of a strike itself as something to be desired, an expression of liberty and power against their captors.

In her work *Understanding Institutional Diversity*, Ostrom discusses how cultural belief systems affect how individuals view their circumstances and make decisions. As discussed above, the effect of the prison system serves to instill a mental model of individualization and isolation. This can lead to differences in how inmates view their current plight as well as their potential solutions, an issue that is exacerbated by the inability to frequently engage in open communication. Thus, it is the task of the strike leaders to disrupt that mental model in order to achieve cooperation. One effective way to do this is by spreading information and ideology (Lichbach 1998; Ostrom 2005). This allows individuals to begin sharing the same mental models and view their plights as collective rather than individual. Put another way, cultivating a shared ideology is a way of reducing inmates' revolutionary thresholds by altering public opinion, thus lowering the costs and increasing the benefits of participation (Kuran 1991; Lichbach 1998).

Strike leaders are concerned with not just the mental models of individuals, but the information that inmates have. Part of cultivating a shared ideology is having a common knowledge in order to develop a similar framework within which to think about strategies and potential solutions (Lichbach 1998; Ostrom 2005). An example of such information dissemination is the letter titled "An Anatomy of the Laundry," written by Sam Melville while in Attica. Originally convicted of bombing multiple government buildings, Melville began his internment at The Tombs, the informal name for the Manhattan Detention Center, where he organized an inmate strike. He was later transferred to Sing Sing, where he started another strike (Melville 1972). Ultimately he ended up in Attica after helping lead a strike at the Auburn Correctional facility. Before he took up a leadership position in the Attica Uprising, an act that would ultimately lead to his death, he wrote a letter titled *Anatomy of the Laundry*. It was a treatise on the economic exploitation of the inmates in Attica explaining how the pay and commissary pricing systems kept them in a state of exploitation and deprivation. One of the major divides between inmates in Attica was the privileges of work assignments. Working in the laundry was one of the more favorable assignments. The letter initially paints this divide between the laundry workers and the rest of the inmates by referring to laundry workers as "docile slaves." It goes on to break down the math on the wages of the laundry system and expenses of commissary, asserting that, whether they realize it or not, the laundry workers were exploited just like the rest of the prisoners and that collectively failing to participate in that oppressive system would cause major financial stress on the prison itself. *Anatomy of the Laundry* is often attributed with sparking the uprising that would eventually take the life of its author (Thompson 2016).

While Melville is an example of a radical leader who entered the foray and spread his own ideologies, other strike leaders cultivated ideologies within prison based on information from other inmates. Once the initial riot at Attica had settled, one of the first things strike organizers did was create an area where inmates could express grievances (Thompson 2016). Before the B Block strike at San Quentin, leaders held inmate meetings to gather information on grievances (Berger 2014). In this way, leaders incorporated the voices of other inmates into the ideology of the strikes. Both were tactics to increase the value of and instill a greater preference for the strike (Lichbach 1998).

Communication Innovation

Ostrom stresses communication as essential for the successful achievement of collective action (Ostrom 1989, 1990, 1998, 2000, 2005, 2010). Communication not only serves a functional purpose of sharing information on systems and processes of the collective action, but also serves the purpose of building trust so that individuals can make credible commitments. At the heart of collective action problems is a lack of credible commitment. How do individuals trust that others will cooperate when the norm is to act opportunistically? According to Ostrom, this is achieved through communication and reputation building (Ostrom 1990, 2010). In this section, I focus on communication. While face-to-face interactions are those most effective at building the trust necessary to foster cooperation (Ostrom 2010), communication generally, even when costs are high, leads to some measure of cooperation (Ostrom and Walker 1989). Given the high level of control over communication exerted by prisons, it may seem as though inmates are doomed to fail at this hurtle alone. I argue that the attempts of prisons to control communication can often backfire and allow communication to spread. And when control by the prison actually does hamper inmates' ability to communicate, innovation in communication techniques allows them to overcome this barrier.

I conceive of *communication innovation* as the use of unconventional techniques to pass information from one person to another. This would include anything outside the primary modes of communication used by the average person. Communication innovation is a long-recorded phenomenon inside prisons. Images of notes tied to the legs of birds come readily to mind. However, it would be disingenuous not to recognize that a lot of communication happens through legitimate conventional channels such as visitation, phone calls, and letter writing. Additionally, while there is an extremely high rate of solitary confinement among prisoners, most experience some measure of freedom to mingle among other inmates and gather in groups (Hassine 2004). As mentioned above, during the planning phase of the demonstrations at San Quentin, prisoners formed coalitions between racial groups and created venues for prisoners to come together and express their collective grievances against the system. These actions did not appear to be sanctioned by the prison system, nor did they seem to require large amounts of clandestine activity (Berger 2014).

However, attempts by prison officials to control communication often allow information to spread. As previously discussed, transferring inmates between prisons is a tactic used by officials to control communication. This instead can have the effect of allowing prisoners to transfer information between prisons, contributing meaningfully to the presence of strikes that include multiple prisons. Recall that Sam Melville was transferred to Attica to stave off more strikes at Auburn. Yet his presence at Attica allowed him to disseminate information that was instrumental in the uprising. The Folsom Prison Workers Strike is another notable example of crackdowns on communication backfiring. When leaders of the San Quentin B Block strike were sent to Folsom to avoid more demonstrations, they simply took their demands and ideologies to another prison. The Folsom Manifesto released during the nineteen-day Folsom strike was actually an updated draft of the list of demands created by those from San Quentin B Block (Berger 2014).

When communication is strictly controlled, however, inmates are able to find innovative ways to overcome barriers. Not only can inmates often shout under the door of SHU and AdSeg cells to speak with other inmates when guards are not present, they have developed a practice called "fishing" to pass messages. Inmates will use string pulled from their bedding and tie them to notes before sliding the notes under their cell door toward another (Frontline 2014). These tactics do not just serve to perpetuate communication between inmates in solitary confinement, but also with the broader prison population. The use of SHU is primarily to keep gang leaders separate from other gang members. However, SHU is also used as punishment for prisoners from the general population (Wallace-Wells 2014; Calavita and Jenness 2015). Thus, communication via gang networks is a useful mode of transferring information to the broader population. Some gang members set up a system of coded messages transferred in library books. Gang members even intentionally provoke disciplinary charges to be put in SHU so they can engage in one of the above mentioned interactions. Once their SHU sentence is done, they can carry that information back to the general population (Wallace-Wells 2014).

The practice of "hooping" is another common tactic that is used to, among other things, enhance communication with the outside world. "Hooping" is simply a modern slang term for the common practice of smuggling contraband into and out of prisons in the rectum. Bobby Sands and his IRA comrades used this technique to smuggle notes written on cigarette paper out of British prison to help coordinate and publicize their several demonstrations (Beresford 1987). With the technological advancement of cell phone cameras, prisoners have even more diverse options. In fact, cell phone footage and calls are a major way that modern prisoners are fighting back against information blackouts by prison officials. In April 2018, a riot broke out in the Lee Correctional Institution of South Carolina that left seven inmates stabbed to death. While officials claimed that this was due primarily to gang tensions and fighting, prisoners were able to tell a different story via the use of cell phone footage. After riots broke out, emails, phone calls, videos, and pictures came pouring out of the prison with footage of metal plates placed over the small windows of inmates' cells, restricting light and air flow, nutritionally inadequate food that prisoners say is often moldy, and putrid water that "smells like feces" coming straight out of the sinks in inmate cells. Inmates claimed that it was not racial tensions that erupted into a riot, but mistreatment by the prison itself (Thompson 2018).

So, while face-to-face communication can be limited, prisoners are able to overcome many communications barriers. This is extremely important for the successful coordination of a strike. Humans experience enhanced feelings of trust and solidarity when they can communicate in front of each other. In repetitive games, this becomes more important because if you promise to cooperate in the first round but instead defect, you then have to face the other players in the second round and explain your defection (Ostrom 2010). This basic principle can still hold true in prisons. While some individuals may be segregated from the wider population, those in the general population know that they will eventually run into everyone. There is almost no avoiding it (Hassine 2004).

Game Repetition and Information of Past Actions

One major way that trust can be built, especially in the face of communication barriers and uncertainty, is through the building of reputation. Reputations are built when games are repeated and people can gather information about other players (Ostrom 2005, 2010). This seems to be a tactic commonly used among strikers.

Most large-scale strikes are preceded by smaller, repeated strikes. This was the case, as mentioned above, with the Folsom Prison Labor Strike that was preceded by several smaller strikes in San Quentin. These strike leaders were able to build a reputation for being committed not only to the action, but to the ideology that backed it up (Berger 2014). Strike leaders from Auburn Correctional facility brought their knowledge and reputation to Attica. Even the ill-fated Attica prison uprising was preceded by several smaller strikes. Inmates had engaged in multiple work stoppages to protest wages. They even performed a sit-in at the medical unit.

Repetition of strikes also served as a learning tool. Strikers often study previous strikes and strikers to get ideas, learn what went wrong, and what they might expect. Attica strikers learned from the Folsom strikers (Thompson 2016). Folsom strikers learned from George Jackson, the Founder of the Black Guerilla Family gang and prominent political prison figure (Berger 2014). The 2016 and 2018 National Prison Labor strikers learned from Folsom and Attica (Speri 2016; Gross 2018).

CASE STUDY: THE SHORT CORRIDOR COLLECTIVE

On July 8th of 2013, four alleged rival gang leaders collectively kicked off the largest prison hunger strike in American history from their cells in solitary confinement. Todd Ashker, Sitawa Jamaa, Arturo Castellanos, and Antonio Guillen, allegedly high-ranking leaders of the Aryan Brotherhood, Black Guerrilla Family, Mexican Mafia, and Nuestra Familia, respectively, had formed the most unlikely of alliances. Their alleged gang affiliations spoke more of a dedication to the hate and eradication of each other than a tight bond of solidarity. Their confinement to 8 x 10-foot windowless cement cells, where they were fed through slots in the door, did not lend itself to cooperation and friendship. Yet over the course of five years, these men meticulously planned, practiced, and coordinated a strike to protest their shared experience, decades-long sentences in solitary confinement (Wallace-Wells 2014).

Prisoners in the Pelican Bay SHU are confined to their cells for twenty-three hours a day, let out only once a day for an hour of recreation, which is carried out in a different solitary cement cell. While in SHU they are not allowed contact visits. There are three ways out of the SHU: parole, snitching, or death. Since the primary use of SHU is to separate gang members from alleged leaders, snitching entails denouncing gang affiliations and providing information to authorities on their members and operations, an act that is likely to get a person killed when back in the general prison population. Thus, many are interned for decades leading to mental breakdowns, hallucinations, suicidal thoughts, social withdrawal, and disassociation (Wallace-Wells 2014).

These four leaders found themselves housed in what was called the Short Corridor, the corridor of the Pelican Bay SHU with the fewest cells. In 2006, the prison moved what they believed to be the most influential gang leaders to the Short Corridor in an attempt to cut them off from mid-ranking gang members in other areas of SHU. So, by trying to minimize communication within the SHU unit, they housed who they believed to be the most influential prisoners within shouting distance of each other. And shout they did. Under doorways, and over and through walls, the group that was eventually known as the Short Corridor Collective talked about family and life and the shared plight of solitary confinement (Wallace-Wells 2014; Camon 2016).

Ashker formed a bond with another white inmate named Danny Troxell. They began reading books like *A People's History of the United States* and the biography of Irish hunger striker Bobby Sands. Others read Goffman, Foucault, and Wolfe. The men would discuss these books and engaged in debates, shouting under the doors of their cells or over the walls of the recreation cells. They devised systems of passing notes from cell to cell and even learned the sewer piping system and developed a method of shouting through toilet pipes to speak with inmates in faraway cells (Wallace-Wells

2014; Camon 2016). Though it is important to note that while this seems like a plethora of communication, it happened in short, disjointed conversations shouted in bursts (Camon 2016). As their relationships grew, so did their collective sense of grievance. They began to latch onto the idea of the prisoner class, that they were not just a hodgepodge arrangement of gang members; rather, they were all united under their shared plight as prisoners. Eventually, the idea of a hunger strike caught on (Wallace-Wells 2014).

The next step was figuring out how to get other prisoners involved. The Black Guerrilla Family was born out of revolutionary ideology and was by far the most politically active gang. Their members could be counted on to participate. The Nuestra Familia gang had developed a system of communication with SHU residents. First, the SHU inmate would write a message in the pages of a book from the law library. They would then send coded messages to family members in the mail informing them which book to look in. The family member would then inform other gang members in general population of the location of the message. Orders from gang leaders were followed without question in the Mexican Mafia and the Familia. So, all Castellanos and Guillen had to do was get the order out in one of the law books. The Aryan Brotherhood was more democratic, with all gang decisions being decided by a vote, but word got out that Ashker and Truxell were willing to sacrifice their lives for the cause. The fact that over the last few years Ashker had also earned his paralegal degree and successfully sued the prison fifteen times (Wallace-Wells 2014) helped to build his reputation as a force against the prison system.

The hunger strike idea began gaining traction in 2011 after SHU was put on lockdown. Jamaa contacted outside advocacy groups, understanding the importance of their support and participation. Some members of the Collective staged private fasts to figure out how long they might survive and how much water they would need. Jamaa fasted for thirty-three days, while Ashker calculated his need for 240 ounces of water a day to keep his heart pumping. In the summer of that year, the Collective staged two smaller hunger strikes (Wallace-Wells 2014; Camon 2016). The first strike involved about 6,000 prisoners across thirteen prisons and lasted thirteen weeks. They were promised concession, but when none materialized they staged another strike, this time doubling the participation. It was clear that prisoners were learning the ins and outs of hunger striking, both the coordinated effort it took and how to manage the physical effects of such a tactic (Camon 2016). By the end of the second strike, they gained small but significant concessions: a hand ball and pull-up bar in the recreation cells, as well as revisions to the "snitching rule," a method for getting out of SHU by snitching on other inmates. Then, in 2012 the Collective released a letter calling for a cessation of gang violence in Pelican Bay. It was a call for solidarity among the prisoner class. Prison officials refused to circulate it, but it made its way around the California prison system anyway (Wallace-Wells 2014; Camon 2016).

Eventually, with the help of advocacy groups and family members, the message of the hunger strike spread. Some later reported that many had been ordered by gang leaders to participate, though prison officials reported only one incidence of violent coercion. On the first day of the strike, 30,000 inmates across the California prison system refused food for twenty-four hours. A week in roughly 11,000 prisoners were still participating. The leaders of the Collective had no way of truly knowing how many people were still participating, but Jamaa knew they needed encouragement. When the leaders were transferred from SHU to AdSeg shortly after the strike began, Jamaa began hollering "40 days and 40 nights!" a reference to Moses leading the Israelites through the desert. He continued shouting this slogan through the space under his door. More strikers were moved to AdSeg and the hopes of the Collective heightened (Wallace-Wells 2014).

The strike had five core demands including the abolition of the snitching rule, adequate food, elimination of group punishments, an end to long-term solitary confinement, and expanded programs and privileges for SHU inmates. The California Department of Corrections and Rehabilitation (CDCR) tried to spin the strike, saying that SHU was not solitary confinement and that the strike was nothing more than coordinated gang activity. But the call for solidarity by the Collective and their insistent referral to the SHU as solitary and torturous delegitimized a lot of these efforts. The strikers were gaining ground. The CDCR began discussing potential reforms while refusing the strikers demands to meet with high-level state officials. The Center for Constitutional Rights was drafting a class action lawsuit against the CDCR on behalf of prisoners (Camon 2016). Over forty days into the strike and the sixty-nine remaining strikers had begun experiencing the worst parts of hunger. Not only were their bodies beginning to consume their muscles, they were no longer able to regulate their body temperature. Their energy was completely drained. On the forty-third day, a judge handed down an order allowing for the forced feeding of prisoners and the disregard for any Do Not Resuscitate orders. But along with this announcement was the promise by two state legislators to hold special hearings on the conditions of SHU (Wallace-Wells 2014).

There was debate among the leaders, but by day fifty-nine the remaining forty or fifty strikers agreed to cease their protest and begin the dangerous process of refeeding (Wallace-Wells 2014; Camon 2016). But their hopes that they had gained some political ground would not come to fruition for a few more years. In 2015, a settlement was reached in the class action lawsuit, where the CDRC agreed to move long-term SHU inmates to less restrictive areas. They also were required to review all prisoners placed in SHU for gang affiliation. Additionally, gang affiliation alone could no longer land you in the SHU. Inmates must be found guilty of a severe rules violation and be given a SHU term of no more than five years instead of indefinite placement. Since the settlement the California SHU population dropped from 3,045 in 2015 to 594 in 2018.

Many members of the Collective were not so lucky. For his participation in the 2011 and 2013 strikes, Ashker was moved to a different area of SHU. When he was moved, guards discovered a picture of Truxell given to him as a gift from his friend. They confiscated it as contraband, issued Ashker a severe rules violation and took his TV as punishment (Wallace-Wells 2014). After the 2015 settlement, Ashker was moved into the general population, but after thirteen months he was placed back into solitary confinement, this time in AdSeg. He filed suit challenging his confinement. As of July 2018, he was still waiting for a settlement conference date (Law 2018).

CONCLUSION

"In broad outline, it is a picture of late-modern society that has expanded civil and legal rights, yet deprives people of their liberty on an unprecedented scale" (Calavita and Jenness 2015, 3). Inmates of American prisons find themselves in a paradoxical situation. They are inmates of a total institution, subject to both the near-complete control of their wardens as well as the shear chaos and uncertainty of the prison society of which they are now members. The prison institution, including the norms established by the officials and other inmates, present seemingly insurmountable barriers to cooperation and collective action. Yet there is a rich history of inmates coming together and engaging in the nonviolent collective action of prison strikes.

The work of Elinor Ostrom helps illuminate some of the most important factors to the successful execution of prison strikes. The presence of strike leaders as heterogeneous participants with high levels of preference for collective action are able to spread ideology and information in order to establish new institutional norms. Inmates develop innovative ways to overcome communication barriers presented by their interment. The repetition of strikes then allows leaders and inmates to build reputations and learn in order to overcome the issue of credible commitment.

This chapter presents a unique application of Ostrom's scholarship on collective action. While this is a first attempt at applying this framework to such circumstances it illuminates the usefulness of Ostrom's work at exploring how people in extremely decollectivized circumstances overcome barriers to achieve cooperation. It suggests that Ostom's theory of collective action could be useful in other such unique circumstances, such as Uber driver strikes in

Nirobi (Ngugi 2019), strikes in US Immigration and Customs Enforcement detention centers (Stein 2019), and children staging hunger strikes in French refugee camps (Grierson 2019).

NOTES

1. These institutional changes can either be policies specific to a prison, such as facility changes and disciplinary policies, or policies that affect a larger system of prisons at the county, state, or federal level, such as prison regulations and minimum wage laws for prisoners.

2. There is a third option, which is to help the current regime, in this case the prison. However, attempting to explain this course of action and its repercussions fall outside the scope of this chapter.

REFERENCES

American Civil Liberties Union. 2019. "The Nationwide Prison Strike: Why It's Happened and What It Means for Ending Mass Incarceration." Retrieved from https://www.aclu.org/blog/smart-justice/mass-incarceration/nationwide-prison-strike-why-its-happening-and-what-it-means.

Anderson, James. 2014. "Hunger Strike at Menard Correctional Facility Draws Solidarity, Support." *Truthout.* Retrieved from https://truthout.org/articles/hunger-strike-at-menard-correctional-center-draws-solidarity-support/.

Beresford, David. 1987. *Ten Men Dead: The Story of the 1981 Irish Hunger Strike.* New York: Atlantic Monthly Press.

Berger, Dan. 2014. *Captive Nation: Black Prison Organization in the Civil Rights Era.* Chapel Hill: The University of North Carolina Press.

Brown, Dalvin. 2018 "Nationwide Strike by Prisoners Set to End Sunday after Weeks of Protest." *USA Today.* Retrieved from https://www.usatoday.com/story/news/2018/09/08/prison-strike-state-state-look-protests-behind-bars/1225268002/.

Bureau of Justice Statistics. 1982. Bulletin: Prisoners 1925-81. U.S. Department of Justice.

Calavita, Kitty, and Jenness, Valerie. 2015. *Appealing to Justice: Prisoner Grievances, Rights, and Carceral Logic.* Oakland, CA: University of California Press.

Camon, Alessandro. 2016. "The Short Corridor: How the Most Isolated Prisoners in America Took on the System, and Won." *Los Angeles Review of Books.* Retrieved from https://lareviewofbooks.org/article/short-corridor-isolated-prisoners-america-took-system-won/#!

Chen, Michelle. 2010. "Georgia Prison Strike: A Hidden Labor Force Resists." *In These Times.* Retrieved from http://www.commondreams.org/print/63604.

Cole, Daniel H. 2017. "Laws, Norms, and the Institutional Analysis and Development Framework." *Journal of Institutional Economics* 13: 829–847.

Denzin, Norman K. 1968. "Collective Behavior in Total Institutions: The Case of the Mental Hospital and the Prison." *Social Problems* 15 (3): 353–365.

Dilawar, Arvind. 2018. "Following a Nationwide Strike, Prisoners Say They Face Repressive Repercussions." *Pacific Standard.* Retrieved from https://psmag.com/news/following-a-nationwide-strike-prisoners-say-they-face-repressive-repercussions.

Edwards, Richard Autour. 1979. *Contested Terrain: The Transformation of the Workplace in the Twentieth Century.* New York: Basic Books.

Federal Bureau of Prisons. "About Our Facilities." *U.S. Department of Justice.* Retrieved from https://www.bop.gov/about/facilities/federal_prisons.jsp.

Frontline. 2014. "How Inmates in Solitary Confinement Trick the Guards." *PBS.* Retrieved from https://youtu.be/2CvDpAvJR84.

Grierson, Jamie. 2019. "Calais Child Refugees Went on Hunger Strike after UK Transfer Delays." *The Guardian.* Retrieved from https://www.theguardian.com/world/2019/mar/31/calais-child-refugees-hunger-strike-uk-transfer-delay.

Gross, Danile. 2018. "An Inside Account of the National Prisoners' Strike." *The New Yorker.* Retrieved from https://www.newyorker.com/news/as-told-to/an-inside-account-of-the-national-prisoners-strike.

Hager, Eli. 2016. "Does the First Amendment End at the Prison Gate? An Inmates Novel is the Latest Test." *The Marshall Project.* Retrieved from https://www.themarshallproject.org/2016/10/25/does-the-first-amendment-end-at-the-prison-gate.

Hardin, Russell. 1982. "Exchange Theory on Strategic Bases." *Social Science Information* 21 (2): 251–272.

Hassine, Victor. 2004. *Life Without Parole: Living and Dying in Prison Today.* New York: Oxford University Press.

Incarcerated Workers Organization. 2016. "Announcement of Nationally Coordinated Workstoppage for Sept 9, 2016." Retrieved from https://iwoc.noblogs.org/post/2016/04/01/announcement-of-nationally-coordinated-prisoner-workstoppage-for-sept-9-2016/.

Jackson, George. 1994. *Soledad Brother: The Prison Letters of George Jackson.* Chicago: Lawrence Hill Press.

Kuran, Timur. 1991. "Now Out of Never: The Element of Surprise in the East European Revolution of 1989." *World Politics* 44 (1): 7–48.

———. 1995. *Private Truths Public Lies: The Social Consequences of Preference Falsification.* Boston: Harvard University Press.

Lavender, George. 2014. "Alabama Prison Work Strike 'Stalls' But Wins Support from Wobblies." *In These Times.* Retrieved from inthesetimes.com/prison-complex/entry/16607/alabama_prisoners.

Law, Victoria. 2018. "As Long As Solitary Exists, They Will Find a Way to Use It." *The Nation.* Retrieved from https://www.thenation.com/article/long-solitary-exists-will-find-way-use/.

Legal Information Institute. "Wex Legal Dictionary." Retrieved from https://www.law.cornell.edu/wex/prisoners%27_rights.

Lichbach, Michael I. 1998. *The Rebel's Dilemma.* Ann Arbor: The University of Michigan Press.

Melville, Samuel. 1972. *Letters from Attica*. New York: William Morrow, Harper Collins Publishing.
Ngugi, Brian. 2019. "Uber, Bolt Riders Pay Double Rate as Digital Taxi Drivers Strike." *Business Daily*. Retrieved from https://www.businessdailyafrica.com/news/539546-5197946-57c5n4z/index.html.
Ostrom, Elinor. 1990. *Governing the Commons: The Evolution of Institutions for Collective Action*. Cambridge: Cambridge University Press.
———. 2000. "Collective Action and the Evolution of Social Norms." *Journal of Economic Perspectives* 14 (3): 137–158.
———. 2005. *Understanding Institutional Diversity*. Princeton: Princeton University Press.
———. 2010. "Analyzing Collective Action." *Agriculture Economics* 44 (1): 155–166.
Ostrom, Elinor, and James Walker. 1989. "Communication in a Commons: Cooperation Without External Enforcement." Presented at American Political Science Association Meetings, Atlanta, GA, August 31–September 3, 1989.
Rabuy, Bernadette, and Peter Wagner. 2015. "Screening Out Family Time: The For-Profit Video Visitation Industry in Prisons and Jails." *Prison Policy Institute*.
San Francisco Bay Review. 2018. "The Folsom Manifesto for the California Statewide Prison Strike, 1970." Retrieved from https://sfbayview.com/2018/10/folsom-manifesto-for-the-california-statewide-prison-strike-1970/.
Silver, Morris. 1974. "Political Revolution and Repression: An Economic Approach." *Public Choice* 17: 63–71.
Skarbek, David. 2014. *The Social Order of the Underworld: How Prison Gangs Govern the American Penal System*. New York: Oxford University Press.
Sparks, R., A.E. Bottoms, and W. Hay. 1996. *Prisons and the Problem of Order*. Oxford: Oxford University Press.
Speri, Alice. 2016. "Prisoners in Multiple States Call for Strikes to Protest Forced Labor." *The Intercept*. Retrieved from https://theintercept.com/2016/04/04/prisoners-in-multiple-states-call-for-strikes-to-protest-forced-labor/.
Stein, Michel I. 2019. "Hunger Strikes at ICE Detention Centers Spread ss Parole, Bond are Denyed." *National Public Radio*. Retrieved from https://www.npr.org/2019/04/19/713910647/hunger-strikes-at-ice-detention-centers-spread-as-parole-bond-is-denied.
Sykes, Gresham M. 1958. *The Society of Captives: A Study of a Maximum Security Prison*. Princeton: Princeton University Press.
Thompson, Heather Ann. 2016. *Blood in the Water: The Attica Prison Uprising of 1971 and Its Legacy*. New York: Pantheon Books.
———. 2018. "How a South Carolina Prison Riot Really Went Down." *New York Times*. Retrieved from https://www.nytimes.com/2018/04/28/opinion/how-a-south-carolina-prison-riot-really-went-down.html.
Timm, Jane C. 2018. "Most States Disenfranchise Felons. Maine and Vermont Allow Inmates to Vote from Prison." *NBC News*. Retrieved from https://www.nbcnews.com/politics/politics-news/states-rethink-prisoner-voting-rights-incarceration-rates-rise-n850406.

Tullock, Gordon. 1971. "The Paradox of Revolution." *Public Choice* 11: 89–99.

———. 1995. "Rationality and Rebellion." *Rationality and Society* 7 (1): 116–128.

Wallace, Samuel E. 1971. "On the Totality of Institutions." From *Total Institutions*, edited by Samuel E. Wallace. New Brunswick, Canada: Transaction Publishers.

Wallace-Wells, Benjamin. 2014. "The Plot From Solitary." *New York Magazine*. Retrieved from http://nymag.com/news/features/solitary-secure-housing-units-2014-2/.

Wheaton, Sarah. 2010. "Prisoners Strike in Georgia." *New York Times*. Retrieved from https://www.nytimes.com/2010/12/12/us/12prison.html?mtrref=www.google.com&gwh=A7B21982F3F3611A7B411C43DB054533&gwt=pay.

Chapter 8

The Cantinas Network of Terra do Meio

A Case of Institutional Learning in the Amazon Forest

V. Miranda Chase, Raquel Rodrigues dos Santos, and Augusto Postigo

INTRODUCTION

Indigenous and traditional populations of the Amazon have historically maintained their livelihoods by preserving forest resources. However, particularly after the 1960s the region saw many "development" projects, most of which were based on destructive activities. In response to that, starting around 1980, several groups challenged the mainstream notion of development and tried to create alternatives so that making a living off a vibrant forest would be more attractive and profitable than making a living by destroying it. These initiatives envisioned an economic modus operandi where local communities protect the forest, generate income, and engage in trade, while maintaining their cultural traditions. This goal runs counter both to the recent trend marked by environmental destruction and to the prior economic system based solely on subsistence.

These initiatives followed different ideologies and strategies. Many have failed quickly, others endured for a little longer, and few are still standing. Creating this new modus operandi is challenging not only because there are strong incentives to cut down the forest, but what makes it extremely hard is the fact that no one knows exactly what it looks like. These initiatives had different arrangements, and people involved believed that the initial setup would be able to accomplish their desired goal. Unfortunately, it is virtually impossible to achieve such an ambitious goal on a first trial. It is thus imperative that people imbued in this mission learn from changing circumstances and adapt their strategies.

This chapter analyzes one such attempt: the Cantinas Network of Terra do Meio (south of Pará state, Brazil). We tell the story of how local communities in this part of the Amazon have learned to keep things flexible and yet persist in their goal of making a living off the forest. We use Ostrom's Institutional Analysis and Development (IAD) framework (2005) to assess this initiative. We analyze several aspects of the cantinas as an action arena and investigate the elements that render this system adaptable and resilient at the same time. We ask how the cantinas network has emerged and, given its structure, how was it possible to maintain flexibility and perseverance? In other words, why were people in this case able to learn from their changing circumstances and adapt their strategies, while maintaining their goal, especially considering that many other initiatives tried similar things and failed? What sets this case apart?

The cantinas network is a solution to several collective action problems, the main one being the challenge that river dwellers face putting forest products in the market. Making a living off the forest requires that people use natural resources for their subsistence and income generation, and it is imperative that they do so sustainably. This includes commercializing nontimber forest products. Local communities face several challenges when trying to sell these products in the market. The most significant ones are market placement with stable prices and liquidity. These challenges are collective action problems: no one's harvest is big enough to make it worth it for this person alone to hire a boat to transport his/her products to the city, so alone no one is able to negotiate a contract and secure good prices with potential buyers. Liquidity is important because very few people have enough resources to make it through a harvesting season and only get paid in the end. Thus, they need to collectively negotiate with buyers for a better payment system.

The solution they found was securing buyers that agreed to pay a better price for their products, and who were willing to sign purchase contracts with favorable conditions to local river dwellers. In order to administer the finances and bureaucracy involved with such contracts, people in these communities created the institution of "cantinas." Cantinas are not profit-oriented private enterprises. They are owned and managed by communities. They are physically located inside rural villages, and on a day-by-day basis they function as a place where people can buy industrialized goods from the city and get paid for delivering their harvest of forest products. Cantinas are, however, much more than a small store where people buy and sell things. They are ultimately a social institution that lowers coordination costs for transportation and market placement, and it increases the social capital for those involved with it. They are a system that offers greater liquidity for forest products, allowing community members to learn more about the value chain of these resources, resulting in income generation options that bring additional incentives for river dwellers to protect the forest.

This chapter presents the cantinas network, highlighting key elements that characterize this social institution. We argue that a distinctive feature of the cantinas system is its resiliency. Actors involved have managed to create a system that is constantly changing and nonetheless never loses sight of its ultimate goal. We give examples of situations when things have almost gone seriously wrong, but people involved acted quickly and responded adequately—changing the system and adapting to new circumstances. We show that cantinas have emerged out of a context where local communities in the Amazon were looking for better options to live autonomously off forest resources, and we point to how this system respects traditional norms and values. This is because communities have developed their own rules-in-use to establish self-governing mechanisms.

The chapter is structured as follows: First, we review the IAD Framework and discuss why it is useful to analyze the cantinas network. We then provide an overall context of Terra do Meio and the cantinas, giving the reader important information about the biophysical characteristics of the region, the attributes of the communities and their rules-in-use. Following that we explain how the first cantina emerged, and we analyze cantinas as an action arena. In the last few sessions we explain the patterns of interactions among cantinas, the outcomes they have achieved, and we evaluate this system according to six criteria suggested by Ostrom (2011). In the conclusion, we explain why we believe this system is likely to endure overtime.

Before we proceed, we would like to offer a quick note about our data. As the reader will notice, we present a wealth of information without providing bibliographical references for some of it. The reason for that is because not much has yet been published about the Cantinas Network of Terra do Meio. We have access to this data through first accounts and participant observation.[1] All the stories we present here are real. To protect the privacy of those involved, we use names of trees as pseudonyms to identify communities and of fake initials to identify people.

REVIEW OF THE IAD FRAMEWORK

The IAD framework was developed by Elinor and Vincent Ostrom and their colleagues as a way for scholars to conduct a guided analysis of any kind of social institution. According to E. Ostrom, institutions are complex networks of rules-in-use, which "operate upon many people, [and] explain the aggregate social, economic, and political outcomes that we observe" (Tarko 2017, 6). People follow these rules for various reasons. According to Tarko (2017, 11), "individuals accept membership to a community because the benefits they receive outweigh the personal costs of having to obey some collective decisions with which they disagree." Institutions are not necessarily formal legal arrangements that gather people in a building—they "exist in a language shared by some community of individuals rather than as the physical parts of some external environment" (Kiser and Ostrom 2000, 56).

Even though the IAD framework has been most ubiquitously used in the study of common pool resources (CPRs), it can be used to analyze a much wider variety of institutions. "The IAD framework is a diagnostic tool that can be used to investigate any broad subject where humans repeatedly interact within rules and norms that guide their choice of strategies and behaviors" (Hess and Ostrom 2006, 41). As explained by McGinnis (2000, xi), the framework is most useful for scholars "to understand and strengthen the foundations of self-governance." He contends that there is a core message promoted by this form of analysis: "Politically, the goal is to establish and sustain capacities for self-governance, by which is meant the structured ways communities organize themselves to solve collective problems, achieve common aspirations, and resolve conflicts. Methodologically, the goal is to understand the institutional foundations of self-governance, that is, to determine which conditions strengthen and which conditions undermine community capacities for self-governance" (McGinnis 2000, xi–xii).

The framework was first created in the 1970s, and it developed over time with slightly modified iterations in later publications. This analytical tool can be used in conjunction with theories from different social sciences, given that the framework is not meant to explain, interpret, or predict any specific problems or issues faced by social institutions. Rather, the framework is an aid for analysts (using whatever theory seems most appropriate) to conduct a thorough check into specific units of social institutions. Thus, looking carefully at these units can yield interesting insights about the institution as a whole (Ostrom 2005).

These basic units of analysis (also known as building blocks) in the IAD framework are: biophysical characteristics, attributes of the community, rules-in-use, the action arena, patterns of interactions, outcomes, and the evaluative criteria. All units have subdivisions—for instance, the action arena is often broken down into action situation and actors. The framework has been depicted in different graphs, but figure 8.1 is the most widely used illustration. Different publications about the IAD have offered many variations of how each unit can be subdivided. There is not one correct subdivision or one way the framework ought to be used—rather, the many iterations are meant to better suit the analysis in question. The IAD framework "contains a nested set

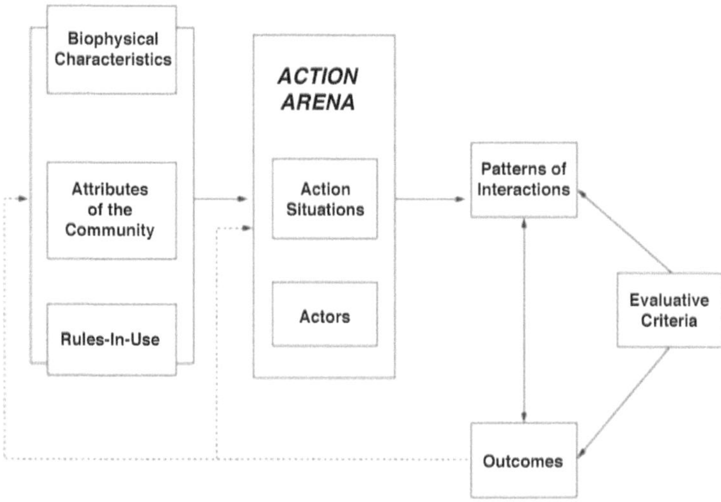

Figure 8.1 The Institutional Analysis and Development Framework. *Source*: Hess and Ostrom 2006.

of building blocks that social scientists can use in efforts to understand human interactions and outcomes across diverse settings" (Ostrom 2009, 413).

Even though all building blocks in the framework are important for a complete analysis, the action situation is often regarded as a central piece of the investigation. This is where people interact under the rules-in-use, where actors cooperate (or not) in underusing, overusing, or maintaining a resource they share. After all, studying institutions is an attempt to understand how people come together to achieve a common goal and why do they sometimes succeed, and others fail.

It is not useful to break down the IAD framework and look only at one building block or another. It is the combined understanding of how each of these parts work in conjunction with one another that offers a more thorough understanding of the situation in question. Each block has particular characteristics and they influence one another. To explain the multifaceted interaction among juxtaposed blocks, McGinnis (2000, 4) suggests the term "polycentricity," because it "nicely conveys an image of a network of overlapping and interlinked arenas of choice." He contends that "a basic tenet of institutional analysis is that multiple arenas, or centers, of interactions and participation need to be considered simultaneously. Self-governance works best if the overall governance structure is polycentric. . . . Governance does not require a single center of power, and governments should not claim an exclusive responsibility for resolving political issues. Instead, politics should be envisioned as an activity that goes on in many arenas simultaneously, at many scales of aggregation" (McGinnis 2000, xii).

Here we use the IAD framework to analyze the cantinas network. The cantinas system is polycentric (there is no central command), and cantinas have emerged out of a context when local communities in the Amazon were looking for better options to live autonomously off forest resources (so it respects traditional norms and values). These communities have developed their own rules-in-use to establish self-governing mechanisms, considering the broader constraints they face in their physical environment and larger political system. The central part of this analysis is the action arena. However, before we describe how cantinas operate from within, we would like to give the reader a better perspective about the context of this institution. In the next section, we provide further information on the biophysical characteristics, the attributes of the communities, and their rules-in-use. This will yield a better understanding of the conditions under which people interact at the cantinas.

THE OVERALL CONTEXT OF TERRA DO MEIO AND THE CANTINAS

Biophysical Characteristics

Terra do Meio is an 8.5-million hectares mosaic of ten protected areas in the Eastern Brazilian Amazon. It is divided in strict nature reserves, protected areas with sustainable use of natural resources and indigenous lands. In the 1990s the government, local communities and environmental nongovernmental organizations (NGOs) were struggling to thwart deforestation, predatory logging and informal land occupation in the region (Doblas 2015). After many years, the Brazilian Park Service (Chico Mendes Institute for Biodiversity—ICMBio) turned Terra do Meio into the protected mosaic it is today (Velásquez, Villas-Boas, and Schwartzman 2006). Currently, there are 267 families of river dwellers (locally called *beiradeiros*) living in more than 100 small communities, and another 100 or so indigenous families in their own territories, all relying on natural resources for their survival and income generation. The region is very isolated and some people can be as far as 250 miles from the nearest urban center (Altamira), a journey that can take many days by boat since there are no roads in the area. As a consequence, these communities have limited access to the market. It is hard for them to acquire basic goods, and it is even more challenging to sell their products and earn some income. It is with this background that the cantinas have emerged. It is possible to make an argument based on Vogler (2019) that, when the state does not provide public services or public goods in a specific area, citizens have significant incentives to provide these public goods and services themselves. The cantinas network may serve as a good empirical example of such a dynamic.

Attributes of the Community

In order to understand the main characteristics of these communities, it is imperative to briefly review the history of migration and settlement in this territory. This section provides a brief historical overview of how families established themselves there, and how their economic livelihoods changed over time.

The Amazon region lived through two rubber booms. After the car industry started to grow internationally in the mid-1800s, the demand for rubber to produce tires peaked. Given that rubber trees at the time could only be found in the Amazon, a large influx of migrants from other regions of Brazil settled there to explore the valuable resource. The peak of the first boom was around 1910, when latex was 40 percent of all the revenues Brazil earned in its foreign trade exchanges (Villas-Boas, Ribas Guerreriro, Junqueira, and Postigo 2017). The first cycle ended because a few decades earlier Britain had taken rubber tree seedlings and planted them in Malaysia. After the production of rubber in Asia took off, international prices fell and rubber tappers in the Amazon found themselves without their main source of income. After Japan invaded Malaysia during World War II, prices went up and latex from the Amazon was again in high demand. This was the second rubber boom, which ended quickly after the victory of the Allied forces over Axis powers (Villas-Boas et al. 2017).

When migrants from other regions of Brazil settled in the Amazon, they incurred in large debts with rubber barons who financed the initial settlement costs. Barons placed rubber tappers along the riverbanks with only one or two houses in each place to make sure that tappers didn't have to compete for rubber trees. Tappers were expected to extract and stock the latex, and boats sent by barons would come every few months to pick up the production. Boats also brought goods, and these were the moments when tappers could exchange their production for whatever they needed to buy (Postigo and Rezende 2017).

Rubber barons established depots (*barracões dos seringais*) along riverbanks to stock rubber production and supply boats with nonperishable goods. Tappers could exchange their production of rubber for other goods both at these depots or where they lived when boats came by. The prices of the latex and of the goods were set by boat owners and depot managers, often leaving tappers with little bargaining power. This established a process of debt accumulation, given that tappers would buy more than what they could sell and would promise to deliver more rubber the next time around. Tappers did not have the option to sell their latex to other buyers, both due to their isolated conditions and due to retaliation from the regular buyers with whom they had debts. After the collapse of latex prices in the international market, rubber barons went bankrupt and tappers were left with large debts and no clear means of economic productivity that could yield them an income. It was then that other forest products became more economically attractive and started being explored commercially (Postigo and Rezende 2017).

Families living along the riverbanks have always practiced farming, fishing, and hunting for their own consumption. After latex prices went down, the surplus from these activities became commodities that started to be traded in rubber depots and when boats went by. Rubber depots would eventually disappear, but boats continued to navigate through the region trading a smaller production of rubber and mostly other goods. Middlemen were already working in the area since the second rubber boom and became more important after this economy collapsed. They own boats and became the bridge for social and commercial relations between river dwellers and the urban world. They started to fulfill the role of rubber barons, in the sense of providing river dwellers with an option to sell forest products and purchase industrialized goods.

Today, river dwellers have their own cultural identity, which is a mixture of the regions where they came from with elements of Amazonian indigenous cultures. They live in small communities, all of them connected through strong kinship relations who share a narrative of a past marked by hard work under the rubber barons, and a pride identity as people who can survive in the forest protecting it at the same time. Aside from river dwellers, Terra do Meio also houses several indigenous communities which have inhabited the region since immemorial times. Indigenous groups maintain, to a large extent, their traditional practices and customs. Many of them, however, have had a long history of contact with the surrounding nonindigenous society and have incorporated many of their habits. The next section explains how all these groups developed social rules to guide their economic relations.

Rules-in-Use

Assistance is a practice rooted in the rubber tapping period and remains an important compass to orient social relations; thus, it is possible to frame it as a key rule-in-use. It prescribes that barons ought to offer logistical and financial assistance to families in the forest who need to go to the city for medical or other reasons. After rubber barons went bankrupt, boat owners began to undertake several social roles in the region, including the provision of assistance. Over time these relations developed far beyond an exchange of products and favors, encompassing relations of marriage, friendship, and compaternity (Postigo and Rezende 2017). In exchange for their assistance, middlemen expect that families save all forest products to be traded exclusively with them. All families in these remote regions depend, to a greater or a lesser extent, on the assistance of middlemen.

Another important rule-in-use in this context is *aviamento*. It is a form of economic exchange which also dates back from the rubber period and is still present. People living along the riverbanks depend on the transportation services offered by barons (in the past) or middlemen (nowadays) to exchange forest products for goods coming from the city. In the *aviamento* system, prices are set so that river dwellers have to buy things on credit, and some people later find themselves in permanent debt. Both rules-in-use (*aviamento* and assistance) have fostered an economic system that enabled these families to remain in this remote territory (Postigo and Rezende 2017).

In this system, river dwellers find themselves in a "catch-22" situation: on the one hand, it is in their interest to maintain amicable relations with middlemen because of their social connections and the possibility that they might need assistance. On the other hand, dwellers are trapped in a system where middlemen and their bosses set prices (often deemed inadequate) and deter them from looking for other buyers. This tension forecloses several opportunities for river dwellers to pursue economic growth.

When cantinas were established, it was crucial to take that expectation of assistance and the *aviamento* system into consideration. Cantinas are today an alternative to the *aviamento* system, offering river dwellers another option to sell their forest products and buy industrialized goods, with the main difference being that prices are set in a more advantageous way to those living in the forest. But people in the communities still expect the cantinas system to offer them some form of assistance when needed. If someone is in dire financial conditions, they expect to be able to buy things on credit at the cantina.

HOW CANTINAS HAVE EMERGED

This section describes how people living in the forest were struggling under the *aviamento* system and were looking for alternatives to sell their products for prices better than those offered by middlemen. To explain this process, we tell the story of Mr. A, a community leader and the person who opened the first cantina in Terra do Meio.

Mr. A was born and raised along the westernmost part of Terra do Meio. His region is rich with Copaiba trees, which produce a natural oil valuable to the cosmetics and pharmaceutical industries and also commonly used for medicinal purposes in the region. He used to collect copaiba oil and sell it to middlemen, always for a price he deemed inadequate. One day, in the early 2000s, he decided to take his production to Altamira, the nearest town which nonetheless requires an expensive journey of many days on a boat. There he put his bottles of copaiba oil on a wheelbarrow and went door-to-door trying to sell them. By the end of his journey, he broke even. The money earned from selling the oil was barely enough to offset his travel costs. But he did not give up. He was convinced that there had to be a better way for him to put his product in the market with a larger profit margin. He reached out to ISA (Socio-environmental Institute), an NGO that had been working in Terra do Meio for several years. He asked them to help him look for alternatives.

ISA is a nonprofit organization driven by the purpose of defending social and environmental rights, supporting local communities, monitoring public policies, and offering alternatives aligned with principles of sustainable development. When Mr. A approached them, they knew that top-down initiatives by outsiders were doomed to fail. They also knew of some pioneer initiatives of cantinas in Acre (an Amazonian state in West Brazil) which could potentially inspire him. In 2009, the nonprofit raised resources and financed a trip for him to go to Acre and learn directly from other communities there. Social movements and other grassroots initiatives in Acre had created co-ops in the late 1990s. The idea was to collect products harvested by people in the communities and sell them in the market bypassing middlemen. These were the first cantinas in the Amazon region, but unfortunately very few succeeded (Villas-Boas et al. 2017).

They faced a number of issues: first, people there were also used to buying goods from middlemen on credit, expecting to pay for them later and often embroiling themselves in life-long debts. When cantinas were created, the culture of buying on credit persisted, which later drove several cantinas bankrupt. Second, cantinas worked by collecting everyone's production first, selling it in bulk to outside buyers, collecting payment, and then redistributing it to local producers. In most cases, it would take months for a person to get paid for a product they had harvested. This delay would further increase the problem of buying things on credit and accumulating debts. Third, in some cases cantinas would collect forest products without knowing ahead of time who would buy them, and often these products ended up being sold in the local market for prices just as low as people would have gotten from middlemen. Fourth, running the day-to-day administrative aspects of these enterprises requires minimal levels of literacy, management, and business skills, which most people in the region lacked.

When Mr. A returned from his trip to Acre, he was inspired by the initiative and was empowered by the lessons learned. What followed was a process through which he and his peers tried to address problems very similar to the ones faced by communities in Acre, but they did it in a more creative way. The first demand he identified among his peers was the need to find potential buyers. Local markets could not absorb the entire volume of products that families in Terra do Meio had the potential to supply. It became imperative to find outside buyers who could absorb all that production. In that same year

(2009), Mr. A and his ISA supporters made contact with a cosmetic company named Atina Ativos Naturais. He knew that no company would negotiate solely with him to buy the relatively small amount of oil he could collect himself, so he also contacted other river dwellers in his area who harvested copaiba oil in order to channel the overall production. After some negotiations, Atina Ativos Naturais agreed to buy the entire production of copaiba oil for a price that river dwellers deemed adequate.

There were, however, some complications. The main one was receiving a payment. After harvesting the oil, river dwellers had to compile the entire production and bring it to Mr. A. He would take it to Altamira, and then send the oil to the city where the company was located. After that, the company had to issue a payment order, and once it was deposited, Mr. A would return to the city, withdraw it, bring it back to the community, and make the final redistribution according to the amount of oil every person had harvested. This process took about five months, and that was the main reason why the partnership with Atina Ativos Naturais did not last very long. Mr. A, his peers in the community, and their ISA supporters learned many lessons along this process which they applied later in future attempts to sell copaiba oil.

In 2011, ISA and the NGO Imaflora (Forestry and Agricultural Management and Certification Institute) organized meetings between representatives from a Swiss cosmetic industry named Firmenich and Mr. A together with other community members. After negotiations, Firmenich agreed to buy the entire production of copaiba oil for a price that community members considered adequate. That time around, Mr. A and peers negotiated an initial working capital. This was important because many people were interested in harvesting forest products but lacked basic resources. The harvesting season can be several months long, and people did not have enough financial means to provide for their families without getting paid for long periods of time. They needed to receive a payment when they delivered their product. Firmenich donated the initial working capital—a crucial step that responded to challenges learned in previous experiences.

Mr. A and his peers were satisfied, but there were still two challenges that had to be addressed for them to overcome the aviamento trap. The first was price instability. Prices set by middlemen for industrialized goods and other forest products were very volatile. Even during one harvesting season, prices could vary as much as 60 percent, creating a high degree of uncertainty. People would go to the forest expecting to get paid one price for their products and would later find themselves having to sell for a much lower value. Of course, prices vary in the market and there are many reasons that influence that. The idea was not to freeze prices, but rather to curb volatility. This problem was addressed when Firmenich agreed to purchase the entire oil production for a fixed priced negotiated yearly before the harvesting season starts.

The second challenge was that they knew they could not base their incomes solely on copaiba oil. They needed to organize a similar system for other forest products in order to ensure greater sustainability for their initiative. To do that, they had to reproduce with other buyers the negotiations they had just had with Firmenich. Their key problem was lack of liquidity, so they had to jumpstart a working capital that could provide them with enough cash flow to get paid for their forest products soon after harvesting them. They created the first cantina to manage this working capital, to coordinate the transactions with buyers, and to internally organize everyone's production. Mr. A was chosen by his fellow community members to be the manager of this first cantina in Terra do Meio, which was officially established in 2012. The place is still running, and it is now a template for several other enterprises in the area.

More cantinas opened in other locations, including some in indigenous territories, and all of them are modeled after Mr. A's one. Cantinas expanded their portfolio beyond copaiba oil to include a wide variety of nontimber forest products, including Brazil nuts (sold as fresh produce and nut oil), latex from rubber trees (sold as rubber mats and blocks), and babaçu (sold as nut oil and flour), among others. Today Terra do Meio has twenty-one cantinas, and the expectation is that more will be opened soon. There is no community that has more than one cantina, and most communities have none. Communities that do not have their own cantina must rely on the nearest cantina for buying and selling their products. The idea to create a cantina responded to several challenges faced by local communities. This process was not linear; rather, it combined overlapping interests and demands. The cantina was not set up since the beginning to operate exactly the way it currently does. This was a learning process, and Mr. A and other fellows had to adapt to changing circumstances as things went on. The next section elucidates in greater details how cantinas operate.

ANALYZING CANTINAS AS AN ACTION ARENA

According to Ostrom, Gardner, and Walker (1994, 28), "one of the first steps that can be taken in an institutional analysis using the IAD approach is the identification of a conceptual unit called the action arena." Here cantinas are this analytical unit. They are the social space where community members exchange forest products and industrialized goods. To analyze an action area, Ostrom and colleagues divide it in two parts: the action situation and the actors involved. First, we provide an overview of how cantinas operate, then we analyze the actors and how they interact in this action situation.

How do Cantinas Operate?

Considering just one cantina by itself, it is possible to summarize its operation as follows: harvesters go into the forest, collect various kinds of natural resources, and bring them to the cantina. Managers need to register three things in their accounting books: the amount of forest product that was delivered, who delivered it, and whether it was paid for with cash, industrialized goods or a combination. When harvesters buy industrialized goods, managers need to write down what was bought, who bought it, and whether it was paid for with cash, forest products, or a combination. Managers then send forest products to the nearest town, which are later sent to large company buyers. Managers are also responsible for purchasing industrialized goods to supply stocks at the cantinas. Bookkeeping notes are later presented to everyone in the community and to other managers who are part of the network.

It is important to emphasize that cantinas are not private enterprises. They are not businesses owned by managers who earn profits. They are a social institution and the solution to a collective action problem: putting forest products on the market for a price that gives river dwellers an incentive to harvest these products and live autonomously off the forest.

This might seem complicated to understand, but it is actually quite simple. In a profit-seeking logic, someone who produces a good determines what are his/her costs of production and sets the price above that. If the product is sold, the producer makes a profit. In this nonprofit-seeking logic, communities first estimate what they consider a reasonable price for their products and add to that all other fixed costs they will incur (transportation, packaging, occasional loses, management fees, etc.). Once the community has an estimated price, they negotiate with the buyers and finally come to a final price—which can be lower or even higher than the one originally proposed by the community. After the final purchase price is set, communities calculate the unit price of each product by taking the final purchase price and subtracting the fixed costs they will incur. This process determines how much cantinas will be able to pay people for each product they harvest. Then every community member makes their own calculations to determine whether they are willing to go into the forest and harvest a product for the price offered by the cantina. Managers receive a fee for their services but earn no profits.

Here is an example of how prices are established. Brazil nuts are one of the most important forest products traded in cantinas. For the 2018–2019 harvesting season, communities had estimated first that an adequate price for a bucket of Brazil nuts would be 100 BRL (this includes the price paid for harvesters plus the fixed costs). They then negotiated that price with their main buyer, and the company agreed to pay this amount. After this price was confirmed, they deducted back their known fixed operating costs which were 12 BRL (this covers things like burlap bags to pack the nuts, transportation and storage costs, etc.). The remaining 88 BRL were divided so that managers receive 8 BRL for each bucket of Brazil nuts, and harvesters receives 80 BRL—the original payment estimated by communities. As a general rule, managers receive 10 percent of the amount paid to harvesters. This 10 percent management fee is important because managers need to forgo working in the forest as harvesters to run the cantina. So the amount they receive for this community service needs to be roughly equivalent to what they would otherwise make harvesting themselves.

In economic terms, cantinas are club goods. When one community member sells his/her forest products there, this does not impede others from doing the same. Cantinas, however, are restricted to communities in Terra do Meio. People living just outside the region are not allowed to sell their products there. One of the most important balances that cantinas must strike is proper management of the working capital. When well managed, cantinas have enough cash to pay harvesters for their regular delivery of forest products. However, when managers act poorly, they can drain a cantina's working capital and harm members in that community. To illustrate the challenges surrounding the working capital, we give three examples. They portray the complex set of incentives, constraints, and mutual social monitoring faced by those involved with the cantinas. The next section describes the examples first, and then it analyzes the actors in the cantinas action arena.

Harvesters and Managers: The Main Actors in the Cantinas Action Arena

The two main actors in this analysis are harvesters (*extrativistas*) and managers (*cantineiros*). They each face a different set of incentives and preferences, as we outline here.

All communities in Terra do Meio have a high degree of kinship among its members, but in the Andiroba community this feature is even more accentuated. After the community decided to open a cantina and chose Mr. B as manager in 2014, they put him in a very complicated position. Soon he realized how difficult it was to say no to his own family. People would come to the cantina with no or little forest products and wanted to buy more industrialized goods than they could afford. He started selling things on credit, expecting that eventually people would pay back. They did not.

Cantinas at the time were only at their very beginning and managers did not have enough working capital to pay harvesters. ISA was trying to raise more money to create a collective fund which cantinas could pool from. But at the time the fund's management was mostly centralized around ISA, so managers would often ask ISA for more funds whenever their working capital was low. Managers who ran cantinas well only asked for enough funds to cover the amount of forest products they were getting from harvesters (and then used the sale from forest products to purchase industrialized goods for the cantinas). Managers who ran cantinas not so well asked ISA for more funds than they needed. In these cases, they used the funds both to pay harvesters for forest products and to buy more industrialized goods. The problem was that there were people "buying" industrialized goods on credit and never paying back. Mr. B used up all the working capital available, eventually ran out of industrialized products, and found himself with almost no forest products that could be sold to replace the stocks.

When others in the cantinas network and at ISA got a hold of the situation, the Andiroba cantina was on the verge of declaring bankruptcy. For the cantinas system, it would have been really difficult to deal with a failed cantina. This could potentially spread the word that this initiative was not working well, people could start selling their forest products exclusively to middlemen again, and company buyers could lose interest in purchasing things from Terra do Meio. The cantinas network decided to pull together resources and make this cantina solvent again (we talk more about how the cantinas operate as a network in the "Patters of Interaction" section below). This case was an important lesson for Mr. B, for this community, and for managers in other places. It shows the struggles that managers go through when dealing with a collective working capital, and how they can overexploit this common financial resource.

Later a similar situation happened at another community, however with a different outcome. Mr. C was the cantina manager at the Cumaru community and was also finding it challenging not to sell things on credit. Just as Mr. B he continued to withdraw funds from the working capital to cover for things he was selling on credit, and soon enough the cantina was selling more industrialized goods than it was buying forest products. When Mr. C realized the dire situation, he called a community meeting. He knew that people who owed money at the cantina could hardly afford paying it back, but it was imperative for them to collectively find a solution to this problem. They organized a task force to produce cassava flour. This is not something usually sold at cantinas, but it is a staple food in the region. Mr. C received part of the flour as payment. Part of it was sold in the nearest town, and the profits were also sent to him. So in addition to buying industrialized goods at the cantina, harvesters for a period also had the option of purchasing cassava flour. This was a temporary solution that worked in this situation: those who had outstanding debts at the cantina payed them off with cassava flour, either delivering it directly at the cantina or selling it in the town and paying cash to the manager. The cantina received enough cash to pay harvesters and had enough flour to sell and make up for the loss. After a few months, the cantina was solvent again and another lesson was learned.

Eventually, it became clear to ISA and managers that having a collective fund from which cantinas could pool from was not working well. The collective fund was meant to be used as working capital for managers to pay harvesters when delivering forest products at the cantinas. This is the main purpose of the cantina-paying harvesters in cash for forest products. Given that the collective fund was quite substantial, this made it extremely hard for managers to deal with social relations at the community level. People had the expectation of receiving assistance, considering that managers had access to such a large volume of resources. But every time when a manager withdrew money from the fund, that meant that those funds were not available to pay harvesters. In 2015, they decided to split the collective fund, so each cantina would have its own working capital, and there would be a much smaller collective reserve that could only be used in extreme emergencies and with everyone's consent. This solution helped many managers better run the cantinas, because the division of the funds was proportional to the amount of forest products harvesters circulated in each cantina.

The third example we would like to discuss is, in a sense, the opposite situation of the previous two. In the Maçaranduba community, there are comparatively not as many Brazil nuts as in other places in Terra do Meio. This means that during the nuts harvesting season, this cantina receives fewer forest products, which lead to a smaller cash flow and fewer industrialized goods. More importantly, this means that the manager, Ms. D, does not have too many opportunities to earn her 10 percent management fee (the 8 BRL per bucket of Brazil nut in this case). In 2017, she decided to partner with Mr. E, a community member who works as a middleman in the region. He does regular trips to several places in Terra do Meio, so he started buying Brazil nuts from people in other communities and delivering them to Ms. D. He claims to have paid people the regular 80 BRL per bucket of Brazil nut as any cantina manager would. She paid him 80 BRL as she would pay to any other community member delivering nuts at the cantina (the accounting books show it). This allowed her to earn her 10 percent management fee (which certainly was later split with him), allowed him to sell his industrialized goods to people who did not have a cantina nearby, and allowed the Maçaranduba cantina to have an inflated cash flow. People in this community benefited from having a cantina with more cash and more industrialized products, so they turned a blind eye.

The situation would have gone unnoticed had it not been for the managers in regions rich with Brazil nuts. They realized people in their communities were delivering fewer nuts than expected. This means that those managers were missing out on the opportunity of receiving their management fee. The other problem is that this situation violated the principle of transparency, which is a guiding foundation of the cantinas network. There was at the time no rules to address situations like this. In a collective meeting, managers created a new rule: if forest products are not delivered at the cantinas directly by harvesters, whoever delivers it must be able to prove that the harvester received the regular payment and that products came from a legitimate area (from within Terra do Meio and not from invaded areas). This rule makes it much harder for middlemen to operate under their regular business model and encourages them to partner with the network if they can abide by cantinas rules.

These examples set the stage for an IAD analysis of the actors involved with cantinas. According to Ostrom, Gardner, and Walker (1994), there are four components to analyze actors: individual preferences, individual information-processing capabilities, individual selection criteria, and individual resources.

Based on the examples above, it is possible to see that managers' preferences vary from being in good terms with their family and community members (as in the case of Mr. B and Mr. C), to finding ways to increase the cantinas revenues and their own management fee (as in the case of Ms. D). These actions must be weighed against the likelihood of others in the cantinas network finding out what is going on and taking appropriate measures. Given that all transactions are recorded in the accounting books, the network is very transparent, and managers know their actions are monitored. In these examples, it was clear that Mr. B and Mr. C were selling too many things on credit, and that Ms. D was buying a disproportionally large amount of Brazil nuts from Mr. E.

The examples above also speak to the perspectives of harvesters. Members in Andiroba and Cumaru communities had to evaluate the advantages of buying on credit things they could not afford, versus the disadvantage of having their cantinas shut down. Harvesters generally prefer selling their forest products at a cantina rather than to a middleman because of price stability, liquidity and access to cheaper industrialized goods. When push came to shove, harvesters opted to restrain themselves and keep the cantinas running. In the case of the Maçaranduba cantina, harvesters in other communities had to decide between selling their nuts to Mr. E or to their local cantinas. Given that many of them had outstanding debts with Mr. E, they probably felt coerced into selling nuts to him and using the money to buy his more expensive industrialized goods. It is true that they did not have to incur in costs transporting nuts to their nearest cantina, but by trading with him they were indirectly draining resources away from their local cantinas. Managers in those cantinas now had fewer nuts, which decreased their working capital and consequentially the amount of industrialized products available.

Cantinas as an Action Situation

In this section we analyze the relations among actors in the cantinas as an action situation, which is defined as "the social space where individuals interact, exchange goods and services, engage in appropriation and provision activities, solve problems, or fight" (Ostrom, Gardner, and Walker 1994, 28). There are seven components to analyze an action situation: participants, positions, actions, potential outcomes, transformation functions, information, and payoffs (Ostrom, Gardner, and Walker 1994). Because of lack of space, in this section we will focus only on some of these components.

There are several positions that constitute the cantinas system: harvesters, managers, representatives of each community association (those who legally represent the communities in contracts with company buyers and other business transactions), ISA technicians (those who provide support for managers and the communities at large), private company buyers (those who buy forest products), and ICMBio (the park service). The most important positions are those of harvesters and managers.

Actions are identified by asking, "[What are] the set of actions that participants in particular positions can take at different stages of a process (or, nodes in a decision tree)" (Ostrom, Gardner, and Walker 1994, 30)? Regular actions undertaken by harvesters include determining how often and how much they are willing to harvest and sell at a cantina. Harvesters also participate in management decisions at their local cantina, for instance determining what price they should bid in negotiations with buyers. Actions related to the manager's position require him/her to coordinate transportation logistics; receive, safely store, and manage forest products; control stocks of industrialized goods, administrate the working capital, maintain the accounting books updated, make sure not too many people buy things on credit, and run the cantina according to rules agreed upon by community members. Managers have an interest in keeping the cantina solvent, because they receive a fee which is proportional to the transactions. If a cantina is poorly managed, harvesters could look for a different one to exchange their forest products, or people in the community could decide to replace the manager altogether.

Information is identified by asking, "How much information do appropriators have about the condition of the resource itself, about other appropriators' cost and benefit functions, and about how their actions cumulate into joint outcomes" (Ostrom 2011, 12)? Harvesters have firsthand information about the conditions of forest resources. During the season, they can estimate the flow of resources through their local cantina by communicating with the manager. Every four months on average, ISA technicians and representatives from the community association visit each cantina and audit the accounting books. The information in the books is verified against the stocks and the

technicians who train cantina managers, they fund a large part of the costs related to organizing events such as Semex, and they write grants and fundraise to attract more donations to the cantinas network. There are no doubts that ISA's role in the cantinas network has been instrumental. The network, however, is not an invention by ISA. The cantinas network emerged out of a long history of *aviamento* in the region, and it grew organically due to the efforts of several community members in a response to struggles they were facing. The goal of living autonomously off forest resources is deeply ingrained in the local culture. ISA's mission to support sustainable development was not imposed there, but rather it became a strong ally when combined with a previously existent aspiration.

Considering all the effort required to run this system, is it worth asking whether the cantinas network has been successful or not. The next session discusses the main results achieved and offers an evaluation of this enterprise.

OUTCOMES AND EVALUATION CRITERIA

What are the main results achieved by the cantinas network? Harvesters nowadays enjoy greater economic standards. They get paid more for their forest products and have more liquidity for these products (i.e., receive payment right away). They have access to cheaper industrialized goods, and prices fluctuate much less than before. Cantinas have created an alternative economic modus operandi that allows harvesters to have a reliable source of income, living autonomously off forest resources. Cantinas provide a concrete example that living off a vibrant forest is economically viable. This enterprise shows the importance of keeping things flexible, transparent, and participatory while maintaining a strong commitment to creating a self-governing system. These outcomes are puzzling especially because when the first cantina of Terra do Meio was created, there was no laid out plan that a network of cantinas would follow. These outcomes are surprising precisely because they have evolved organically, driven by the demands of local communities.

To evaluate these results, we use six criteria suggested by Ostrom (2011): economic efficiency, fiscal equivalence, redistributional equity, accountability, conformance to values of local actors, and sustainability. "The evaluative criteria allow us to assess outcomes that are being achieved. . . . Evaluative criteria are applied to both the outcomes and the interactions among participants that lead to outcomes" (Hess and Ostrom 2006, 62).

Economic Efficiency is "determined by the magnitude of net benefits associated with an allocation of resources" (Ostrom 2011, 16–17). We consider the cantinas network to be an economic system more efficient than the previous forms of commerce through middlemen. Through this system, communities negotiate sales contracts directly with company buyers without intermediaries, which yield them better prices and more transparency. Cantinas also bring industrialized goods to community members at a cheaper price than middlemen. In the system run by middlemen, they buy products from communities and sell them in the city to their bosses, who then sell these products to processing companies. They in turn sell products to company buyers, resulting in a much longer commercial chain. By reducing this chain, cantinas cut costs which are reflected in higher pay for community members.

Fiscal Equivalence can be assessed in two ways: "(i) on the basis of the equality between individuals' contributions to an effort and the benefits they derive and (ii) on the basis of differential abilities to pay" (Ostrom 2011, 16–17). The cantinas network does not differentiate people based on their abilities to participate in the system: elder people with less physical strength are paid the same amount for the forest products they harvest as young people. However, the cantinas do offer a system that is fiscally equivalent precisely because people extract benefits from the cantinas based on their efforts and contributions. If someone works hard, spending long hours and many days in the forest harvesting a large amount of forest products, then that person will receive more than someone who only spent minimal efforts collecting these products.

Redistributional Equity is characterized by "policies that redistribute resources to poorer individuals. . . . Thus, although efficiency would dictate that scarce resources be used where they produce the greatest net benefit, equity goals may temper this objective, and the result is the provision of facilities that benefit particularly needy groups" (Ostrom 2011, 16–17). As explained above, the network is a club good and cantinas must pay a toll to participate in this system. This toll is best illustrated by cantinas that are closer to urban centers paying the same amount to transport their goods as those located further away. This policy is a form of redistributional equity, because it supports communities which would have to incur in greater costs to send their products to the market.

Accountability is characterized by leaders being held "accountable to citizens concerning the development and use of public facilities and natural resources" (Ostrom 2011, 16–17). One of the hallmarks of the cantinas network is its transparency. Managers are held accountable to their fellow community members, all accounting books are open for scrutiny, and shared costs undertaken by the network are made public to managers and community members during Semex meetings.

Conformance to Values of Local Actors is an important criterion to evaluate the network. It is a consideration that assess "how the outcomes fit the values of those involved" (Ostrom 2011, 16–17). We explained that the cantinas emerged organically in a social context characterized by a history of assistance and *aviamento*. The cantinas network created an alternative option to the *aviamento* system, which allows harvesters to put their products in the market for a better price. Cantinas have also managed to meet the expectations for assistance that local communities had (e.g., managers do occasionally sell things on credit to families who are in need). Thus, the network operates in line with values and customs that were already in place.

Sustainability is the characteristic of "institutional arrangements [that] are able to respond to ever changing environments" (Ostrom 2011, 16–17). According to McGinnis, sustainability is also a measure of how adaptable, resilient and robust a system is. "Loosely speaking, [it is] a system's capacity to suffer a disturbance and yet still continue to function, without losing its basic structural or functional integrity" (McGinnis 2011, 176). Even though the cantinas network has not yet withstood the test of time for hundreds of years or even decades, this system has been put to test numerous times and managed to respond adequately to many challenges as illustrated by the examples given here.

CONCLUSION

This chapter analyzed the Cantinas Network of Terra do Meio. This is a social institution that emerged out of isolated rural communities in the Amazon region, because those involved were struggling to make a living off forest resources. The cantinas network emerged out of a long history of *aviamento* in the region, and it grew organically due to the efforts of several community members in a response to struggles they were facing on a daily basis. The cantinas network is a solution to a collective action problem, namely the challenge that river dwellers face to put forest products in the market. This problem was solved by creating a club good that provides its members with better market access, giving incentives for river dwellers to harvest and commercialize forest products sustainably. Companies purchasing these products agree to pay above-market prices because forest products from protected areas come with sustainability labels that can be advertised and yield a better final consumer product.

One of the premises of the IAD framework is that people are fallible yet capable learners (Ostrom and Ostrom 2004). This case is certainly an example of that. Cantinas are not successful because things always work out as expected. They are successful because of their high levels of resilience and their ability to learn and adopt new strategies. Local communities are perseverant in their goal of creating a modus operandi that allows them to live autonomously off forest resources. This has always been the goal behind their initiatives, since they have first started articulating the first cantina. As things evolved, the specific rules and strategies had to adapt. Nowadays, the cantinas network operates in a transparent way, that allows participants to adapt and create new rules, shift strategies when needed, which render the system quite flexible. Nonetheless, those involved never lose sight of their higher purpose. Community members now have higher income levels in a modus operandi that protects forest resources.

The goal of creating a self-governing system led local communities to create the cantinas network. This system is most certainly not going to remain as it is in the long term. We believe that community associations are likely to gain a more influential role, able to build even more partnerships with other organizations, and to eventually no longer rely so heavily on ISA's support to run the cantinas network. Given that communities have legal protection over their territories, they are extremely likely to remain there. But given that Terra do Meio is a protected area, it is certain that these communities will continue to live in an isolated setting (i.e., there will never be a network of roads cutting through the forest). This will always impose challenges for them to access the market. Thus, the collective problems examined here are likely to persist. The shift from a commerce based on middlemen to one where communities own cantinas and have access to a working capital has taught people the advantages of not relying on a long trading chain that drains profits at each link. Given that this system is resilient and adaptable, the day-by-day operations of cantinas might change in the future, but communities are likely to keep relying on this institution to trade directly with large company buyers which yields them more revenues for their forest products.

NOTE

1. Augusto Postigo is an anthropologist who has been working in this area since 2011 and has participated in the design and implementation of the cantinas system since its initial conception. Raquel Rodrigues dos Santos worked in Terra do Meio between 2007 and 2018, traveling to several communities in the area and assisting managers and community members with the daily challenges involved with commercializing nontimber forest products and running cantinas. Miranda Chase worked for several months in 2018 as an assistant to the associations that represent these communities, revising their accounting books and organizing contract documentation and other paperwork. The authors thank ISA, AMORA, AMOMEX and AMORERI.

REFERENCES

Doblas, Juan. 2015. *Rotas do Saque: Violacoes e Ameacas `a Integridade Territorial da Terra do Meio (PA)*. Edited by Natalia Ribas Guerreiro and Mauricio Torres. Sao Paulo: Instituto Socioambiental (ISA).

Hess, Charlotte, and Elinor Ostrom. 2006. "A Framework for Analyzing the Knowledge Commons." In *Understanding Knowledge as a Commons: From Theory to Practice*, edited by Charlotte Hess and Elinor Ostrom, 41–81. Cambridge: MIT Press.

Kiser, Larry L., and Elinor Ostrom. 2000. "The Three Worlds of Action: A Metatheorical Synthesis of Institutional Approaches." In *Polycentric Games and Institutions: Readings from the Workshop in Political Theory and Policy Analysis*, edited by Michael D. McGinnis, 56–88. Ann Arbor: The University of Michigan Press.

McGinnis, Michael D., ed. 2000. *Polycentric Games and Institutions: Readings from the Workshop in Political Theory and Policy Analysis*. Ann Arbor: The University of Michigan Press.

———. 2011. "An Introduction to IAD and the Language of the Ostrom Workshop: A Simple Guide to a Complex Framework." *Policy Studies Journal* 39 (1): 169–183. doi: 10.1111/j.1541-0072.2010.00401.x.

Ostrom, Elinor. 2005. *Understanding Institutional Diversity*. Princeton: Princeton University Press.

———. 2009. "Beyond Markets and States: Polycentric Governance of Complex Economic Systems." The Nobel Prize Award Ceremony, Stockholm.

———. 2011. "Background on the Institutional Analysis and Development Framework." *Policy Studies Journal* 39 (1): 7–27. doi: 10.1111/j.1541-0072.2010.00394.x.

Ostrom, Elinor, Roy Gardner, and James Walker. 1994. *Rules, Games and Common-Pool Resources*. Ann Arbor: The University of Michigan Press.

Ostrom, Elinor, and Vincent Ostrom. 2004. "The Quest for Meaning in Public Choice." *American Journal of Economics & Sociology* 63 (1): 105–147. doi: 10.1111/j.1536-7150.2004.00277.x.

Postigo, Augusto, and Roberto Rezende. 2017. "O Aviamento e o Modo de Vida Beiradeiro." In *Xingu: Historia dos Produtos da Floresta*, edited by Andre Villas-Boas, Natalia Ribas Guerreiro, Rodrigo Gravina Prates Junqueira and Augusto Postigo, 235–260. Sao Paulo: Instituto Socioambiental (ISA).

Tarko, Vlad. 2017. *Elinor Ostrom: An Intellectual Biography*. New York: Rowman & Littlefield.

Velásquez, Cristina, Andre Villas-Boas, and Stephan Schwartzman. 2006. "Desafio para a Gestão Ambiental Integrada em Território de Fronteira Agrícola no Oeste do Pará." *Revista de Administração Pública* 40 (6): 1061–1075.

Villas-Boas, Andre, Natalia Ribas Guerreiro, Rodrigo Gravina Prates Junqueira, and Augusto Postigo, eds. 2017. *Xingu: Historia dos Produtos da Floresta*. Sao Paulo: Instituto Socioambiental (ISA).

Vogler, Jan P. 2019. "The Entanglement of Public Bureaucratic Institutions: Their Interactions with Society, Culture, Politics, and the Economy." In *Interdisciplinary Studies of the Political Order: New Applications of Public Choice Theory*, edited by Donald J. Boudreaux, Christopher J. Coyne and Bobbi Herzberg, 99–129. New York: Rowman & Littlefield International.

Chapter 9

Community, State, and Market

Rethinking Social Capital in Transitional Authoritarian Regimes

Wanlin Lin

Elinor Ostrom's lifework made considerable contributions to the literature on the operation and performance of the community mechanism as the third solution, beyond the supposedly dichotomous market and state, to the collective action problem (Ostrom 1990, 2005a, 2010). She and her colleagues, constituting the Bloomington school, have created and developed the institutional analysis and development (IAD) framework, which systemically identifies the attributes of the physical world, rules in use, and community attributes as three institutional elements that shape the institutional situation facing actors and become powerful tools to examine community-based self-governance and informal institutions (Ostrom, Gardner, and Walker 1994; Kiser and Ostrom 2000). They also focus on context and the roles of community attributes by associating them with social capital—an attribute of individuals and their relationships, such as trustworthiness, networks, and norms, that enhances individuals' ability to solve collective action problems (Ostrom and Ahn 2009, 20).

No doubt, the Bloomington school pioneered and facilitated our understanding of community governance, an understanding that besides rules on property rights enforcement (including mechanisms of [re]definition, allocation, appropriation, and provision), community attributes such as group size, network, trust, and shared norms can exert a significant effect on the level of cooperation (Ostrom 1998, 2003). Ostrom's approach has inspired a large body of thought-provoking research on community-based governance and institutions that not only expands our empirical understanding of institutional arrangements and change, but promotes theoretical advancements on such topics as the typology and mechanisms of social capital (Chamlee-Wright 2010; Richman 2017; Skarbek 2014; Storr, Haeffele-Balch, and Grube 2016).

But past research on the institutional implications and effects of social capital has primarily focused on institutional contexts in democratic regimes or systems with weak governments rather than those in transitional authoritarian regimes, which have been underexplored both theoretically and empirically. This chapter applies the concept of social capital to the redevelopment of urban villages in China, where village communities attempt to solve coordination problems in a context in which community, market, and state interact. It aims at better understanding the role of social capital as a set of institutional resources and mechanisms of community governance. Such governance is embedded in an imperfect but rapidly emerging market in which communities' bridge with the market can bring them informal bargaining power and make them simultaneously subject to a powerful and even predatory state that might grant political privileges only to certain groups. I draw on the insights of Chamlee-Wright (2010), Putnam (1993), Storr, Haeffele-Balch, and Grube (2016), and Woolcock (2001) on the definition and typology of social capital in the background of democratic regimes: social capital is structural in nature and made up of a wide array of heterogeneous resources along three structural dimensions—bonding, bridging, and linking. I attempt to answer the question: To what extent and how does social capital develop and function in transitional authoritarian regimes?

The rest of the chapter is organized as follows. First, it introduces the institutional environments and essence of urban-village redevelopment in China, which is a process of community governance and enforcement of collective property rights involving market and state. Second, it provides a theoretical examination of social capital in transitional authoritarian regimes. It elaborates on the subsets of bonding, bridging, and linking social capital by associating them with the institutions of urban-village redevelopment. Third, it examines three relationships among community, market, and state from the perspective of social capital. Finally, it summarizes the interaction of the three structural dimensions of social capital.[1]

REDEVELOPMENT OF URBAN VILLAGES: COMMUNITY GOVERNANCE BETWEEN MARKET AND STATE

Urban villages are the by-product of rapid urbanization and collective landownership under the dual-track land system in China (Lin 2009). They constitute a decentralized and spontaneous order composed of high-density residential buildings (Webster and Lai 2003). Land institutions and collective-economy organizations (CEOs) are two crucial institutional arrangements spurring and underlying the emergence and redevelopment of urban villages. The constitution stipulates that the property rights to urban land are assigned to the state, while rights to rural land are assigned to the villages as collectives.[2] The land in villages comprises farmland, unused land, and construction land (including housing plots). On paper, village households are allocated housing plots on which to build houses for self-use.[3] In practice, village committees (VCs) or CEOs often are in charge of the applications for permits and the administrative affairs concerning the housing plots.[4] Neither the villagers nor the CEOs are allowed to sell their land to people or institutions outside the villages.

Governing and enforcing villagers' collective property rights, particularly rights to collective construction land, is the primary purpose of CEOs. Some CEOs also enter the industrial or commercial sector to seek profits. Their start-up funds are often raised from the villagers or previously collected revenues from land. In some cities, such as Guangzhou and Shenzhen, the CEOs have a more institutionalized stock structure. Most of them have become entrepreneurial by adopting the mechanism of "collective of shareholding economy," which calculates the total value of the village's collective assets (particularly collective land) and turns them into stocks to be distributed among all the villagers (Chen 2016, 828–849). This implies that all villagers benefit from a growing collective economy while losing from a collective economy with internal rent-seeking. Further, the social capital of urban villages is fostered (corroded) by the development (failure) of the collective economy.

Rapid urbanization has significantly increased the land values of villages in and around urban areas. Facing the constraints of formal property rights, some villagers or their CEOs enter the informal land-rental market (Ho 2013; Liu, He, Wu, and Webster 2010). Villagers construct residential buildings and lease them to migrant laborers (Wu, Zhang, and Webster 2013). CEOs lease the collective land to some enterprises or cooperate with them by offering land-use rights. Nonetheless, their land use is still less efficient compared with that of developed urban land in the same or similar areas. In the eyes of local governments, insufficient land-use planning detracts from urbanization and industrial progress (Hao, Sliuzas, and Geertman 2011).

Therefore, the redevelopment of urban villages presents profit opportunities and incentivizes the villagers, their CEOs, real estate developers, and local governments to seek mechanisms to enforce the rights to the increasingly valuable land. Traditionally, the reconstruction of urban villages has followed the government-domination pattern. Governments expropriate the collective-owned land and convey the land-use rights to developers using the auction mechanism. But this pattern frequently triggers resistance.

Two new patterns have emerged in such cities as Beijing, Shenzhen, and Guangzhou. In the first pattern—autonomous redevelopment—the villagers' CEOs are independent bodies governing all redevelopment issues. In the second pattern—collaborative redevelopment—the villages cooperate with external developers to redefine the use of village land. Villages invest in their land, developers take responsibility for construction, and both groups may formulate land-use plans and distribution rules together, while local governments provide support instead of monopolizing the land market. The redistribution rules are often at the core of the negotiation between villagers and developers (Zhou 2014).

The redevelopment of urban villages essentially is an attempt to overcome the villages' coordination problem and a process of redefining, redistributing, and reusing collective-owned land. Urban villages attempt to design and develop rules compatible with the incentive structures that could allow them to depart from a less efficient equilibrium to a more efficient one. The set of rules mainly concerns land-use planning, the mechanism to collect the funds to implement the planning (particularly to construct the new buildings), and the rules to distribute the redeveloped properties to villagers (including resettlement apartments for villagers and profits from collective land operated by CEOs).

Nonetheless, incentive-compatible rules, while necessary, are not sufficient. The social capital features of urban villages can significantly facilitate or handicap the enforcement of the rules. The enforcement of rules and the performance of the collective economy operated by CEOs and villagers before conducting urban-village redevelopment serve as fertile (poor) soil for cultivating (eroding) the social capital of village communities. The accumulation of social capital greatly affects the redevelopment of urban villages (Baland and Platteau 1996; Whiting 1998). In other words, shared experience in community governance affects community members' subsequent decision-making (Ostrom and Kiser 2000). Therefore, we should examine the mechanisms of social capital in village redevelopment along with the development path of the collective economy.

SOCIAL CAPITAL IN TRANSITIONAL AUTHORITARIAN REGIMES

Scholars have developed numerous and even contradictory definitions of social capital. Governance structure (shaped by various institutional elements and characterized by multiple nested levels) and divided knowledge and institutional entrepreneurship are both causes and effects of heterogeneous social capital. I adopt the broad definition of social capital provided by Chamlee-Wright (2010, 42) and Hayami (2009, 98): social capital is structural in nature, consists of a wide array of heterogeneous relational resources, and

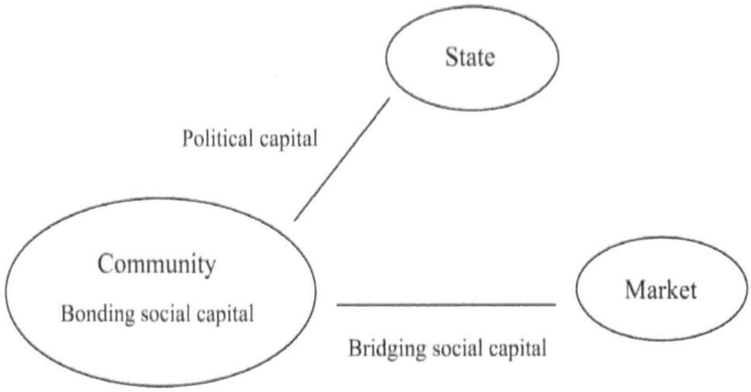

Figure 9.1 Community between Market and State.

is conducive to enhancing cooperation or overcoming collective action. It accrues to people in certain social relationships.

There are three types of social capital based on social structure: (1) bonding social capital, or relational resources that bind individuals in a homogeneous group (this includes community network, norms, trust, and leadership); (2) bridging social capital, or relational resources that connect the members of horizontal and heterogeneous groups; and (3) linking social capital, or relational resources linking individuals in varying positions of power in a vertical (hierarchical) structure (Aldrich 2012; Putnam 1993; Storr, Haeffele-Balch, and Grube 2016; Woolcock 2001).

The definition and typology allow me to draw insights from the study of social capital in democratic regimes to study its mechanisms in transitional authoritarian regimes while providing an institutional mapping tool to identify their (sub)categories and capture their role in an institutionally complex system of community governance between market and state (see figure 9.1). As Ostrom (2010, 665) notes, researchers have to "be willing to deal with complexity instead of rejecting it."

BONDING SOCIAL CAPITAL IN TRANSITIONAL AUTHORITARIAN REGIMES

Bonding social capital generally points to strong ties between individuals in homogeneous communities and ensures a sense of social solidarity. It is what villagers in clan-based village communities have (Meadowcroft and Pennington 2007; Putnam 1993). And it can help people coordinate and overcome collective action problems through a variety of causal mechanisms associated with the subcategories described below (Aldrich 2012; Ostrom and Ahn 2009; Putnam 1993). Though the subcategories of bonding social capital in transitional authoritarian regimes are similar to those in democratic regimes, the former has distinctive features.

Network

A dense and small network enables members of the network to communicate and exchange information at low cost and encourages reciprocal behaviors because more frequently repeated interaction motivates members to move from one-shot games to long-term cooperative relationships (Aldrich 2012; Ostrom and Ahn 2009). Generally, it is more costly for large groups than small ones to negotiate and reach agreements (Olson 1965; Baland and Platteau 1996). But as Hardin (1982) and Ostrom (1997) remark, the impact of network size on collective action is usually mediated by many other variables. The size of urban villages has two components: village population and land area.

Trust within Villages

Drawing from Coleman (1994), Levi (1998, 2000), and Ostrom and Ahn (2009), I define trust as a trustor's beliefs—at a particular level of subjective probability—about the trustworthiness of the trustee, where the beliefs inform the trustor's decision on how to act. Trust affects the trustor's calculation concerning the probability that he or she will be not made worse off by taking a risk (Coleman 1990). The beliefs are based on the trustor's knowledge about credibility, competence, and incentive structure given the past and present institutional situation (Whiting 1998). Trust might reduce the transaction costs of collective action in communities, where contracts are likely to be incomplete and bargaining less formal than elsewhere. Trust in urban villages does not only include villagers' trust of other villagers, but, more importantly, their trust of the leaders and members of the CEOs. The trust level varies across urban villages.

Leadership

As stated above, trustworthiness is an important feature of leadership. The credibility of the leaders of CEOs in urban villages often means that those leaders can develop and enforce fair rules for distribution of profits from the collective properties. The credibility of CEOs might not be sufficient to enable collective action, but the villagers' beliefs that the CEOs are untrustworthy can be a considerable obstacle. Unfair elections for selecting CEO members and clan collusion to extract rents are often the causes of distrust in CEOs (Manion 2006; He 2007; You 2018).

Public Entrepreneurship

This is a particular form of leadership focused primarily on problem-solving and putting heterogeneous elements and resources together in complementary ways in nonmarket institutional contexts (Ostrom 2005a, 2005b). As Chamlee-Wright (2010, 75) defines it, it is "the ability to see a situation in ways that most others have missed—to recognize the grain of opportunity in a sea of political obstacles—and then act to seize that opportunity." In transitional authoritarian regimes, the obstacles include lack of formal protection of property rights, government predation, and a market environment lacking a supportive credit market or encouraging fraud. Regarding urban villages, public entrepreneurship of CEO leaders is the capacity to discover opportunities and coordinate villagers' efforts and investments to improve the collective economy and increase the efficiency of collective-owned land and even deter governmental intervention where exchange of collective-owned land is illegal.

Community Norms

Community norms are informal behavioral rules that are common beliefs combining empirical and normative expectations of certain groups of people (Aoki 2007; Bicchieri 2006; Elster 1989). Basu (2000) provides a useful distinction between three kinds of community norms: rationality-limiting norms, preference-changing norms, and equilibrium-selection norms. Some community norms have emerged and evolved in some urban villages. One category is distribution norms, which concern the mechanism to allocate property or distribute collective profits. Another category is cooperation norms—such as "Harmony makes a clan prosperous" or "Avoid trouble whenever possible"—which regulate how villagers interact with other villagers or people outside the village. The existence of community norms implies that an urban village is relatively ethnically homogeneous, which might alleviate the coordination problem.

BRIDGING SOCIAL CAPITAL IN TRANSITIONAL AUTHORITARIAN REGIMES

"Bridging social capital" refers to the weak ties between the members of horizontal, heterogeneous groups (Putnam 1993; Woolcock 2001). Bridges between people from diverse groups allow people to exchange information and discover reciprocal opportunities. As Meadowcroft and Pennington (2007) emphasize, a bridge between a certain community and the market, such as one between villagers and external developers, is crucial for people to engage in cooperation at larger scale and benefit from the exchange of goods and services even though their ties might be looser than those inside the communities.

The urban villages, to some degree, were born of rapid economic growth and urbanization. Many CEOs and villagers enter the informal housing-rental market and connect with businesspeople (industrial or commercial land users) and migrant laborers (tenants). Though strong ties (bonding social capital) are formed among villagers, the highly respected informal contracts suggest that villagers and migrant laborers also have loose ties (bridging social capital) (He et al. 2010; Wu, Zhang, and Webster 2013). In other words, the market mechanism is generally honored. Some urban villages have developed more robust bridges with the market through specific cooperative patterns. Meanwhile, in some villages, the bridges are fragile because the capture of CEOs leads villagers to distrust market forces. But given the considerable demand for funds and the surging value of the redeveloped property, the redevelopment of urban villages always implies that a larger scope of market activities, and more institutionalized arrangements, such as a formalized collaborative pattern bridging community and market, might be required (Leeson 2007; Meadowcroft and Pennington 2007).

LINKING SOCIAL CAPITAL IN TRANSITIONAL AUTHORITARIAN REGIMES

Linking social capital refers to relational resources connecting individuals in a vertical power structure (Aldrich 2012; Putnam 1993; Storr, Haeffele-Balch, and Grube 2016; Woolcock 2001). When linking social capital refers more specifically to an individual/community's political bargaining power, endowment, and privilege as resources that can affect the interaction between individuals/communities and governments in the policy formation or enforcement process and therefore help them realize outcomes serving their perceived interests, it can be termed "political capital" (Birner and Wittmer 2003; Turner 1999). Political capital, as a subset of linking social capital, encompasses some subcategories playing more pronounced roles in transitional authoritarian regimes than in democratic ones.

Governmental Tolerance

The first subcategory is governments' tolerance of individuals/communities' rule breaking, which can result from the latter's strong bargaining power and collective action capacity. It allows individuals/communities to make a credible commitment to the state that though their rule breaking is unlawful, suppressing it would trigger violent collective resistance, bring considerable enforcement costs, and even undermine the legitimacy of the state or prove (local) officials to be administratively incompetent (Cai 2010; Chen, Pan, and Xu 2016). Governments' tolerance can be seen as a form of political privilege. Groups with such bargaining power often also have a high stock of bonding (and probably also bridging) social capital.

Attention-Based Political Trust

Political trust points to ordinary citizens' beliefs about the trustworthiness of either local governments or the authoritarian state. As Hardin (1999) contends, besides expecting consistent behavior of governments, trustors also expect that the governments intend to further the trustors' interests. Government performance, administrative competence, and procedural fairness jointly shape citizens' evaluation of political trustworthiness (Levi and Sacks 2009).

In authoritarian regimes, to demonstrate their efficiency and political legitimacy, governments may concentrate their administrative attention and resources on presenting model communities/cities or hosting international events. Given public and international attention, governments highly value administrative competence and social order. Realizing this, villagers involved in these projects believe they will enjoy political privilege or be given greater political endowments and tend to increase their trust in the governments, which serves as an "encapsulated interest" for themselves (Hardin 1998, 9–15). I term this trust "attention-based political trust."

Cooperation-Enhancing Policies

"Cooperation-enhancing policies" refers to the rules or mechanisms provided by local governments that grant freedom and reduce costs of local decision-making, allow the self-governance of communities (including introducing market mechanisms and cooperating with enterprises), and maybe also improve monitoring. The policies in Shenzhen's special economic zone, such as tax exemption for foreign enterprises and weak regulation of high-tech industries, are examples (Moberg 2017). As Bowles and Gintis (2002) argue, some distributions of property rights and public policies are better than others at fostering community governance and ensuring complementarity among communities, states, and markets. Cooperation-enhancing policies have a twofold nature as rules and political capital.

Take the cooperation-enhancing policies concerning the collaborative redevelopment of urban villages. The redevelopment of urban villages, as a collective action, requires a series of institutionalized rules and mechanisms that are difficult to implement in land institutions in China. Rules and supervision are public goods and likely to be undersupplied privately (Landes and Posner 1975; Ostrom 1990). Not all village communities are able to develop appropriate rules. And though interjurisdictional competition stimulates local governments to enhance regional economic growth by providing preferential policies, such governments' heavy reliance on land-use fees might stop them from loosening control over land use and turning to community-based governance. Nonetheless, they might take such actions in regions where local governments can benefit from it. Compared with village communities in regions without these policies, urban villages equipped with the cooperation-enhancing policies have economic freedom to cooperate with external developers and exchange land property rights and public goods as political resources. The cooperation-enhancing policies might allow some urban villages lacking enough funds or advantageous community attributes to redevelop anyway (Levi 2000). Nonetheless, as such policies are not sufficient conditions, some urban villages still fail to redevelop.

The interaction of community, market, and state, to a large degree, can be explained by the interactions among bonding, bridging, and linking social capital. By examining the process and institutional patterns of redevelopment of four urban villages in China, I explore the formation, transformation, and interaction of social capital in transitional authoritarian regimes through mapping institutional complexity (Aligica 2014; King, Keohane, and Verba 1994; Small 2009; Ostrom 2010).

POLITICAL ATTENTION REINFORCING BONDING AND BRIDGING SOCIAL CAPITAL

Yumin is located in the Luohu District in Shenzhen, along the Shenzhen River and adjoining Hong Kong. It is the first village in Shenzhen to have engaged in autonomous redevelopment, and its villagers and CEOs now redefine and enforce their property rights to land without external assistance. Urban villages need to develop informal but centralized institutional arrangements in order to reach agreement on alternative land-use planning, to collect funds for constructing new buildings, and to allocate the redeveloped property. The institutional arrangements should be compatible with the incentives of villagers, but that alone is insufficient. The enforcement of the institutional arrangements also rests on social capital that can coordinate villagers' belief that engaging in the redevelopment project will be feasible and efficient.

The bonding social capital of Yumin, including a tightly knit network, a norm of fairness, internal trust derived from the development of a collective economy and the past experience of housing allocation, and the village's bridge with the market, has significantly increased the villagers' participation in their village redevelopment. First, the villagers form a small, tight network. In 1980, there were thirty-four households and 140 villagers (Hu and Wu 2011). The villagers mainly have the family names Wu and Deng. Most of them are relatives or in-laws. The small size and high cohesion of the community reduce the costs of collective action (Baland and Platteau 1996).

Second, the strong bonding social capital of Yumin has been fostered by the village's history as a collective economy and its allocation of housing plots and houses, which brought the villagers internal trust, property and ethnic homogeneity, and appreciation for the market mechanism. Yumin villagers entrepreneurially discovered beneficial opportunities in the construction market and made use of their advantageous location along the Shenzhen River (SMD 2013). The villagers raised money, purchased such instruments as tractors and dumpsters, set up transport crews and flotillas, transported construction materials, and, of course, benefited from their investment. About half of the villagers' income was allocated to individual households, and the rest was saved in the collective account for the provision of public goods, particularly public infrastructure (Hu and Wu 2011).

Third, the fairness norm of equal distribution emerged and was followed when the village allocated housing plots and houses. In 1981, Yumin's VC decided to appropriate 700,000 yuan from the collective account to build new houses for every household. The house block constituted thirty-four identical small villas with two floors each and arranged in an orderly way. The rule used to allocate the house was drawing lots. Whether a household was able to acquire a house at a favorable location purely depended on luck.

Succeeding at operating the collective economy through collective action not only has brought the villagers wealth, reminded them of the uncertain but real opportunities in market activities, and fostered the village's bridging social capital, but also has enhanced trust among villagers, thereby endowing them with the confidence to invest.

The achievement of Yumin attracted special attention from governmental officials as a spillover effect. The attention, in turn, served as political capital. In 1984, Deng Xiaoping, the leader of China who reformed the country and opened it up, visited Yumin when he inspected Shenzhen, the frontier city of economic development and reform. Deng highly praised the achievements of Yumin and its way of cooperating in the interest of common prosperity. His visit signaled the central government's determination to stick to the path of economic reform and political decentralization (Vogel 2011). To continue the signal and to express respect and loyalty to the central government, the succeeding national presidents, including Hu Jintao and Xi Jinping, and other officials from the central and local governments have visited Yumin. Yumin has served as a symbol of success in the special economic zone and of the legitimacy of the central government. Serving as such a symbol, in turn, has brought the villagers the common understanding that government regards them highly, and therefore they have been more confident in engaging in collective action since they believe governments would provide either political or financial support (SMD 2013). In other words, they have attention-based political trust in the state.

Yumin's redevelopment pattern provides convincing evidence. Though the thirty-four identical small villas significantly improved the villagers' living conditions, they failed to provide external tenants affordable housing as more and more migrant laborers sought job opportunities starting in the late 1980s. Hence, nearly all the households added several floors to their villas, which increased the villagers' incomes but simultaneously led to disorderly land use (SMD 2013). In 1999, encouraged by the leaders in the Shenzhen government, Yumin's VC decided to attempt to redevelop the village, particularly by replanning and reusing villagers' housing plots.

Through the discussion among villagers, under Yumin's CEO, they settled on a set of institutional arrangements for land redevelopment that included land-use planning, a mechanism to collect funds to implement the plan, and rules to distribute the redeveloped properties to villagers. The thirty-two households collectively took out loans from the bank and rebuilt an apartment building with eleven floors for each household (totaling thirty-two buildings). Drawing lots was the method adopted to allocate the buildings, as before. Moreover, a multiple-use building with eighteen floors—Yufeng Dasha—was built as a combination of rentable collective property (from fifth to eighteenth floors) and public facility (first to fourth floors). The loan amounts of the households ranged from 2,650,000 yuan to 2,850,000 yuan, much more than their existing wealth. But the villagers believed that it would be beneficial in the long term because the values and rents of the redeveloped property would significantly increase. Shenzhen's government provided support by subsidizing interest payments on the loans during the period of construction, but the majority of loans were borne by the individual household.

The redevelopment of Yumin is characterized by risk-taking and a high level of coordination among villagers. It took the villagers just five years (1999–2004) to finish the redevelopment project (from establishing the rules to resettling in the new buildings). The rules were effective because of the villagers' "internalized belief" that the redevelopment project was promising and the "behavioral belief" that other villagers would also engage in the project (Greif 2006, 36). Their strong bonding social capital (tight network, fairness norms, and internal trust) and bridging social capital (cooperation with commercial banks and favorable experience with the market mechanism) contributed to their belief systems (Alesina and Spolaore 2003).

Moreover, Yumin's special political position as a symbol of the success of the special economic zone and the opening-up policy and the steady positive attention from the state functioned as political trust and enhanced villagers' confidence. When asked why the redevelopment was successful, many villagers stated that they believed that the state (including Shenzhen's government) stood by them. In Yumin's small but well-organized museum are artifacts and photos relating to the history of economic development and land use in Yumin; also exhibited are indications of the visits of leaders from both central and local governments. The museum demonstrates that the villagers are proud of their institutional patterns and are being praised by the state, indicating the high level of both internal and political trust in the villages. The attention-based political trust has been the spillover effect of Yumin's bonding and bridging social capital, and it in turn reinforces the latter types of capital.

GOVERNMENTAL TOLERANCE AS BY-PRODUCT OF BONDING AND BRIDGING SOCIAL CAPITAL

Zhenggezhuang is another village that engaged in autonomous redevelopment, but the mechanisms the villagers adopted and social capital they stocked and fostered were significantly different from those of Yumin. Zhenggezhuang is bigger than Yumin. Its land area is about 2,888,000 square meters, and the number of its households increased from 318 in the early 1980s to 415 in the late 1990s. There have been more than 1,000 villagers. The large size implied the organizational costs for collective action might have been higher than in Yumin, and it called for effective leadership (Webster and Lai 2003, 44). The village's social capital has been characterized by powerful leadership and a close bridge with the market, which is associated with the development of the village's collective economy.

Fushui Huang has been the major manager and operator of Zhenggezhuang's collective economy for more than three decades. In 1986, Huang established a construction crew, Tushifang, which was renamed and registered as Beijing Hongyuan Jixie Construction Crew (BHJCC) in 1993. All the members are Zhenggezhuang villagers. Through hard work, it developed despite confronting a variety of problems, such as fraud and a shortage of transportation equipment (Zhao, Huang, and Liu 2013).

Through undertaking shareholding reforms, Huang further connected BHJCC with the villagers, and the construction crew bridged the village community with the market. In 1996, Huang decided to establish the Hongfu Group with registered capital of 30,000,000 yuan. Among the contributors of capital, BHJCC invested tangible goods accounting for 67.67 percent of the corporate shares, the VC of Zhenggezhuang contributed tangible goods accounting for 16.67 percent, and 116 villagers contributed cash accounting for 16.67 percent (Li and Yang 2015). Therefore, Hongfu Group is not an enterprise of Huang, but of the CEO of Zhenggezhuang. Huang has been acting as the chairman since Hongfu Group was established.

Moreover, Hongfu Group placed individual shares in 1999 and 2003. The shareholders were 189 households, accounting for 46 percent of the total households of the village; their investments ranged from 2,000 yuan to several million yuan out of a total value of 241,370,600 yuan. In addition, Hongfu Group has provided job opportunities to more than 400 villagers according to their educational status. To increase human capital, to signal its concerns about the villagers, and to demonstrate its leadership's credibility, it reimburses villagers for all tuition fees. Villagers over the age of 70 years can live in the apartments newly built specifically for the aged, where they get free housing and food and 2,000 yuan a month as a subsistence allowance (Brennan 1998; Wang and Ren 2014).

The establishment and development of Hongfu Group to a large degree shaped the community attributes of Zhenggezhuang. First and most importantly, the strong leadership of Huang is reflected in the fact that he is not only a market entrepreneur discovering opportunities and overcoming problems in the emerging, imperfect market, but also a public entrepreneur connecting his enterprise with the village by placing individual and collective shares and providing villagers job opportunities and welfare services. Second, the increasing number of households investing individual shares suggests that villagers' trust in Hongfu Group has been enhanced through observing its performance. Third, the socioeconomic statuses of the villagers have been tightly bridged with the market. The better the performance of Hongfu Group in the market and industries, the higher and more stable is the investment return of individual shares and villagers' salaries. The bridge was further reinforced by the land redevelopment project.

As a public entrepreneur, Huang also pioneered a pattern to recognize, redefine, and distribute the property rights of the collective-owned land (Anderson and Hill 2004). In 1997, though Hongfu Group had continued to grow, it faced the problem of triangular debts. To recover the capital, Huang asked its debtors to pay debts in construction materials, such as cement and steel, and it built four apartment buildings on the unused land in Zhenggezhuang before selling them. These apartments were extralegal and informal housing without legal titles and termed "small-property-right housing" (SPRH) (Qiao 2015). But it was a time when the real estate market began to thrive. The apartments were all preordered by villagers and employees of Hongfu Group. The successful trial not only brought Hongfu Group cash flow, but also reminded Huang of the opportunities latent in reusing the collective-owned land. Simultaneously, more and more villagers, observing that those who moved into the apartments were enjoying improved living conditions, such as central heating instead of coal burning, recognized the advantages of living in the apartments (Zhang 2005).

The four apartment buildings could be regarded as a favorable beginning of the redevelopment of Zhenggezhuang. But not all villagers believed it would benefit them. Therefore, the redevelopment pattern of Zhenggezhuang was characterized by five phases guided by Hongfu Group, which allowed it to gradually raise funds and allowed villagers to increase their confidence in the redevelopment project (Zhao, Huang, and Liu 2013). By associating the institutional arrangements of land reuse with the growth and profit distribution of Hongfu Group and the provision of welfare services, Huang and the villagers developed three rules governing the village's autonomous redevelopment.

First, to increase the land-use efficiency, the major objective of the new land-use plan was to move the villagers from their one-story houses to the apartment buildings. In this way, massive housing plots (about 533,333 square meters) would be saved and could be, for example, leased to other enterprises or institutions instead. Moreover, the apartments, though without legal title, were affordable compared with the formal housing and were attractive for employees of Hongfu Group and, in general, nonvillager buyers with lower incomes. One hundred forty apartment buildings, more than the number the villagers needed, were planned to be built and to constitute an apartment complex called Hongfu Yuan (Wang and Ren 2014).

This land-use plan and the fund collection, land-use, and profit distribution rules were nested and complementary mechanisms. Every married adult villager was allocated 40 square meters, and unmarried ones were allocated 120 square meters. One square meter was about 600 yuan, a reasonable price (Zhao, Huang, and Liu 2013). Villagers were also paid for the reuse of saved housing plots and unused farming land. They were compensated with 405,000 yuan for every housing plot (as large as about 180 square meters) in the form of cash or individual shares in Hongfu Group. But it was not until 2009 that all the compensation was paid (Liu 2008). In practice, the villagers often got paid or were charged for the difference between the compensation and the costs of the new apartments.

Second, Hongfu Group played a crucial role in increasing the efficiency of the saved housing plots and unused farming land and has created an increasingly strong bridge between the market and Zhenggezhuang. From 1998 to 2007, Hongfu Group rented 273,333 square meters of land to its eighteen subsidiaries, rented 343,333 square meters of land to eight partnerships, and leased 40,666 square meters of land to twenty-seven general enterprises, which were rarely observed in other villages at similar locations. Enterprises in such sectors as tourism, education, and technology have business activities in Zhenggezhuang. All payments were made to the VC and then equally distributed to the villagers involved in the redevelopment program. Per capita land income increased from 50 yuan in 1998 to 3,110 yuan in 2012 (Wang and Ren 2014).

Third, the redevelopment project attempted to enhance the bridge between the village community and the market by selling apartments to nonvillagers including the employees of Hongfu Group and general buyers. Employees were offered 30 to 40 percent discounts. This not only generated more profits for the collective economy, but also served as an effective way to accumulate the human capital and bridging social capital of Hongfu Group. Apartments totaling 447,700 square meters of floor area (81.49 percent of the total) were sold to nonvillagers. In brief, Huang's public entrepreneurship has been the most remarkable form of Zhenggezhuang's bonding social capital, which enhances the village's solidarity and also underlies its accumulation of bridging social capital and therefore promotes the collective economy and redevelopment of the collective-owned land.

The combination of bonding and bridging social capital, which indicates the strong collective action capacity and bargaining power of Zhenggezhuang villagers, Hongfu Group employees, and nonvillager buyers, increases the security of property rights to the apartment buildings. Constructing and selling SPRH violates the legal provision that collective-owned land, including housing plots, cannot be exchanged.[5] Therefore, local governments, as the legal bodies enforcing the formal land institutions, have both the legal duty and the power to intervene in the extralegal housing market. However, the Beijing government has only selectively intervened. In 2013, it announced that there were about 103 SPRH projects, but it only demolished 25 of them. The demolished projects were always run by external developers who bought land from villagers, whereas projects governed by VCs or CEOs were tolerated even though illegal. The Hongfu Yuan project, the largest SPRH project, has proven to be robust and secure.

Government's selective tolerance resulted from the multiple incentives and concerns of local governments and villagers along with SPRH buyers' potential collective resistance as a credible threat. Local governments are sometimes criticized by the state for not fully implementing the formal property rights, and they lost their monopoly power over land-use orders, which implied the loss of considerable land-conveyance fees, an important source of off-budget revenue for them (Qun, Yongle, and Siqi 2015). However, such losses must be traded off against the huge enforcement costs. Intervening in such a project as Hongfu Yuan would very likely trigger the violent and collective resistance of villagers and buyers seeking to preserve their shared benefits from the security of their land and housing property rights.

As a result, the Beijing government opted for diverse strategies against different SPRH operators: be strict with respect to SPRH operated by external developers with a loose bridge to buyers and local villagers, but be tolerant with respect to SPRH operated by VCs or CEOs, which entails strong ties among village communities and a close bridge to buyers. Specifically, many buyers of apartments in Hongfu Yuan are also the employees of Hongfu Group or other enterprises whose bases are in Zhenggezhuang. If the Beijing government demolished Hongfu Yuan, not only would it have to respond to social unrest and the villagers' need to resettle, but it would also damage the enterprises and industrial sectors in Zhenggezhuang. The huge enforcement costs and negative spillover effect on economic development follow from the strong group solidarity (bonding social capital) and close bridge to market forces (bridging social capital). Such social capital further increases villagers' informal bargaining power when faced with governmental intervention and expropriation, and it forces Beijing to make a concession as a political privilege.

SUPPLEMENTARY BUT INSUFFICIENT COOPERATION-ENHANCING POLICIES AND THE MARKET MECHANISM

The villages conducting autonomous redevelopment were not only able to design incentive-compatible rules, but also to enforce them with their strong bonding, bridging, and even linking social capital. However, not all the villages have these institutional conditions of self-governance. Therefore, external forces might be needed to reduce the costs of collective action and enhance collaboration. Another redevelopment pattern—the collaborative pattern, guided by cooperation-enhancing "urban renewal" policies and involving state and market—emerges to attempt to solve the problem (Hao, Sliuzas, and Geertman 2011; Schoon 2014).

Although governments are important in the pattern, they do not play dominant or decisive roles. Instead, they provide rules and supervision, which are public goods and likely to be undersupplied privately (Landes and Posner 1975). First, they are the main sources of a series of rules ranging from land-use planning (such as floor area ratio and the standards for public-infrastructure provision), to the allocation and use of land transfer benefits, to regulations on the distribution of redeveloped apartments among villagers (Lai, Wang, and Lok 2017). Second, local governments function as third-party monitors of the redevelopment proposals.

Real estate developers, as a market force, cooperate with village communities and engage in village redevelopment. Introducing the developers is a solution to financial difficulties (Li et al. 2014). They assume nearly all the relevant costs, such as costs of constructing new buildings and villagers' housing costs during the redevelopment process, and many of them also construct all the new buildings and infrastructures. In exchange, they acquire the use and development rights to some parcels of land in the village (Hao, Sliuzas, and Geertman 2011). The redevelopment proposals including the land-use planning and distribution rules often come from the negotiation and agreements between developers and CEOs based on government approval. CEOs serve as the representatives of villagers. But given the principal–agent problem, collusive bargaining between CEOs and developers might occur. If villagers believe CEOs and developers are colluding, they might hesitate or even decline to join the redevelopment project. In the form of collaborative redevelopment partners of village communities, the market, which was extralegal before the adoption of cooperation-enhancing policy, plays a role.

Therefore, the stock of social capital of urban villages matters, as is the case in the autonomous redevelopment pattern. Their leadership and norms along with villagers' trust in their CEOs, local government, and developers are important institutional variables in the context of the interplay among community, market, and government (compared to an isolated community). Despite living under the same set of redevelopment rules, villages with different attributes of social capital experience different performance from the rules, as the villages of Liede and Xiancun in Guangzhou show. The cooperation-enhancing policy of the Guangzhou government drove the redevelopment in the former, but it seemed insufficient in the latter.

LIEDE: COOPERATION-ENHANCING POLICY AND POLITICAL TRUST

Liede is the first urban village that adopted the collaborative pattern for village redevelopment in Guangzhou. The ties among villagers have been characterized by a large network, credible leadership, and the norm of conflict avoidance. Consider, first, that Liede is large. Its land area is around 336,300 square meters, and the floor area is 686,000 square meters. There are more than 3,000 households and 10,000 villagers.[6] It is located in the central area of Tianhe District in Guangzhou. Second, as with urban villages in general, the informal rental market has been villagers' main source of income. About 74.8 percent of household revenues come from the collective-owned properties operated by its CEO—Liede Economy Development Limited Company (LEDLC)—and 25.1 percent from the villagers' private housing (Wang 2011). Third, the villagers acknowledged that they tended to follow simple folkways, which served as norms for reducing conflict with others, including other villagers and nonvillagers. Though Liede failed to conduct autonomous redevelopment—because of the large village network and because the cost, 3,000,000,000 yuan, was too high for the villagers to bear by themselves—the villagers' main income from the collective properties indicated their relatively high level of property homogeneity, the credible leadership of LEDLC, their norm of avoiding conflicts (a form of supportive bonding social capital), and their positive experience with and confidence in the market mechanism, all of which were "activated" when combined with other forms of social capital and driven by appropriate rules.

Liede's bonding and bridging social capital did not function well until the state and market collaborated with it. Although the Guangzhou government realized that the land use was less than efficient, the fact that the government domination pattern might be strongly resisted by the villagers and therefore enforcement costs would be considerable meant that land was not redeveloped until Guangzhou won the privilege to host the 2010 Asian Games (Lin 2015). The venues at Haixinsha Square were planned to be on the island of Haixinsha, which is close to Liede. Hosting the international games suggested that Guangzhou would be the focus during the event. Not only would people evaluate its public services and infrastructures, but they would also heatedly discuss its economic development, urban planning, and appearance (Ren 2009). To enhance its reputation and prove to the superior governments—Guangdong and the central government—that its administration was competent, the Guangzhou government decided to adopt the collaborative pattern to promote the redevelopment of Liede (Xu 2011).

The institutional arrangements of the pattern contained three sets of rules. The first one is the rules on raising redevelopment funds. LEDLC sold the parcel of land located on the west side of Liede Bridge (more than 20,000 square meters). R&F Properties and KWG Property Holding (a conglomerate) won the bid for the plot in Liede through an auction. The price was 4,600,000,000 yuan, which could have financed the costs of the redevelopment projects—3,000,000,000 yuan—that the villagers could not bear without external support.

Second, the land use of the village was replanned. The floor area ratio increased from 2.06 to 5.13. Besides the exchanged parcel of land that was set to be used as commercial land, the parcel of land located on the west side of Liede Bridge (316,294 square meters) was to be made residential. Forty-one apartment buildings (5,662 apartments), a kindergarten, a primary school, and a clan temple were to be provided to the villagers (Tan, Yuan, and Lü 2012). As in Yumin, the sizes of the apartments varied. Additionally, the parcel of land located on the north side of Liede Bridge (207,731 square meters) was reserved as collective-owned land (Li et al. 2014). A large mixed-use building called Liede Center was designed to include a five-star hotel, a serviced apartment building, a shopping mall, an advanced office building, and a banquet center. Liede Center was expected to bring annual revenue of 100,000,000 yuan to Liede, which would approximately triple that before redevelopment (Wang 2011).

The third set of rules concerned the distribution of apartments to the villagers: "one-to-one (in square meters) exchange" (Lin 2015, 879). Specifically, for the land with legal title, an apartment with equal area would be redistributed to villagers. For the informal floors, or houses without legal title, villagers would be paid 1,000 yuan per square meter. Villagers demanding more floor area could purchase it at the price of 3,500 yuan/square meters. Moreover, the location and floors of the apartments were decided by drawing lots. Households with legal title to more gross area were given more apartment space.

The redevelopment proposal was quickly agreed to by most of the Liede villagers (95 percent) at the first village conference, and the Guangzhou government approved it in May 2007. Just two months later, 98.6 percent of the villagers agreed to it at the second village conference. Only four households rejected it when the demolition of the original buildings was to take place in October 2007. But in the end, they all agreed in January 2008. The villagers' quick and almost-unanimous acceptance of the redevelopment proposal implies that the vast majority of the villagers believed that the distribution rules were fair.

The cooperation-enhancing policy provided by the Guangzhou government, which introduced the market mechanism, rules, enforcement, and monitoring (public goods), gave the villagers more autonomy and compatible incentives. It expanded the strategy set of the villagers, offering a more efficient equilibrium. As discussed above, the policy consists not only of rules but also political capital. But whether the villagers could deflect from the existing equilibrium depended on the stock and features of social capital in the village. Several other categories of social capital have contributed to the efficient performance of the collaborative redevelopment pattern in Liede.

First, the convergence of villagers' beliefs was facilitated by its stock of bonding and bridging social capital before the redevelopment project—their community norms of conflict avoidance along with their trust in other villagers, the CEO, and developers. Furthermore, the villagers admitted that the leaders of LEDLC were generally credible when the latter enforced the collective land and operated the informal rental-housing market. Relevantly, they gained confidence in market mechanisms. Moreover, since the rental housing operated by the CEO instead of individual households was the main income source of the villagers, their beliefs tended to converge.

Second, villagers' attention-based political trust in the Guangzhou government further coordinated their decisions. When asked the primary reason for the success of the village redevelopment, many villagers stressed that to host the Asian Games, the Guangzhou government created a beneficial policy experiment by allowing the enforcement of collaborative redevelopment without expropriating villagers' collective-owned land (Broudehoux 2012). This trust resembles Yumin villagers' political trust based on privileged attention (i.e., their encapsulated interest).

XIANCUN: THE STATE'S FAILURE TO RESCUE A TRUST-COLLAPSING COMMUNITY

Liede finished the redevelopment project—from when it was launched to when villagers moved into the new apartments—within three years. This seems to prove that the sets of rules were robust and could be copied by and applied to other villages. However, when the rules were enforced in the villages of Yangji and Xiancun, the rules were not efficient. The erosion of bonding, bridging, and linking social capital in the village of Xiancun might account for the divergent performances.

Xiancun is similar in size to Liede. It has about 1,400 households, and its land area is about 162,800 square meters (about one-third that of Liede). Even though the village is smaller than Liede, it has taken longer to complete the redevelopment project (launched in 2009 but not yet completed as of 2019).[7] In 2012, less than 80 percent of the households agreed to the project. Even in 2019, many villagers remain opposed to it. They have planted red flags on their roofs to express their strong dissatisfaction with the redevelopment proposal.

The villagers in Xiancun rejected the project since they had lost trust in their CEO, Xiancun Economic Development Company (XEDC), and consequently they distrusted the developers and local government. First, internal trust in Xiancun collapsed. Though Xiancun is close to Liede (in the Central Business District in Guangzhou), household revenue from collective-owned property in Xiancun was merely one-third that in Liede, making it the second lowest in Tianhe District. Villagers used to suspect the members of XEDC of collusive rent-seeking, but the problem remained because of lack of legal evidence until Lu Suigeng, secretary of the Xiancun branch of the Communist Party of China , was removed from his position in the anticorruption campaign (Feng and Zhao 2015). Xian Zhangming (the brother-in-law of Lu) and three members of XEDC were arrested and investigated by the Guangzhou Commission for Discipline Inspection.

The investigation showed that XEDC, monopolized by the Lu clan, has a history of appropriating the Guangzhou government's payments meant to go to the villagers in compensation for the government's expropriation of the village's collective-owned land. In 1985 and 1995, the Guangzhou government compensated the villagers with 600,000,000 yuan and 3,8871,000 yuan, respectively, but the money was all captured by the members of XEDC. Even more seriously, XEDC colluded with external businessmen and sold or leased the collective property at a low price. In 2007, a time when the real estate market in Guangzhou was very hot, XEDC transferred 48 percent of the stock equity of a large parcel in Zhujiang New Town (a commercial real estate project covering about 68,000 square meters) to Guangzhou Jiayu Real Estate Development Co. at a fairly low price of 60,000,000 yuan. Likewise, it leased collective property—hotels, stores, commercial office buildings—at the well-below-market price of 15 to 18 yuan per square meter (the average market rent was 400 to 1,000 yuan per square meter). The corruption and graft of XEDC members led to severe dissatisfaction and anger among the villagers.

Second and related, the villagers also began to distrust the local government and the market. Conflicts and acts of resistance occurred frequently. In 2009, when Kingoli Group, the external company partnering with XEDC to operate the hotels, was about to lay the cornerstone, villagers came to disrupt the ceremony. Even five years later, the construction was incomplete. Additionally, the investigation of the Guangzhou Commission for Discipline Inspection found that Lu had bribed Guangzhou officials, which further reduced the villagers' trust in the state (Feng and Zhao 2015).

The significant lack of trust in the CEO combined with declining confidence in the market and government resulted in the dysfunction of the collaborative redevelopment pattern in Xiancun even though the village was located at a commercially advantageous site. When the redevelopment project was launched by XEDC in 2009, villagers rejected the redevelopment proposal and required the company to disclose its account and return the revenues that belonged to the villagers. Their collective resistance was characterized by "rightful resistance," in which they resorted to legally and politically legitimate methods (O'Brien and Li 2006, 1–24). Two hundred villagers engaged in a collective march from Xiancun to the Guangzhou government. Instead of targeting the distribution rules, they appealed to recover the governance order of the XEDC and redefine the collective property. Additionally, they raised money and hired Cailiang Wang, a lawyer specializing in land conflicts, to defend against the potential coercive implementation of the village redevelopment project (Wang 2015).

The villagers opposed to the redevelopment project believed that the enforcement of the distribution rules would be unfair given that the members in XEDC were likely to collude with the developer and secretly compensate themselves or the villagers belonging to their clans with more apartment space than what the written rules prescribed. Similarly, they suspected that

XEDC's distribution of revenues for the redeveloped collective property would be unfair.

Restocking and fostering social capital and therefore changing the villagers' beliefs would be time consuming and costly. Though the collective resistance of the villagers and the delay of the redevelopment project incited the new members of XEDC to change the previous rules governing the collective property, the villagers' preferences for alternative arrangements were heterogeneous. In 2014, XEDC held a village meeting concerning the governance of eleven collective properties of Xiancun that had been leased at prices well below market rates. About 4,000 villagers voted for two sets of proposals while 1,806 (42.53 percent) were in favor of the first proposal (increasing the rent first and then seeking an opportunity to take back the properties) and 2,401 (56.55 percent) supported the second proposal (taking properties back directly regardless of the cost and risks) (Zhang and Liang 2014).

As a villager said, it was worth celebrating that the vote involving many villagers, which broke the tradition in which major decisions were monopolized by a certain powerful and corrupt clan, took the first step toward democratic self-governance (Zhang and Liang 2014). Nonetheless, we might expect that it would take some time for the villagers to converge on the belief that the redevelopment rules were acceptable. In other words, cooperation-enhancing policy is insufficient to drive the redevelopment of villages lacking internal trust, but it might provide an opportunity for villagers to reshape the rules governing their collective-owned properties, to restore their bonding social capital, and to bridge to the market again.

CONCLUSION

Following Ostrom's IAD framework on community governance and collective action, this chapter tried to develop our understanding of the formation, structure, and evolution of social capital and the interaction of community, state, and market in authoritarian regimes in economic transition. By studying and comparing the redevelopment of urban villages in China, it examined the forms of and interplay among three structural dimensions of social capital: bonding, bridging, and linking. The bonding and bridging social capital in transitional authoritarian regimes share some subcategories with those in democratic regimes, such as network, leadership (public entrepreneurship), trust, and norms as bonding social capital along with bridges to the market as a typical form of bridging social capital, but their specific institutional contexts and mechanisms differ. For instance, public entrepreneurship in authoritarian systems might require local leaders to be able to organize credible collective action to deter state predation or avoid strong regulation. The community–market bridge in a transitional economy might rely on heterogeneous groups to develop and respect informal or even extralegal contracts not protected by formal institutions. Political capital, a form of linking social capital owned by the community when interacting with a state, might have such specific categories as purposive tolerance, attention-based political trust, and liberal cooperation-enhancing policies in authoritarian regimes characterized by governmental monopolization of resources, strong economic regulation, and high dependence on political legitimacy of a type undermined by social unrest.

My research does not aim at understanding all relationships among community, state, and·market. Instead, I hope that via examining the land redevelopment of urban villages in China, it expands our empirical understanding of the role of social capital in community governance in transitional authoritarian regimes. The first of my three empirical findings is that by closely connecting with each other and seeking market opportunities in the emerging construction and land market, Yumin villagers successfully developed their collective economy, improved housing conditions, and attracted special state attention and praise, which in turn brought them political trust in government and encouraged their autonomous redevelopment.

Second, although facing a powerful state, some communities are still able to entrepreneurially discover and seize opportunities and defend against governmental expropriation. Many people have realized that SPRH can be profitable, but many SPRH projects are fragile when government intervenes. In contrast, Hongfu Yuan, the largest SPRH project in the village of Zhenggezhuang, was made possible because the villagers have formed strong bonds with each other and have a strong community–market bridge such that the local government faces heavy potential enforcement costs. The government's tolerance, a political privilege, is a by-product of the villagers' bonding and linking social capital.

Third, even the cooperation-enhancing policies might not be able to mitigate the coordination problem in communities lacking bonding social capital, as we see from the fact that the policy in Xiancun is dysfunctional despite being the same as that in Liede. A more efficient and fair community order might first rely on the villagers to reshape alternative institutional arrangements and cultivate their bonding social capital.

Though the forms of social capital I examined might significantly allow some communities to realize their interests to some degree, they do not necessarily enhance the robustness of community governance. From a normative perspective, we should be careful about recommending them because of their dark sides, particularly the exclusive bonding ties and attention-based political privilege (Dasgupta 2000, 356; Meadowcroft and Pennington 2007). Governance in a community that is characterized by strong but exclusive solidarity or relies on anticompetitive rent-seeking can generate pernicious social consequences (Rajan 2019). In terms of political capital, governmental mechanisms attempting to promote robust community governance should motivate local cooperation and enhance political trust by providing public goods, such as monitoring and punishment mechanisms and information-sharing platforms, while discouraging local communities from diverting resources from self-governance to lobbying or engaging in bribery to seek such political privileges as special attention or selective enforcement (Chamlee-Wright and Storr 2011). As Aligica, Boettke, and Tarko (2019) highlight, community governance is robust only when it is based on the diversity, heterogeneity, dynamism, and complex division of power and knowledge; organized for production, cooperation, and conflict resolution; and cultivated for learning, resilience, and adaptability.

NOTES

1. I thank Peter Boettke, Bobbi Herzberg, and Brian Kogelmann for providing useful comments. I am also grateful to the participants in the Adam Smith Fellowship program. This research has been funded by the Centre for the Study of Governance and Society at King's College London.

2. National People's Congress, 2004, Constitution of the People's Republic of China.

3. National People's Congress, 2007, Property Law of the People's Republic of China.

4. Government of Guangzhou Municipality, 1995, Temporary Provisions of Guangzhou Municipality for Administration of Land Use for Construction of Dwellings for Rural Villagers.

5. National People's Congress, 2004, Constitution of the People's Republic of China; Standing Committee of the National People's Congress, 2009, Urban Real Estate Administration Law of the People's Republic of China.

6. Guangzhou Urban Renewal Bureau, 2018, Report of Guangzhou Urban Renewal Bureau on the Reconstruction and Demolition of Unlicensed Buildings in Old Villages.

7. Guangzhou Urban Renewal Bureau, 2018, Report of Guangzhou Urban Renewal Bureau on the Reconstruction and Demolition of Unlicensed Buildings in Old Villages.

REFERENCES

Aldrich, Daniel P. 2012. *Building Resilience: Social Capital in Post-disaster Recovery*. Chicago: University of Chicago Press.

Alesina, A., and E. Spolaore. 2003. *The Size of Nations*. Cambridge: MIT Press.

Aligica, Paul Dragos. 2014. *Institutional Diversity and Political Economy: The Ostroms and Beyond.* Oxford: Oxford University Press.

Aligica, Paul Dragos, Peter J. Boettke, and Vlad Tarko. 2019. *Public Governance and the Classical-Liberal Perspective: Political Economy Foundations*. Oxford: Oxford University Press.

Anderson, Terry L., and Peter J. Hill. 2004. *The Not So Wild, Wild West: Property Rights on the Frontier.* Stanford: Stanford University Press.

Aoki, Masahiko. 2007. "Endogenizing Institutions and Institutional Change." *Journal of Institutional Economics* 3 (1): 1–31.

Baland, Jean-Marie, and Jean-Philippe Platteau. 1996. *Halting Degradation of Natural Resources: Is There a Role for Rural Communities?* Oxford: Clarendon Press.

Basu, Kaushik. 2000. *Prelude to Political Economy: A Study of the Social and Political Foundations of Economics*. Oxford: Oxford University Press.

Bicchieri, Cristina. 2006. *The Grammar of Society: The Nature and Dynamics of Social Norms.* Cambridge: Cambridge University Press.

Birner, Regina, and Heidi Wittmer. 2003. "Using Social Capital to Create Political Capital." In *The Commons in the New Millennium: Challenges and Adaptation,* edited by Nives Dolšak and Elinor Ostrom, 291–334. Cambridge: MIT Press.

Bowles, Samuel, and Herbert Gintis. 2002. "Social Capital and Community Governance. *Economic Journal* 112 (483): F419–36.

Brennan, Geoffrey. 1998. "Democratic Trust: A Rational-choice Theory View." In *Trust and Governance*, edited by Valerie Braithwaite and Margaret Levi, 197–217. New York: Russell Sage Foundation.

Broudehoux, Anne-Marie. 2012. "Civilizing Beijing: Social Beautification, Civility and Citizenship at the 2008 Olympics." In *Olympic Games, Mega-events and Civil Societies*, edited by Christopher J. Bailey, 46–67. London: Palgrave Macmillan.

Cai, Yongshun. 2010. *Collective Resistance in China: Why Popular Protests Succeed or Fail.* Stanford: Stanford University Press.

Chamlee-Wright, Emily. 2010. *The Cultural and Political Economy of Recovery: Social Learning in a Post-disaster Environment.* Vol. 12. London: Routledge.

Chamlee-Wright, Emily, and Virgil Henry Storr. 2011. "Social Capital, Lobbying and Community-Based Interest Groups." *Public Choice* 149 (1–2): 167–185.

Chen, An. 2016. "The Politics of the Shareholding Collective Economy in China's Rural Villages." *Journal of Peasant Studies* 43 (4): 828–849.

Chen, Jidong, Jebbifer Pan, and Yiqing Xu. 2016. "Sources of Authoritarian Responsiveness: A Field Experiment in China." *American Journal of Political Science* 60 (2): 383–400.

Coleman, James S. 1990. "Commentary: Social Institutions and Social Theory." *American Sociological Review* 55 (3): 333–39.

———. 1994. *Foundations of Social Theory.* Cambridge: Harvard University Press.

Dasgupta, Partha. 2000. "Economic Progress and the Idea of Social Capital." In *Social Capital: A Multifaceted Perspective*, edited by Partha Dasgupta and Ismail Serageldin, 325–424. Washington DC: World Bank.

Elster, Jon. 1989. "Social Norms and Economic Theory." *Journal of Economic Perspectives* 3 (4): 99–117.

Feng, Lu, and Ruixi Zhao. 2015. "The Aftershocks of Corruption Cases Spreaded in Xiancun Village, Guangzhou—Various Bribery Methods of the Former Deputy Secretary of the Party Committee of Guangzhou Cooperation Office." *Xinhuanet*, April 30. http://www.xinhuanet.com//politics/2015–04/30/c_1115148395.htm.

Greif, Avner. 2006. *Institutions and the Path to the Modern Economy: Lessons from Medieval Trade*. Cambridge: Cambridge University Press.

Hao, Pu, Richard Sliuzas, and Stan Geertman. 2011. "The Development and Redevelopment of Urban Villages in Shenzhen." *Habitat International* 35 (2): 214–224.

Hardin, Russell. 1982. *Collective Action*. Baltimore, MD: Johns Hopkins University Press.

———. 1998. "Trust in Government." In *Trust and Governance*, edited by Valerie Braithwaite and Margaret Levi, 9–27. New York: Russell Sage Foundation.

———. 1999. "Do We Want to Trust in Government?" In *Democracy and Trust*, edited by Mark Warren, 22–41. New York: Cambridge University Press.

Hayami, Yujiro. 2009. "Social Capital, Human Capital and the Community Mechanism: Toward a Conceptual Framework for Economists." *Journal of Development Studies* 45 (1): 96–123.

He, Baogang. 2007. *Rural Democracy in China: The Role of Village Elections*. New York: Springer.

He, Shenjing, Yuting Liu, Fulong Wu, and Chris Webster. 2010. "Social Groups and Housing Differentiation in China's Urban Villages: An Institutional Interpretation." *Housing Studies* 25 (5): 671–691.

Ho, Peter. 2013. "In Defense of Endogenous, Spontaneously Ordered Development: Institutional Functionalism and Chinese Property Rights." *Journal of Peasant Studies* 40 (6): 1087–1118.

Hu, Aimin, and Jinquan Wu. 2011. *Yumin Cun Cunshi* [History of Yumin Village]. Shenzhen: Golden Island Publishing Service Center.

King, Gary, Robert O. Keohane, and Sidney Verba. 1994. *Designing Social Inquiry: Scientific Inference in Qualitative Research*. Princeton: Princeton University Press.

Kiser, Larry L., and Elinor Ostrom. 2000. "The Three Worlds of Action: A Metatheoretical Synthesis of Institutional Approaches." In *Polycentric Games and Institutions: Readings from the Workshop in Political Theory and Policy Analysis*, edited by Michael Dean McGinnis, 56–88. Ann Arbor: University of Michigan Press.

Lai, Yani, Jiayuan Wang, and Waiming Lok. 2017. "Redefining Property Rights over Collective Land in the Urban Redevelopment of Shenzhen, China." *Land Use Policy* 69: 485–493.

Landes, William M., and Richard A. Posner. 1975. "The Independent Judiciary in an Interest-Group Perspective." *Journal of Law and Economics* 18 (3): 875–901.

Leeson, Peter T. 2007. "An-arrgh-chy: The Law and Economics of Pirate Organization." *Journal of Political Economy* 115 (6): 1049–1094.

Levi, Margaret. 1998. "A State of Trust." In *Trust and Governance*, edited by Valerie Braithwaite and Margaret Levi, 77–101. New York: Russell Sage Foundation.

———. 2000. "When Good Defenses Make Good Neighbors: A Transaction Cost Approach to Trust, the Absence of Trust Distrust." In *Institutions, Contracts and*

Organization, edited by Claude Menard, 137–157. Cheltenham, UK: Edward Elgar Publishing.

Levi, Margaret, and Audrey Sacks. 2009. "Legitimating Beliefs: Sources and Indicators." *Regulation & Governance* 3 (4): 311–333.

Li, Jun, and Xu Yang. 2015. "Chengzhenhua Beijing Xia Shequ Gufen Hezuozhi Xingtai Yanjin Yu Zhongjie-yuanzi Beijingshi Zhenggezhuang De Anli Jiedu" [Evolution and End of Community-based Share-holding Cooperation Against Urbanization Background: Based on Interpreting Case of Village Zhengezhuang in Beijing]. *Journal of Nanjing Agricultural University (Social Sciences Edition)* 15 (2): 17–25.

Li, Ling Hin, Jie Lin, Xin Li, and Fan Wu. 2014. "Redevelopment of Urban Village in China: A Step towards an Effective Urban Policy? A Case Study of Liede Village in Guangzhou." *Habitat International* 43: 299–308.

Lin, George C.S. 2009. *Developing China: Land, Politics and Social Conditions.* London: Routledge.

———. 2015. "The Redevelopment of China's Construction Land: Practising Land Property Rights in Cities through Renewals." *China Quarterly* 224: 865–887.

Liu, Shouying. 2008. "Jiti Tudi Zibenhua Yu Nongcun Chengshihua—Beijingshi Zhenggezhuangcun Diaocha" [Collective Land Capitalization and Urbanization: A Survey on Zheng GE Zhuang Village]. *Journal of Peking University (Philosophy and Social Sciences)* 45 (6): 123–132.

Liu, Yuting, Shenjing He, Fulong Wu, and Chris Webster. 2010. "Urban Villages under China's Rapid Urbanization: Unregulated Assets and Transitional Neighbourhoods." *Habitat International* 34 (2): 135–144.

Manion, Melanie. 2006. "Democracy, Community, Trust: The Impact of Elections in Rural China." *Comparative Political Studies* 39 (3): 301–324.

Meadowcroft, John, and Mark Pennington 2007. *Rescuing Social Capital from Social Democracy*. London: Institute of Economic Affairs.

Moberg, Lotta. 2017. *The Political Economy of Special Economic Zones: Concentrating Economic Development*. London: Routledge.

O'Brien, Kevin J., and Lianjiang Li. 2006. *Rightful Resistance in Rural China.* Cambridge: Cambridge University Press.

Olson, Mancur. 1965. *The Logic of Collective Action*. Cambridge: Harvard University Press.

Ostrom, Elinor. 1990. *Governing the Commons*. Cambridge: Cambridge University Press.

———. 1997. "Self-Governance of Common-Pool Resources." Workshop in Political Theory and Policy Analysis, Indiana University.

———. 1998. "A Behavioral Approach to the Rational Choice Theory of Collective Action: Presidential Address, American Political Science Association, 1997." *American Political Science Review* 92 (1): 1–22.

———. 2003. "Toward a Behavioral Theory Linking Trust, Reciprocity, and Reputation." In *Trust and Reciprocity: Interdisciplinary Lessons from Experimental Research*, edited by Elinor Ostrom and James Walker, 19–79. New York: Russell Sage Foundation.

———. 2005a. *Understanding Institutional Diversity*. Princeton: Princeton University Press.

———. 2005b. "Unlocking Public Entrepreneurship and Public Economies." WIDER Discussion Paper No. 2005/01, United Nations University World Institute for Development Economics Research, Helsinki.

———. 2010. "Beyond Markets and States: Polycentric Governance of Complex Economic Systems." *American Economic Review* 100 (3): 641–672.

Ostrom, Elinor, Roy Gardner, and James Walker. 1994. *Rules, Games, and Common-Pool Resources*. Ann Arbor: University of Michigan Press.

Ostrom, Elinor, and Toh-Kyeong Ahn. 2009. "The Meaning of Social Capital and Its Link to Collective Action." In *Handbook of Social Capital: The Troika of Sociology, Political Science and Economics*, edited by Gert Tinggaard Svendsen and Gunnar Lind Haase Svendsen, 17–35. Cheltenham, UK: Edward Elgar Publishing.

Putnam, Robert D. 1993. *Making Democracy Work*. Princeton: Princeton University Press.

Qiao, Shitong. 2015. "Small Property, Big Market: A Focal Point Explanation." *American Journal of Comparative Law* 63 (1): 197–238.

Qun, Wu, Li Yongle, and Yan Siqi. 2015. "The Incentives of China's Urban Land Finance." *Land Use Policy* 42: 432–442.

Rajan, Raghuram. 2019. *The Third Pillar: The Revival of Community in a Polarised World*. London: William Collins.

Ren, Xuefei. 2009. "Olympic Beijing: Reflections on Urban Space and Global Connectivity." *International Journal of the History of Sport* 26 (8): 1011–1039.

Richman, Barak D. 2017. *Stateless Commerce: The Diamond Network and the Persistence of Relational Exchange*. Cambridge: Harvard University Press.

Schoon, Sonia. 2014. "Three Olds: Experimental Urban Restructuring with Chinese Characteristics, Guangzhou and Shenzhen in Comparison." In *Maturing Megacities*, edited by Uwe Altrock and Sonia Schoon, 105–121. Dordrecht: Springer.

Skarbek, David. 2014. *The Social Order of the Underworld: How Prison Gangs Govern the American Penal System*. Oxford: Oxford University Press.

Small, Mario L. 2009. "'How Many Cases Do I Need?' On Science and the Logic of Case Selection in Field-Based Research." *Ethnography* 10 (1): 5–38.

Southern Metropolis Daily (SMD). 2013. "The Prosperity and Silence of Shenzhen Yumin Village, the First 'Ten Thousand Yuan Village' in China." *Southern Metropolis Daily*, August 13. http://finance.ifeng.com/a/20130813/10415880_0.shtml.

Storr, Virgil Henry, Stefanie Haeffele-Balch, and Laura E. Grube. 2016. *Community Revival in the Wake of Disaster: Lessons in Local Entrepreneurship*. London: Palgrave Macmillan.

Tan, Xiaohong, Qifeng Yuan, and Bin Lü. 2012. "Chengzhpuncun gaizao cunmin canyu jizhi fenxi—yi guangzhoushi liede cun weili" [Analysis of the participation mechanism of villagers in urban village reconstruction: a case study of Liede village in Guangzhou City]. *Tropical Geography* 32 (6): 618–625.

Turner, Robyne S. 1999. "Entrepreneurial Neighborhood Initiatives: Political Capital in Community Development." *Economic Development Quarterly* 13 (1): 15–22.

Vogel, Ezra F. 2011. *Deng Xiaoping and the Transformation of China*. Vol. 10. Cambridge: Belknap Press of Harvard University Press.
Wang, Cailiang. 2015. "2014: Zhongguo chaiqian niandu baogao" [2014: Annual report on demolition and relocation in China]. *Sina*. January 1. http://blog.sina.com.cn/s/blog_49858b220102vc5v.html.
Wang, Linsheng. 2011. "A Case Study of City Village Reconstruction in Guangzhou: Unscramble Liede Village." MA diss., South China University of Technology.
Wang, Su, and Bo Ren. 2014. "The Parable of a Village." *Caixin*, June 3. http://topics.caixin.com/ygczdyy/.
Webster, Christopher J., and Lawrence Wai-Chung Lai. 2003. *Property Rights, Planning and Markets: Managing Spontaneous Cities*. Cheltenham, UK: Edward Elgar Publishing.
Whiting, Susan H. 1998. "The Mobilization of Private Investment as a Problem of Trust in Local Governance Structures." In *Trust and Governance*, edited by Valerie Braithwaite and Margaret Levi, 167–194. New York: Russell Sage Foundation.
Woolcock, Michael. 2001. "The Place of Social Capital in Understanding Social and Economic Outcomes." *Canadian Journal of Policy Research* 2 (1): 11–17.
Wu, Fulong, Fangzhu Zhang, and Chris Webster. 2013. "Informality and the Development and Demolition of Urban Villages in the Chinese Peri-urban Area." *Urban Studies* 50 (10): 1919–1934.
Xu, Chenggang. 2011. "The Fundamental Institutions of China's Reforms and Development." *Journal of Economic Literature* 49 (4): 1076–1051.
You, Jong-Sung. 2018. "Trust and Corruption." In *The Oxford Handbook of Social and Political Trust*, edited by Eric M. Uslaner, 473–496. Oxford: Oxford University Press.
Zhang, Youqiong, and Wenxiang Liang. 2014. "Villagers of Xiancun Village Voted to Take Back Collective Property." *Nanfang Daily,* March 4. http://gd.people.com.cn/n/2014/0304/c123932-20692766.html.
Zhang, Zheng. 2005. "Nongcun Tudi Chanquan Zhidu Chuangxin Moshi De Tansuo—Beijing Jiaoqu Zhenggezhuang Xianxiang Shizheng Fenxi" [Exploration on The Innovation Model of Rural Land Property Rights System—Empirical Analysis of Phenomenon of Zhenggezhuang in Suburban Beijing]. *Chinese Rural Economy* 2: 73–77.
Zhao, Junjie, Huang Huang, and Qing Liu. 2013. *Nongcun Zhudong Chengzhenhua Shijian Tansuo—you 'Zhenggezhaung Xianxiang' Yinfa De Sikao* [*Practical Exploration of Active Urbanization in Rural: Reflections on "Zhenggezhuang Phenomenon*]. Beijing: China Social Science Press.
Zhou, Zhihua. 2014. "Towards Collaborative Approach? Investigating the Regeneration of Urban Village in Guangzhou, China." *Habitat International* 44: 297–305.

Chapter 10

Under Emergency Management

Community Responses to the Flint Water Crisis

Sawyer Phinney

On April 25, 2014, the City of Flint, Michigan, switched their water source and began to pump poorly treated water from the Flint River into residents' homes. For several months following the switch, Flint citizens had complained that their tap water was discolored and polluted, and that there was a foul-smelling fluid coming from their taps (Gostin 2016). It was only after Flint residents and communities organized their own campaign—attracting scientists, doctors, citizen activists, and journalists—that the state finally acknowledged the scale of the issue and began steps to resolve Flint's unsafe drinking water issue (Drum 2017).

The poisoning of Flint's water is not an isolated nor random incident; it is an event historically and socially rooted and reflective of the city's political and economic conditions. By studying the events which took place in Flint, from the time when city officials began to search for alternative water sources until the present, as well as by analyzing the academic literature regarding such events, this chapter shows that the poisoning of the City of Flint is complex and indicative of systemic failures. These failures include lack of government accountability, ignoring local communities in the regulation and oversight of Flint water services, and disinvestment in the city and people of Flint by multiple levels of government. By applying varying perspectives through which to analyze this crisis, I was able to unpack and piece together the structural causes of the events in Flint to understand the deep source of the events that took place.

In this first section, I provide an analysis of theories of polycentricism, local knowledge and social capital from an Ostromian perspective applied to the case of Flint and theorize the importance of communities in being included in the governing of the provision of goods and services. In the second section, I offer a background of events leading to the poisoning of Flint's water system. Firstly, I examine the more recent history of the events immediately preceding the mass contamination of Flint's water. Foremost, I place Flint in a larger context of emergency manager laws being placed upon fiscally distressed cities, and the consequences when local communities are not involved in the decision-making processes of public service provision. This portion includes my analysis of the perspective of the importance of bridging and bonding social capital to encompass local knowledge, proposing that decentralized responses to health/environmental crises are more effective, as is reflected in the activism and organizing work of local individuals and groups of Flint to exchange information and resources to force political action on behalf of the state and to, most importantly, creating mechanisms to effectively monitor their water systems.

CONCEPTS FROM OSTROMIAN POLITICAL ECONOMY

Polycentricity and Local Knowledge

Polycentricism is described as a system with many decision-making powers independent of one another, and that involves multiple, overlapping systems of autonomous governments (Ostrom, Tiebout, and Warren 1961). A fundamental feature of polycentricism is that not just government levels, but also civil society and nongovernmental community organizations have a degree of autonomy within such system of governance. In their work on polycentric systems, both Vincent and Elinor Ostrom have also focused extensively on the ways in which communities solve complex challenges within polycentric orders (V. Ostrom 1999). According to Hess and Ostrom (2007, 53), local knowledge plays a vital cultural component, as well as intellectual, economic, and political functions. Elinor Ostrom envisioned such polycentric systems to also be sites of learning and innovation, and where aspects of social capital and cooperation can be enhanced. From the Ostroms' perspective, polycentric system should be one of cultivation, not control. This means that policies should focus on the enabling environment and serve to capture the local knowledge of social actors directly involved (E. Ostrom 2005). One important benefit of polycentrism is having better access to local knowledge to be able to successfully match policy to context and, thus, reducing the risk that a public service provision will fail (Carlisle and Gruby 2017, 5).

Postindustrial, declining cities like Flint present a challenge to the public provision of goods and services due to reduced economic activity and decreasing government revenue to pay for and provide an adequate level of goods and services. There are strong incentives for community self-governance when there is a degree of nonprovision of public goods and services on behalf of the state. By drawing on literature in public choice theory, this chapter argues that social capital and local knowledge are important elements in the functioning of governance and the delivery of public services. What is the role of local communities in the functioning of polycentric systems when it comes to the delivery of public goods?

To answer this question, my focus is primarily to better understand the interactions between society, the bureaucracy, and their environment, and how this informs the types of interactions of self-governance that emerged in the context of Flint. It has been discussed in the literature, polycentricism fosters both cooperation and coordination between public bureaucracy and civil society, which can contribute to a more efficient provision of public services (Ostrom and Ostrom 1977). V. Ostrom (1999) finds that monocentric orders crowd out social capital and local efforts to respond to challenges versus polycentric orders, which increase the social coordination capacity of community by allowing them to use local knowledge and respond to challenges.

Cross-sector collaborative network governance is argued to resemble polycentrism (Aligica, Lewis, and Storr 2017, 51). This includes the intersecting decision-making powers of civil society, the state at various levels, private firms, and nongovernmental organizations (NGOs). It is emphasized that well-informed individuals with rights of autonomy and mutual monitoring could undertake collective action to protect public resources at a localized scale and solve collective action problems without the involvement of top-down state intervention (Ostrom 1990, 1991, 2007a). For instance, Boettke, Lemke, and Palagashvili (2016) find that the centralization of police services in the United States made it very challenging for citizens to voice their concerns and change the conduct of police services. This created a lack of incentives for communities to participate in coproduction, leading to alienation between community members and police forces, and less effective at being able to provide public safety to communities—a local public good. As Vogler (2019) argues, it is crucial to analyze the underlying conditions of coproduction, where the adequate delivery for public goods and services is predicated upon citizen engagement and cooperation (116). When examining governments experiencing tight public budgets post-2008 financial crisis, Jimenez (2017) argues that drawing on local knowledge from civil society and stakeholders, such as business groups, unions, organizations, and neighborhood organizations, can have a positive impact on a local government's fiscal recovery through the coproduction of networking and development strategies.

In a similar vein, Uzochukwu and Thomas (2018) examine what the determinants are for citizen participation in public service provisions. What they found was that those from lower incomes and racial backgrounds were more likely to engage in forms of coproduction. Consulting with civil society will have an impact on public service delivery performance (Vogler 2019, 116). Thus, coordinating with the public is a way of drawing on local knowledge and multiple experiences into account thereby influencing the operation of bureaucracy and how services are delivered. Both Vincent and Elinor Ostrom places great emphasis on the everyday empirical knowledge of people as important transformative tools leading to beneficial outcomes and the emergence of institutions and, also, for the effective delivery of goods and services (Aligica, Lewis, and Storr 2017, 5). From this view, increased community involvement aligns with wider discourses of "good governance," and the normative view that the knowledge and input of nonstate actors such as citizens and NGOs improve the legitimacy, quality, and sustainability of decisions-making institutions (Gunningham and Shearing 2013; Newig and Fritsch 2009).

Bonding and Bridging Social Capital

Social capital has been employed as a concept to understand different values of network relationships for specific communities in various sociopolitical contexts. E. Ostrom, in particular, has described social capital as the resources that are associated with membership in some particular network that individuals use as they pursue their goals (1999, 173). Moreover, it is used by academics to understand strengths of families, communities, and interactions with public bureaucracy and the market. Social capital is unique in its ability to bridge the theoretical gap between individual and community that spans from the micro to the macro in an interactive manner more effectively than many previous socioeconomic/sociopolitical theories. Social distinctions have been made in the literature about the kinds of social capital that exist.

Bonding social capital refers to trust and social networks within a group, whereas bridging social capital refers to various links between seemingly different groups (Puntam 2000). It is argued that homogeneous communities exhibit more bonding social capital and less bridging and linking social capital at societal levels (Lin 2001). Moreover, Gitell and Vidal (1998) conceptualize bonding social capital as referring to trusting as well as cooperative relations, between members of a network who view themselves as having a "shared social identity" (655). In contrast, bridging social capital encompasses networking and relations of mutuality between people who are aware they are not alike in some sociodemographic social identity (age, class, ethnicity, group, etc.). According to Gitell and Vidal (1998), it is the nature of the social identity boundaries, along with the political salience of bonding and bridging groups that make such relations context specific. It is argued that homogeneous communities exhibit more bonding social capital but less bridging at societal and institutional levels (Lin 2001; Costa and Kahn 2003). However, both bonding and bridging social capital refer to social relationships that form for the purpose of shared interests or goals but both including different ties (strong or weak). It has been suggested that urban communities tend to have strong bridging but weaker bonding capital, whereas rural communities more typically have strong bonding but weaker bridging capital (Woolcock 2002). These various forms of social capital contribute to successful collective action. In the case of postindustrial cities like Flint, bridging capital is not necessarily stronger as it would be for other urban communities. With the loss of industry, jobs, and capital, drawing on external networks and working through weakened institutions can be a challenge.

In the literature on social capital, community-based organizations have been found to play an important role in helping loosely connected communities leverage the extra-community connections and other resources of their members. It is argued that the reason why community and local organizations play such a key role in recovery is because governments face a knowledge problem. In this way, the element of social capital provides a way for evaluating the benefits of local knowledge (E. Ostrom 1999).

Social actors, including organizations and individuals, pursue their goals in polycentric institutional settings where they comply with multiple governance rules at different levels and scales embedded in local knowledge and particular settings (Ostrom 1990). Elinor Ostrom's work on common pool resource (CPR) situations demonstrates the significance of different form of social capital, and, also, ways in which communities can self-govern themselves through designing various rules for monitoring one another based on being the experts of their own community, and overcome problems related to the tragedy of the commons (overuse/misuse of public goods and resources) (Ostrom 1990). Studies have looked at how social capital aids recovery in communities with a focus on "bonding" and "bridging," which serve as a way to help communities overcome collective actions problems related to the provision of public goods.

There is a clear link in the literature that discuses the link between social capital to community redevelopment. Scholars place great emphasis on the importance of community actors in responding to recovery efforts, particularly when the government or public sector is absent, and how systems of self-governance emerge out of these actions. From their empirical work following the post-disaster recovery of Hurricane Katrina, Storr, and Haeffele-Balch (2012) found that community-based organizations make it more likely that community members be able to coordinate collective action plans. They also discovered that by keeping community-based organization acting as a common network and space to coordinate and funnel activities and organizing to address a community crisis, it makes it easier for the community to rebound.

Moreover, in their research, Bolin and Stanford (1991) outline the benefits of this through their discovery that community-based organizations aided in an earthquake recovery by coordinating with government agencies to provide the necessary resources to redevelop impacted infrastructure and support families affected. Similarly, Nakagawa and Shaw (2004) found that high levels of social capital in earthquake rehabilitation and reconstruction programs and with lineages of community activities led to faster recovery. Lastly, Hurlbert et al. (2000, 2001) and Aldrich (2011) acknowledge that networks comprised of weak ties (particularly links to extra-community institutions) can be important; they nonetheless stress the importance of bonding and bridging social capital in bringing about post-disaster recovery. In sum, researchers examining disaster recovery, or a crisis recovery, suggest that the balance should shift further toward community actors (Quarantelli 1998, 56).

There is little research that focuses on how communities utilize forms of social capital to manage the nonprovision of public goods and services, and the elements which can make communities the best agents to respond to government failures. More studies are needed to better understand collective action problems and the benefits of social capital as tools to improve local self-governance when the public sector fails in providing such goods. In my case, how do communities work toward solving collective action problems and developing patterns of private organization to deliver services to their communities in a political environment where their legitimacy and decision-making power is being suppressed by the state? Social resiliency includes social capital, particularly such features as community norms and networks. From the Flint case, it is clear that households and organizations had strong incentives to use social capital and develop ways to monitor the provision of their water systems. Such incentives were based on their individual expected return from social capital—accessing clean drinking water.

The Flint Water Crisis: A Brief Overview

Scholars, along with various think tanks, theorize and attribute the root of the Flint Water Crisis to the failures of deindustrialization, global economic restructuring, urban planning, and political mismanagement. The Michigan Civil Rights Commission, a state-established body, concluded that the poor governmental response to the Flint crisis was a "result of systemic racism"

(MCRC 2017). Other studies have linked the causes of the Flint water crisis to the interventionism of financial emergency management (Hammer 2017; Pulido 2016). Because of the consequences of deindustrialization, the City of Flint has suffered from depopulation and a series of fiscal crises (Highsmith 2015; Scorsone 2011). As thousands of people in Flint lost their jobs and many were forced to move away for employment, loss of industry kickstarted an urban decline in the region. From 1960 to 2010, Flint lost half of its population, and has since declined nearly a quarter from 2000 to now (Trounstine 2016). Additionally, with the decline of wealth comes the decrease of tax revenue in such cities, and hence the quality of education and other public resources and services is seen to have dramatically fallen. Flint's fiscal health worsened following the 2008 housing crisis, forcing thousands of housing foreclosures and subsequently draining the city's tax base (Bianco 2008). What was once an economically thriving middle-class industrial city was left to devolve into a declining, fiscally distressed city.

Flint's water and wastewater systems is considered one of the city's most valuable assets, so it was no surprise that it was a target for restructuring as a way to help balance their municipal budget. However as with many postindustrial US cities, Flint has miles of old water pipes underground that are deteriorating and in need of replacement (Hanna-Attisha 2017, 80). Lead-based water infrastructure, particularly for older and distressed US cities, is quite common. A 2003 study finds that eight out of ten cities with the highest childhood lead poising were in postindustrial, declining cities: Cleveland, Philadelphia, Buffalo, Providence, Milwaukee, St. Louis, Detroit, and Baltimore (Markowtiz and Rosner 2013, 6). Flint is an extreme case, but, nationally, there is a lack of investment in water infrastructure (AWWA 2012). More concerning is that Flint's water distribution lines have never been replaced unless they outright failed. This has meant that over the last several years the City of Flint has been forced to raise water rates and also issue private bonds to deal with decrepit infrastructure (Wisley 2016). Water rates in the city are expensive and increasing annually because pipes are in poor condition and in need of replacement. Moreover, Flint is losing population yet still needs to provide water services within the same boundaries, so this places a strain on current ratepayers. Water and sewerage bills in Flint in 2014 were $140 per month—$35 more than the city with the second-highest rates in Genesee County and $90 more than the lowest (Clark 2017, 34). Costly bills have been a factor tempting residents to move to the suburbs. Because of the fact that there are fewer paying into the system, it means that there is less money to maintain it, which means water rates continue to increase. Because of these issues, it was easy to understand the desire to make Flint's water more affordable. Therefore, the switch of the Detroit system that was pitched by Flint's emergency management team served as a way to do just that.

Switching Water Sources

Since 1967, Flint had purchased water from the City of Detroit, its water source being Lake Huron. However, in 2012 a decision was made by Flint's emergency manager Ed Kurtz to change the source of the city's water from the Detroit Water and Sewerage Department to the Karegnondi Water Authority (KWA) to save costs while the city was undergoing financial restructuring following 2008 (Stanley 2017, 34). Still under construction, KWA would not ready to deliver the water until 2016 as they were in the process of building a new pipeline to bring water from nearby Lake Huron (the Center for Michigan 2016). This meant that officials in the city of Flint needed to find a short-term solution while the new pipeline was being built. They decided to use water from the local Flint River in the meantime that they would clean in water treatment plants (Dingle 2016, 1). As a result of Flint switching its water supply, this meant that they were using different water mains to deliver drinking water to its residents which needed to be assessed as different pipes depending on their material components are treated in different ways. This is standard protocol, according to the Environmental Protection Agency (EPA), when switching to a new water source as a way to deal with the changing chemistry of the water in the pipes (US Environmental Protection Agency 2018; Flint Water Study Group 2015a). Without an assessment meant officials failed to apply corrosion inhibitors to the water.

Because of pressure for city to cut costs to balance their budget by the State of Michigan, impulsive decisions were made without consultations with residents and the community, and with little time and space for regulatory oversight on whether the new water source along with the different water infrastructure that was being used was safe. It was reported that upgrades were needed for water infrastructure (for water plants, mains, and lines) to ensure that drinking water quality was safe. A Rowe Engineering report estimated that nearly $60 million of new maintenance and upgrades was needed to be able to treat the water properly; however, the city only had spent $3.8 million before the switch was made to the new water source (Egan 2016). This meant that the system was underfunded and not equipped to ensure the river treatment plant was a safe, drinking water source and sufficiently upgraded to an adequate capacity. The Flint River water that was treated improperly caused lead from aging pipes to leach into the water supply. The Flint Water Advisory Task Force (2016, 52) concluded in fact: "There was and remains no justification for MDEQ not requiring corrosion control treatment for the switch of water source to the Flint River." It was the lack of corrosion control that resulted in the corrosion of water service lines and interior lead-based plumbing in houses (solder, fixtures, faucets) in Flint, which in turn resulted in contaminated drinking water. As a result, between

6,000 and 12,000 children have been exposed to drink water with high levels of lead during the time of the switch (Gross 2018; Hanna-Attisha et al. 2015). Because of changes to the water source, the percentage of Flint children with elevated blood-lead levels doubled between 2013 and 2015 (Hanna-Attisha et al. 2015, 282). Although the Flint water crisis has now reached national headlines across the globe, it took the resilience of Flint residents to make this possible.

The next section will outline the ways in which emergency management created strong incentives for Flint citizens to self-organize and develop patterns of private organization around the provision of clean water. Social action became absolutely necessary to counter policies of emergency management and as a way of monitoring their water sources, as possibilities for democratic collective action within a local public realm were being severely curtailed in a democratic sense. This chapter argues the ways in which social capital helped the recovery of the Flint water crisis and led to the emergence of self-governance institutions to monitor their water systems. This worked to expose the inefficiencies and failures of public service provision through bridging and bonding social capital.

THE IMPORTANCE OF COMMUNITY AND CITIZEN RESPONSES TO THE CRISIS

Polycentricity and Local Knowledge: Technocracy vs. Community Engagement

Consequences of switching water systems to the Flint River were quickly realized. Residents complained that their water smelled foul and looked discolored and that they were breaking out in rashes (Clark 2018b). Residents' concerns of their drinking water are well documented in local media reports. For instance, Melissa Mays claimed her water had a foul smell, "and a strange tint when coming out of the faucet, sometimes blue, sometimes yellowish" (Samuels 2015). Another resident, Bethany Hazard, says her water started coming out of the faucet brown and smelling like a sewer, and when she called the city to complain, she was told the water was fine. More concerning, LeeAnne Walters noticed that her children were getting rashes between their fingers, on their shins, on the back of their knees. Her four-year-old son, who has a compromised immune system, started breaking out into scaly rashes whenever he swam in their saltwater pool, which he'd used since birth (Samuels 2015; Wisley 2016). Residents and community members were bringing forth their concerns to local government, state, and federal officials that their water was unsafe to drink and the health risks they were experiencing went on for months. In an early protest, some residents brought their discolored water bottles to City Hall—however, their actions were largely ignored or framed as unfounded.

Department of Public Works Director Howard Croft asked residents to be patient, acknowledging how hurried the process had been: "City water plant workers have had a crash course in learning how to treat river water" (Fonger 2014). As it was reported, "Many residents were avoiding the tap and drinking bottled water instead" (Fox 2016). Some Flint residents began to purchase bottled water and filters; however, many did not have the means and continued to drink, cook with, and bathe in the city water. The state's top drinking water officials, Prysby and Stephen Busch, insisted that consistent testing was conducted on Flint's drinking water and that it meets all EPA standards (Denchak 2018). When the city was asked to respond to these concerns, their response also confirmed "the water met all safety requirements and legal drinking water standards." Moreover, the city authorities further said in a statement to a local news outlet, "Residents in the affected areas may see increased water cloudiness for a short time, but the water is safe to drink" (Spitznagel 2017). Since not every household was impacted to the same extent in terms of levels of lead in their drinking water, skepticism and protesters' complaints were viewed as exaggerated—this served to discredit residents' concerns and their local knowledge and deprive them of avenues for reparation.

How do theories of local knowledge as the main catalyst for the functioning of polycentric systems help us to understand what went wrong in the Flint water crisis from a governance perspective? What is first important to consider is the implication of technocratic policies to financially restructure the city, thereby excluding community members from the decision-making processes. This involves dissolving the power of city council and elected government officials, sidestepping community engagement, and expunging public consultation within city government. The requirements embedded in Michigan emergency management law cede power to external financial consultants that are appointed and have crowded out opportunities to involve the Flint local community and their empirical, everyday knowledge in decisions being made to their water services.

In 2011, the City of Flint was declared in a state of financial emergency by the State of Michigan due to risk of defaulting on city bonds and falling into fiscal solvency that led to an emergency management takeover (Pulido 2016, 6). They did this under Public Act 436, which allows governors to assign emergency managers to municipalities with the goal of restructuring the city's finances. As a result, emergency managers were appointed by the State of Michigan to take over the city government and restructure their municipal finances. In some US states, when cities fail to be self-sufficient, state and national governments have the power to employ legal tools, such as emergency management laws, and impose top-down restructuring policies.

Between 2011 and 2015, Flint was placed under emergency management, and four consecutive emergency managers (EMs) were appointed by Michigan Rick Snyder. EMs are unelected and hired and contracted by the state to get the city out of financial troubles and restructure the city's finances and government services, which includes local elected officials' powers being usurped by the State of Michigan (Pulido 2016; May 2018; Abbey-Lambertz 2013). EMs have broad powers to intervene in financially struggling municipalities with full control over restructuring finances the way they see fit—this includes selling public assets or transforming the ways in which public services and goods are delivered. EMs also hold the power to make executive decisions related to the governance arrangements and delivery of municipal goods and services. According to Michigan state officials, emergency manager law serves as an important tool of governance because it allows for government intervention by providing relief and third-party assistance from financial experts when a city is distressed (Nickels 2016, 195–196).

Governor-appointed EMs can take extraordinary measures, such as supersede local ordinances, sell city assets, void collective bargaining agreements, and relieve city councillors of their political duties (Amromin and Chabot 2013, 1). EMs are only accountable to the state governor and State Treasury Department officials, rather than city council members and local voters. Thus, this reduces opportunity for citizens to influence local policy decisions and decimates local democracy (Lewis 2013). Moreover, under emergency management and under state control, local elected officials can only exercise the powers of their offices only with the manager's written approval.

Michigan is one of sixteen states with a provision for the state government to shift local decision-making powers away from local elected officials to an appointed EM under conditions of financial distress (Scorsone and Bateson 2014). However, the level and nature of the intervention vary widely (Mattoon 2013: 3). Richard Mattoon, a senior economist and financial adviser, writes, "Some states (e.g., Michigan, North Carolina, Pennsylvania, and Rhode Island) are more aggressive than others when they intervene" (Mattoon 2013, 3), which can act as a vehicle allowing unrestricted and absolute authority into the policy agendas of local governments during periods of economic failure.

Because of the EM, such a decision to switch Flint's water system did not require a vote by city council and likely would have not received public support due to the widespread perception that the river was contaminated by decades of industrial waste (Longley 2011). Flint residents faced some difficult challenges with emergency management impeding their capacity to monitor decisions being made to their public services, such as water but this also has included housing, education, police, and fire services during the time of emergency management (Fehr and Murphy 2016). Restructuring to these services was solely done by the EM and his team and did not follow the usual democratic processes under city government.

During the process of switching Flint's water, and the implementations of new policies and programs to complete such process, minimal information was released to the public about changes being made to their water, steps that will be taken to ensure water quality, and how their water systems were being monitored. This served as a way to curtail community engagement and disagreements that may have reversed such decisions, or, at the very least, brought media attention to such decisions being considered. Moreover, from reports it shows that officials did not immediately treat the Flint River water to ensure it did not cause corrosion in the pipes (lead contamination), and, instead, they took a "wait-and-see approach" (Kennedy 2016). These policy changes and approaches to how the city is assessing and addressing water quality did not need to be accountable or transparent to the public, or even city council, as details were only known and decided upon by emergency managers (Lewis 2013).

What is important is that as the water quality became worse, residents in Flint had few outlets to report their concerns. One, because the city council had limited authority, and, two, the Office of the Ombudsman had been completely eliminated. Lack of citizen engagement and opportunities for citizens to participate in public consultations with representative groups, along with the prohibition of city council meetings to vote on new implementations and policies on public services, emergency management by law, served as a way to sidestep municipal democratic processes when it comes to changes to Flint's water services. This meant Flint's local government was acting over communities, rather than through them. An absence of facilitating and coproducing management strategies drawn from local knowledge and excluding local community members from not only the decision-making processes, but from local bureaucracy spaces to voice their concerns, created the conditions for the Flint water crisis.

In this case, local knowledge was suppressed via centralized efforts to restructure the city. Because of this, information regarding decisions being made to switching water systems was distorted and being mediated through convoluted networks that did not include the local community. During the process of switching water sources, emergency managers did not consult local residents, association, businesses, or organizations to take part in evaluating benefits/costs in utilizing different water systems. Such consequences may have been avoided if emergency managers did not presuppose knowledge of local circumstances. As has been argued by scholars like Stanley

(2017), emergency management in Michigan served as technocracy as a democratic alternative to achieve financial efficiency. In this way, concentrated authority was understood by policymakers and state officials as being more efficient in improving the fiscal health of the city than its own residents. As is further argued by Stanley (2017), emergency management served as a form technocratic governance that justified under the narrative being put forth—Flint's fiscal problems are far too technically complicated and need to involve "financial experts" that is beyond ordinary citizens' capacity to understand (10). The ideal of technocracy is financial efficiency. In this case of Flint, "financial emergencies" require "financial experts" to find solutions (Stanley 2017, 12). Technocratic governance as opposed to more polycentric systems is attractive, then, because it offers a neutral resolution to pluralist, conflicting interests in a financial crisis and a set of programs and ideals in place to negotiate between conflicting parties.

The conceivable benefits that were understood to be obtained by emergency management were outweighed by the potential harms of unsafe drinking water that resulted from the implementations of policy that failed to incorporate localized community knowledge in the decision-making processes. The limited and unsound knowledge on which the decision was based on amplified the resultant harm beyond what it might have been in a decentralized system that prioritized localized power from community members who possess valuable knowledge of their environment to decide on the best ways to deliver their public goods and services. Should we think of the failure of public service provisions, such as unsafe drinking water, as a by-product of technocracy forced upon Flint rather than polycentricism? Could a more polycentric forms of governance, which includes local self-determination and local communities involved in the decision-making processes, prevented such a crisis? What eventually led to the switch back to the more safer water system?

BONDING AND BRIDGING SOCIAL CAPITAL: EXTERNAL PARTNERSHIPS AND MAKING SCIENTISTS OUT OF CITIZENS

Because of circumstances that led to public sector inefficiency and the nonprovision of water services—emergency management created strong incentives for Flint citizens to self-organize and develop patterns of private organization around the delivery of clean water. Such example demonstrates the importance of drawing on local knowledge and the everyday experiences of people as a way for public administrations to deliver public goods and services most effectively, particularly at the local level.

After Flint residents' concerns were not taking seriously and action was not taken to address the drinking water or test the water on behalf of government officials, communities and organizations coming from various different backgrounds worked together to create political action in a few ways. Citizens organized a grassroots movement among themselves (bonding social capital) and, secondly, allied themselves with outside/national drinking water experts in the field to get the necessary equipment to test the water themselves (bridging social capital) and published their results to draw in national attention. This also included working with health organizations and nurses who tested blood samples to find levels of lead. Through drawing on ways of utilizing "citizen scientists," social capital helped bond and bridge resources and information from various local residents, individuals from different professional fields, and organizations to triangulate local knowledge and information and collectively work together to expose unsafe drinking water in Flint and pressure the local, state, and federal government to act. There was no onus to act if there was no proof. Community actors reorganized their social networks and used bonding (within the community of Flint) and bridging (drawing on resources and people from outside of Flint) to expose lead poisoning in the community and collaborate transformative political action. This section uses research findings from local and national media reports of the Flint Water Crisis, online sources from Flint's Water Study Group, along with some scholarly work on the topic. This section demonstrates the ways in which social capital facilitated community governance following events of the crisis. Because of the fact that social capital can aid information flow and enforcement, it has served as a way to help the Flint community overcome collective action problems related to government failures of the delivery of public goods.

In the literature on social capital, several characteristics have been used to investigate and assess social capital and its relationship to community-level emergency resiliency. Based on Murphy's (2007, 305) study, these include the following:

> (1) An assessment of the presence and capacity of, and participation in, community groups and organizations (e.g., presence of strong ties), (2) the positive/negative views about communities that exist within and between groups, (3) the horizontal and vertical interaction among the groups and their relative social positioning (e.g., presence of weak ties and power structures), (4) the congruence (or lack thereof) between municipal and community boundaries and interests, (5) the extent to which community group organization and dynamics is incorporated into local government emergency management planning, and (6) in the wake of a disaster, organizational and community response, development and change.

Historically speaking, the city has strong ties with community groups linking together and organizing. Flint has a culture of organizing that began with United Auto Workers and their historic sit-down strikes in Flint in the 1930s. Following that, citizens bonded together against segregation and racial discrimination in real estate with sleep-ins on the law of city hall, drawing in thousands of supports for a fair housing vote (McCloud 2012). More recently, when fiscal emergency management came to Flint, residents founded groups such as the Democracy Defense League to challenge it.

In the case of the water crisis, it was not a surprise that when individuals and groups knew that their water switch had gone badly, the people of Flint worked together and got organized. In many ways, bonding and bridging social capital served as creating the conditions and necessary tools for coproduction where members of civil society began participating in their own delivery of public goods. The absence of clean water (as an essential public good/service) created strong incentives for residents to develop networks and connections among themselves, while also drawing on external personnel and resources to create their own monitoring mechanisms to measure the quality of their water around the community.

There are several ways in which the community bonded and bridged social capital to deal with their CPR problem of unsafe drinking water: (1) created and handed out petitions to community members; (2) organized public meetings; (3) kept detailed notes on the quality of their water; (4) collected water samples, and also blood samples that detected lead; (5) created social media pages to share this information to residents; (6) sought out public documents.

In 2015, a number of individuals and groups banded together to form the Coalition for Clean Water to better coordinate their resources. They spent time distributing information about the dangers and health risks of lead contamination and were the center point in connecting with households and families who were experiencing health concerns as a result of contamination or suspected their water was unsafe to drink. The activists in this group also repeatedly made trips to the governor's office to make their case to the Michigan's Department of Environmental Quality—however, during these trips nothing was done. The State Michigan didn't budge from its position and further emphasized that from their tests the water was safe. However, neither the local emergency management government in Flint nor the State of Michigan would release their findings to the public or allow the broader public to take part in the process.

The most important element of social capital was using information and resources from the organization and community residents to independently monitor and test lead contamination in Flint themselves. These tests spanned the entire city to make little room for error, or discredit from the State of

Michigan. By raising funds from various organizations, such as American Civil Liberties Union (ACLU) and the National Science Foundation, and from contributions and support from community organizations in Flint, they raised enough money for 100 samples for a scientifically valid test.

They contacted Marc Edwards, who worked as an environmental engineer and expert on water treatment and corrosion at Virginia Tech. Edwards recruited undergraduates, graduate students, and postdoc researchers. Thirty students, along with local activists, and Marc Edwards formed the Flint Water Study group. This group collaborated with homeowners on something they called, "citizen testing" (Hanna-Attisha 2017, 92). Sampling kits were given out to households all throughout the city with instructions of how to use them. Samples were needed from across all zip codes of the city to give a comprehensive picture of Flint's water. Additionally, a degree of trust was needed. Residents needed to trust the organizers who were going door-to-door on knocking on households' doors for sampling. This is where bonding social capital and strong horizontal ties of Flint's community excelled in demonstrating the city's capacity of community resilience. When volunteers were taught and learned of the process of how to use the sampling kit correctly, they passed on their training to their neighborhoods, and broke down the city into zip codes as they coordinated pickups and deliveries of samples. Social bonding served as an important tool to encapsulate local knowledge. Additionally, residents doing the testing implemented procedures on their own to prevent any accusations and to counter any accusations that they tampered with the results to make the problem seem worse than it really was. For example, they developed a way of having each homeowner seal and sign the kit, so that no one but the homeowner could have opened the bottle before the Flint Water Study Group could check the deal at Virginia Tech (Flint Water Study 2015b).

In a span of a few weeks, the coalition distributed over 300 samples of lead-sampling kits to Flint residents and collected back 277 (Roy 2015). Several other organizations worked with residents in the community (Water You Fighting For, Concerned Pastors for Social Action, ACLU of Michigan, Democracy Defense League) to maximize distributing sample kits , collecting the kits and returning to the study group (Flint Water Study 2015a). Analysis of the kits showed that lead poisoning was spread across the entire city. Most of the lead was found in the central belt of the city according to work conducted by the Coalition for Clean Water and the Flint Water Study group (ACLU 2016). Many samples exceeded 100 parts per billion, which was over twice the federal action level, and ten times the safety standard of the World Health Organization (10 parts per billion). The highest tested sample was 1051 parts per billion, and in a few hard-hit zip codes in Flint, one in five homes had high lead. After these tests were conducted, a report was compiled by the Flint Water Study Group and the Coalition for Clean Water outlining the results of their testing, emphasizing that Flint has a serious lead problem, further noting that "because of the very serious and permanent health damage that arises from lead exposure, we feel that this problem requires immediate public health warning and interventions" (Flint Water Study 2015b).

At the same time, local pediatric nurses at Hurley Medical Center collaborated with nonprofit health coalitions in the Flint area to access data on blood-lead levels obtained by other clinics and doctors in Flint. Local pediatric nurses started noticing more than unusual problems from child patients that they suspected could be from the lead drinking water. They were able to pull electronic medical records for children under the age of 5 years in seven Flint zip codes to analyze (Hannah-Attisha 2018, 184), and compare their findings with the water-lead levels testing that was completed by the Flint Water Study Group. Nurses at the Hurley Medical Center studied two periods: preswitch blood-lead levels from January 1 to September 15, 2013, and post-switch levels during the same months of 2015. Their findings showed that post-switch, the percentage of children with blood-lead elevation was almost double (Hulett 2015; Hannah-Attisha 2018, 226)

It is important to note that this was in contrast to every national state trend (lead levels have been coming down every year). Moreover, by looking at water-lead levels in each zip code, the team of nurses and researchers were able to show a causal relationship: the zip codes with the highest water-lead levels saw the greatest increases with the percentage of children with elevated blood levels (Hannah-Attisha 2018, 227). While also accessing and testing children blood samples, local pediatric nurses in Flint organized townhall meetings to bring awareness to families with young children of the risks associated with children drinking water with lead and worked to raise funds and resources to provide "ready-to-feed" formula for babies to deter families form having to use their tap water. These nurses worked with the Genesee County Health Department's Women, Infants, and Children (WIC) program to provide ready-to-feed formula and discuss the risks health and developmental risks associated with babies who are drinking formula mixed with tap water in Flint (Hannah-Attisha 2018, 242).

The report that was produced by the Flint Water Study Group, along with the findings of blood-lead sampling, was given to a local news source which released the findings to the public. Through findings from the Flint Water Study, due to insufficient water treatment (the city not using corrosive control) and aging water pipes from the Flint River, lead leached from the water pipes into the drinking water, exposing over 100,000 residents to lead poisoning (Hacker and Pierson 2016; Gostin 2016). Once the news got out, it spread quickly, and the State of Michigan and the local government were forced to finally admit that there was a lead poisoning epidemic in Flint, Michigan, and the water was unsafe to drink—this was after eighteen months of the local and state governments discrediting lead as an issue (Bosman and Smith 2016). Governor Rick Snyder held a press conference in January 2016 to declare Flint in a State of Emergency and plans to switch their water source back to Lake Huron (Dolan and Egan 2016; Filson 2017).

By highlighting both vertical and horizontal relationships, the differentiated yet interrelated roles played by community members, and, also, the bridging of knowledge and resources among groups to resolve problems related to Flint's drinking water, this chapter demonstrates the ways in which the social capital construct provides an important lens through which to assess the important role of communities in responding to crisis events. This section highlights a range of factors and relationships that contribute to our understanding of community resiliency in Flint. Furthermore, I place emphasis on the role of community members as active agents rather than passive victims by demonstrating how communities in Flint are self-organized when the public sector was absent in adequately delivering public services (i.e., clean water), highlighting the vital importance of everyday local knowledge to the provision of public goods.

SUMMARY AND CONCLUSION

Municipal financial constraints and economic decline, in combination with limited avenues for citizen opposition, motivated decisions that climaxed the Flint water crisis. In this chapter, I have outlined the importance of local knowledge for the functioning of polycentric systems as demonstrated by the Elinor and Vincent Ostrom to better understand why communities and their everyday knowledge serve as unique tools for governance at the local level and the consequences that were produced in Flint when this was not done. The importance of communities in local governance was also demonstrated in regard to community responses to self-organize to raise awareness and retake control over their water services by creating enforcement and monitoring mechanisms on their own when it was not being done by local or state government agencies. This was done by utilizing social capital both internally within their community, and also externally, by drawing on resources and assistance across the United States for the purpose of regaining control of being able to determine the quality of their drinking water and that it met certain standards for everyone in the community.

I argue that the characteristics of the emergency management governance structure that existed in Flint at the time are compatible with a form of technocratic governance, and not a polycentric system that would have encouraged local residents to be involved in the decision-making process for the delivery of public goods and services. Future research in public choice theory would benefit from examining the root of public sector service provision inefficiencies and failures by measuring ways civil society can impact public service delivery performance.

REFERENCES

Abbey-Lambertz, Kate. 2013. "Michigan Emergency Manager Law in Effect in 6 Cities after Detroit Appointment (MAP)." *HuffPost*, March 15, 2013. http:// www.huffingtonpost.com/2013/03/15/michigan-emergency-manager-law-cities_n_2876777.html.

Adams, Dominic. 2014. "City to Get Drinking Water from River as Pact with Detroit Ends." *The Flint Journal*, March 6, 2014. http://www.mlive.com/news/flint/index.ssf/2014/03/ flint_drinking_water_to_come_f.html.

Aldrich, Daniel. 2011. "The Externalities of Strong Social Capital: Post-tsunami Recovery in Southeast India." *Journal of Civil Society* 7 (1): 81–99.

American Civil Liberties Union of Michigan. 2016. "Here's to Flint: Documentary on Flint Water Crisis." March 8, 2016. http://www.aclumich.org/herestoflint.

American Water Works Association (AWWA). 2012. "Buried No Longer: Confronting America's Water Infrastructure Challenge." *AWWA*. https://www.awwa.org/Portals/0/files/legreg/documents/BuriedNoLonger.pdf.

Amromin, Gene, and Benjamin Chabot. 2013. "Detroit's Bankruptcy: The Uncharted Waters of Chapter 9." *Chicago Fed Letter* 313: 1–4.

Aligica, Paul, Paul Lewis, and Virgil Storr. 2017. "Austrian Economics and the Bloomington School: An Introduction and Overview." *Advances in Austrian Economics* 22: ix–xxi.

Bianco, Katalina. 2008. "The Subprime Lending Crisis: Causes and Effects of the Mortgage Meltdown." *Walters Kluwer Law & Business*. https://business.cch.com/images/banner/subprime.pdf.

Boettke, Peter J., Jayme S. Lemke, and Liya Palagashvili. 2016. "Re-Evaluating Community Policing in a Polycentric System." *Journal of Institutional Economics* 12 (2): 203–25.

Bolin, Robert, and Lois Stanford. 1991. "Shelter, Housing and Recovery: A Comparison of U.S. Disasters." *Disasters* 15: 24–34

Bosman, Julie, and Mitch Smith. 2016. "Gov. Rick Snyder of Michigan Apologizes in Flint Water Crisis." *New York Times*, January 19, 2016. https://www.nytimes.com/2016/01/20/us/obama-set-to-meet-with-mayor-of-flint-about-water-crisis.html.

Carlisle, Keith, and Rebecca L. Gruby. 2017. "Polycentric Systems of Governance: A Theoretical Model for the Commons." *Policy Studies Journal* 42 (4): 1–26.

Clark, Anna. 2018a. *The Poisoned City: Flint's Water and the American Urban Tragedy*. New York: Metropolitan Books.

———. 2018b. "'Nothing to Worry about. The Water Is Fine': How Flint Poisoned Its People." *The Guardian*, July 3, 2018. https://www.theguardian.com/news/2018/jul/03/nothing-to-worry-about-the-water-is-fine-how-flint-michigan-poisoned-its-people.

Costa, Dora, and Matthew Kahn. 2003. "Understanding the American Decline in Social Capital, 1952-1988." *Kyklos* 56 (1): 17–46.

Denchak, Melissa. 2018. "Flint Water Crisis: Everything You Need to Know." *National Resource Defence Council.* Accessed May, 01 2019. https://www.nrdc.org/stories/flint-water-crisis-everything-you-need-know.

Dingle, Adrian. 2016. "The Flint Water Crisis: What's Really Going On?" *ChemMatters.* https://www.acs.org/content/acs/en/education/resources/highschool/chemmatters/past-issues/2016-2017/december-2016/flint-water-crisis.html.

Dolan, Matthew, and Paul Egan. 2016. "Top Snyder Aides Urged Going Back to Detroit Water." *Detroit Free Press*, February 26, 2016. http://www.freep.com/story/news/local/michigan/flint-water-crisis/2016/02/26/flint-water-crisis-snyder-detroit/80926138/.

Drum, Kevin. 2017. "The Water in Flint Is Now Officially Safe to Drink." *Mother Jones*, January 25, 2017. https://www.motherjones.com/kevin-drum/2017/01/water-flint-now-officially-safe-drink/.

Egan, Paul. 2016. "Flint Will 'Lose Everything' If It Leaves KWA." *Detroit Free Press.* Accessed May 09, 2019. http://cqrcengage.com/iapmo/app/document/14295636;jsessionid=d0xba59r-hyd11uli0ncvqyl7u.

Fehr, Stephen, and Mary Murphy. 2016. "Flint Water Crisis Could Spur Changes to Michigan's Emergency Manager Law." *The Pew Charitable Trusts*, March 23, 2016. https://www.pewtrusts.org/en/research-and-analysis/articles/2016/03/23/flint-water-crisis-could-spur-changes-to-michigans-emergency-manager-law.

Filson, Jackie. 2017. "The Latest on the U.S. Water Crisis." *Food and Water Watch*, July 11, 2017. https://www.foodandwaterwatch.org/news/latest-us-water-crisis-its-still-happening-fyi.

Flint Water Advisory Task Force. 2016. "Final Report." *State of Michigan,* March 2016. http://www.michigan.gov/documents/snyder/FWATF_FINAL_REPORT_21March2016_517805_7.pdf .

Flint Water Study Group. 2015a. "Flint River Water Is Very Corrosive to Lead, and Causing Lead Contamination in Homes." September 2, 2015. Accessed November 22, 2018. http://flintwaterstudy.org/2015/09/flint-rivers-water-is-very-corrosive-to-lead-and-causing-lead-contamination-in-homes/.

———. 2015b. "Lead Testing Results for Water Sampled by Residents." Accessed November 22, 2018. http://flintwaterstudy.org/2015/12/complete-dataset-lead-results-in-tap-water-for-271-flint-samples/.

Fonger, Ron. 2014. "Flint River Water Complicating City's Efforts to Battle Contamination, Boil Advisories." *MLive*, September 19, 2014. http://www.mlive.com/news/flint/index.ssf/2014/09/dpw_director_ says_flint_river.html.

Fox, Maggie. 2016. "CDC Confirms Lead Levels Shot Up in Flint Kids after Water Switch." *NBC News*, June 24, 2016. http://www.nbcnews.com/storyline/flint-water-crisis/cdc-confirms-lead-levels-shot-flint-kids-after-water-switch-n598496.

Gostin, Lawrence. 2016. "Lead in the Water: A Tale of Social and Environmental Injustice." *Journal of American Medical Association (JAMA)* 19: 2053–2054. DOI:10.100/jama.2016.5581.

Gross, Terry. 2018. "Pediatrician Who Exposed Flint Water Crisis Shared Her 'Story of Resistance.'" *NPR*, June 25, 2018. https://www.npr.org/sections/health-shots/2018/06/25/623126968/pediatrician-who-exposed-flint-water-crisis-shares-her-story-of-resistance.

Gunningham, Neil, and Cameron Holley. 2013. *The New Environmental Governance*. New York: Routledge.

Hacker, Jacob, and Paul Pierson. 2016. "The Real Cause of the Flint Crisis." *The Atlantic's Politics & Policy Daily*, March 7, 2016. https://www.theatlantic.com/politics/archive/2016/03/the-real-cause-of-the-flint-crisis/472305/.

Hammer, Peter. 2017. "The Flint Water Crisis, The Karegnondi Water Authority and Strategic Structural Racism." *Critical Sociology* 45 (1): 103–119.

Hanna-Attisha, Mona. 2018. *What the Eyes Don't See: A Story of Crisis, Resistance, and Hope in an American City*. New York: One World.

Hanna-Attisha, Mona, Jenny LaChance, Richard Sadler, and Allison Schnepp. 2015. "Elevated Blood Lead Levels in Children Associated with the Flint Drinking Water Crisis: A Spatial Analysis of Risk and Public Health Response." *American Journal of Public Health* 106 (2): 283–290.

Hess, Charlotte, and Elinor Ostrom. 2007. *Understanding Knowledge as A Commons: From Theory to Practice*. Cambridge: MIT Press.

Highsmith, Andrew. 2015. *Demolition Means Progress: Flint, Michigan, and the Fate of American Metropolis*. Chicago. University of Chicago.

Hulett, Sarah. 2015. "High Lead Levels in Michigan Kids after City Switches Water Source." N*ational Public Radio*, September 29. Accessed September 27, 2018. http://www.npr.org/2015/09/ 29/444497051/high-lead-levels-in-michigan-kids-after-city-switches-water-source.

Hurlbert, Jeanne S., Valerie Haines, and John Beggs. 2000. "Core Networks and Tie Activation: What Kind of Routine Networks Allocate Resources in Nonroutine Situations?" *American Sociological Review* 65 (4): 598–618.

Hurlbert, Jeanne S., Beggs, John J., Haines, Valerie A. 2001. "Social Networks and Social Capital in Extreme Environments" in *Social Capital: Theory and Research* edited by Lin, N., Cook, K., Burt, R, 209–31. New York: Aldine de Gruyter.

Jimenez, Benedict S. 2017. "When Tied Bind: Public Managers Networking Behavior and Municipal Fiscal Health after the Great Recession." *Journal of Public Administration Research and Theory* 27 (3): 450–467.

Kennedy, Merrit. 2016. "Lead-Laced Water in Flint: A Step-By-Step Look at the Makings of a Crisis." *NPR*, April 20, 2016. https://www.npr.org/sections/thetwo-way/2016/04/20/465545378/lead-laced-water-in-flint-a-step-by-step-look-at-the-makings-of-a-crisis?t=1563379685974z.

Lewis, Chris. 2013. "Does Michigan's Emergency-Manager Law Disenfranchise Black Citizens?" *The Atlantic*, May 9, 2013. https://www.theatlantic.com/politics/archive/2013/05/does-michigans-emergency-manager-law-disenfranchise-black-citizens/275639/.

Lin, Nan. 2001. *Social Capital: A Theory of Social Structure and Action.* Cambridge: Cambridge University Press

Longley, Kristin. 2011. "Water Pipeline vs. Flint River: City of Flint Studying Its Drinking Water Options." *MLive*, January 2, 2011. http://www.mlive.com/news/flint/index.ssf/2011/01/water_pipeline_vs_flint_river.html.

Markowitz, Gerlad, and David Rosner. 2013. *Lead Wars: The Politics of Science and the Fate of American's Children.* Berkeley: University of California Press

Mattoon, Richard. 2014. "What Happens after Detroit's Bankruptcy? Lessons in Reform." *Essays on Issues: The Federal Reserve Bank of Chicago* 318a: 1–4.

May, Jake. 2018. "Flint's History of Emergency Management and How It Got to financial freedom." *MLive.* https://www.mlive.com/news/flint/index.ssf/2018/01/city_of_the_state_flints_histo.html.

McCloud, Brandi. 2012. "Solidarity Forever: The Story of the Flint Sit-Down Strike and the Communist Party from the Perspective of the Rank and File Autoworkers." PhD diss., East Tennessee State University.

Michigan Civil Rights Commission. 2017. "The Flint Water Crisis: Systemic Racism through the Lens of Flint." *MCRC*, February 27, 2017. https://www.michigan.gov/documents/mdcr/VFlintCrisisRep-F-Edited3-13-17_554317_7.pdf.

Murphy, Brenda. 2007. "Locating Social Capital in Resilient Community-Level Emergency Management." *Nat Hazards* 41: 297–315.

Nakawaga, Yuki, and Rajib Shaw. 2004. "Social Capital: A Missing Link to Disaster Recovery." *The International Journal of Mass Emergencies and Disasters* 22 (1): 5–34.

Newig, Jens, and Oliver Fritsch. 2009. "Environmental Governance: Participatory, Multi-Level – and Effective?" *Environmental Policy and Governance* 19 (3): 197–214.

Nickels, Ashley. 2016. "Approaches to Municipal Takeover: Home Rule Erosion and State Intervention in Michigan and New Jersey." *State and Local Government Review* 48 (3): 194–207.

Ostrom, Elinor. 1990. *Governing the Commons: The Evolution of Institutions for Collective Action.* New York: Cambridge University Press.

———. 1991. "Rational Choice Theory and Institutional Analysis: Toward Complementarity." *American Political Science Review* 85 (1): 237–243.

———. 1999. "Social Capital: A Fad or Fundamental Concept?" *Social Capital: A Multifaceted Perspective. World Bank*, 172–214.

———. 2005. *Understanding Institutional Diversity.* Princeton: Princeton University Press.

———. 2007. "A Diagnostic Approach for Going beyond Panaceas." *PNAS* 104 (39): 15181–15187.

Ostrom, Elinor, and Vincent Ostrom. 1977. "Public Goods and Public Choices." In *Alternatives for Delivering Public Services: Towards Improved Performance*, edited by E. Savas, 7–49. Boulder, CO: Westview Press.

Ostrom, Vincent. 1999. "Polycentricity." In *Polycentricity and Local Public Economies: Readings from the Workshop in Political Theory and Policy Analysis*, edited by Michael McGinnis, 52–74. Ann Arbor: University of Michigan Press.

Ostrom, Vincent, Charles M. Tiebout, and Robert Warren. 1961. "The Organization of Government in Metropolitan Areas: A Theoretical Inquiry." *American Political Science Review* 55: 831–842.

Pulido, Laura. 2016. "Flint, Environmental Racism, and Racial Capitalism." *Capitalism, Nature, and Socialism* 27 (3): 1–16.

Putnam, Robert. 2000. *Bowling Alone: The Collapse and Revival of American Community*. New York: Simon & Schuster.

Quarantelli, E.L. 1988. "Assessing Disaster Preparedness Planning: A Set of Criteria and their Applicability to Developing Countries." *Region Dev Dialog* 9: 48–69.

Roy, Siddhartha. 2015. "Complete Dataset: Lead Results from Tap Water Sampling in Flint, MI." Accessed 28 November 2018. http://flintwaterstudy.org/2015/12/complete-dataset-lead-results-in-tap-water-for-271-flint-samples/.

Samuels, Alana. 2015. "Aging Pipes Are Poisoning America's Tap Water." *The Atlantic*, July 19, 2015. https://www.theatlantic.com/business/archive/2015/07/dont-drink-the-water/399803/.

Scorsone, Eric, and Nicolette Bateson. 2011. "Long-Term Crisis and Systemic Failure: Taking the Fiscal Stress of America's Older Cities Seriously. Case Study: City of Flint, Michigan." *Michigan State University*. https://www.cityofflint.com/wp content/uploads/Reports/MSUE_FlintStudy2011.pdf.

Spitznagel, Eric. 2017. "Letter of Recommendation: Michigan." *New York Times*, April 20, 2017. https://www.nytimes.com/2017/04/20/magazine/letter-of-recommendation-michigan.html .

Stanley, Jason. 2016. "The Emergency Manager: Strategic Racism, Technocracy, and the Poisoning of Flint's Children." *The Good Society* 45 (1): 1–45.

Storr, Virgil Henry, and Stefanie Haeffele. 2012. "Post-Disaster Community Recovery in Heterogeneous, Loosely-Connected Communities." *Review of Social Economy* 70 (3): 295–314.

The Center for Michigan. 2016. "Michigan Truth Squad: Who Approved Switch to Flint River? State's Answers Draw Fouls." *Bridge Magazine*. https://www.mlive.com/politics/index.ssf/2016/01/michigan_truth_squad_who_appro.html.

Trounstine, Jessica. 2016. "How Racial Segregation and Political Mismanagement Led to Flint's Shocking Water Crisis." *The Washington Post*, February 8, 2016. https://www.washingtonpost.com/news/monkey-cage/wp/2016/02/08/heres-the-political-history-that-led-to-flints-shocking-water-crisis/?noredirect=on&utm_term=.173d4083e6ef.

U.S Environmental Protection Agency. 2018. "Office of Inspector General: Ensuring Clean and Safe Water Compliance with the Law." Accessed December 01, 2018. https://www.michigan.gov/documents/mdcr/VFlintCrisisRep-F-Edited3-13-17_554317_7.pdf.

Uzochukqu, Kelechi, and John Clayton. 2018. "Who Engages in Coproduction of Local Public Service and Why? The Case of Atlanta, Georgia." *Public Administration Review* 78: 514–526.

Vogler, Jan P. 2019. "The Entanglement of Public Bureaucratic Institutions: Their Interactions with Society, Culture, Politics, and the Economy." In *Interdisciplinary Studies of the Political Order: New Applications of Public Choice Theory*, edited by Donald J. Boudreaux, Christopher J. Coyne, and Bobbi Herzberg, 99–129. New York: Rowman & Littlefield International.

Wisley, John. 2016. "Flint Residents Paid America's Highest Water Rates." *The Detroit Free Press*, February 8, 2016. DTD. https://www.washingtonpost.com/news/monkey-cage/wp/2016/02/08/heres-the-political-history-that-led-to-flints-shocking-water-crisis/?noredirect=on&utm_term=.173d4083e6ef.

Woolcock, Geoffrey. 2002. "Social Capital and Community Development: Fad, Friend or Foe?" Presented at Queensland Local Government Community Services Association Annual Conference, Rockhampton, Australia.

Chapter 11

The Expressive Commons

Freedom of Expression as a Collective Action Problem

Alexander Schaefer

But the peculiar evil of silencing the expression of an opinion is, that it is robbing the human race.

—John Stuart Mill, *On Liberty*

Despite enjoying praise from nearly all corners, freedom of expression faces a battery of challenges. Populist regimes around the world undermine media freedom while universities grow ever-more hostile to ideas with the potential to offend the political sensibilities of their students and faculty. How do we explain these crisscrossed attitudes toward freedom of expression? How do we reconcile an avowed support for freedom to express oneself with a demonstrated effort to suppress disagreeable expressions? This paradox largely dissolves, I argue, once one identifies the operant incentives.

The conflict over freedom of expression involves, primarily, two goods: (1) expressive freedom and (2) the congeniality of one's expressive environment, or, for short, *expressive agreeableness*. These two goods must be traded off against one another: a society with a high degree of expressive freedom will exhibit lower degrees of expressive agreeableness, at least for some groups in society. Or equivalently, improving the expressive agreeableness for one or more groups entails a society-wide diminution of expressive freedom. Though involved in a rather simple trade-off relationship when viewed aggregately, for the individual embedded in a choice scenario, these two goods exhibit a crucial distinction. The good of expressive freedom produces benefits indiscriminately for the entire "human race," as Mill puts it. Expressive agreeableness, on the other hand, concentrates its benefits on the particular individual or group that manages to restrict free expression according to its standards. For such a group, the banned or "appropriated" expressions represent no loss, while the increase in expressive agreeableness that results is obvious. For example, if Rabbinic Jews wished to remove the word "God" from everyday use, this would come at no cost to them. The cost would fall entirely on other users of that term: Christian gospel singers or perhaps foul-mouthed atheists.

Employing an Ostromian perspective, the objective of this chapter is to analyze the incentives that structure our choices with respect to the trade-off between expressive freedom and expressive agreeableness. The first section considers two paradigmatic collective action problems—the production of a common pool resource (CPR) and of a public good—concluding that a public goods model better illuminates the qualitative features of the problem of expressive freedom. The elaboration of this model occurs in the second section, which offers a detailed explanation of how expressive freedom resembles a public good, what predictions this yields, and lays out a simple numerical example. The remainder of the chapter is devoted to exploring the normative implications of this analysis. Following Elinor Ostrom, in the third section I consider and reject both state and market solutions, ultimately advocating a more promising third alternative, namely informal enforcement of social norms. The final section considers the analysis from a purely moral perspective, arguing that our fairness-related social norms apply quite directly to the problem of expressive intolerance. The moralistic framing of this section suggests that existing fairness norms may provide a valuable safeguard for expressive freedom once individuals correctly conceptualize the issue of expressive freedom.

PUBLIC GOOD OR COMMON POOL RESOURCE?

To capture the features of the trade-off between expressive freedom and expressive agreeableness, two models present themselves: (a) a CPR model and (b) a public goods model. CPRs are defined as goods that exhibit rivalry of consumption and nonexcludability (or costly excludability) (Ostrom 2015, 32). Standard examples include a shared fishing area or Garrett Hardin's cattle-nourishing commons (Hardin 1968). Public goods, on the other hand, exhibit nonrivalry of consumption, despite sharing the feature of nonexcludability with CPRs. Standard examples include lighthouses, weather forecasts, and national defense.[1] Thus, although CPRs and public goods both possess the characteristic of nonexcludability (or costly excludability), only CPRs are rivalrous—there are a finite number of resource units in a CPR system, and using one of those resource units precludes its use by others. By contrast, all can enjoy the use of a public good without diminishing the ability of others to likewise enjoy it.

The good of expressive freedom exhibits features of both CPRs and public goods. On the one hand, there are a finite number of expressions, and subtracting one from the common pool of acceptable expressions poses little to no harm to the appropriator. That is, since only the most odious expressions will be removed, the appropriator stands to gain little to nothing from leaving that expression in the pool. This makes the incentives similar to a CPR, but unlike a public good, in which contributing to the resource provides benefits for all individuals, including the contributor. On the other hand, there exists an intrinsic value in the resource system. People value the existence of a large stock of expressions, that is, expressive freedom is valuable in and of itself. In contrast to the appropriation of particular expressions, the value of the common stock of expressions is nonrivalrous. All can enjoy the right to express themselves without diminishing the rights of others to do the same. The more expressions it contains, the more freedom of expression individuals enjoy. This makes the incentive structure similar to a public good, where producing the good benefits all. This is unlike a CPR, however, where only the extracted "resource units" enter into individuals' utility functions.

The question is: What sort of model will provide the most insight into the problem? Is it worse to ignore the public benefits of a large stock of permitted expressions or to suppose that restricting expressive freedom hurts, to some degree, even the appropriators? For my purposes, the latter assumption, though unrealistic, is not just benign—it actually strengthens my argument. Assuming that the appropriating faction values all freely available expressions, and thus bears a cost when it appropriates them, exaggerates the extent to which parties are willing to tolerate expressive *dis*agreeableness. The thrust of my analysis is that expressive freedom will be overrestricted. If this result holds even in a model that exaggerates the incentive to facilitate expressive freedom, then my result will hold a fortiori in real-life situations, where this incentive is not exaggerated. Accordingly, I adopt the public goods model, including the (often unrealistic) assumption that removing expressions from the common pool imposes some cost on the appropriator. This unrealistic assumption frames the argument charitably for those who might disagree.[2] There is no harm (and some rhetorical benefit) in adopting this model, rather than some modified CPR model.

In brief, the model considers language and expression (both verbal and nonverbal) as a public good in which the number of available or permitted expressions measures the level of its provision. Individuals choose between varying levels of two values: (1) expressive agreeableness and (2) expressive freedom. Individuals pursue the value of (1) by appropriating (banning) distasteful expressions. The value of (1) therefore comes at some cost of undermining the value of (2). This cost is smaller for the individual than for society, since this cost extends to all other individuals in the collective. If all individuals ban expressions, therefore, the result is a severe restriction of the pool of acceptable expressions, that is, a great expense in terms of (2).

Conceptualizing freedom of expression in this manner has several benefits. First, it opens up a wide collection of analogies that lay bare the logic of the problem. This logic illuminates why expressive repression has been so common throughout history and why expressive freedom seems under constant threat even in today's political environment, where most proclaim it as a great political value. Secondly, this conceptualization suggests a host of solutions that might be effective in protecting freedom of expression. In particular, markets, states, and informal institutions have all been proposed as ways to resolve such problems.

Most importantly, construing the issue this way generates a perspective in which attempts to limit freedom of expression are tantamount to uncooperative advantage-seeking. "Appropriating" behavior thus becomes subject to charges of unfairness, allowing social norms to perform their work in curtailing such behavior by generating attitudes of disapprobation. The conceptualization of the problem proposed by this chapter may, therefore, function as an important aspect of the solution to the very problem it analyzes (see the third and fourth sections).

FREEDOM OF EXPRESSION AS A PUBLIC GOOD

In order to expose the logic that undergirds the restriction of free expression, the model developed here analyzes freedom of expression as a public good that corresponds to the number of expressions in the "common pool," that is, the stock of expressions that can be made without the threat of formal or informal punishment. In a standard public goods model, an individual i must expend money, or some other "numeraire" good, y_i, indexing i's consumption of private goods, in order to secure additional quantities of the public good, x. Here, y_i represents the private good in our choice scenario: the agreeableness of one's expressive environment. One can maintain or increase the extent of expressive freedom, x, only by forgoing improvements in one's expressive environment y_i. Therefore, more y_i means less x and vice versa.

Normal consumption goods are modeled without externalities: if I enjoy some ice cream, this has no effect on the welfare, preference satisfaction, or utility of any other consumer. In this case, all consumers will consume ice cream up to the point where the marginal cost of doing so, in terms of other goods which are forgone, is equal to the marginal benefit. That is, an agent will continue to buy ice cream until she believes that more ice cream is no longer worth the cost, measured in terms of other possible uses of her money. By acting in this manner, individuals achieve a socially optimal allocation of resources: each has maximized his or her utility, subject to a budget constraint, by making choices that have no effect on the utility functions of other individuals. Thus, by aligning private marginal cost with private marginal benefit, individuals have also achieved an alignment between aggregate or social marginal cost and benefit.

In the case of public goods, similar reasoning applies with one crucial modification: when you demand a public good x, this benefits other consumers as well, even though the cost in terms of forgone y_i falls entirely on you as the decision-maker (this is why good x is not indexed with an i). When individuals align marginal cost with marginal benefit therefore, they fail to align *social* marginal benefit with marginal cost. The marginal cost is accurately appraised and taken account of by the decision-maker, since he or she alone feels its sting. The marginal benefit, on the other hand, is underappraised, since the benefits are diffused among all individuals, and the decision-maker therefore enjoys only a fraction of the total benefits provided by increased levels of x. When marginal benefit is underappraised, the quantity of x that sets the individual's marginal benefit equal to marginal cost will come at an inefficiently low level of x. Put simply, if somewhat inaccurately, the individual decision-maker is unwilling to bear costs in order to provide benefits for others. Therefore, if costs are marginally increasing or benefits are marginally decreasing, or both, the decision-maker will not take on all the costs that are "worth it," that is, will not forgo all fully compensated decreases in y_i, when all individuals are taken account of.

The inefficient alignment of marginal cost and marginal benefit may sound abstract and removed from daily life, but in fact individuals face this problem in almost every social setting. In my experience, when roommates share a living space, while also each having their own room, the cleanliness of the shared space often deteriorates to an alarmingly low level, even while the private rooms exhibit no such downward spiral of filth. The explanation of this phenomenon, perhaps, lies in the public goods nature of clean living space: if I clean, then my roommates enjoy the cleaning as much as I do. However, I enjoy 100 percent of the benefit derived from crunching Cheetos into the carpeting. If all roommates reason in this way, the result is predictable and widely observable in college living situations. The issue of littering, though often corrected in various ways (see the third section), presents another clear example of this unfortunate incentive structure. Emptying the contents of my vehicle onto the street offers me a convenient way of tidying my immediate surroundings. Waiting until I am near a designated disposal area is less convenient and, therefore, imposes a cost on me. I alone bear this cost. By doing so, I contribute to maintaining a clean, aesthetically pleasant environment. This benefit, however, is diffused. Some napkins or a plastic bottle on the side of the street might bother me slightly, but will it bother me more than driving around with that same garbage next to me in my car for an additional hour or two? Doubtful. However, if we could somehow add up the total "bother" that my litter imposes on all passerby, then the total litter-caused "bother" might greatly outweigh my personal, garbage-in-car-caused "bother." My utility function, though, presents littering as less bothersome than careful disposal. When this phenomenon scales up, we get Bourbon Street.

In the model of expressive freedom, an individual may choose to remove certain expressions from the stock of acceptable expressions, by threatening either formal punishment or informal social intimidation. I assume that individuals can do so only at the expense of reducing the quantity of the public good of expressive freedom. This reduction of expressive freedom, however, affects all individuals—only a fraction of the cost of expression banning is borne by the decision-maker. Or equivalently, the decision-maker enjoys only a fraction of the total benefit of expressive freedom produced by reducing private good y_i, expressive agreeableness. Toleration is like waiting to throw your garbage away: if we all do this, the total benefits will normally outweigh the total costs. Yet, doing it alone looks irrational. If all others are refraining, then I can enjoy a very clean environment even if I throw my personal garbage out the window. If others aren't refraining, then I'd be a sucker if I kept my garbage in the car, experiencing both a littered environment and a garbage-ridden automobile. Similarly, if others are tolerant, and expressive freedom is high, why not go ahead and ban the expressions that I find detestable? If others are intolerant, I appear to have even less reason to sit by and tolerate their offensive expressions.

A specific numerical example will justify and precisify these intuitions. The example will clarify the choice logic and highlight the tendency to overrestrict freedom of expression, providing an instance where the above reasoning applies as a mathematical certitude. Consider a society of four individuals—Akerlof (A), Buchanan (B), Coase (C), and Deaton (D)—$N=\{A, B, C, D\}$. Each individual i in N values expressive freedom, x, but also values expressive agreeableness, y_i. And although everyone values freedom of expression, all four people in this community value it to different degrees. In fact, their valuations increase in ascending order: Akerlof values freedom of expression the least, all the way up to Deaton, who values it the most. This ordering expresses itself through their utility functions (see figure 11.1).

These utility functions yield the following marginal rates of substitution (see figure 11.2).

The marginal rate of substitution measures how many units of y an individual would need in order to willingly forgo one unit of x. So, for example, when 5 units of x are already being produced, Akerlof is willing to purchase another unit as long as he can do so for less than $(19 - 5) = 14$ units of y.

$$u^A(x, y_A) = y_A - \frac{1}{2}(19 - x)^2$$

$$u^B(x, y_B) = y_B - \frac{1}{2}(22 - x)^2$$

$$u^C(x, y_C) = y_C - \frac{1}{2}(25 - x)^2$$

$$u^D(x, y_D) = y_D - \frac{1}{2}(30 - x)^2$$

Figure 11.1 Utility Functions.

$$MRS^A = 19 - x$$

$$MRS^B = 22 - x$$

$$MRS^C = 25 - x$$

$$MRS^D = 30 - x$$

Figure 11.2 Marginal Rates of Substitution.

As x increases, each individual becomes less willing to purchase more. This is because x has diminishing marginal utility. When the environment is already extremely free, then more expressive freedom is less valuable.

Now suppose the exogenously given price of acquiring an additional unit of free expression is $p = 40$—that is, by giving up 40 units of y_i, an individual can acquire an additional unit of free expression, x, shared by the entire community.[3] Using these marginal rates of substitution, we can easily calculate the Pareto-efficient level by determining the level of x at which the sum of each individual's marginal value of x in terms of y_i is exactly equal to the price of acquiring an additional unit of x in terms of y_i[4] (see figure 11.3).

Nevertheless, at a price of 40, we have $MRS^i < p$, for all i in N. Consequently, the amount of x that will actually be provided in this community is exactly 0. The public good nature of free expression has thus reduced a community of freedom-loving individuals to a situation of total censorship.

$$\sum_{i=A}^{B} MRS^i = MC$$

$$96 - 4x = 40$$

$$x = 14$$

Figure 11.3 Optimality Conditions.

NORMATIVE IMPLICATIONS

Identifying freedom of expression as a collective action problem calls forth an arsenal of solutions. As a species, Homo sapiens excel at resolving collective action problems through formal and informal institutions. Elaborate legal systems counteract the benefits of aggression; orderly lines form at the grocery store. In the case of public goods, as well as CPRs, the classic institutional response goes one of two ways. Garrett Hardin exemplifies the view that to resolve commons tragedies we must implement either a system of "socialism" or a "private enterprise system" (Hardin 1978, 1247). That is, states or markets must rise to the challenge of internalizing the costs and benefits of resource use. On the level of individual conduct, human beings employ informal norms, enforced through social disapprobation and internalization (Hume 1978, 499). These norms often arise to resolve collective action problems that exhibit a "prisoner's dilemma"–incentive structure. This section explores the normative implications of conceptualizing freedom of expression as a collective action problem. While perhaps promising among a populace committed to norms of tolerance, formal institutions do not appear capable of supporting freedom of expression without support from informal norms. Today's political landscape, I will argue, is particularly inimical to freedom of expression. The reconceptualization offered here may provide part of the solution: moving beyond mere theoretical classification, the reconceived structure of the problem invites the application of fairness norms to uproot the motivation to restrict free expression.

FORMAL INSTITUTIONS: MARKETS AND STATES

Leviathan

From the very inception of modern economics, government action has provided a solution to the problem of public goods. Thus, Adam Smith writes that a key function of government is

> erecting and maintaining certain publick [sic] works and certain publick [sic] institutions, which it can never be for the interest of any individual or small number of individuals, to erect and maintain; because the profit would never repay the expense to any individual or small number of individuals, though it may frequently do much more than repay it to a great society. (Smith 1976, Bk. 4 Ch. 9)

On this view, the government can address the issue of public goods provision by coercing individuals into contributing. As a consequence, all are better off than if left to choose their own contribution levels, in which case free riding would have been the dominant strategy.[5]

In the context of free expression, this approach would involve the government requiring citizens to pay the price of tolerance in exchange for a well-protected right, or set of rights, to free expression. In particular, constitutional law might proscribe a wide range of contexts in which one could express a wide range of sentiments with impunity. Attempts to suppress language or symbolic actions that one dislikes are met with sanctions, which undermine any attempt to benefit from intolerant free riding.[6] This Smithian solution, though prima facie plausible, faces serious limitations, especially in the particular case of expressive freedom.

One issue plaguing all attempts to efficiently provide governmental goods and services concerns the lack of information-conveying prices to reveal the preferences of individuals. Recent discussions of public goods provision have responded to Paul Samuelson's program, which, having proven the existence of an optimal provision of public goods, concedes that "the problem is how to 'find' it" (Samuelson 1954, 389). Samuelson is clear that the failure of decentralized prices does not entail the success of governmental conjecture. Simply asking consumers, Samuelson points out, is futile: "it is in the selfish interest of each person to give *false* signals, to pretend to have less interest in a given collective consumption activity than he really has" (388–399). Accordingly, economists have sought mechanisms to elicit the preferences of consumers with respect to public goods. Although such attempts have produced theoretically interesting conclusions (Vickrey 1961; Clarke 1971; Groves 1973), practical solutions have not materialized.[7]

Apart from *determining* the optimal quantity of freedom of expression, there is the daunting issue of *implementing* this ideal policy. Political decisions do not issue forth from an economist king who aims to satisfy first-order optimality conditions. Rather, in most relevant contexts, the basis of public policy is a complex of political institutions, usually grounded in democratic decision. Consequently, many economists and political scientists have turned to the study of likely voting equilibria, rather than mechanisms for eliciting the true preferences of consumers—for, even with these preferences in hand, the political process may still fail to provide adequate rights protection. Analyses of voting equilibria have tended to provide fodder for pessimism. The conditions required for such an equilibrium to exist tend to be unattractive in the context of public goods.[8]

Of course, no system should be held to the standard of optimal efficiency and rejected once we realize that it will not meet this standard (Boettke 1997). Yet, with respect to freedom of expression, the issue goes beyond the tendency of government policy to miss the efficient provision point. The alarming rise of intolerant political factions suggests not just suboptimality, but the utter inadequacy of a political solution to the issue of securing expressive freedom. Although media freedom often proves instrumental in their rise to power, populist leaders around the world have not returned the favor, instead working to undermine such freedom. In Venezuela, Hugo Chavez nationalized or refused licenses to opposing news stations; Maduro followed soon after by neutralizing opposition newspapers. In India, Prime Minister Narendra Modi, leader of the populist Bharatiya Janata Party, has made use of outdated sedition laws to silence political opponents (Bellur 2016). In Turkey, under Erdogan, hundreds of media outlets have been closed and journalists arrested en masse. Nor do things look particularly good in the United States, where an overt enmity between the current administration and major media outlets raises deep worries about President Trump's ability to curtail media freedom, for example, by "loosening libel laws" as he vowed to do in 2016 (Jacobs 2016) or by revoking media licenses in response to "fake news" as he suggested in 2018 (Mindock 2018).[9] Trump's overt hostility toward the press continues into 2019, a year in which he has referred to American media sources as an "enemy of the people" (Grynbaum 2019). These anecdotes constitute part of a measurable trend. In 2015, a study on populism and liberal democracy concluded that two terms of populist leadership led to, on average, a decline in media freedom of 13 percent (Allred 2015). Another study has recently reached similar conclusions (Ruth-Lovell, Doyle, and Hawkins 2019).

Though the recent surge in populist politics should concern us, the attitudes of populism's opponents provide yet further grounds for pessimism regarding democratic ability to protect freedom of expression. University communities and elite educated classes are among the staunchest opponents of populist politics. Yet, despite praising free expression in the abstract, their behavior and policy stances exhibit open hostility toward free expression.[10] On university campuses, student and faculty protesters frequently aim to deter speakers with diverse ideologies from appearing and presenting their views. The list of speakers recently prevented from appearing due to pressure from protesters includes Larry Summers, Hillary Clinton, Tony Kushner, Charles Murray, George W. and Laura Bush, and Christine Lagarde.[11] A recent survey, drawn from 2,300 participants, reveals that the majority of Americans support laws that punish hate speech.[12] Another study from 2018, focusing on American students, concludes that while "students strongly support protection of their rights and liberties—and of freedom of speech, in particular—when asked questions about them in general terms," the same does not hold when the implications of free speech are made explicit: "when students are asked more specific questions about the limits of free speech or the content of speech, their support for the protection of speech declines. This occurs most notably when students are asked questions about expression that is offensive or intolerant. We believe this is why more than half of students (57 percent) think colleges and universities should be able to restrict student expression of political views that are hurtful or offensive to certain students" (Naughton 2019). According to Public Policy Polling, those on the far left overwhelmingly believe that punching Nazis is "acceptable," with 78 percent of Jill Stein voters feeling this way, and 49 percent of the general population feeling this way.[13] This attitude is perfectly logical given the intellectual influence that persists among many on the far left. In academic publications as well as popular op-eds, many academics equate unpleasant speech to physical violence. As Professor Stanley Fish once put it, "The speech that is being assaulted is itself assaultive speech."[14] Or more recently, Columbia law professor, Kayum Ahmed, claimed that allowing a right-wing speaker to present his views on campus "constitutes an act of violence" (Sauve 2017). From this point of view, acts of violence against speakers expressing unpopular or hurtful ideas constitute, not unwarranted assault, but justified self-defense.

The groups most staunchly opposed to the populism therefore exhibit (a) lack of commitment to freedom of expression, as well as (b) widespread (though not universal) acceptance of coercion as a means of improving expressive congeniality. Together, (a) and (b) suggest that the principle of restriction faces little to no threat from populism's opponents. All parties appear to be pursuing restrictive policies. The debate circles around the specific content of the pool of permissible expressions, rather than whether there should be any restriction in the first place. Given that governmental decisions originate from democratic elections, this lack of strong support for freedom of expression and the apparent devolution of politics into a zero-sum game where the winner determines what counts as valuable speech and what counts as "violence" or "fake news," provide strong reason for thinking that governmental provision of expressive freedom will be inadequate. That is, it will fall disastrously below the optimal level.

Behemoth

If governmental provision of freedom of expression will falter, economic instinct may suggest private provision as a superior alternative.[15] Many economists have suggested privatization and enclosure as the most effective way to solve the collective action problems that arise from CPRs or public goods (e.g., Demsetz 1967; Johnson 1972; Smith 1981; Ostrom 2003, 2014). Of course, if freedom of expression is a pure public good, then its nonexcludable nature renders private provision unprofitable and hence infeasible. However, as Elinor Ostrom notes, excludability is a matter of degree, and few (if any) goods exhibit pure nonexcludability (Ostrom 2003, 2014). Rather, the issue is typically one of cost; though not impossible, excluding free riders is relatively expensive. As Robert Staaf explains, "All so called public goods could be transformed into private goods if relative costs were ignored" (Staaf 1983). Staaf's claim is actually more encompassing, since it applies not just to private goods, but also to goods that are excludable, though nonrivalrous, such as a musical performance or a swimming pool.[16] As Ostrom notes, saying that goods like a swimming pool are "non-rivalrous" is at best imprecise. She offers a more accurate, though less catchy, description of such goods as exhibiting "low subtractability of use" (Ostrom 2014, 172). If freedom of expression could be "enclosed," then it would exhibit the features of this latter type of good, sometimes referred to as "club goods" (Buchanan 1965), since one person's enjoyment of freedom of expression would not subtract from another's enjoyment of that freedom.[17]

The theory behind the efficiency of private provision is straightforward: privatization internalizes externalities.[18] To be concrete, suppose we have a park (a traditional, if wrongheaded, example of a public good). Any time or money spent maintaining the park by one individual benefits every other individual who might use the park. This is a positive externality. If the park is open and accessible to anyone who wishes to use it, then individuals have no incentive to contribute time or money to maintain it. They will bear the full cost of such contributions while only enjoying a small fraction, *1/n*, of its benefit. The park, under this institutional structure, will likely revert to a trash-laden dirt patch. Imagine, however, an entrepreneur bought the park and built a fence. Now, since the park manager can charge an entry fee, all benefit to park users translates into additional revenue for the entrepreneur. If putting in ten hours of maintenance generates a net benefit to the population of prospective park users, then the entrepreneur will profit by doing so. In effect, every action that generates a social benefit greater than the cost of the action becomes private economic profit and will thus be rationally undertaken—this is the effect of internalizing the positive externality of park maintenance.

Does it strain credulity to imagine such a scheme applying to a good as abstract as freedom of expression? It shouldn't. Private associations, such as businesses, schools, and churches, often empower or restrict free expression according to the preferences of their members or the goals of their institution. Although, as discussed above, many universities appear to be trending toward restriction of speech, the classic ideal of a university casts it as a pure example of benefit internalization. In ideal type, universities guarantee freedom of expression in order to draw in students who, seeking an enlarged worldview, see benefits in a diverse, even if uncomfortable, expressive environment. In addition, professors desire to work for such establishments in virtue of the protected platform that the university offers. In this idealization, university administrators resemble the park entrepreneur: by making all entrants accept the cost of toleration, universities can provide the good of expressive freedom. In fact, some believe that this idealized conception actually approaches reality, and that such institutions might rebuff the challenge posed by anti-free-expression activists. One could cite, for example, the fact that enrollment at universities exhibiting restrictionist trends plummeted in 2017, or that Gallup polls indicate that the perceived value of education has collapsed among conservative voters who do not share the political or philosophical views of university activists. Universities, then, may respond to profit incentives as the market model predicts, and push back against restrictionists in favor of a more optimal level of free expression.

The idealized university, however, differs from reality in too many ways to present a convincing case for private provision of expressive freedom. Most notably, university administrators are not profit-seeking entrepreneurs and face a very different incentive structure. Furthermore, faculty and students are able to select universities on an ideological basis, enabling them to enjoy environments cleansed of expressions they find odious without needing to capitulate by relinquishing expressions they see as nonodious. But still, the private provision of expressive freedom occurs in less ideal forms. For example, short of harassing other customers, one can rant about politics, utter profane terms or expressions, make inappropriate jokes, and so on in most private establishments. Not in churches, of course, but certainly at Walmart. Such expressions see only mild restrictions. For example, shouting the N-word will likely get one escorted out of Walmart by a security guard. Yet taking coercive action to stop another from using the N-word is also likely to get one kicked out. This permissive stance results partly from the costs of enforcing speech codes, but private establishments may also have some sense that customers value the freedom to express themselves. An average individual deciding between two identical stores would, after all, feel more comfortable at the one that doesn't have a list of restricted expressions posted on the door.[19]

The most basic objection to the enclosure of the commons or to the privatization of public goods concerns the cost of exclusion (Demsetz 1967; Ostrom 2015). The problems we've been considering only arise in virtue of high exclusion costs. Of course, *pace* the caricature of Chicago school of economics, there often exist inefficiencies to be corrected. Governments sometimes treat perfectly privatizable goods as though they were public.[20] The question is whether freedom of expression can feasibly exclude prospective free riders.

Both empirically and theoretically, the answer appears to be "no." As noted above, we now observe a mass of overtly intolerant groups falling all along the political spectrum. Moreover, these groups are vociferous: they take full advantage of freedom of expression, even while their aim is to break down and restrict such freedom. A free rider, recall, is one who enjoys a public good without covering any of its costs. If the cost of freedom of expression is tolerance, then from neo-Nazis to social justice warriors to *New York Times* op-eds, free riders appear abundant. Empirically, then, institutions that might monetize the benefits of free expression, thus internalizing the externalities, have not done so.

The explanation of this fact, lies partly in the logic of freedom. The theoretical reason why exclusion is difficult in the case of expressive freedom is because freedom of expression, in its full purity, requires that *all* expressions receive the same protections.[21] By logical entailment, this includes intolerant expressions. In other words, the very provision of freedom of expression, unless qualified in some way, requires the admission of free riders into the ambit of its provision.[22]

The associations tasked with providing freedom of expression may, of course, simply qualify their stance on freedom: permit and protect all ideas except for intolerant ones. Though superficially plausible, such an approach faces insurmountable hurdles. First, the classification of groups into the categories of acceptable and unacceptable, even if purportedly based on the tolerance of their worldviews, is ripe for political opportunism. Conservatives will scramble to brand proponents of gay marriage as intolerant toward their religious moral convictions; liberals will accuse reasonable pro-lifers of exhibiting aggressive misogyny. Who is permitted to speak will likely depend more on the politics internal to the association than on any bona fide intolerance.[23] Second, note that many of the most important areas in which free expression occurs are public, not private, zones: streets, sidewalks, outside of government buildings, public universities, and so on. Society will inevitably face a decision as to how to manage the rules that govern activity in such spaces. These rules, as pointed out above, are ultimately at the whim of democratic decisions, making the private solution to providing expressive freedom largely inapplicable to many of its most prominent arenas.

Worsening the issue, the influence of politics penetrates deeper into human affairs than merely the governance of spaces deemed "public." If private associations are to offer the benefits of extensive freedom of expression, while denying entry to intolerant free riders, they will require a legal framework that permits them to do so. Such a framework, many have noted, is itself a public good. In this way, it is impossible to sever the private provision of freedom of expression from its public provision. All of the issues identified with respect to governmental provision thus plague private institutions that would offer an extensive package of free expression. If major political factions—populists, conservatives, radical leftists, and so on—desire the curtailment of speech, this will inevitably affect the type of speech that must be prohibited or permitted within associations such as universities or churches. For example, if the radical left were to achieve a winning coalition, would universities be free to filter out intolerant leftist activism? Would the controversial ideas of intellectuals like Charles Murray be permitted to pass through the filters? Even if we could somehow constrain government to follow a policy of restricting only intolerant expressions, the ambiguities of language render the meaning of "intolerant" subject to various interpretations. This combines with the vagaries of human motivation to create a choice scenario ripe for corruption by those in charge of determining which views to accept and which to exclude.[24] Ultimately, then, the private provision of expressive freedom appears woefully dependent on political vicissitudes.

Thankfully, many constitutional governments are relatively robust to the whims of winning coalitions. President Trump cannot shut down CNN at will or decide who gets to protest on university campuses. Yet, the past few decades have demonstrated that constitutions can collapse in the face of majority opposition. When publicly opposed, constitutions are reduced to paper and ink. As jurist Learned Hand once put it, "Liberty lies in the hearts of men and women; when it dies there, no constitution, no law, no court can save it" (Hand 1944). The weak support of freedom of expression among society at large, not to mention the fierce onslaught it receives from prominent political factions, suggest that freedom of expression—whether protected governmentally or by private associations—lacks the political basis of support that it requires. A constitutional amendment is no protection from a mass acutely aware of the benefits of restricting disagreeable expression and apparently unaware of, or unwilling to work collectively to achieve, the benefits of expressive freedom.

Informal Institutions

As collective action problems are set up, game-theoretical reasoning logically entails an unhappy outcome. As Hardin puts it in discussing the tragedy of the commons, "Every way in which I can 'win' involves, in some sense, an abandonment of the game, as we intuitively understand it" (Hardin 1968, 1243). The creation of governmental punishment structures or of market reward structures are both attempts to abandon the game in favor of one that's more fun to play. However, we've seen that the games generated by these modifications are fundamentally unaltered and that the incentive to defect (to behave intolerantly) remains in force. Markets and states alone will not come to the rescue.

To capture the essence of the game, consider a simple prisoner's dilemma. Letting T stand for "tolerate," letting B stand for "ban," and letting the numbers in each cell represent some weighted average of freedom of expression, x, and environmental congeniality, y, we generate a game form (figure 11.4a).

(a)

1 \ 2	T	B
T	2, 2	0, 3
B	3, 0	1, 1

(b)

1 \ 2	T	B
T	2, 2	4, 1
B	1, 4	3, 3

Figure 11.4 (a) Free Expression Game Form. (b) Free Expression Game.

If individuals' utility functions are increasing in both goods, then the numbers in each cell, representing an objective quantity, will also be an accurate measure of utility if goods *x* and *y* are properly weighted.[25] However, experimental game theorists often fail to adequately distinguish objective consequences ("payoffs" in terms of some numeraire good) and subjective utility. For our purposes, this distinction will be critical. We must therefore construct a separate matrix to represent subjective preference rankings, yielding the following normal-form game in figure 11.4b.

The numbers in this matrix do not represent some objective measure of good *x* and *y*, but rather, the order in which each player ranks the outcome specified by each cell of the matrix. So, for example, player 1 most prefers the outcome $(s_1, s_2) = (B,T)$—that is, player 1 most prefers to free ride by banning while player 2 tolerates. Her second most preferred outcome is where both players tolerate, and so on. The preference ordering in this matrix corresponds to the objective payoff specified in figure 11.4a. The best option for both players is to free ride, to ban while enjoying the toleration of others. The worst option is to tolerate others who refuse to tolerate you, that is, who ban expressions even though you have refrained from doing so. In this game, the so-called Prisoner's Dilemma, banning is a strictly dominant strategy: whatever the other player chooses, my payoff and my utility are greater when I ban. The only Nash Equilibrium in such a game is mutual banning of expressions. The unhappy logic of this problem is that all players end up with their third choice even while cooperating would enable them to obtain their second best choice. "Winning" this game, as Hardin points out, implies abandoning it. But how?

We have already examined two standard solutions: states and markets. We noted that they don't appear to offer a satisfactory solution. State intervention is premised on democratic decision-making, and the provision of good governance itself is a public good. It might even be modeled as a prisoner's dilemma: let players 1 and 2 be voting factions. With sufficient volatility in the makeup of factions, we cannot rely on repeated interactions to provide a cooperative solution. Consequently, factions have an incentive to ban rather than tolerate. Nor do markets provide a promising cure: free-speech zones would be patchy, at best, and the heavy influence of politics on public affairs renders private provision heavily dependent on responsible governmental policy—something we have found unlikely with respect to expressive freedom. In essence, potential providers of free-expression zones require a cooperative solution to the same prisoner's dilemma game. Political decisions need to establish their right to discretion regarding the permissible views, which is unlikely when "free riding" allows a faction to curtail this right.

In her work on social norms, Elinor Ostrom has suggested an alternative to market or state solutions. Her starting point is the observation that "a substantial gap exists between the theoretical prediction that self-interested individuals will have extreme difficulty in coordinating collective action and the reality that such cooperative behavior is widespread, although far from inevitable" (Ostrom 2000, 138). In particular, individuals tend to contribute in public goods games, especially when able to communicate during play. This, of course, contradicts the prediction of the game in figure 11.4b, suggesting that something has been left out when translating between game form and full-fledged game. Ostrom suggests that norms provide the missing element. These "shared understandings about actions that are obligatory, permitted, or forbidden" transform individuals' utility functions, since failing to follow a norm prompts negative feelings of guilt and shame (Ostrom 2000, 143; Ostrom and Crawford 1995, 583). Thus, maintaining the game form of figure 11.4a, proper social norms allow us to avoid playing the game of figure 11.4b. But how can society create or leverage social norms to achieve a better outcome? In particular, how can individuals protect freedom of expression without relying on states or markets, but, instead, on social norms?

Since social norms rarely emerge through top-down imposition, the key is to leverage already-existing norms. Rather than attempting to generate new norms, we can change how we conceptualize different scenarios. For example, suppose *n* is a rule of etiquette that applies to circumstance *C* in virtue of some *application rule*, which I consider to be internal to a given norm itself, and the features of *C*. Perhaps *n* is the rule of sending a thank-you letter after receiving a gift. Let *n'* be a different norm, for example the social norm against initiating aggression, which applies in circumstances *C* and *C'* in virtue of its own application rule and the features of *C* and *C'*. Now, *C* may represent a situation of interacting with a coworker, while *C'* may be one's relationship to one's sister. Norms of etiquette apply within one's relationship with one's coworker and one's professional acquaintance, but not within one's relationship with one's sister. So *n* links to *C* but not to *C'*.

To take another example, suppose that *n** is a norm that governs relationships between members of the Jewish community. The norm *n** might say that taking legal action against a fellow Jew is inappropriate.[26] Suppose further that one Jewish employee comes to learn that a coworker is Jewish. The relationship toward the coworker, *C*, is also a relationship with a fellow Jew. Under this new description, *C* is reconceptualized, resulting in the new application of an already-existing norm, *n**.

Such reconceptualization provides an avenue toward behavioral change without the invention new norms. Underlying the scientific purpose of this chapter—namely, demonstrating that the incentive structure characterizing freedom of expression reflects a public goods collective action problem—is the practical purpose of providing a mental model that will work with pre-existing norms to sway public preferences toward the support of freedom of expression. Social scientists and psychologists have identified fairness norms as fundamental to human interaction.[27] Such norms can function as an important element of self-governance, a way of altering the game in order to achieve a more optimal outcome. As Elinor Ostrom puts it:

> individuals vary in regard to the importance they place on acting in ways that they and others view as right and proper. Norms of behavior reflect valuations that individuals place on actions or strategies in and of themselves, not as they are connected to immediate consequences. When an individual has strongly internalized a norm related to keeping promises, for example, the individual suffers shame and guilt when a personal promise is broken. If the norm is shared with others, the individual is also subject to considerable social censure for taking an action considered to be wrong by others. Norms of behavior therefore affect the way alternatives are perceived and weighed. (Ostrom 2015, 35–36)

If the provision of freedom of expression is a public good, then intolerance is a form of unfair free riding. Conceptualizing it in this way allows norms to work both internally and externally to incentivize lower levels of free riding: internally through guilt and shame, the feeling that one has done something wrong by acting intolerantly, and externally through social disapprobation, the feeling that one has fallen in public esteem by acting intolerantly.

Imagine, then, that the objective payoffs depicted in figure 11.4a can give rise to multiple subjective rankings, based on the extent to which norms are able to "affect the way alternatives are perceived and weighed." For our purposes, we will posit two possible games: one where the preference ranking corresponds to the objective payoff and one where norms exert a sufficient influence to make free riding less preferred than mutual cooperation.

In figure 11.5, the game has become sequential. We are not *just* choosing strategies within a game, but are also choosing the sort of game that we will play. Thus, player 3 can be understood as a *global* perspective, adoptable by any citizen. Here, I intend it to represent the perspective of theorists and

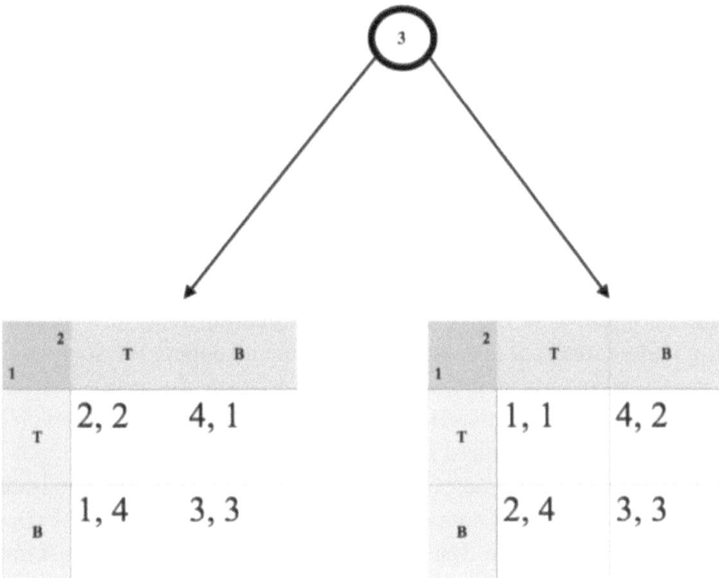

Figure 11.5 Choosing the Game.

activists deciding how to conceptualize a problem: choosing left is some conceptualization which will leave out the public goods nature of freedom of expression and in which norms will therefore fail to provide incentives to refrain from antisocial, intolerant behavior. Choosing right will lead to a situation in which conceptualizing the problem as one of collective action allows norms to make mutual cooperation more attractive than free riding.

The payoffs for player 3 have been left undefined, since I am inviting the reader insert his or her own preference ranking into the game structure. For the sake of analysis, however, let's assume that player 3 is reasonably benevolent and define the utility function of player 3 as an inverse function of the average of player 1 and player 2's numeric ranking of the outcome: $u_3(p_1,p_2) = 2/(p_1 + p_2)$, where p_i is player *i*'s numerical preference ranking of the outcome. This entails that player 3's preference ranking is increasing in the preference satisfaction between both players 1 and 2, and that player 3 equally weights the interests of each player. Since the subgame on the right has two possible *pure-strategy* Nash equilibria, the game as a whole has three possible subgame perfect Nash equilibria:

SPNE #1: (s_1^*, s_2^*, s_3^*) = (*BB, BB, L*)
SPNE #2: (s_1^*, s_2^*, s_3^*) = (*BB, BB, R*)
SPNE #3: (s_1^*, s_2^*, s_3^*) = (*BT, BT, R*)

The subgame on the left has only one possible Nash equilibrium: mutual ban (both choose *B*). The game on the right, due to the influence of norms, has become a coordination game, rather than a prisoner's dilemma. It therefore has two pure-strategy Nash equilibria: mutual toleration and mutual banning.[28] If players latch onto the second of these two possible pure-strategy equilibria, then player three is indifferent between the two games. If they happen upon the first, then the right subgame is clearly preferable. The crucial point is that the right subgame, where a mental model allows norms to incentivize toleration, possesses a cooperative equilibrium, whereas the left subgame does not. This simple model, therefore, illustrates how reconceptualization and its itinerant norm-response enable a cooperative solution. Even in the model, which assumes a strong norm-response, this is not a silver bullet. It requires an equilibrium selection process, something about which game theory has traditionally offered little guidance.[29]

Yet, if only from a commonsense perspective, the right subgame is clearly superior: the possibility of cooperation defeats the impossibility of cooperation. Moreover, even if the right subgame is unattainable through reframing the problem and drawing on norms—that is, even if norms are insufficiently strong to make mutual cooperation the most preferred choice for all players—it remains the case that approaching the right subgame represents an improvement in our prospects for attaining a cooperative solution. Firstly, those on the margin may need only a small push to reverse the ordering between free riding and mutual cooperation. So even if conceptual reframing does not achieve mass preference reversal, it can at least achieve marginal improvements in public opinion. Secondly, conceptual reframing and norm response need not be a solution unto itself. There are various other tactics that might also push us toward a cooperative equilibrium. I highlight norms and conceptual reframing because it seems like the most obvious way in which academic discourse can exert a positive influence on the nature of the game (more on this below). Finally, examples of conceptual reframing suggest that such a strategy is capable of generating a tremendous response under the right conditions. What those conditions are and whether they are satisfied in the case of freedom of expression is beyond the scope of the present chapter. However, journalists and other opinion leaders have a clear interest in freedom of expression. This suggests that a conceptual reframing that empowers this cause could have an enthusiastic uptake in popular discourse.

Whether or not this solution provides the main means of securing expressive freedom, it remains highly relevant to the academic profession. Academics have little power to control policy. They constitute a tiny minority of the voting population. Through their work, they communicate with the public only indirectly, if at all. However, they do exert a disproportional amount of influence over the framing of policy issues. They provide mental models that structure the public perception of various important issues. For example, the economic theory of monopoly behavior and its associated deadweight loss has generated a framework of thought that portrays large, monopolistic firms as social parasites. This framework generates notable political and cultural consequences: support for antitrust laws, for example, or the proliferation of CEO supervillains in films and novels. To take another example, the theory of anthropogenic climate change has furnished a mental model that posits direct causation between using fossil fuels and warming global temperatures. Obviously, the academy utilizes more complicated theories than the mental models that get adopted by the public. Nevertheless, many of the pedestrian mental models that proliferate among nonspecialists clearly have their source in academic discourse. Who would have connected warming temperatures to automobiles and cattle farms without a climatological theory of greenhouse gases and energy storage?

Importantly, the mental models that permeate down from the ivory tower can work in tandem with preexisting social norms to produce significant changes in behavior, both individual and collective. For example, the mental model that arose from the theory of anthropogenic global warming has had major repercussions in personal and political decision-making. In effect, polluting—even minor acts of littering—has become connected in the public imagination with the horrors of species extinction and massive flooding in poverty-stricken nations. Engaging in unnecessary polluting is no longer benign; many social circles treat it as an egregious act of free-riding defection.[30] The mental model that links pollution and littering to ecological destruction has thus tapped into our preexisting norms of fairness to elicit strong moral emotions. Leaving your water running isn't just wasteful anymore; for many, it's downright unjust. The connection to norms of fairness has had visible consequences: high-efficiency automobiles, reusable shopping bags, products made from recycled materials, organic produce—these and other such products have flooded consumer markets. In the political arena, as well, we see major effects: regulations receive widespread support and some politicians run on platforms that prioritize climate change as a major issue. Some of these products and some of these policies are, of course, completely inefficacious, functioning more as a marketing scheme than as a legitimate solution to the problem. Nevertheless, the eagerness of consumers and voters to support such an agenda, and to shame those who do not, demonstrates the power that mental models, and hence academics, have in affecting public behavior.

FAIRNESS AS GENERALITY

One way in which political philosophers have traditionally sought to elicit reliable moral intuitions may prove useful here. The idea is to characterize a point of view—an "Archimedean Point" as Rawls phrases it—from which the

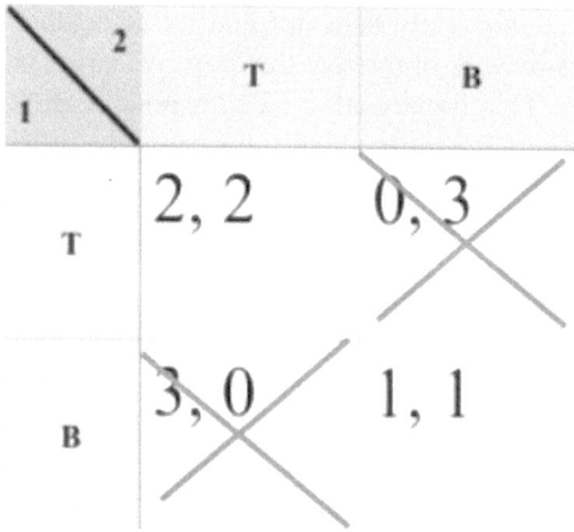

Figure 11.6 Free Expression Game with a Generality Constraint.

normatively relevant features of interpersonal relationships (or some subset of these relationships) become more salient. By applying this constructivist approach here, we may precisify the notion of "fair" behavior, thereby clarifying where norms for punishing unfair free riding readily apply.

The basic idea of fairness is that of rejecting double standards: rules that I apply to you must also apply to me.[31] In the context of our simplified prisoner's dilemma model, this is rather easy to model: we simply require that all action profile be symmetric, leaving only (*T,T*) and (*B,B*) as the possible action profiles, as in figure 11.6.

The only equilibrium in figure 11.6 is $(s_1^*, s_2^*) = (T,T)$. Although we are here considering only a thought experiment to aid in identifying fair behavior, it is worth noting that this game can be attained via an "assurance contract" in which no party pays for a public good unless all other parties also pay. Each potential contributor is thus pivotal and protected from the grim prospect of being a sucker.[32]

We can also apply the generality condition to our more sophisticated (though still simple) numerical example. Suppose that when any individual i in $N = \{A, B, C, D\}$ exhibits tolerance by "purchasing" units of the expressive freedom, the x-good, then all other members of N, denote N_{-i}, also purchase that same amount of the x-good. Applying the generality condition in this way, we can reconsider the individual choice problem and derive a very different result. Still assuming that $p = 40$, the utility functions change to reflect the fact that when one chooses a certain amount of x-good, one also chooses that quantity for all others: $u_i(x,y_i) = y_i - 1/2(c_i - nx) = -40x - 1/2(c_i - 4x)$\$, for some constant c_i. Recalling abovementioned utility functions, we see that even the most intolerant individual, Akerlof, improves his utility by purchasing a positive amount of expressive freedom. His utility is maximized at $x^* = 2.25$. Thus, every individual gains utility as the quantity of x-good purchased by all i in N increases from 0 to 2.25 (0 to 9 units total). Deaton, who values expressive freedom the most, maximizes his utility when all purchase 5 units of the x-good. Hence, all parties lose utility as the amount of x-good purchased moves beyond 5 units per person (beyond 20 units total). The set of Pareto optimal allocations, therefore, consists of all allocations in the range (9, 20).

We have already established that if choosing alone, without the generality condition, each individual maximizes utility by choosing $x = 0$. Further analysis can identify allocations that are at least as good for every single i in N as leaving the group and thus purchasing no x-good. For example, Akerlof is better off with no x-good at all if the group attempts to supply expressive freedom above the level of 4.5 units per person (18 units total). Anything above $x = 18$, therefore, would fail to benefit all individuals in the group. A similar analysis could be conducted for all coalitions in society to identify the set of "core" allocations in the economy—that is, the set of allocations that are at least as good for every individual and every subset S of N as the allocation they could independently achieve by leaving the group. Restricting ourselves to such allocations guarantees that no individual or faction is made worse off by being a part of our community. This is a basic condition of fairness, since violating this condition entails exploitation.

To summarize, fairness means applying rules in a satisfactorily general way. If individuals value expressive freedom, the above analysis shows that a fair rule would involve producing a positive amount of x-good, expressive freedom. Thinking in these terms clarifies the concept of fairness and should thus help us to reconceptualize intolerance as a form of unfair free riding. If this reconceptualization is apt, then norms of fairness apply and support for free expression should increase once this fact is realized.

CONCLUSION

Social living presents an opportunity for massive gains; society at its best is a "cooperative venture for mutual advantage" (Rawls 2009, 79). Yet, collective action problems can stunt our capacity to realize these gains. They can even render society oppressive, unjust, or—in the extreme—worse than being alone. One of the massive advantages that society offers appears only once we secure freedom of expression. With such liberty guaranteed, individuals have the opportunity to learn from one another, to sharpen their own understanding of their beliefs and values, and to escape loneliness by expressing these beliefs and values through communicative action.

Yet, tolerating diverse worldviews is difficult. In fact, as psychologists will explain, it is literally painful. By taking advantage of power, some individuals may seize the opportunity to restrict opposing views—the cost to them is negligible, and the benefit substantial. As an isolated action, therefore, intolerance may seem quite rational. On a social level, however, this strategy is destructive for all but the most powerful faction. And if power is a volatile asset, then in the long run this strategy is to the detriment of all.

To employ such a strategy should therefore invite blame and disapprobation. Moreover, it should engender guilt and shame. By recognizing that intolerance is an affront to the proverbial social contract, we can alter our perspective on and evaluation of the various outcomes that arise from our decisions. Armed with this new perspective, we can avoid entering the prisoner's dilemma of free expression. Or, if it's too late for that, we might progress toward abandoning this perverse game.

Elinor Ostrom identified four levels of decision-making, each structured by a different set of rules: (a) metaconstitutional choice, (b) constitutional choice, (c) collective choice, and (d) operational choice (Ostrom and Ostrom 2004, 134; see also Ostrom 2015, 53). Metaconstitutional choice, the most removed from the day-to-day arena of action, produces behavioral rules, norms, that guide our choices in all subsequent levels. This includes the constitutional level, where agents determine the structure of collective decision making. For example, individuals may latch upon two-thirds majority as the proper decision rule to govern changes in permissible grazing behavior for their cattle. Then, on the collective level, individuals determine rules that will structure their day-to-day decisions on the operational level. For example, one can graze their cattle for only four hours each day. This classification underlies Ostrom's key insight into the nature of collective action problems. It is not true, as Hardin puts it, that we are "locked into" a game in which "ruin is the destination toward which all men rush" (Hardin 1958, 1244). On the contrary, human choices take place "beyond the operational level," that is, on levels that will determine the rules and incentives that structure our choice problem on the operational level. The rules themselves become, in some contexts, the objects of choice (Ostrom 2015, 53). Since ideas and norms structure choice scenarios that decision-makers face at the operational level, they must be analyzed as an arena of rule selection. However, they are not formally chosen, like democratic processes are. Rather, they arise and operate through a web of informal decisions. This web of decisions, I propose, is the action arena of academic discourse.[33]

NOTES

1. But see (Coyne 2016).

2. Moreover, treating the common pool of expressions as unlimited is a harmless simplification given the vast number of expressions currently available and the constant stream of novel expressions that culture produces.

3. The choice of $p = 40$ is arbitrary. For any price higher than $p = 30$, individuals will demand 0 x-good. And even for $p = 1$, an inefficiently low level of x-provision would result.

4. This condition is quite intuitive, but (Samuelson 1954) provides a formal proof that this equation does, in fact, yield a Pareto-efficient outcome. He also proves the inefficiency of the equilibrium for a more general class of utility functions than this simple example can encompass.

5. As Schmidtz 1991 points out, the issue is rarely, if ever, so clean cut. One man's public good is another lady's public bad, and in practice it is impossible to discern the "honest hold-outs" from those that are merely trying to game the system (Schmidtz 1991). Another way of putting this is that public goods do not necessarily exhibit the incentive structure of a prisoner's dilemma, since some may prefer mutual defection to mutual cooperation. I thank Rachel Mannahan for alerting me to this point.

6. In addition, adequate provision of freedom of expression will require enforcement costs beyond the requisite tolerance itself: police services, for example, would protect communist protesters from assault or nonviolent Nazis from getting punched. These costs could be incorporated in the model by expanding our understanding of the private y-good.

7. At least, this is the view expressed by Agnar Sandmo in his discussion of the literature in *The New Palgrave Dictionary of Economics* (Sandmo 1987, 745).

8. For a timely analysis, see (Healy and Malhotra 2009). For a brief survey, see (Sandmo 1987).

9. The president, of course, cannot simply "loosen libel laws," which are determined separately by each state. Nor does he have the power to revoke media licenses. There exist, however, other channels by which he could prove a menace to freedom of expression, for example the vaguely worded Espionage Act.

10. And recent surveys reveal that students praise free expression while denying that this implies the right to utter offensive statements (Naughton 2019).

11. Information on disinvited speakers has been carefully collected and presented in a database hosted by the Foundation for Individual Rights in Education (FIRE), accessible on the web at https://www.thefire.org/resources/disinvitation-database/.

12. In fact, around 40 percent of them believe that it is already illegal to make racist statements in public. Tellingly, over 50 percent of democrats think it should be punishable to refer to a transgender person by his/her nonpreferred pronoun (Friedersdorf 2017).

13. This poll has been amply corroborated by my Facebook feed.

14. Quoted in (Rauch 1993, 131).

15. Hardin considers private and state ownership of CPRs as the only two options (Hardin 1978). Alchian and Demsetz present a similar dichotomy (Alchian and Demsetz 1973, 23).

16. Such goods are referred to by Elinor Ostrom as "toll goods" (Ostrom 2003, 2014) and by James Buchanan as "club goods" (Buchanan 1965).

17. This is not to forget, of course, that enjoying higher levels of expressive freedom does come at the cost of expressive agreeableness.

18. As Alchian and Demsetz put it, "private rights can be socially useful precisely because they encourage persons to take account of social cost" (Alchian and Demsetz 1973, 24).

19. Seinfeld's "soup Nazi" presents a vivid illustration of an entrepreneur's awareness that restricting free expression results in lower revenues—though, in this case, the entrepreneur is comically willing to accept those losses.

20. Examples here are bound to be controversial, though each individual can probably find some example that they would recognize as public provision of an excludable good. Some candidates: transportation, parks, health care, postal service, or utilities systems with close substitutes.

21. While this tolerance has limits, these limits are quite extensive. For a nuanced discussion, see (Rawls 2009, 190–194).

22. The issue of providing freedom of expression is therefore deeply connected to a fundamental issue in liberal politics, the "paradox of liberalism," namely the issue of tolerating the intolerant (Judd 2005). To be a liberal means to tolerate the illiberal. In the extreme, however, this generates an insoluble conflict between one's liberal values and the stability of one's liberal society.

23. Self-sorting is one way to ensure the economic viability of these faux-tolerant associations. For an idea of how this may work, see (Schelling 1971).

24. Though this is somewhat orthogonal to the argument here, a great value may be lost by filtering out extreme critics of our institutions, including critics of freedom. As Mill argued, such critics, even if they do not change our minds, provide an invaluable opportunity to clarify the nature and sources of our beliefs, without which opportunity liberals might hold their commitment to free speech with "a dull and torpid assent, as if accepting it on trust dispensed with the necessity of realising it in consciousness . . . [this commitment] doing nothing for the mind or heart, except standing sentinel over them to keep them vacant" (Mill 1989, 42).

25. This is because any monotonic transformation of a utility function represents the same preference ranking.

26. This norm and its fascinating contractual consequences are discussed by Lisa Bernstein (1992).

27. Christina Bicchieri, for example, has provided ample evidence for the existence of a human "taste for fairness" (Bicchieri 2005, ch. 3).

28. It also has a mixed-strategy equilibrium, which I ignore for the purpose of concise exposition.

29. Though recent work in game theory explores some fascinating approaches to this problem. See, for example, (Romero 2015).

30. Once, a friend of mine spit his gum onto the asphalt of a parking lot. A horrified spectator immediately scolded him: "People like you are the reason the earth is being destroyed!" Clearly, mental models are not the same as the scientific theory that generates them.

31. This idea is more easily stated than applied. Consider the rule. "If you are black, then you do not receive a trial following accusation." Applying this rule to everyone in society, including me and African Americans, would be patently unfair, despite its general framing.

32. See (Schmidtz 1991) for a philosophical analysis of this subject.

33. Of course, other opinion leaders also interact within this web. I am only claiming that this is the action arena in which academics are best represented and exert the most influence.

REFERENCES

Alchian, Armen A., and Harold Demsetz. 1973. "The Property Right Paradigm." *The Journal of Economic History* 33 (1): 16–27.

Allred, Nathaniel, Kirk A. Hawkins, and Saskia P. Ruth. 2015. "The Impact of Populism on Liberal Democracy." In *ALACIP Annual Congress*. Lima (Peru).

Bellur, Poorvi. 2016. "Free Speech and Populism." *Columbia Political Review*. http://www.cpreview.org/blog/2017/1/free-speech-and-populism.

Bernstein, Lisa. 1992. "Opting Out of the Legal System: Extralegal Contractual Relations in the Diamond Industry." *The Journal of Legal Studies* 21 (1): 115–157.

Bicchieri, Cristina. 2005. *The Grammar of Society: The Nature and Dynamics of Social Norms*. Cambridge: Cambridge University Press, 2005.

Boettke, Peter J. 1997. "Where Did Economics Go Wrong? Modern Economics as a Flight from Reality." *Critical Review* 11 (1): 11–64.

Buchanan, James M. 1965. "An Economic Theory of Clubs." *Economica* 32 (125): 1–14.

Clarke, Edward H. 1971. "Multipart Pricing of Public Goods." *Public Choice*, 11 (1): 17–33.

Coyne, Christopher J., and David Lucas. 2016. "Economists Have No Defense: A Critical Review of National Defense in Economics Textbooks." *Journal of Private Enterprise* 31 (4): 65–83.

Demsetz, Harold. 1967. "Toward a Theory of Property Rights." *American Economic Review* 62: 347–59.

Friedersdorf, Conor. 2017. "America's Many Divides over Free Speech." *The Atlantic*. https://www.theatlantic.com/politics/archive/2017/10/a-sneak-peek-at-new-survey-data-on-free-speech/542028/.

Groves, Theodore. 1973. "Incentives in Teams." *Econometrica* 41 (4): 617–631.

Grynbaum, Michael M., and Eileen Sullivan. 2009. "Trump Attacks the Times, in a Week of Unease for the American Press." *New York Times*.

Hardin, Garrett. 1968. "The Tragedy of the Commons." *Science* 162 (3859): 1243–1253.

———. 1978. "Political Requirements for Preserving our Common Heritage." *Wildlife and America* 31: 1017, 1978.

Healy, Andrew, and Neil Malhotra. 2009. "Myopic Voters and Natural Disaster Policy." *American Political Science Review* 103 (3): 387–406.

Hume, David. 1978. *A Treatise of Human Nature*, edited by L.A. Shelby Bigge, revised by P.H. Nidditch. Oxford: Oxford University Press.

Jacobs, Ben. 2016. "Donald Trump Pledges to Curb Press Freedom through Libel Laws." *The Guardian.* https://www.theguardian.com/us-news/2016/feb/26/trump-pledges-curb-press-freedom-libel-laws-first-amendment.

Johnson, Omotunde E.G. 1972. "Economic Analysis, the Legal Framework and Land Tenure Systems." *The Journal of Law and Economics* 15 (1): 259–276.

Lewis, Paul, Clarke Seán, and Caelainn Barr. 2019. "Revealed: Populist Leaders Linked to Reduced Inequality." *The Guardian.* https://www.theguardian.com/world/2019/mar/07/revealed-populist-leaders-linked-to-reduced-inequality

Mill, John Stuart. 1989. *On Liberty and Other Writings.* Edited by Stefan Collini. Cambridge: Cambridge University Press.

Mindock, Clark. 2018. "Trump Suggests Revoking NBC's Broadcast License Amid Attacks on 'Fake News.'" *The Independent.* https://www.independent.co.uk/news/world/americas/us-politics/donald-trump-nbc-broadcast-license-fake-news-attack-a8522651.html.

Naughton, Kelsey Ann. 2019. "Student Attitudes Association Survey." *FIRE.* https://www.thefire.org/research/publications/student-surveys/student-attitudes-association-survey/.

Ostrom, Elinor. 2000. "Collective Action and the Evolution of Social Norms." *Journal of Economic Perspectives* 14 (3): 137–158.

———. 2003. "How Types of Goods and Property Rights Jointly Affect Collective Action." *Journal of Theoretical Politics* 15 (3): 239–270.

———. 2014. "Beyond Markets and States: Polycentric Governance of Complex Economic Systems." In *Choice, Rules, and Collective Action: The Ostroms on the Study of Institutions and Governance*, edited by Filippo Sabetti and Paul Dragos Aligica, 167–209. Colchester, UK: ECPR Press.

———. 2015. *Governing the Commons.* Cambridge: Cambridge University Press.

Ostrom, Elinor, and Sue E.S. Crawford. 2000. "A Grammar of Institutions." In *Polycentric Games and Institutions: Readings form the Workshop in Political Theory and Policy Analysis*, edited by Michael D. McGinnis, 114–155. Ann Arbor: Michigan University Press.

Ostrom, Elinor, and Vincent Ostrom. 2004. "The Quest for Meaning in Public Choice." *American Journal of Economics and Sociology* 63 (1): 105–147.

Owen, J. Judd. 2005. "The Tolerant Leviathan: Hobbes and the Paradox of Liberalism." *Polity* 37 (1): 130–148.

Rauch, Jonathan. 1993. *Kindly Inquisitors: The New Attacks on Free Thought.* Chicago: University of Chicago Press.

Rawls, John. 2009. *A Theory of Justice.* Cambridge: Harvard University Press.

Romero, Julian. 2015. "The Effect of Hysteresis on Equilibrium Selection in Coordination Games." *Journal of Economic Behavior & Organization* 111: 88–105.

Ruth-Lovell, Saskia, David Doyle, and Kirk Hawkins. 2019. "Consequences of Populism Memo for *The Guardian's* "The New Populism"." Accessed at: http://populism.byu.edu/Pages/Publications.

Samuelson, Paul A. 1954. "The Pure Theory of Public Expenditure." *The Review of Economics and Statistics* 36 (4): 387–389.

Sandmo, Agnar. 1987. "Public Goods." In *The New Palgrave Dictionary of Economics*, Vol. 3, edited by Steven N. Durlauf and Lawrence E. Blume, 1061–1066. London: Palgrave Macmillan.

Schmidtz, David. 1991. *The Limits of Government: An Essay on Public Goods Argument*. Boulder, CO: Westview Press.

Simon, Carl P., and Lawrence Blume. 1994. *Mathematics for Economists, Viva-Norton Student Edition*. New York: Norton New York.

Smith, Adam. [1776] 2000. *An Inquiry into the Nature and Causes of the Wealth of Nations*. New York: The Modern Library.

Smith, Robert J. 1981. "Resolving the Tragedy of the Commons by Creating Private Property Rights in Wildlife." *Cato Journal* 1: 439.

Soave, Robby. 2017. "Columbia Law Professor: Letting a Right-Wing Activist Speak Is 'An Act of Violence'." *Reason Magazine*. https://reason.com/2017/10/23/columbia-law-professor-letting-a-rightwi.

Staaf, Robert J. 1983. "Privatization of Public Goods." *Public Choice* 41 (3): 435–440.

Vickrey, William. 1961. "Counterspeculation, Auctions, and Competitive Sealed Tenders." *The Journal of Finance* 16 (1): 8–37.

Chapter 12

Are American Immigrant Processing Institutions Surviving or Thriving?

Large-Scale Immigration as a Shock to Institutional Robustness

Emily VanMeter

In 2014, there was a dramatic uptick in the number of unaccompanied minors (68,451) originating from Mexico, Guatemala, El Salvador, and Honduras and apprehended at the Southern US border. Called the "American Immigration Crisis," this increase in the number of unaccompanied minor apprehensions was nearly 180 percent of the previous year's numbers. The increasing strain on the United States–Mexico border was not only made up of unaccompanied minors but families as well—68,445 family units[1] were apprehended in 2014 (US Border Patrol 2016). This increase was attributed to a number of factors, including: (1) high rates of gang-related crime in their countries of origin, (2) a booming smuggler economy, and (3) a growing awareness of H.R. 7311, a 2008 law that grants substantial protection from removal for unaccompanied children from countries that do not share a border with the United States (Greenblatt 2014). Numbers have not improved since 2014. In 2016, 59,692 unaccompanied minors and 77,674 family units were apprehended at the Southern US border (US Border Patrol 2016).

In this chapter, I will argue that the institutions created (1) for detaining apprehended persons on the border and (2) for placing detained persons before immigration courts have been challenged in historically unparalleled ways. I will refer to these institutions, collectively, as an "immigration processing institution," or IPI, for consistency throughout the rest of the chapter. I argue that the institutional framework currently in place has been found to be insufficient, but due to the nature of citizen responsibility, the institutions in place are currently being bolstered by external enterprise at great personal cost. This ad hoc solution is unsustainable without institutional revision to integrate these new enterprises and to ensure some basis of quality control and accountability to citizens. From this case, we can learn a great deal about the value of the polycentric vision put forward by the Ostroms, and the role that multifaceted governance can play in avoiding humanitarian crises.

In the first section of the chapter, I discuss Ostromian guidelines for institutional robustness. In the second section, I address the failure of the United States' current system to meet these guidelines, and how this was showcased by an exogenous shock to the institution. In the third section, I describe the ways in which the institutions in place have been bolstered by the communities most affected, at high personal cost. In the fourth section, I propose two theories as to why this has not been considered a viable alternative. Finally, I will conclude by discussing the normative implications this has for institutional survival and what best fits the Ostromian model of institutional robustness going forward.

THE OSTROMS ON INSTITUTIONAL ROBUSTNESS

It is important to first understand the definition of a robust institution from a political economy viewpoint in order to evaluate the ways in which the United States' IPI was ill-prepared for the "Migration Crisis." Elinor and Vincent Ostrom's work focuses heavily on the meaning of institutions, institutional creation, and institutional persistence, and is entrenched in a rich subfield of related work on institutionalism. Within this subfield, there are many possible qualifications for "robust" institutions. As with all scientific progress, consensus does not follow from the number of citations or publications, even consensus on a definition of the term "robust" institution.

In her 1986 work, E. Ostrom noted that to date there had been a large degree of ambiguity and variety in the formal definition of an institution. Lack of definitional consensus, she argued, had led to scientific stagnation—scholars were talking past each other rather than engaging in a productive dialogue. She then noted that rules persist across the definitions of "institution" put forward by several scholars, including Plott (1979), Schotter (1981), and Riker (1982). If we are considering institutional robustness from the Ostromian framework, it is therefore important to know that Elinor and Vincent Ostrom saw institutions as collections of rules. This is, of course, not very productive by itself, and she also tried to answer epistemological questions about (a) where these rules came from and (b) the types of action that we expect rules to take.

Given that the operational definition of "institutions as rules" requires little further explanation, I will move onto a discussion of where these rules originate. E. Ostrom (2014) asserts that they come from attempts to achieve order and predictability within specific situations by: (1) creating positions, (2) stating how participants enter or leave positions, (3) stating which actions participants in these positions are required, permitted, or forbidden to take, and (4) stating which outcomes participants are required, permitted, or forbidden to influence. Given that rules come from these predefined desirable attributes of institutions, we should expect that robust institutions, in practice, serve to bring these results to fruition.

These rules shape behavior in such a way as to create a hierarchical network in which some actors have given positions that enable them to perform specific roles. It is not surprising, then, that she breaks these verbs into nominal categories. These rules, once created, become (1) position rules, (2) boundary rules, (3) scope rules, (4) authority rules, (5) aggregation rules, (6) information rules, or (7) payoff rules. The type of action we expect a rule to take is contingent on which type of relational rule is being developed. For example, position rules "specify a set of positions and how many participants hold each position," and boundary rules "specify how participants are chosen to hold these positions and how participants leave these positions" (E. Ostrom 2014, 113).[2]

Shepsle (1989) goes on to expand E. Ostrom's work on rules, saying that in order to be *robust*, as one typically thinks of institutions, they must be devised and modified over time in accordance with collective and constitutional choice regulations. That is, they must be Pareto optimal to the decisive actors. Pareto optimality is defined as the set of conditions where none of the actors can be made better off without making at least one actor worse off. North (1990) argues that it is the relationship between institutions and the organizations formed to exploit them that leads to Pareto improvement. However, he also adds that less optimal institutions may persist if the transaction costs of change are high enough to serve as barriers to entry for organizations hoping to deliver change.

A crucial measure of true institutional success is not just persistence, but a given institution's ability to endure within changing circumstances, such that the decisive actors do not have incentive to renegotiate the terms of the institution—a characteristic which Shepsle (1989) called renegotiation proofness. In *Governing the Commons*, E. Ostrom (1990) gives eight design principles that she argues are related to long-term institutional renegotiation proofness (henceforth institutional robustness). These are: (1) well-defined boundaries, (2) proportional equivalence between costs and benefits, (3) collective choice arrangements, (4) monitoring, (5) graduated sanctions, (6) conflict resolution mechanisms, (7) recognition of rights to organize, and (8) nested enterprises.[3]

Combining the Shepsle (1989), North (1990), and Ostromian (1986–2014) models of institutions, one arrives at a picture of institutions that are Pareto optimal rules for the decisive actors (voters in the United States' model) and maintain their robustness by permitting organizations to operate efficiently within them in a way that collectives do not have incentive to change the institutional framework. It is also important that actors would be able to Pareto improve the institutional framework if the institution is no longer desirable. As previously discussed, change should occur when organizations, and the voters that ultimately make up organizations, realize that they would benefit from a new set of rules. In the Ostromian framework, institutions should also have well-defined boundary rules, proportionally equivalent costs and benefits, monitoring and enforcement proportional to any potential violations at hand, a way to resolve disputes fairly, and overlapping levels of procedure to simultaneously permit the institution to benefit from economies of scale as well as represent local interests.

If one considers this working model of institutions and the implementation of these features in the real world, it is easy to see that the role of the citizen is performing the hidden legwork behind institutional robustness. Citizens have the power to formally make and remake the rules in democratic societies, and the power to informally remake them in nondemocratic ones. This comes with great responsibility: rules need to be enforced, and if the probability of agreement on the rules is small, the probability of agreement on what constitutes just enforcement of the rules is even smaller (Rawls 2001; Rousseau 2002). Without delving into the philosophical complexities of citizen consensus and how that plays out in a given institutional framework, we know that for the sake of this context citizen decision-making is taking place under the complex voting rules of the United States' government and the "town hall" model of local governance. Influencers, according to North (1990), are those that shape themselves into organized collectives. These organized collectives are expressions of preference over a given issue area that are easily observable to fellow citizens and government officials alike. Because of the large size of the United States, it would be impossible to observe every individual citizen's complete preferences, so we can only observe where the design principles and practice of institutions fall short of the characteristics described above, and the responses that groups of individuals have to these failures.

When robustness is not met and there are no visible organizational responses, V. Ostrom (1979, 14–5; 1997, 294–5) argues, there is one of two possible underlying causes—each with a very different ultimate outcome. The first possible cause is that citizens are ignorant of the principles of self-governance and lack the capability to do so. The second is that citizens wait until conflict occurs to address grievances, at which point threat to the system is necessary for change to occur. While the first is more pessimistic about citizen engagement than the second, I argue that there is little need for concerns about incapability in the case of IPI.

THE UNITED STATES' IMMIGRATION FRAMEWORK AS A NONROBUST, ENDURING INSTITUTION

Following from Shepsle's definition of renegotiation proofness, we should expect that viable institutions would be Pareto optimal even in the presence of exogenous shocks. In fact, in describing changing water institutions, E. Ostrom (1990: 109–10) demonstrates that CPR organizers maintain Pareto optimality by endogenizing future uncertainty. We should expect the same from IPI in the United States. E. Ostrom argues that water institutions would not need to endogenize future uncertainty if assessing the amount of resources currently available was cheap. However, the reality is that operationalizing resource consumption is difficult and labor intensive. Even if there is enough workforce available to collect the data and analyze it, resource assessment prevents the institution from using its labor force for monitoring, resource provision, and maintenance (E. Ostrom 1990). Sustainable solutions are made even more difficult due to limited information about future demand. These are problems faced by all institutions with finite resources and not just water access CPRs, so it is not difficult to argue that the institutions designed to respond to migration in the United States might suffer the same shortcomings. I argue that by failing to sufficiently endogenize future uncertainty, the United States' IPI missed an opportunity to better meet Ostromian design principles under current strain.

To take a Northian (2000) view, the probable cause of the United States' immigration policy failure is a high cost of entry for organizations that would want to change the institution. In this case, it is credible that entry might be difficult because border decisions are made by the Department of Homeland Security (DHS), and as a part of the executive branch of the national government they are in possession of many resources and a monopoly of the legitimate use of force. These constraints make it nearly impossible for third-party organizations operating inside the rules set by the DHS to influence them. As such, inefficient policies that would be renegotiated have been allowed to persist for over a decade.

The evidence that these policies would in fact have been renegotiated if left to the voters is clear in the wake of the public opinion data. While it is not always clear exactly which institutional arrangements constituents would prefer, it is clear that they are discontent with the status quo—the current institution is hardly in alignment with citizens' preferences. An NBC News and Wall Street Journal poll (2019) found that only 18 percent of respondents felt the border was secure in 2013, and when repeated in January of 2019, this number had only increased to just over a third.[4] Likewise, a Gallup poll (January 2019) revealed that 75 percent of respondents felt that the border patrol was understaffed, but 83 percent of a different sample (June 2018) were strongly in favor of allowing immigrants brought to the United States illegally as children the chance to become US citizens if they met certain requirements over a period of time. On the whole, it seems that US citizens favor increased border security and a mixed approach on illegal immigrants residing within the country. Poll results indicate support for safe access to citizenship for illegal immigrants and some degree of deportation, most likely for criminals (Newport 2019).

At the same time that these nonrobust institutions have been allowed to exist due to high costs of entry, border apprehensions have remained high. In fiscal year 2016, there were 553,378 Southern border apprehensions, in fiscal year 2017 there were 415,517 apprehensions, and in 2018 there were 521,090 (US Border Patrol 2019). From October to June in fiscal year 2019, the US Border Patrol has apprehended 688,375 individuals, nearly ten percent of which were unaccompanied minors (US Border Patrol 2019). The resulting strain has highlighted the inefficiencies present within the IPI. Societal pressure has increased as it has become more and more apparent that this institution is not robust, particularly in the face of large shocks such as political and economic disturbances in Latin American countries. In the wake of these crises, institutional inefficiency presents as escalated backlog in immigration courts and overflow in immigrant detention centers (Lu and Watkins 2019). Compounding the problem, the so-called catch and release policies limit the number of days that children can be held in confinement. As the average number of days until an immigration court date continue to grow, so do the number of pending families being released into the streets.

As confidence in the DHS's ability to handle the flux of immigrants has dropped, so have the barriers to entry for organizations seeking change. As a result, policies in place have been called into question by both the presidency (presidents 43–45 in particular) and Congress (Jordan 2006; Bump 2016; Baker 2019; Rose 2019). While ordinarily this would be cause for hope of institutional adaptation, President Obama's policy changes, in an attempt to elicit reform, just increased the burden on the institution (Rose 2019). Overcrowded detention centers are now the center of media attention due to alleged human rights abuses (Joung 2019; Paul and Miroff 2019; Sergent et al. 2019).

The current immigrant processing institutions do possess some of the Ostromian design principles: clearly defined boundaries, monitoring, and recognition of rights to organize. However, they lack proportional equivalence between costs and benefits, as well as nested enterprise. In best-case scenarios, they feature collective choice arrangements, graduated sanctions, and conflict resolution mechanisms, but this is not always the case. A discussion of how I arrived at these evaluations follows.

Clearly defined boundaries are, according to E. Ostrom (1990: 90), created when those that have rights to benefit from resource units are clearly defined, as well as the presence of clear boundaries to the resource itself. There are certainly boundaries between the United States and Mexico, and though not flawlessly enforced, there is little doubt that there are clear definitions of legal versus illegal immigrants, refugees versus immigrants, and a variety of other consumer distinctions. The procedural aspect of current immigrant processing is very clear—As I will discuss in the coming pages, the shortfalls lie predominantly in institutional implementation.

Monitoring is simply defined as the presence of monitors who actively audit conditions as well as the behavior of those involved in the exchange and are accountable to the people. "Accountable to the people" is the dubious aspect of this definition when applied to the United States' immigrant processing monitors. It is very difficult for immigrants, particularly vulnerable populations like children, to hold the monitors accountable. If, however, we are talking about the citizenry of the United States, then due to the nature of democracy, it seems fair to assess that they are accountable to the people. Even if those monitoring the institution are bureaucrats, citizens may call for their resignation if they behave inappropriately.

Discussing "rights to organize" in the case of a government organization is trivial. The overarching Cabinet seat, the DHS, was given the right to organize in 2002, when following the terrorist attacks on 9/11, different agencies were stripped of their duties to serve in a domestic security capacity. Since then, there have been no serious challenges to DHS authority by external government authorities.

Areas of nonrobustness, where the IPI currently in place falls short of Ostromian design principles, are also present. For example, the concept of proportional equivalence of costs and benefits is intended to ensure that restrictions imposed by the institution are aligned with conditions on the ground and that they have the resources necessary to maintain the regulations being imposed. I argue that the rapid-fire media attention garnered by the IPI and the subsequent involvement of collective action organizations to meet the needs of citizens and immigrants alike as the IPI falls short of its desired goals suggest that this design principle has been found lacking for some time. It has clearly not been met since the start of the "Migration Crisis," and will likely continue to worsen so long as there is bureaucratic deadlock, but it is possible that there was simply never a need to ensure proportional equivalence due to the nature of national-level government organizations as outside of a competitive market.

This brings into context the next condition that the current IPI fails to meet: nested enterprise. Because DHS runs immigration processing from the national level, using national-level immigration courts and national-level enforcement officers, neither is there layering of expertise nor are there differing viewpoints varying in scale and incentive structure. Nested enterprise is a mechanism that the Ostroms intended to prevent problems of detachment from local community needs and desires. Monitoring and provision of IPI have become less credible because there is no outside force beyond the federal government surveilling immigration processing in practice. It could be argued that the media has recently begun to fill this role, but like with all media, there is an underlying incentive to sell copy rather than holding the institution truly accountable.

Less clear is whether or not the institution as it currently stands is open to collective choice arrangements. While local citizens are not allowed a weighted sample in representation due to their level of exposure, the principle behind democratic institutions is that all voting members of society have a say in government. By choosing their leaders to represent them, citizens are able to raise concerns through community organization measures. Additionally, they can sanction leaders that have placed inefficient or corrupt bureaucrats within the system by threatening to revoke their votes in the next election. When democracy is working well, one would expect that individuals affected by the rules would be able to participate in changing the rules. However, when democracy is bogged down in red tape and partisan stalemates, it becomes easier for institutions to maintain operational rules counter to the will of the people.

Graduated sanctions are nominally in place for those immigrants that violate operational rules. This is often showcased in conversations about deporting illegal immigrants. Border Patrol and politicians alike are often found highlighting cases where they have deported criminally minded immigrants in order to garner approval. Immigration and Customs Enforcement (ICE) Spokesman Matthew Bourke revealed to *USA Today* reporters that "ninety percent of aliens arrested by ICE's Enforcement and Removal Operation component in fiscal year 2018 had either a criminal conviction, pending criminal charge, were an ICE fugitive or illegally reentered the country after previously being removed." However, there is room for concern about the justification of these sanctions—in 2018, only 66 percent of people arrested by ICE had been convicted of crimes in the United States (Bacon and Gomez 2019). It is clear from the opinion data given above that Americans feel threatened by some migrants and not others. As a result, criminals and those that engage in deviant behavior are often subject to increasing penalties. However, in an ideal situation, the officials deciding to impose sanctions would be accountable to those that use immigrant processing institutions. However, due to the nature of sovereignty, the DHS is not going to condition responses on the feedback of would-be immigrants, which is what makes border security such a perilous human rights landscape (Paul and Miroff 2019).

It is also uncertain whether or not there are appropriate conflict resolution mechanisms in place. While in principle there are courts in place to try officials or appropriators that overstep their bounds, it is neither rapid nor low cost to pursue such legal action (Lu and Watkins 2019), two requirements for E. Ostrom's robust design principle. Those in detention centers have little power to hold the officials accountable. For example, during her visit to one such detention center, Alexandra Ocasio-Cortez reported that a detainee told her that in the absence of a functioning sink they should just drink water from the toilet (Porter 2019). This report led to claims of falsehood and overenthusiastic partisanship—an attempt to vilify those that support immigrant detention. However, it should have raised concerns about accountability and justice—is there a way to hold current immigrants and immigrant processing institutions accountable that is easily accessible to both the monitors and those being monitored? If it was easier for immigrants in the detention facility to tell a congresswoman from New York rather than a lawyer that their rights were being violated, the answer is that it is almost certainly inaccessible.

COLLECTIVE ACTION RESPONSES TO INSTITUTIONAL SHORTCOMINGS

Frank and Shockley (2016) argue that social entrepreneurship has microfoundations in the Ostroms' work on polycentricity and Hayek's work on the economics of knowledge. They find that local, decentralized social entrepreneurs are the most appropriate and best-positioned (efficient) actors to solve their communities' social problems. In the case of the United States' immigrant processing institutions, groups of citizens have stepped up to fill the void left by the nonrobustness of the current institutional structure. As will be discussed in greater detail below, as long as these organizations continue to function without Ostromian institutional design principles to support them, this is not a sustainable or even particularly safe option.

Most of the problems resulting from failed immigrant processing institutions are geographically determined, meaning that the whole country does not share equal burden. The reality is that different communities within the United States bear different loads. For example, the pressures on North Dakota are very different than the pressures on Texas and Arizona, though all three are border states. As a result, individuals tend to be most engaged in remedying shortcomings in regions of heavy immigration—Southern border communities. Within border communities, citizens seem to have a variety of concerns stemming from the influx of immigrants. These concerns vary from public safety to resource provision to the human rights of the immigrant populations, and any combination of quandaries in between.

As I discussed above, when citizens do not share incentive to set and enforce similar rules, particularly under the start-up costs of institutional organization, they tend to splinter—most of the groups that I will discuss in this work are not large. In terms of normatively acceptable governance, they are not all beneficial either. Unregulated paramilitaries are generally considered a detriment to state sovereignty, and in historic cases members of these types of organization have been known to commit human rights abuses and even murder (Prendergast 2018).

In Phoenix, churches have organized to take in migrants and have created an informal network. This organization formed in response to the failure of the immigration processing institution to provide food and water to recently released immigrants, awaiting immigration hearings. Some have maximized the number of days they can be detained under "catch and release" laws, while others arrive to overcrowded containment facilities that choose to release them. These vulnerable populations are without temporary housing as they travel to destinations throughout the country, and often any money they traveled with has been confiscated or stolen. Previously, these immigrants had been released at Greyhound stations, often with no buses coming until the next morning. However, Greyhound has recently forbidden immigrants from staying in their stations without having purchased a ticket (Galvan 2019). The Phoenix churches have stepped in to provide temporary shelter, food, and water.

At its peak, the Phoenix network had fifteen churches, but has dropped down to ten as resources depleted. These ten to fifteen churches housed over 40,000 migrants within a six-month period (Leon and Samore 2019). By cooperating and working in tandem, churches can request community members outside of their congregations to provide assistance and can manage migrant overflow by sending migrants to other organizations that might still have food and beds available. Another option that organizations have used in cases of overflow is appealing to citizens to let migrants stay in their own homes (González 2019a, 2019b).

Annunciation House is another collective action organization designed to address institutional shortcomings once immigrants are released. A poverty relief organization based out of El Paso, Texas, the nonprofit called for local churches to provide aid using local news outlets once it became apparent that there could be as many as 600–700 migrants being released by ICE a day from the Juarez border region. Though Annunciation House is a shelter in its own right, the number of additional immigrants beyond fire code that it has taken in require large monthly motel bills which are paid for by extensive fundraising and donations (Favela 2019). The City of El Paso had originally volunteered to open up public facilities to aid migrants, but this plan was found to be a violation of state and federal guidelines mandating that a state of emergency be declared by the Texas governor before local tax dollars could be spent on aid. It was not until the estimated number of migrants released to churches and nonprofits totaled approximately 1,800 in one weekend that the municipal government reconsidered this stance and is now scheduling a meeting to find legal pathways to provide assistance to these overwhelmed voluntary organizations (Montes 2019).

Not all collective action responses pertain to newly released immigrants, however. Several collective action organizations have formed around the idea of increased border security, and as such have formed paramilitary units throughout the country, sending them to the border to alert Border Patrol of potential illegal border crossings. While paramilitary do not have a legitimate use of force within the United States, self-defense laws and the right to bear arms provided by the US Constitution mean that these organizations pack weaponry that ranges from pistols to semiautomatic rifles.

One such organization is Arizona Border Recon, or AZBR, is a border patrol group in Arizona, composed of former military, law enforcement, and private security contractors. Formed in 2011, the group had approximately 250 volunteers operating in the area surrounding Sasabe, Arizona, in 2018. While it was formed with the intention to curtail undocumented immigration, in 2015 it changed its goal to disrupting drug smuggling and trafficking across the United States–Mexico border, as well as preventing infiltration by foreign terrorists (Steller 2012). AZBR, like other paramilitaries in the area, provide intelligence to US Customs and Border Patrol. If they spot illegal activity, they carry out citizens' arrests and alert the authorities. Their code of conduct discourages using force "unless no other alternative exists. Deadly physical force is authorized only if no other alternative exists to defend oneself, and if vacating the area would pose a greater risk of injury or death" (Sim 2016).

Another paramilitary organization was the Minutemen Civil Defense Corps (MCDC), which was founded in 2005. The organization was founded with the mission to simply observe the border and report suspected undocumented crossings to border control. However, the open nature of recruitment for this organization and lack of appropriate monitoring by leadership meant that the organization fell prey to factions which were more violent in their intentions. The group disbanded in 2010 following leadership concerns that they would be held responsible if volunteers failed to follow the standard operating procedure (Wagner 2006).

While MCDC was short-lived due to quality control concerns, one of the cofounders of MCDC had organized a similar organization the same year, the Minuteman Project. This group serves as both a border watch patrol and a political action committee, appealing to government leadership to support proactive immigration law enforcement and other border security concerns (Cabrera and Glavac 2010). Members of this group believe that the existing IPI has fundamentally failed to protect American citizens from a foreign threat (Stewart, Bendall, and Morgan 2015).Within six months of beginning intensive recruiting, the organization had 1,250 volunteers that went to the Arizona–Mexico border in order to "do the job the government failed to do" (Gilchrist 2008; Stewart, Bendall, and Morgan 2015). Unlike MCDC, the Minuteman Project continues to thrive. In fall of 2018, the leader of the Texas Minutemen was interviewed by *The Independent* and reported that he had placed members at three points of the Texas–Mexico border, and that due to the then-impending "Migrant Caravan" he intended to be able to add up to 100 more patrolmen (Dalton 2018).

The relationship between the DHS, nonprofit aid organizations, and paramilitary units is complex, although they are all responding to the problems of large-scale apprehensions in their own way. Even without taking into account other aid organizations operating in the area such as legal aid organizations, housing initiatives, and soup kitchens, we can see that the systems of exchange are based upon implicit agreements of behavior. The relationship between religious and aid organizations is such that the churches each function as a decision-making body, agreeing to take in a certain number of migrants, and using a finite amount of funding. McGinnis and E. Ostrom (2012)[5] point out that polycentric governance, as established by Ostrom, Tiebout, and Warren (1999), bears resemblance to cross-sector collaborative network governance, which is exactly what is happening in these conditions. However, this is not an ideal case of polycentric governance due to the extreme disparity between the amount of resources available to each group and the disproportionate amount of influence held by the government. There are still aspects of monocentric governance, a system where "governmental prerogatives for determining, enforcing, and altering legal relationships are vested in some single office or decision structure that has an ultimate monopoly over the legitimate exercise of coercive capabilities in some particular society" (V. Ostrom 1999, 55).

There is, however, growing cross-sector pressure as religious organizations issue more and more pleas through television, radio, and print media for constituents to hold their local governments accountable for providing at least buildings for shelter to aid in the largest influxes of asylum seekers (Villasana 2018; González 2019a, 2019b; Montes 2019). At the same time that these organizations were garnering media attention trying to gain support both financially and in terms of workforce, Greyhound withdrew from housing migrants in its bus depots (Galvan 2019). While immigrants sleeping in the Greyhound station had never been official policy, it had become one ex post, as ICE officers dropped off busloads of immigrants at the doors of the

Greyhound station, often without buses departing until the next morning at the earliest.

On the other end of the spectrum, paramilitary groups, which have not been officially recognized by the US government, are under increasing scrutiny of the military and Border Patrol, organizations which paramilitary members feel have fallen short of their responsibilities (Stewart, Bendall, and Morgan 2015; Wagner 2006). Leaked military documents suggest that this concern is namely out of potential to steal equipment from military organizations such as the National Guard while Guard members are deployed (LaPorta and da Silva 2018), though the ultimate demise of MCDC suggest that there are also concerns regarding the violent tendencies of the sort of person that joins a paramilitary. The leaked military report suggests further institutional disdain by suggesting that these are "unregulated militias" that "operate under the guise of citizen patrols supporting CBP [Customs and Border Protection] (LaPorta and da Silva 2018)." This may not be the case throughout all police and military forces, however—a reporter who went undercover as a paramilitary patrolman revealed that in his experience there was support for paramilitary patrols among local police (Bauer 2016). This flux of immigrants has forced a relationship between public, private, and third-sector organizations to solve a collective action problem—meeting the needs of border communities in the face of an increasing, vulnerable immigrant population to prevent undesirable consequences such as crime, illness, and death.

WHY A POLYCENTRIC SYSTEM HAS NOT BEEN FORMALLY ADOPTED

To cite Aligica (2013), "It is uncontroversial that some sets of beliefs and attitudes make for good governance, some don't. Citizenship matters. In an era of scientism, we tend to forget that many institutional pathologies of modern governance may be in fact the result of 'the superficial way we think about citizenship in democratic societies' (V. Ostrom 1997, 3)." The institutional pathologies we see in the IPI stem in part from the legwork these organizations are doing. The organizations described above have arisen due to dissatisfaction with the immigration processing institutions currently in place. However, as they operate right now, they form a de facto polycentric system within the IPI framework, where each node is formally independent from the others and there are multiple levels of decision-making between them. The government has not, thus far, publicly responded to these organizations arising at the peripheries to meet the needs left unmet by the current, formalized institution. Leaked military briefings showed concern over the potential dangers of paramilitary organization (Dalton 2018; LaPorta and da Silva 2018), but there has not been formal government action to discourage these groups from forming.

The reasons for failing to publicly address these organizations is more than likely multifaceted. Firstly, if the DHS was to claim responsibility for these institutional failures and the rise of unregulated organizations to fill what were intended to be government functions, they would have to reform current institutions. The costs of institutional change are not insignificant (E. Ostrom 1990; North 1990), and under the current de facto system the institution itself does not have to pay the costs of change in order for these roles to be fulfilled by third-party organizations.

Secondly, and more pessimistically, as an institution with many bureaucratic measures and safeguards, it is easy to deflect blame for inflexibility on other aspects of the institution (Hood 2010). For example, interviews with border patrol suggested that the politicians responsible for signing H.R. 7311 into law were to blame for early releases and lack of housing for immigrants (Gonzales 2019a). Likewise, DHS and Health and Human Services (HHS) have taken turns blaming each other for the detention of immigrant children past legal limits (Caldwell 2019). This intergovernmental deflection serves to complicate reform efforts—it is difficult to know which agencies should be improved for the institution to fulfill more of the Ostromian design principles.

As such, a permanent solution such as institutional reform or decentralization of the current institution is unlikely. The adverse incentives of formal institutional actors encourage stagnation. The best chance of reform seems to be top-down, with the head of the executive branch, the president, pressuring the secretary of Homeland Security into absorbing the costs of reform. It would be necessary to change the incentive structure for actors within the institution in order to create lasting change. Without reform, there are normative human rights concerns to be raised by letting unmonitored nonprofit and security organizations handle immigrant processing on their own terms. Additionally, the crowd-sourced funding and workforce provided by these organizations is constantly under strain, there are no guarantees of resource renewal once given resources have been depleted—the uncertain future of these organizations mean that they are not a reliable solution to the institutional problem.

CONCLUSION

In this work, I have outlined the Ostromian qualifications for institutional robustness. I have argued that current US IPI falls short of this model of institutional robustness, and this failing has been made particularly apparent due to political and economic turmoil in Guatemala, El Salvador, and Honduras leading to large numbers of economic and political asylum seekers flooding the IPI. Having historically failed to properly endogenize future uncertainty, the strain placed on the institution highlights the places that the institution falls short. In response, under growing risk of human rights violations and decreased border security, collective action organizations such as religious organizations and paramilitaries have formed in order to address concerns of priority to them.

I address the ways in which this can lead to an additionally insecure future plagued by security and human rights problems for the volunteer organizations and for the vulnerable immigrant populations. I argue that the solution to this problem is government accountability and increased multilevel governance within the realm of immigrant processing. This is in line with the work of the Ostroms (E. Ostrom 1983, 2007, 2008, 2009, 2010a; V. Ostrom 2006, 2009), which generally advocates for small, direct-service producers, which are more effective and occasionally more efficient than large producers. By allowing state and local governments to have a say in the issues affecting them, there will hopefully be more accurate future planning with more fine-grained data about needs. Closer proximity would make it harder to overlook the strain placed on the institution. Likewise, such a change would make it easier for citizens to hold politicians and bureaucrats alike accountable to their actions. This institutional revision would alleviate strain on Southern border communities, provide long-term stability in terms of funding and workforce, and help the IPI currently in place to acquire the design principles that it has struggled to meet thus far. By critically examining and addressing institutional shortcomings using the Ostromian institutional robustness framework, I highlight shortcomings to ameliorate within the United States' immigrant processing institution, bypassing institutional opacity, and hopefully creating a path forward for improving human rights within complex institutional frameworks.

NOTES

1. US Border Patrol defines a family unit as "the number of individuals (either a child under 18 years of age, parent, or legal guardian) apprehended with a family member by the U.S. Border Patrol" (U.S. Border Patrol 2016).

2. For more on the type of actions that we can expect rules to take, see E. Ostrom (2014, 113 in *Choice, Rules, and Collective Action*).

3. In E. Ostrom (1983), she puts forward (1) economies of scale in production, (2) coproduction, (3) measurability, (4) size and location of the group of individuals who jointly consume the service, and (5) the degree of choice that citizens have concerning

their consumption of a service as an earlier attempt at the design principles. It is easy to see how these are interrelated with the design principles from *Governing the Commons* and how they might be pertinent to a conversation about immigrant processing institutions.

4. Nine hundred interviews with a margin of error of 3.27 percent.
5. See also Aligica (2016) and Aligica and Tarko (2013).

REFERENCES

Aligica, Paul Dragos. 2013. "Citizenship, Political Competence and Civic Studies: The Ostromian Perspective." Forthcoming in *Civic Studies*, edited by Peter Levine and Karol Soltan. SSRN: https://ssrn.com/abstract=2242205.

———. 2016. "Neither Market nor State Domain: Nonprofits from the Ostroms' Theoretical Perspective." *Nonprofit and Voluntary Sector Quarterly* 45 (4S): 43S–60S.

Aligica, Paul Dragos, and Vlad Tarko. 2013. "Co-production, Polycentricity, and Value Heterogeneity: the Ostroms' Public Choice Institutionalism Revisited." *American Political Science Review* 107 (4): 726–741.

Bacon, John, and Alan Gomez. 2019. "Immigration Advocates Brace for ICE Round-ups Across the Country: 'The Goal Is to Terrorize'." *USA Today*. Accessed July 22, 2019. https://www.usatoday.com/story/news/nation/2019/07/11/ice-raids-round-up-immigrants-deportation-sunday-nyt-reports/1701549001/.

Baker, Peter. 2019. "Trump Declares a National Emergency, and Provokes a Constitutional Clash." *The New York Times*. Accessed July 22, 2019. https://www.nytimes.com/2019/02/15/us/politics/national-emergency-trump.html.

Bauer, Shane. 2016. "I Went Undercover with a Border Militia. Here's What I Saw." *Mother Jones*, November/December Issue. Accessed May 24, 2019. https://www.motherjones.com/politics/2016/10/undercover-border-militia-immigration-bauer/.

Bump, Philip. 2016. "Here's What Donald Trump Said in His Big Immigration Speech, Annotated." *Washington Post*. Accessed July 22, 2019. https://www.washingtonpost.com/news/the-fix/wp/2016/08/31/heres-what-donald-trump-said-in-his-big-immigration-speech-annotated/.

Cabrera, Luís, and Sonya Glavac. 2010. "Minutemen and Desert Samaritans: Mapping the Attitudes of Activists on the United States' Immigration Front Lines." *Journal of Ethnic and Migration Studies* 36 (4): 673–695.

Caldwell, Alicia A. 2019. "Federal Agencies Trade Blame over Detention of Migrant Children." *The Wall Street Journal*. Accessed July 22, 2019. https://www.wsj.com/articles/federal-agencies-trade-blame-over-detention-of-migrant-children-11562929201.

Dalton, Jane. 2018. "Armed US Militia Groups Prepare to See Off Migrant Caravan at the Mexico Border." *The Independent*. Accessed March 21, 2019. https://www.independent.co.uk/news/world/americas/migrant-caravan-us-armed-militia-groups-mexico-texas-border-trump-immigration-a8604371.html.

Favela, Tatiana. 2019. "Annunciation House Calling on Local Churches to Help House Migrants." *KTSM.com*. https://www.ktsm.com/news/local/

el-paso-news/annunciation-house-calling-on-local-churches-to-help-house-migrants/1864683067.

Frank, Peter M., and Gordon E. Shockley. 2016. "A Critical Assessment of Social Entrepreneurship: Ostromian Polycentricity and Hayekian Knowledge." *Nonprofit and Voluntary Sector Quarterly* 45: 61S–77S.

Gallup. 2019. "Immigration." *In Depth: Topics A to Z.* Accessed July 22, 2019. https://news.gallup.com/poll/1660/Immigration.aspx?g_source=link_newsv9&g_campaign=item_246665&g_medium=copy.

Galvan, Astrid. 2019. "NewsBreak: Greyhound Won't Let US Drop Migrants in Depots." *Associated Press.* Accessed July 23, 2019. https://www.apnews.com/8a3c7c2feefe4b2189efb97596e79384.

Gilchrist, Jim. 2008. "An Essay by Jim Gilchrist." *Georgetown Immigration Law Journal* 22 (3): 415–428.

Greenblatt, Alan. 2014. "What's Causing the Latest Immigration Crisis? A Brief Explainer." *NPR News.* Accessed July 22, 2019. https://www.npr.org/2014/07/09/329848538/whats-causing-the-latest-immigration-crisis-a-brief-explainer.

Gonzales, Richard. 2019. "Migrant Families Arrive in Busloads As Border Crossings Hit 10-Year High." *NPR All Things Considered*, March 5. Accessed March 24, 2019.

González, Daniel. 2019a. "Customs and Border Protection Says U.S. Laws, Court Rulings to Blame for Migration Spike." *AZcentral, Part of the USA Today Network.* https://www.azcentral.com/story/news/politics/border-issues/2019/03/06/cbp-says-us-laws-court-rulings-blame-border-migration-spike-senate-judiciary/3072257002/.

———. 2019b. "ICE Released 84,500 Migrant Family Members since Dec. 21, Including 14,500 in Arizona." *AZcentral, Part of the USA Today Network.* https://www.azcentral.com/story/news/politics/immigration/2019/03/07/ice-has-released-84-500-migrant-family-members-since-dec-21/3095755002/.

Hood, Christopher. 2010. *The Blame Game: Spin, Bureaucracy, and Self-Preservation in Government.* Princeton: Princeton University Press.

Jordan, Lara Jakes. 2006. "U.S. Ends 'Catch-And-Release' at Border." *Washington Post.* Accessed May 23, 2019.

Joung, Madeleine. 2019. "What Is Happening at Migrant Detention Centers? Here's What to Know." *TIME.* Accessed July 22, 2019. https://time.com/5623148/migrant-detention-centers-conditions/.

LaPorta, James, and Chantal da Silva. 2018. "Migrant Caravan: Border Troops Preparing for Threat of Armed, Unregulated Militias, Leaked Documents Show." *Newsweek.* Accessed March 23, 2019. https://www.newsweek.com/trump-administration-migrant-caravan-border-troops-1196855.

Leon, Nailea, and Peter Samore. 2019. "Valley Pastor Pleased for Help Housing Asylum Seekers Released by ICE." *KTAR.com.* http://ktar.com/story/2492992/valley-pastor-pleads-for-help-housing-asylum-seekers-released-by-ice.

Lu, Denise, and Derek Watkins. 2019. "Court Backlog May Prove Bigger Barrier for Migrants Than Any Wall." *New York Times.* January 24. https://www.nytimes.com/interactive/2019/01/24/us/migrants-border-immigration-court.html.

McGinnis, Michael D., and Elinor Ostrom. 2012. "Reflections on Vincent Ostrom, Public Administration, and Polycentricity." *Public Administration Review* 72 (1): 15–25.

Montes, Aaron. 2019. "El Paso City Council to Consider Providing Migrant Services." *El Paso Times: Part of the USA Today Network.* March 23. Accessed March 24, 2019. https://www.elpasotimes.com/story/news/2019/03/23/el-paso-city-council-consider-providing-help-migrant-services/3245711002/.

NBC News and Wall Street Journal. 2019. *Study #19020.* Conducted by Hart Research Associates/Public Opinion Strategies. Accessed July 22, 2019. https://www.wsj.com/public/resources/documents/19020NBCWSJJanuary2019Poll.pdf?mod=article_inline&utm_source=link_newsv9&utm_campaign=item_246665&utm_medium=copy.

Newport, Frank. 2019. "Immigration, Public Opinion and Congress." Gallup: *Polling Matters.* Accessed July 22, 2019. https://news.gallup.com/opinion/polling-matters/246665/immigration-public-opinion-congress.aspx.

North, Douglass C. 1990. *Institutions, Institutional Change and Economic Performance.* Cambridge: Cambridge University Press.

Ostrom, Elinor. 1983. "Analyzing Institutions for the Delivery of Local Collective Goods." Presented at the American Society for Public Administration Meetings, New York.

———. 1990. *Governing the Commons: The Evolution of Institutions for Collective Action.* Cambridge: Cambridge University Press.

———. 1994. "Constituting Social Capital and Collective Action." *Journal of Theoretical Politics* 6 (4): 527–562.

———. 2000. "Crowding out Citizenship." *Scandinavian Political Studies* 23 (1): 3–16.

———. 2005. *Understanding Institutional Diversity.* Princeton: Princeton University Press.

———. 2007. "Collective Action and Local Development Processes." *Sociologica* 3: 1–32.

———. 2008. "Polycentric Systems as One Approach for Solving Collective-Action Problems." Bloomington, IN: School of Public & Environmental Affairs Research Paper No. 2008-11-02. Available at SSRN: https://ssrn.com/abstract=1936061.

———. 2009. "A General Framework for Analyzing Sustainability of Social-Ecological Systems." *Science* 325 (5939): 419–422.

———. 2010a. "The Challenge of Self-Governance in Complex Contemporary Environments." *The Journal of Speculative Philosophy* 24 (4): 316–332.

———. 2010b. "Beyond Markets and States: Polycentric Governance of Complex Economic Systems." *American Economic Review* 100 (3): 641–672.

———. 2014. "An Agenda for the Study of Institutions." In *Choice, Rules and Collective Action,* edited by Filippo Sabetti and Paul Dragos Aligica, 97–120. Colchester: ECPR Press. Originally published in 1986 in *Public Choice* 48 (1): 3–25.

Ostrom, Elinor, and J.M. Walker. 1991. "Communication in a Commons: Cooperation without External Enforcement." In *Contemporary Laboratory Research in Political Economy*, edited by T. Palfrey. Ann Arbor: University of Michigan Press.

———. 2000. "Neither Markets Nor States: Linking Transformation Processes in Collective-Action Arenas." In *Polycentric Games and Institutions: Readings from the Workshop in Political Theory and Policy Analysis*, edited by M.D. McGinnis. Ann Arbor: University of Michigan Press.

Ostrom, Elinor, J.M. Walker, and R. Gardner. 1992. "Covenants With and Without a Sword: Self-Governance is Possible." *American Political Science Review* 86 (2): 404–417.

Ostrom, Elinor, and Roger B. Parks. 1999. "Neither Gargantua nor the Land of Lilliputs: Conjectures on Mixed Systems of Metropolitan Organization." In *Polycentricity and Local Public Economies: Readings from the Workshop in Political Theory and Policy Analysis*, edited by Michael D. McGinnis. Ann Arbor: University of Michigan Press.

Ostrom, Elinor, and Vincent Ostrom. 1986. "Analytical Tools for Institutional Design." In *Institutional Development: Improving Management in Developing Countries: Reports on a Seminar Series*, edited by John L. McGruder. Washington, DC: American Consortium for International Public Administration.

Ostrom, Vincent. 1979. "A Conceptual-Computational Logic for Federal Systems of Governance." In *Constitutional Design and Power-Sharing in the Post-Modern Epoch*, edited by D.J. Daniel, 2–22. Lanham, MD: University Press of America.

———. 1997. *The Meaning of Democracy and the Vulnerability of Democracies: A Response to Tocqueville's Challenge.* Ann Arbor: University of Michigan Press.

———. 1999. "Polycentricity (Part 1)." In *Polycentricity and Local Public Economies,* edited by Michael D. McGinnis, 52–74. Originally prepared for delivery at the 1972 annual meeting of the American Political Science Association.

———. 2006. "Citizen-Sovereigns: The Source of Contestability, the Rule of Law, and the Conduct of Public Entrepreneurship: The 2005 John Gaus Award Lecture." *Political Science and Politics* 39 (1): 13–17.

———. 2009. "Why Were There So Many Governance Failures in the Twentieth Century?" In *Community Governance from Multicultural Perspectives: Theory and Practice*, edited by Y. Chen. Beijing: Peking University Press.

Ostrom, Vincent, Charles M. Tiebout, and Robert Warren. 1999. "The Organization of Government in Metropolitan Areas: A Theoretical Inquiry." In *Polycentricity and Local Public Economies*, edited by Michael D. McGinnis, 31–51. Ann Arbor: University of Michigan Press. Originally published in 1961 in *American Political Science Review* 55: 831–842.

Paul, Deanna, and Nick Miroff. 2019. "U.N. Human Rights Chief 'Deeply Shocked' by Migrant Detention Center Conditions in Texas." *The Washington Post.* Accessed July 22, 2019. https://www.washingtonpost.com/immigration/2019/07/08/un-human-rights-chief-deeply-shocked-by-migrant-detention-center-conditions-texas/?utm_term=.d2d82b249e29.

Plott, C.R. 1979. "The Application of Laboratory Experimental Methods to Public Choice." In *Collective Decision Making: Applications from Public Choice Theory*, edited by C.S. Russell, 137–160. Baltimore, MD: Johns Hopkins University Press.

Porter, Tom. 2019. "Photo Shows Hybrid Toilet and Drinking Fountain in Migrant Detention Centers, Where Ocasio-Cortez Says Women Had to Drink from the Bowl." *Business Insider.* Accessed July 24, 2019. https://www.businessinsider.com/photo-hybrid-toilet-drinking-fountain-cbp-centers-2019-7.

Prendergast, Curt. 2018. "Armed Vigilantes bring Unease to Arizona Border Town Haunted by Killing of Girl, Dad." *Arizona Daily Star.* October 8. Accessed March 22, 2019. https://thisistucson.com/news/local/armed-vigilantes-bring-unease-to-arizona-border-town-haunted-by/article_338c98ba-1850-5540-8e6a-571351366b70.html.

Rawls, John. 2001. *Justice as Fairness: A Restatement.* Cambridge: Harvard University Press.

Riker, William H. 1982. "Implications from the Disequilibrium of Majority Rule for the Study of Institutions." In *Political Equilibrium*, edited by P.C. Ordeshook and K.A. Shepsle, 3–24. Boston: Kluwer-Nijhoff. Originally published in 1980 in *American Political Science Review* 74: 432–447.

Rose, Joel. 2019. "President Obama Also Faced a 'Crisis' At the Southern Border." *NPR.* Accessed March 23, 2019. https://www.npr.org/2019/01/09/683623555/president-obama-also-faced-a-crisis-at-the-southern-border.

Rousseau, Jean-Jacques. 2002. *The Social Contract and The First and Second Discourses.* New Haven, CT: Yale University Press. Originally published in 1762.

Schotter, A. 1981. *The Economic Theory of Social Institutions.* Cambridge: Cambridge University Press.

Sergent, James, Elinor Aspegren, Elizabeth Lawrence and Olivia Sanchez. 2019. "Chilling First-Hand Reports of Migrant Detention Centers Highlight Smell of 'Urine, Feces,' Overcrowded Conditions." *USA Today.* Accessed July 22, 2019. https://www.usatoday.com/in-depth/news/politics/elections/2019/07/16/migrant-detention-centers-described-2019-us-government-accounts/1694638001/.

Shepsle, Kenneth A. 1989. "Studying Institutions: Some Lessons from the Rational Choice Approach." *Journal of Theoretical Politics* 1 (2): 131–147.

Sim, David. 2016. "Heavily Armed Civilian Vigilantes Patrol US-Mexico Border for Illegal Immigrants." *International Business Times.* November 16. Accessed March 20, 2019. https://www.ibtimes.co.uk/heavily-armed-civilian-vigilantes-patrol-us-mexico-border-illegal-immigrants-1592087.

Stewart, Julie, Michele Enciso Bendall, and Charlie V. Morgan. 2015. "Jobs, Flags, and Laws: How Interests, Culture, and Values Explain Recruitment into the Utah Minuteman Project." *Sociological Perspectives* 58 (4): 1–22.

United States Border Patrol. 2016. "Family Unit and Unaccompanied Children (0–17) Apprehensions FY16, Compared to the Same Time Period for FY 15 and FY 14." Accessed July 22, 2019. https://www.cbp.gov/sites/default/files/assets/documents/2016-Oct/BP%20Southwest%20Border%20Family%20Units%20and%20UAC%20Apps%20-%20FY16.pdf.

———. 2019. "Southwest Border Migration FY 2019." Accessed July 22, 2019. https://www.cbp.gov/newsroom/stats/sw-border-migration.

Villasana, Jose. 2018. "Annunciation House: ICE Releasing Migrants into El Paso's Streets Unacceptable – Never Again." KVIA. Accessed March 22, 2019. https://www.kvia.com/news/el-paso/annunciation-house-ice-releasing-migrants-into-el-paso-s-streets-unacceptable-never-again/953755439.

Wagner, Dennis. 2006. "Minutemen's Goal: To Shame Feds into Action." *USA Today*. Retrieved July 22, 2019. https://usatoday30.usatoday.com/news/nation/2006-05-24-minuteman-goals_x.htm.

Index

About the Contributors

Dr. Peter J. Boettke is a university professor of economics and philosophy at George Mason University, and director, F.A. Hayek Program for Advanced Study in Philosophy, Politics, and Economics, Mercatus Center at George Mason University.

Joanna Carroll is a PhD student in public affairs at Indiana University, Bloomington.

V. Miranda Chase is a PhD student in global governance and human security at the University of Massachusetts, Boston.

Roland Fritz is a DPhil student in economics at the University of Siegen.

Dr. Bobbi Herzberg is a distinguished senior fellow in the F.A. Hayek Program for Advanced Study in Philosophy, Politics, and Economics, Mercatus Center at George Mason University.

Dr. Nicholas F. Jacobs is a faculty fellow in government at Colby College.

Mili Kalia is a PhD student in sociology at the University of Virginia.

Dr. Brian Kogelmann is an assistant professor of philosophy at the University of Maryland, College Park, and affiliated fellow in the F.A. Hayek Program for Advanced Study in Philosophy, Politics, and Economics, Mercatus Center at George Mason University.

Wanlin Lin is a PhD student in political economy at King's College London.

Pablo Paniagua Prieto is a PhD student in political economy at King's College London.

Sawyer Phinney is a PhD student in urban geography at the University of Manchester.

Dr. Augusto Postigo holds a PhD in anthropology from the University of Campinas UNICAMP

Dr. Veeshan Rayamajhee is an assistant professor of economics at North Dakota State University.

Raquel Rodrigues dos Santos is a PhD student in applied ecology at the University of São Paulo ESALQ-USP.

Alexander Schaefer is a PhD student in philosophy at the University of Arizona.

Emily VanMeter is a PhD student in political science at the University of Rochester.

Dr. Jan P. Vogler is a postdoctoral research associate in political economy of good government at the University of Virginia.

www.ingramcontent.com/pod-product-compliance
Ingram Content Group UK Ltd.
Pitfield, Milton Keynes, MK11 3LW, UK
UKHW012034150926
475560UK00001B/13

9 781786 614346